TRIPOD'S TOOLS FOR LIFE

TRIPOD'S TOOLS FOR LIFE

Streetsmart strategies

for Work, Life—and Everything Else

by Matt Goldberg and the editors and members of Tripod

Foreword by Bo Peabody

NEW YORK

EDITOR: Matt Goldberg
DESIGNER: Adam Smith
ASSOCIATE EDITOR: Marni Davis
TRIPOD STAFF EDITORS: Josh Glenn, Dan Reines, Emma Taylor, Lori Tuckett, Randy Williams
ASSISTANT EDITORS: Alissa Quart, Sarah Blustain, Liza Featherstone
CARTOONIST: Ted Rall
ILLUSTRATIONS: David Miller
ICONS: Federico Jordan
EDITORIAL ASSISTANT: Ben Klipstein

The editors would like to thank the two groups of people without whom this book would have been impossible: the staff and members of Tripod.

Special thanks: Bo Peabody, Dick Sabot, and Scott Walker

And, of course, thanks to Jennifer Lang, our editor at Hyperion, who somehow managed to keep us calm on a consistent basis throughout the lengthy process of producing this book.

Library of Congress Cataloging-in-Publication Data

Goldberg, Matt
Tripod's Tools for Life / by Matt Goldberg and the editors and members of Tripod
p. cm.
ISBN 0-7868-8332-4
1. Life skills—United States—Handbooks, manuals, etc.
2. Generation X—United States—Life skills guides. I. Title.
HQ2039.U6G65 1998
646.7 00973—dc21 98–16300
CIP

FIRST EDITION

10 9 8 7 6 5 4 3 2 1

Contents

The Net

Work

Home

Contents

Food

Health

Money

Foreword

The creation of the book you are holding is a microcosm of the creation of Tripod itself. It is the result of the unique combination of the entrepreneurial drive of a few people and the creative spirit of millions of Tripod members. We (you, your fellow Tripod members, and the Tripod staff) have always done things as a team. This book is just the latest manifestation of our very successful partnership.

So many DIY (do-it-yourself) books operate on the assumption that there most certainly is "one right way," whether you're talking career-building or dinner-building. If there wasn't "one right way" and xyz "how-to" book didn't reveal it, than why on earth would you buy it and read it, right? Not right by us. Our premise is the only right way to do things is the way that doesn't fail and doesn't suck.

It is this premise that lead us to make this DIY book truly DIY. *Tripod's Tools for Life* has hundreds of authors and serves up as much information on as many subjects as possible. It really is do-it-yourself, your way.

Enjoy.

—Bo Peabody, President and CEO

Introduction

What is perhaps the most noteworthy element of *Tripod's Tools for Life* was the last thing to fall into place. In fact, we'd already sold the idea for this "work smart, live smart, streetsmart guide" before the idea of opening its authorship up to the Tripod community at large even occurred to us.

It was in the act of building a homepage for the incipient book that the notion of soliciting participation from our online membership base began to crystallize. The idea behind the homepage had been something along the lines of a glorified press release, a way to alert the users of our Web site that, indeed, we'd gone out and brought home a book deal.

But in the course of writing the letter that would be posted online and would explain to our members just how and why we wanted to explore book publishing on their behalf, I realized I had it sort of backwards. Using the Web to tell people stuff about the way I envisioned the book would be mostly an empty exercise: Sure, some people might get really psyched right away and shoot off a congratulatory E-mail or whatever but that would be about it. No, it dawned on me that the members of our online neighborhood had a hell of a lot more to tell me than I could possibly say to them. Accordingly, our first order of business—on par with actually parceling out to writers assignments to compose the book's forty or so core pieces—became figuring out a way to actively solicit a wide range of feedback from as many of our globe-scattered members as possible on each subject we planned to cover.

Boy, did we hit a nerve. The interactive "book site," as it came to be affectionately known, offered Tripod members several dozen forums in which they could make themselves heard, each one mirroring a particular section in the book. From homebrewing and home painting to homepages, we asked our members to speak up. And by closely analyzing the comments as they came in, day after day, for over six months, a picture of sorts began to emerge, an early not-so-distant warning about what issues really concerned and compelled the denizens of Tripod.

Among the more popular discussion areas residing on the book site were "Credit Card Hell" and "Retirement Planning" from the Money chapter, communicating to us—loud and clear—that we could and actually had to address people's difficulty getting their fiduciary ducks in a row. Same thing with the "Depression" and "Therapy" forums from the Health chapter, which received an extraordinary amount of traffic. Clearly, this, too, was important for us to investigate—we couldn't exclude a Mental Health section from the book and just chalk up our member's urgent communiqués to some sort of so-called slacker ennui.

Such a wealth of close-to-real-time feedback helped us focus in on exactly who we were doing this book for and on how we ought to put it together and present it in order for it to best meet their expectations. Which brings us to another way that signing up a multitude of coauthors pushed the editorial process of this book into uncharted territory. We soon found ourselves cowering at our desks surrounded by towers of printed out E-mails from our members. And we were putting this stuff in the book in much greater quantities than we'd first imagined, to the point where we were stuffing and cramming missives from Tripod members into every unfilled nook and cranny in the book's emerging layouts. Some of these were pithy one-liners, while others submitted much longer messages. When we were finished, we determined that we'd jammed over 30,000 words of "member-generated content" into the book. We couldn't believe it. There were so many voices emanating from this thing that it was starting to seem less a book than a freaking "Hallelujah" chorus.

Well, it seemed kind of providential, at least, when we saw how all the different comments from our members interacted on the page with one another and with the articles, essays, and resource lists comprising the rest of the book. What emerged was, ironically enough, a fairly decent representation, in print, of the dynamic that had always existed on our Web site: real people swapping war stories and offering one another advice, the whole thing fueled by clearly presented information and the incendiary touch of a bunch of really good writers. The result, we think, transcends what many other books on similar enough subjects are able to offer.

In order to sell as many books as possible, the authors behind most DIY books proclaim to have "seen the light": If only you'd buy their book, you'd surely learn the correct way to proceed. But if our efforts collaborating with our members taught us anything it's that there's always an exception, always another way. So, we reasoned, let's simply offer as much information on these subjects as we can, including as many corroborating (and for that matter, dissenting) reports as we can get our hands on.

And it's by giving you the tools to arrive at your own conclusions that we hope to ultimately help you with this book. After reviewing the work of our three dozen or so contributing writers and sampling the actual (and surprisingly well-rendered) experiences of hundreds of other folks like (and not like) you—and following up with some examination of the huge list of Web sites we also make available—we suspect you'll have at the very least a better understanding of the lay of the land. The collective experience and knowledge you've perused will give you a few navigational beacons to call on once you set sail.

Because before you invest all that money, or switch forms of contraception or use that herbal cure or shift job tracks, it's helpful to know what can happen—and courtesy of all the folks featured in the margins of these very pages—what has happened and what it was like.

I guess calling it a "guide" book isn't so off the mark, after all.

—Matt Goldberg

part 1

the Net

Online Shopping

With the advent of full-scale E-commerce, you may never again step into a traditional shopping mall. But is that a good or a bad thing? Actually, that part's up to you.

by Michael Agger

It seems like only yesterday that we were bemoaning the malling of America. Now we have an even faster, cheaper, cleaner, and truly virtual kind of mall, an even better (though some would say an even less active) retail experience than traditional mall shopping that's taking America by storm—Internet shopping. According to Jupiter Communications, Internet sales reached $706 million in 1996 and are expected to top $7 billion by the year 2000. The recent introduction of secure credit card transactions to the Web infrastructure has made it the most far-reaching alternative retail network ever created.

With low overhead and a potentially worldwide customer base, Internet retailers hope to reap high profits from online shopping. Bleeding-edge E-stores are developing new tools—intelligent agents, online auctions, personalization tools—that assist consumers in their search for everything from stretch pants to stretch limos. You can reach thousands of E-stores and online catalogs from your desktop (see sidebar on page 3). No more wading through crowds at the mall or cross-checking several locations to see if the prices are different. Because E-stores can offer their products to the public with very little overhead, their prices are often much cheaper than a comparable "real world" store. And you can find a wildly diverse array of products, too, like homemade ketchup sold by a grandmother in Texas or the antique golf clubs sold by GolfWeb.

Say you're a nervous Nelly and you're wondering right now,

"What's going to stop someone from stealing my credit card number when I transmit it online?" The risk you take transmitting credit card information online is the same as, if not less than, purchasing something with a credit card at a local store. The fear of credit fraud still persists even now that all the major Internet retail sites use the widely accepted Secure Sockets Layer (SSL) protocol. Recognizing this credibility gap, Visa, MasterCard, and American Express are working on developing the Secure Electronic Transaction (SET) protocol, making Internet shopping that much safer for the masses.

But wait: There are other caveats. For one, most of your purchases will arrive by mail. Shopping online lacks the instant gratification of shopping in a real store. It also makes returning merchandise more problematic. Return policies are often buried five or six levels deep on these retail sites. What is true about regular shopping is doubly so about E-shopping: Let the buyer beware. Before you buy, do some basic research on the site you are patronizing: i.e., Where are they located? How long have they been in business? How do they ship the product? Both Excite (http://www.excite.com) and the Better Business Bureau Online (http://www.bbbonline.org) have launched merchant-certification programs to assure consumers that accredited sites have secure transactions, rapid order processing, and exceptional customer service. The best retail sites are often found through word-of-mouth. Ask your friends where they have shopped online or scan newsgroups or Internet magazines for recommendations. Remember: If the deal sounds too good to be true, online as well as off-, it probably is. For many people, shopping online cannot match the serendipity of mingling and browsing with other people in physical stores. There is something pleasurable, they insist, in the display of products, the relationship you develop with the store owner and sales clerks, and the chance conversations you have with fellow customers. But since America's small merchants have been hard pressed by the growth of the suburban megastores, the personal attention they're known for offering is rapidly becoming a fond memory. Surprisingly, many people are finding a new sort of personalized shopping experience online while still enjoying wholesale prices. Shopping "agents" (also called "affinity" technology) allow you to customize your shopping experience by

member: TripodAlyssa
CONFERENCE: HOW DO YOU USE THE INTERNET?
I'm not sure why but I love the idea of buying stuff over the Internet. Maybe it's because there isn't a good mall around here. I can find everything I want online. Of course, I lose out on digging through a big rack of clothes to find the perfect shirt for 75 percent off, but hey—those are the breaks.

alerting you to products similar to the ones you buy that might also appeal to you or by tailoring the display of new products to coincide with your interests.

Firefly (http://www.firefly.com) has been a major innovator of affinity technology and is currently in use at several sites like Bignote, Moviewatcher, and Yahoo!, to name a few. Here's how it works: Let's say you visit Bignote as a first-time user. You will be asked to rate several CDs so that the service gets a sense of your likes and dislikes. The more CDs you rate, the more accurately Bignote will be able to gauge what bands will appeal to you.

> Internet Shopping Guide

Apparel
Bills Khakis
http://www.billskhakis.com
A good example of a specialty item Web site. Stop here to buy what GQ called "the pants of the gods."

Automobiles
Auto-By-Tel
http://www.autobytel.com
A complete resource for buying, leasing, and researching new and used cars.

Books
Amazon.com
http://www.amazon.com
The blue-chip book site. They also locate out-of-print texts as well.

Coffee
Lucidcafé
http://www.lucidcafe.com
Read up on exotic blends of coffee and then order a pound for your own pleasure.

Computers
Cyberian Outpost
http://www.outpost.com
A massive amount of computer hardware, software, and books can be bought here on the cheap.

Finance
StockSmart
http://www.stocksmart.com
Get real-time portfolio tracking at this site for the serious armchair investor.

Flowers
1-800-Flowers
http://www.1800flowers.com
Send fresh flowers to anyone anywhere in the world.

Film
Movie Critic
http://www.moviecritic.com
This site compares your movie tastes with others' to offer new films you might like.

Food
Peapod
http://www.peapod.com
Although it serves only a few areas, this site shows how we all might get groceries in the future.

Hardware
Cornell's Hardware
http://www.cornells.com
A family run hardware store dispenses advice and all kinds of tools.

Music
CDNow
http://www.cdnow.com
Great customer service. Great selection. A top-notch CD site.

Real Estate
CyberRentals
http://www.cyberrentals.com
Find a vacation rental anywhere in the world.

Tickets
Ticketmaster
http://www.ticketmaster.com
Online ticket purchasing for any Ticketmaster event in the United States.

Travel
Expedia
http://www.expedia.com
Find a bargain fare with Expedia's excellent travel services.

Wine
Virtual Vineyards
http://www.virtualvin.com
Order crates of your favorite wine to be delivered to your door.

Eventually, it will acquire the ability to recommend new albums to you with a surprising degree of accuracy.

You can get an "agent" to comparision shop for you, too. Let's say a price for a new CD seems too high. You can easily check three or four other sites to comparison shop. Compare.net (http://www.compare.net) will search the Web for the product you request and return a list of prices. Another site, Jango (http://www.jango.com), will find merchants, prices, and even reviews for any product you enter. With these tools, there is no excuse for not paying the lowest price possible.

E-shopping has also given rise to unique purchasing opportunities. The online auction sites, like ONSALE (http://www.onsale.com), Cyberquest (http://www.bid4it. com), or Zauction (http://www. zauction.com), offer the chance to buy computer equipment, bikes, and myriad other products at bargain prices. Bibliobytes (http://www..bb.com) has taken advantage of the digital quality of E-commerce by offering rare, out-of-print books in electronic format. Also, the once humble classified ad can now be found most everywhere on the Web. National borders and trade pacts are blithely ignored as E-shoppers scour the globe for the products they want.

With this new disembodied purchasing, you may never again step into the perfumey changing room of a Victoria's Secret or push past a sweaty high school jock at Footlocker. In fact, high school kids who want to be seen may be the last people left at the malls, which is bad for business since they never buy anything there anyway.

Net Radio

There's a whole world of netcasted radio content for you enjoy, from local sports and news to experimental performance art. And the beauty is you don't even have to stop typing that proposal to tune in.

by David Kushner

Most DJs must be content playing to whatever audience they can corral into a physical space, be it a sprawling club or a crowded basement. But the advent of Net Radio—audio programming broadcast over the Internet—is making available a seemingly limitless worldwide audience, creating a digital alternative for DIY broadcasters who simply must be heard.

"It's what every music fan wishes he or she could do," says King Koffee, drummer and resident Web guru for neopsychedlic AltRock godfathers, the Butthole Surfers. Since February 1997, Koffee has been hosting his own Net Radio show called "Brainwash" (http://m2.monsterbit.com/brainwash) from his home in Austin, Texas. Whenever he hears the muse banging inside his head, Koffee thumbs through the dusty ribs of his immense record collection, plucks out a few choice cuts, then uploads his program so computer listeners across the world can tune in and enjoy the show. "It's like taking over a radio station and playing anything you want," he says.

Fortunately, one needn't be a rock star to have a Net Radio show. Thousands of broadcasters across the world are getting in on the action, from artists like Koffee to corporations like ABC News. Unlike TV or offline radio, Net Radio is a vastly more accessible enterprise. There's no studio to own, no staff to hire, no airwaves to negotiate (there's also not much money to make . . . yet).

For now, anyone with a computer, speakers, and Internet access can play program director. The key element to Net Radio is audio compression software, available for free on the Internet, which enables surfers to listen to and broadcast sound files over the Internet. The best way to tune in or beam out audio is to start with RealAudio from Progressive Networks, the most popular and easy-to-use compression program (see the RealAudio site, www.real.com).

Prior to RealAudio, files had to be downloaded then played back, meaning that the files had to be super small or they would take forever to pass through the wires. But with the advent of RealAudio, surfers can simply download the free RealAudio player, click on a designated RealAudio file on a Web page, and hear sound clips instantaneously.

At present, there are three types of Net Radio shows: Netcasts (a.k.a. cybercasts), radio station simulcasts, and original programming. Netcasts are live broadcasts of offline happenings like concerts and sporting events. Big-time arena rock artists from Tori Amos to Smashing Pumpkins have had their concerts Netcasted. Even entire festivals, like the Beastie Boys' Tibetan Freedom Festival, have been accessible via the Net. Professional and amateur sports from across the country are increasingly being Netcasted, allowing people to catch their alma mater's football game even if they're on the other side of the planet.

Not surprisingly, offline radio stations have tuned into the potential of Net Radio and have heartily embraced it. "Net Radio is increasingly important for radio stations looking to establish their own brands and to market themselves," notes Walt Wurfel, senior vice president of Public Affairs for the National Association of Broadcasters. News and music stations the world over have been racing to get their programs online. At any given moment, surfers might catch the latest pop from a Top Forty station in Reykjavik, Iceland, or the local news from some small station in rural Canada.

Then, of course, there are the original programs made by and for the people on the Net. One of the leading producers of Internet-only radio is New York's Pseudo Online Network (http://www.pseudo.com), an eclectic company that features dozens of different shows every week. Robert Galinksy, a downtown poet and performer, hosts his own weekly Pseudo show called "Go! Poetry." "I knew nothing about the Net," says Galinsky, "but Josh [Harris, Pseudo's founder] said, 'That doesn't matter: You know how to keep an audience entertained.' "

One plus to Net Radio is that the Internet is currently outside the jurisdiction of the Federal Communications Commission. That means people can wield the infamous "seven dirty words" without

> Internet Radio Guide

Here's a list of some essential Net Radio sites. Stations, networks, companies, and shows are, of course, always in flux.

RealAudio
(http://www.real.com)
The essential Net Radio software site from Progressive Networks. Download RealAudio's latest version; it's free for individual use. Also has RealVideo—live video stream freeware. Check this site frequently for upgrades.

Timecast
(http://www.timecast.com)
RealAudio's comprehensive guide to Net Radio shows and events across the Net.

LiveConcerts
(http://www.liveconcerts.com)
RealAudio's other guide, covering live concert simulcasts on the Net.

AudioNet
(http://www.audionet.com)
A massive Internet broadcasting site. Features live and on-demand sporting events, concerts, and nearly 200 TV and radio station simulcasts. Produces Netcast events from the Super Bowl to Bill Gates's speeches.

Pseudo Online Network
(http://www.pseudo.com)
New York's Subterranean Net Radio Production Company. Nightly shows on sex, music, and computer games. Audience participates through unique "chat radio" programs, combining chat rooms with live Net Radio broadcasts.

ESPN Radio Network
(http://espn.sportszone.com/editors/liveaudio/index.html)
The sports network's popular Web site, SportsZone, features daily radio shows on sports news.

GRIT
(http://www.grit.net)
An Internet broadcasting company in New York that specializes in reviewing Web sites on everything from politics to media.

CNET Radio
(http://www.news.com/radio)
The online news site's audio news magazine, covering high-tech happenings. Three different broadcasts per day, plus an archive.

Net Events
(http://events.yahoo.com/)
Yahoo!'s convenient service for live events on the Net, including Net Radio programs. Search by category, just like the main Yahoo! site.

LA Live
(http://www.lalive.com)
Live alternative music Netcasts from Los Angeles. Past shows, including Beck and Luscious Jackson, are archived for easy access.

NPR
(http://www.real.com/contentp/npr)
National Public Radio's site on the Net, featuring popular programs like "All Things Considered" and "Morning Edition." Past shows are archived.

paying Howard Stern–size fines. At least for now, Net Radio crackles with the "anything goes" chaos of the Old West.

If Net Radio has a downside, it's the medium's dependency on a networked computer. As Wurfel notes, listening to Net Radio requires you to be "tethered by a wire and a computer." (Very few folks can afford the cellular phone–wireless modem–sleek laptop combo that transcends this limitation.) However, Net Radio can reach millions of potential listeners: all those corporate warriors who spend their days chained to a desk. Since RealAudio can play while other programs run, workers can hammer away at the keyboard while simultaneously tuning into their favorite Net Radio shows.

Search Engines

To really make the most of the information explosion that is the Internet, you have to know how to find precisely what you're looking for amidst a sea of irrelevancy.

by Michael Agger

The major search engines—Lycos, Altavista, HotBot, Infoseek, and Excite—receive hundreds of thousands of hits per hour, as does the major Internet directory Yahoo! These search engines, also called "spiders" or "crawlers," are essentially powerful computers that constantly visit Web sites, twenty-four hours a day, seven days a week, and index each page as it's encountered. Seemingly once a week, one or more of these companies introduces a faster means to catalog the Web, a new content partnership, or a more refined search algorithm that will catalog sites with greater accuracy, as they are all constantly reinventing themselves to compete with their challengers. Search engines are in a sense the key to the Web's future growth. They embody the Web's promise as a "new" medium, one that provides a decidedly revolutionary service: all the information you need to know. Now.

With all of this information available, though, a person can get quite lost in the Web hinterlands—a place overflowing with often fruitless minutiae. At one time, the Internet was small enough that if you searched for the band Phish you received a total of maybe 200 sites, and you were reasonably assured of uncovering several useful sites within the first twenty or so listed. Now, a similar search would return over 30,000 hits, and it's possible that some of the more useful Phish sites might appear at the bottom of the list. The Phish test case speaks to the mammoth expansion of the Web as a whole. In

1991, the Web had an estimated 376,000 host sites (i.e., tripod.com = 1 host). In 1997, there were an estimated 19 million hosts.

But there are some tricks you can use to find what you're looking for within this overabundance of content. "Meta" search engines—sites that submit a search query to several engines at once and then collate the results—are tremendous time savers (see sidebar on page 12). Also, by using Boolean operators (remember eighth grade math?) like "and," "not," or "or," you can devise more precise Web searches. To use the Phish example, an advanced search might be Phish AND Junta OR Anastasio, adding in the name of the band's first album and the last name of its guitar player to help refine the search. Another basic time-cutting search technique: Put quotes around words so that the engine will look for them next to each other. For example, entering "Trey Anastasio" will only net you results containing the full name of this band member.

All this computer-assisted magic aside, humans—despite their need for food, clothing, and shelter, and the fact that they can't work twenty-four hours a day—are still better at indexing Web sites than computers. Web directories, likc the ones found at Yahoo!, Excite, and Lycos, are created by human researchers. These people are "professional" Web surfers, browsing sites and categorizing them according to subject, usually with a high degree of accuracy. The directories cannot match the enormous breadth of pages cataloged by a search engine, but they do cover the majority of the more popular and well-trafficked sites. This selectivity can be a great advantage to the average info-seeker.

There are two ways to search using directories. First, you can use them like a standard index: i.e., clicking on the appropriate subject headings. To find the Phish page, I would click on Entertainment then Alternative then Bands. (It's amazing how some of those old library science skills actually come in handy in the wired world.) Second, you can search within these directories by key word. For example, if I search for Phish within Yahoo!, I have a good chance of receiving useful sites about Phish that have been described and reviewed by Yahoo!'s staffers. It's akin to searching for a needle in a sewing bag instead of the proverbial haystack. Because you are searching a select list of sites instead of the entire Web, you often receive more focused and useful results.

How do you decide whether to use a search engine or a directory? If you are searching for a highly specific piece of information, begin with a key word search using a search engine. If you are searching for the best site on a broad topic, begin with a directory. The smart Web researcher plays to the strengths of both types of search tools. If you want to know more about the obscure alternative country band you heard at a club last night, your best option is to search for their name, Scud Mountain Boys, by key word with a search engine. Why? Scud Mountain Boys is an unusual combination of words. Because search engines categorize every word on a

> Searching Skills

1. It's very unusual to find the page with the information you are looking for directly from a search engine or Web directory. Once you've left a search engine or directory behind and are adrift on the Web, you still have to play it smart. This is where surfing skills come into play:

   - If a page does not look promising, do not move on right away. Most pages have a "links" section. Check to see if any of those linked-to pages are relevant.
   - If a page is close to what you need but not exactly right, bookmark it so that you can return to it easily.
   - If a page is extremely deep, a quick way to find if the page has the info you need is to use the Find command on your browser. The Find command lets you search for a word within a Web page.
   - If you fall on a page that covers a topic related to what you are looking for, you might want to return to its "root" page. For example, let's say you visited www.trees.com/birch/, you might want to delete /birch/ and go directly to www.trees.com to find more information on trees.

2. All search engines and directories are not created equal. All of the search engines and directories use different means of sorting the Web. If you are unsuccessful with one search service, try another. You will find that some search tools are more suited to your particular researching style than others. Also, take advantage of "meta" search engines like MetaCrawler (www.metacrawler.com) or Dog pile (www.dogpile.com). These are search services that will submit your queries to many search engines and then collate the results.

3. Evolve. Any time spent learning the advanced search functions of a search engine will be rewarded. With practice, you can become adept at honing in on information with more complex searches. Also, new search services are being introduced all the time. Keep current with the latest developments on Internet news sites and with sites geared to researchers like www.searchengine.com.

4. Think before you click. Imagine walking into a library and saying to the librarian, "Travel." That's roughly analogous to what you are doing when requesting information from a search engine. Now, imagine walking into a travel agency and uttering the same word. You are likely to get some results. That's the advantage of using specialized services like Microsoft's Expedia. Before you start searching with a general directory or search engine, pause to think if you know of any more specific resources that will speed your search.

5. If all else fails, pay someone else to hunt down your info. Send a question to HumanSearch (www.humansearch.com) and their team of researchers will try to find you an answer.

page, they will locate the exact pages were those words appear near each other (as long as you put quotes around the words as described above). You have a good chance of finding the relevant info quickly. Now, if you want to know more about the "alternative country" phenomenon in general, one of the directories is probably best.

Perhaps the biggest boon to Web surfers in need of certain key bits of info is the swelling group of specialized search tools (see sidebar on this page). I can find information about a book much faster by using Bookwire, a books-only site, than I could from a more generic search engine or directory. There are thousands of specialized directories on the Web that tailor themselves to particular genres and interests. If you learn to search and surf well, you'll put yourself in a position to harness the power of the ever-expanding Web.

> Searching Sites

DirectoryGuide
(www.directoryguide.com)
Here is the guide to guides. A listing of over 350 search engines and directories.

MetaCrawler
(www.metacrawler.com)
One of the more established meta search services, MetaCrawler allows you to query several search engines at once and collates the results for you.

Four11
(www.four11.com)
Four11 is an excellent source for locating people's E-mail addresses and phone numbers.

DowJones
(www.wsj.com)
This database contains complete text of articles from major periodicals and newspapers. There is lots of valuable data here, but you will have to pay for it.

DejaNews
(www.dejanews.com)
This site contains a complete archive of all Usenet newsgroup discussions dating back to March 1995. A wealth of information can be tapped by searching the catalog of these discussions.

Shareware

Just giving it away isn't a business model that works well for things like, say, cars. But with software, it's a whole other story.

by David Kushner

All the essential lessons that parents drill into their kids are perfectly applicable to life on the wires: Don't talk to strangers; do unto others as you would do unto yourself; and, of course, share and share alike. Accordingly, shared software, or shareware, has emerged as an essential ingredient of online culture and industry.

Instead of having to go to a store, shell out fifty bucks (or more), peel open a package, and then see how a program really works, shareware lets surfers download the program from the Net for a free trial period. After a couple weeks, the user is expected to pay a fee. It's like the reverse of a money-back guarantee: if you dig the program, you pay for it; if not, you throw it away.

Shareware comes in all forms, from big companies spreading the word on a new product to individuals marketing their home-brewed wares. There's something for everyone: games, screensavers, word processors, virus protectors. "I'm a certifiable shareware junkie," says one thirty-three-year-old communications director. "I can spend hours online, searching through the different programs. It's highly addictive."

Shareware and freeware (essentially shareware you don't ever have to pay for) first came about way back in the pre-Web days of computer-based bulletin board services called BBSs. Systems operators and hackers would use the communities as a market for their personal wares, from neopsychedelic desktop patterns to text-based interactive games. Soon enough, however, big companies copped a clue; here was a simple, effective means of word-of-mouth advertising with which they could reach the elusive market of software buyers.

The higher concept at play was the same philosophy used by drug dealers: Give out samples, get the suckers hooked, then bill them for more down the line.

There are a couple of ways this can work. A shareware distributor can simply ask users to pay a small fee after they have used the program for a certain period of time. Does anyone actually pay? According to Forester Research the answer is usually no. "Software piracy is an inherent part of high-tech culture," says Forester analyst Ted Schadler. Nevertheless, if someone finds a program that's good, it's nice to pay the person who made it (otherwise it's like drinking a kid's lemonade from his stand and not leaving a quarter). "The bottom line is that there are not enough people actually paying to allow these code writers to make any money," Schadler adds, "with one huge exception."

The big corporations. Companies like Microsoft and Netscape are cashing in on shareware's buzz power. These companies offer a scaled-down version of a program for free, then a deluxe version for a price. Computer games like Doom and Quake have capitalized on this form of digital bait. A few levels of a game will be distributed online. Gamers can download and play all they want, but eventually they have to pay to get more levels or to get the complete game.

"We've set a trend by offering shareware," says Barrett Alexander of id Software, the company that created Doom and Quake. "By letting people get a taste of it, they enjoy it, they love it, they get addicted," he says. "In today's society, [that approach] may be considered odd; some people don't understand why anyone would give anything away." Yet when you consider that Doom has sold over 1.5 million copies, shareware makes plenty of sense.

Now, the real challenge is where to find the best shareware. More and more sites are popping up that separate the worthwhile from the worthless. Going through these sites (see sidebar on this page) is also a good way to avoid nasty viruses. As an extra precaution, it's also a good idea to use some kind of virus protection program to scan any and all shareware you retrieve.

> Shareware Sites

Once you've downloaded the essentials (Eudora for E-mail, RealAudio for sound, PGP for privacy), there are countless other wares to help you style out your desktop.

SHAREWARE.COM
(www.shareware.com)
This site is the mini=mall of shareware. Run by CNET, the popular online news service, Shareware.com is the place to browse for wares that might catch your interest or just go searching for something you heard about but don't know where to find. This site is updated daily with news reports and bug warnings. There's also a nifty shareware newsletter that will keep you informed of the latest wares.

HAPPYPUPPY
(www.happypuppy.com)
HappyPuppy features all the latest game demos for the PC and Mac. Don't worry if you can't get past a level of Quake, because Puppy also features plenty of "cheat" programs that can give you unlimited weapons and lives.

BROWSERS

NETSCAPE
(www.netscape.com)
INTERNET EXPLORER
(www.microsoft.com)
The debate wages on between the virtues of Netscape's Navigator and Microsoft's Internet Explorer, but the good news is you can try them both. Keep checking their sites frequently for upgrades. The browser wars are far from over.

SCREEN SAVER HEAVEN
(http://www.galttech.com/ssheaven.shtml)
Everyone goes nuts for screensavers. Screen Saver Heaven boasts almost a thousand screensavers to satisfy your cravings for eye candy.

FREEWARENOW
(www.freewarenow.com)
Guilt-free wares! Since this site features freeware, you can get all the downloads and none of the bad conscience. FreewareNow has everything from sound files to screensavers. This site is updated daily, with a newsletter similar to shareware.com.

Privacy in the Digital Age

If you spend a lot of time online, making sure your business stays your business means understanding who's collecting what kind of information about you and how. Then, you can take matters into your own hands.

by Ethan Zuckerman

Privacy is not an easy subject to talk about. If you express concerns about privacy, people will ask you, "What have you got to hide?" There's a good response to this question: Ask your inquisitors whether they send all their mail by postcard. Everyone needs a little privacy to carry out business, romance, or even a friendship.

How much privacy do you have when using the Internet? Less than you think. That's the bad news. The good news is that, with a little effort, you can keep your business your business.

Getting Personal

Many sites now ask you to register to gain access to some of their services. Information you give a site can be used to make your experience on the Web more "personal." For instance, a site might ask where you live and use this information to give you local news and weather. The same site might also use that information to send you an ad for your local phone company. This sort of personalization is generally useful—even if you don't like ads, you have to admit that it makes more sense to see ads for a product you could buy than for one that doesn't even exist in your area.

Some Web users are becoming very conscious of how the information they've offered is being used. TrustE, a certification board that reviews how Web sites use this kind of information, classifies Web sites into three categories:

No Exchange means that a site will not collect personal information on you—any information you give will be deleted at the end of a session using the site.

One-to-One Exchange means that a site can use the information you give to deliver customized information or advertising to you, but will not exchange this information with another Web site.

One-to-Many Exchange means that a Web site may give or sell any information it gathers on you to other Web sites or offline marketers. You may want to consider looking for TrustE marks on Web sites before deciding to give them personal information, including your E-mail address.

member: Emma

SURVEY: THE FIRST TIME ONLINE

I made the mistake of letting my friend visit the AOL chatrooms using my member name. He must have offended somebody, because over the next few days I started getting obscene phone calls. (OK, not obscene, just sad . . . "What are you wearing, Emma?" etc.) It took me a while to figure out that someone had posted my name and phone number somewhere on AOL with the message: "For a good time, call . . . " That was my first lesson in privacy and the Net! I stopped being quite so diligent about filling out personal information on membership stuff after that.

member: Melosh

SURVEY: PRIVACY

Most companies have it in an agreement that they are allowed to read any E-mail that comes through their system. When I worked at a place where I had E-mail, my password could only be found out by two people with higher clearance than myself. I also changed it every ninety days. Also, thankfully, the big boss wasn't computer savvy enough to have read my E-mail even though it was stored on a local server. If you want private E-mail, get a Hotmail or Rocketmail type account.

Hey Baby, Can I Get Your Number? Your IP Number That Is

Any time you load a page from a Web server, you give certain information to the server's administrator, notably the IP number you're surfing from and the type of computer you're using. An IP number is the closest thing you have to a fingerprint when you're using the Web. Each computer connected to the Internet has a unique IP address, a string of four numbers separated by periods. The first three numbers represent the organization you're logged in from (a university, a corporation, or an ISP), and the last number points to the individual machine you're using. From your IP number, a crafty server administrator can discover what country you're surfing from, who your ISP is, and what company you work for. If you're using a local ISP, a server administrator might even be able to find out the general area in which you live.

All of this sounds somewhat scary and sinister—what are these administrators doing tracking your every move? The truth is a little more benign: Web sites just want to make a buck. By understanding their member base better (20 percent of our page views come from Sweden, 35 percent of our users run WindowsNT) sites can charge advertisers more money for ads. (IP numbers do not correspond to E-mail addresses, so a sleazy marketer can't send you mail saying, "Hey, I saw you visited my Web site!")

IPs turn out to be a lousy way to identify users, though. If I log into a Web site from my office, I'm telling the Web server that I'm IP number 209.23.141.2. When I log in from home that evening, the Web server sees that I'm IP number 204.34.213.23. The server has no way of knowing the same person is using these two different IPs and, therefore, any personalization I've set up based on my work IP won't work using my home IP. Worse yet, if I use an ISP or online service to access a Web site, I'll be given a new IP number every time I dial into my service. The Web server will never know who I am just from my IP.

member: ppparker

SURVEY: PRIVACY

My employer has an acceptable-use policy governing the use of company equipment. It is reasonable at this point, i.e., no surfing porno sites or conducting personal business. Ultimately, a person is at work to work. They have no right to spend that time in personal pursuits, online or not. If you spend your time at work making personal phone calls, you are not upholding your end of the bargain with your employer. The caveat is that in my online time at work, I may pass through places not specifically related to work. If my employer were to use a log of my accesses to then say that I was "not working," and reprimand me for instance without understanding the technology, I would quit. Period.

Cookies . . . Like None Your Mama Ever Baked

One of the most popular ways to identify users session to session is through "cookies." A cookie is a small file written onto your hard drive by a Web site. It might contain a unique identifying number so the site can track you session to session, a date—probably the last time you logged on—and, if the site asks you for personal information, the cookie might contain that information, either encrypted or in readable text.

Want to know what's in your cookies? A little poking around on your hard drive will usually reveal the location of a file called cookie.txt (on PCs) or MagicCookie (on Macs). Start by using the Find utility to search your hard drive. If that doesn't turn up the file, look in the Netscape or Explorer folders. (On a Windows95 PC, you can also look in Program Files; on Macs, try the Preferences folder in your System Folder.) Use a word processor to open the cookie file. You may need to tell your word processor to open all files, not just text documents. You'll see a file that looks something like this:

Netscape HTTP Cookie Fil # http:// www. netscape.com/
newsref/std/ cookie_spec.html # This is a generated file! Do not edit
scores-espn.sportszone.comFALSE/cgi/scoretrackerFALSE
946627200SCOREBOARDSPORT=Major+League+Soccer&
SOUND=on&UPDATE=15+sec&FAVORITES=fbp
GNB%2Cfbp PHI%2C

Each line is a cookie set by a different Web server. For instance, the first cookie in this file was set by scores-espn.sportzone.com, one of the servers making up ESPN's SportsZone site. The last part of each line is the data a server chooses to store about you. ESPN, for instance, has stored the fact that I want updates on a sports score ticker every fifteen seconds, and that I'm interested in major league soccer results and the scores from the Green Bay Packers and Philadelphia Eagles games (GNB and PHI in the last line). Using this stored information, they can set up a customized sports score ticker for me every time I log on to their site.

Oncc you've opened this file, you've got the option to delete any or all of the cookies, just like you'd remove lines from a letter you'd written. There's an even more drastic way to do this: Within Preferences of either Netscape or Internet Explorer there's the option to turn cookies off. Before you turn off cookies or edit your cookies file, a few thoughts. Don't cut off your nose to spite your face. Sites use cookies to track you, but they also use cookies to give you a personalized view of the Web. If you enjoy getting weather for your area when you go to a particular Web site, be careful how you treat that cookie. If you eliminate the cookie, the server won't know who you are and can't tell whether to give you weather for Phoenix, Arizona, or Green Bay, Wisconsin.

Most people's objections to cookies stem from the fact that they're largely hidden from view—none of the Web browsers give you the option to examine your cookies from within the browser. Microsoft and others are trying to address this problem by creating OPS—Open Profiling Standard. Like cookies, your OPS profile would live on your hard drive. But unlike cookies, you could edit it easily, making sure you were comfortable about the information you were presenting to Web sites.

member: jkcummi

SURVEY: PRIVACY

I worked for a company in the computer security area. Their stated policy was as follows: "All computers, media, and correspondence (written or electronic) are property of the company. Do not send anything you do not want read by management or an investigating body." The reason for this policy is the existence of the Federal laws pertaining to anticompetitive policies (price fixing, mononopolies, and market collusion). If a suit is filed against the company by the government or by a competitor, all records *including* electronic ones, must be turned over to the investigating team. If you have a friend at a rival company you have been exchanging E-mail with, you personally can be investigated for anticompetitive practices.

Cookies and OPS share a common problem, however: They're stored on your hard drive. What happens if I want to get my home weather when I'm on the road, using my laptop or logging in from a cybercafe? My cookie is at home on my PC. Enter the "log-in."

Logging In

Sites that really need to know who you are will ask you for a user name and password before letting you work on any personal data (like a personalized stock portfolio). It's annoying but for your protection. If you've got a homepage on Tripod, would you want anyone who sat down at your computer to be able to modify it? By requiring a user name and password before letting you modify a homepage, Tripod can prevent someone from changing your homepage, something that could be really damaging for some people. (How would your boss feel if your homepage began, "I hate my job and I'm looking for another position immediately. Please hire me—here's my résumé.") While log-ins and passwords do give system administrators a reliable way to track your movements on a Web site, they also protect your rights as an online publisher.

member: Carolannie

SURVEY: PRIVACY

I give my employer a great deal of my time and *creativity* and I consistently do an outstanding job. It's unfair and stupid to look over my shoulder every minute to see if I am really working. Because I am a creative person, watching me every moment and forbidding digressions, even if they seem unrelated, would squash and squander the very thing that makes me a valuable employee.

member: rtalada

SURVEY: PRIVACY

As soon as I leave my desk, my boss sits right down and "tinkers" with my computer—reading E-mail, looking at my browser history, you get the idea. The only real consequence is that I always delete any especially juicy E-mail items, and I conduct my job search from home. It sucks, though, but frankly doesn't really surprise me.

Privacy at Work

Whether you're concerned about being watched by Web site administrators or not, there's another cause for Web-surfing worry if you have Web access from work: What does your boss see you doing on the Web?

If you work for a large corporation, there's a good chance that your Web surfing is being watched. Many corporations feel (understandably, perhaps) that they shouldn't finance your extracurricular Web surfing. After all, they are paying you for your time in the office and for your connectivity, to boot. Using tools like Cyberpatrol or Cybersitter, which are usually installed on your hard drive, system administrators are able to keep track of whatever sites you look at.

If you'd like to make sure that your surfing doesn't raise any eyebrows, especially your boss's, here are a few tips:

- Precheck URLs. Responsible companies like Cyberpatrol maintain lists of the sites they block and make them available to the

Web community. By entering a URL into the CyberNot engine (http://www.cyberpatrol.com/cybernot/), you can see whether Cyberpatrol is going to block a URL and why. If you're worried a URL might be blocked, check it out before you visit it.

- It's not just porn that these engines check for. Cyberpatrol can be configured to keep you from browsing sports or entertainment sites as well. If your company Web-use policy bans "recreational surfing," be aware that checking the sports scores could get you into trouble.

There's a solution, of sorts, to the site-blocking problem. It's called The Anonymizer and is located at http://www.anonymizer.com. The Anonymizer loads pages for you, allowing you to access sites anonymously. Imagine your organization prevents you from surfing sports sites. You could load espn.com through The Anonymizer and your system administrator will see you accessing anonymizer.org rather than espn.com, allowing you to acccss blocked pages. Of course, your system administrator may get suspicious if she sees you accessing The Anonymizer several times a day. Lucent Technologies is currently experimenting with a similar service, located at http://wwww.lpwa.com.

member: Nick_Condyles

SURVEY: PRIVACY

Whether someone is looking over your shoulder or doing a keystroke capture, passwords . . . private keys . . . are less and less reliable. There is a great need for biometry schema in addition to key use. Not calling for smart cards or retinal scanners or hand-spread scanners or simply a means of identifying yourself in a personal way. Encrypted streams are great until someone grabs your keyring or a key and suddenly has access and means to illegally obtain services, use password "protected" credit cards.

What About My E-mail?

If you're worried about your employer watching your Web surfing, allow me to share an even more disturbing concern: There's a good chance that your employer reads your E-mail. Isn't this illegal? Nope. Court decisions have determined that employers provide employees with E-mail as a tool to carry out their jobs and that employers have the right to monitor the use of those tools. In the same way that an employer can forbid you from making personal calls from an office telephone, he can also prevent you from using E-mail for private conversations. The difference is that she can monitor your E-mail to make sure you're complying, setting up potentially embarrassing situations.

If you think your work E-mail is being monitored, here's an easy solution—get another E-mail account from an online service or ISP. Use your work account for work only and carry out your personal life on your own account. Never make the mistake of searching for a new job using your work E-mail—there's no easier way to guarantee that you'll need a new job.

Not an underemployed temp slave? You still need to worry about E-mail security, even if you're the CEO of your company. E-mail is not a good medium for sensitive communications because of what we call "The Rogue Sysadmin Problem." An E-mail system administrator needs to have access to the mail of everyone on her system so she can diagnose problems as they arise. She also needs access to all the mail that passes through her system. If you must use E-mail for secure communications, agree on a set of code words with your correspondent—over the telephone, not over E-mail.

Phil Zimmerman to the Rescue

Better than encoding some of your conversation, why not encode the whole thing? Encryption makes the Web a more private place. But how do you send me a coded message? The best solution is known as "public-key encryption." Here's how it works: You want to send me a message that only I can read. You look up my "public key" and feed it into your encryption program along with the message you want to encode. Using my public key, your program creates a message that only I can understand. You then send me the encoded message over the Internet, without fear that anyone can read it. By feeding your message into my encryption program along with my secret "private key," I'm able to decipher your message.

The big innovation in public-key encryption is the fact that I can publish my public key, but you can't decipher a message based solely on the public key. In fact, if you encode a message to me with my public key, you can't read it either! A fellow named Phil Zimmerman created a program called PGP—short for Pretty Good Privacy—which lets you protect documents and E-mail with public-key encryption.

To prevent identity-counterfeiting, PGP keys are signed by other people who've got PGP keys. Your key will only be signed if you can convince the signer that you are who you say you are. In the past, people would get together for "key-signing parties," where the new PGP users would produce passports, driver's licenses, and high

member: WashingtonG
SURVEY: PRIVACY
A boss where I work just mistakenly sent an E-mail to "distribution," i.e., everyone in the 700 person organization. The E-mail was to his honey. Lucky for him it was very innocent.

member: vlemle00
SURVEY: PRIVACY
The case of the snooping boss or anyone else getting into my files raises the anarchist streak in me. I'd probably password protect my personal files. Then I'd copy them to floppy and destroy the originals, being careful to empty the trash bin each time. Then as an added measure I'd change the attributes of the files on the floppy disk to hidden files and defrag the hard drive.

school yearbooks to convince the signers that they were who they said they were. Verisign (www.verisign.com) has tried to make the process a little easier. If you send them certain pieces of information, they'll sign your PGP key and get you on the road toward public-key encryption.

Incidently, public-key encryption is what makes secure transactions possible over the Internet. When you send your credit card number to a virtual florist to pay for flowers for your grandmother, you want to make sure no one intercepts that number and uses your

credit card to buy a new motorcycle. When your browser sends a form to a secure server, it looks up the public key that corporation has registered and encrypts the message using said key, so your form is only readable by the intended recipient. This doesn't prevent the florist shop from defrauding you in a variety of other ways (not sending your grandmother the flowers, overcharging you, etc.), but it does mean that a wily hacker can't intercept your credit card information on the way to the florist's site.

Unfortunately, encryption is harder to use than it should be. Very few of the major commercial programs people use integrate encryption. There's a reason for this; U.S. law makes it very difficult to export encryption software because said software, in the hands of the wrong users, might constitute a threat to national security (or so the government's reasoning goes).

Strong encryption software, therefore, is not exportable, and software companies wishing to use encryption need to create two versions of software—one for domestic use and another for overseas use. Given the trouble of doing this, many companies skirt the problem and don't incorporate encryption into word processors or E-mail software. As the Internet becomes more of a common carrier, software companies may need to take encryption more seriously, and perhaps they'll convince the United States to change its stance on the status of encryption software.

member: Spinnuendo
SURVEY: PRIVACY
Definitely start using Hotmail for personal E-mail. And don't forget to turn off cookies in your browser! This way, even if your boss sits down and notices that you've been to hotmail.com, he can't find out what's there (assuming you've logged off)!

member: glamour
SURVEY: PRIVACY
If the boss owns the computer and pays for Internet access, then he is justified in finding out what his employees are doing while they are on the clock. If you want privacy, buy your own computer.

member: Miranda1
SURVEY: PRIVACY
If I had a boss, I wouldn't care if he read my E-mail. Let him be as bored as me when my brother-in-law E-mails about his latest big purchase.

Conferencing

Long before there was a Web, conferencing was established as the preferred way to concoct an online society.

by David Hudson

Anyone who logged on to the Internet for the first time during the last few years was probably greeted initially by the dazzling face of the Web. It was the Web that sparked the media blitz hyping the Internet in the mid '90s, enticing tens of millions of newbies to look at their personal computers as more than just a tool for the home office. Now it could also be a source of entertainment and information.

Businesses ranging from multinational corporations to the local mom-and-pop store on the corner also discovered the Net (about a quarter of a century after its creation), setting up shop with Web sites and investing in banner ads—those billboards along what we were then calling the Information Superhighway. But as nifty as it was to pull up pages from halfway around the world that looked as if they might have been ripped from a glossy magazine, something vital was missing, something unique to what the online experience had been before the Web.

That something was other people. After surfing aimlessly for a few nights, those newbies may well have wondered what all the fuss was about, while businesses found themselves looking in vain for a quick return on their investments. But if the talk of 1996 was the looming Great Web Wipeout, there was a new rejuvenated buzz the following year. The word for it was "community."

Business Week was impressed enough with the success of Internet communities to feature the phenomenon on its cover. And while other models, such as the online magazine or the Web site as

member: dpadgett1
SURVEY: INTERNET ADDICTION
My ex-wife tells me she divorced me because I spent more time on the computer than on her! Seriously, the Internet is a problem for me, no time for anything else.

member: Mukul
SURVEY: INTERNET ADDICTION
IAD is a *real* problem now. I speak from experience. I have not met any friends for the past two weeks. I am perpetually glued to my computer. My fingers ache from typing and clicking. And I am not the only one. And as in the future our lines become faster, technology gives us better stuff, we'll probably not even need anyone else. My phone bill is going through the roof. I can't concentrate on my job. My social skills are falling. Bad Bad Bad. I think I'll just have to throw away my computer one of these days if I want to live in the physical world.

member: Melosh
SURVEY: ONLINE COMMUNITY
You never really know the person behind those electrons on your screen and people can harrass you in almost total anonymity (spam, flames, impersonation, etc.).

company brochure, bled cash, cut staff, or shut down altogether, business consultants John Hagel and Arthur Armstrong found an incredibly receptive audience for their book, *Net Gain: Expanding Markets through Virtual Communities*.

The world of commerce finally discovered what seasoned Net veterans had known all along. What got people so excited about this many-to-many medium in the first place was the ability to congregate with like minds; what might be lost by not having a face-to-face gathering was more than made up for by the fact that time and distance had been rendered practically irrelevant.

The ways people get together online can be loosely lumped into three basic categories: E-mail, chat, and conferencing. E-mail, still one of the Net's most popular applications, can also be put to use as an ad hoc conferencing system by simply ccing one or more recipients. Then, of course, there are the mailing lists, running on software such as listserv or majordomo, and as primitive (and cheap!) as these may be, some still prefer this version of online conferencing over all others.

When someone on the list has a message to convey, the missive is zapped immediately into your inbox, and if you reply, you reply to everyone at once. In a sense, mailing lists are a cross between the virtual community and push media, though they precede the hype behind both. (A terrific resource for finding out more about how mailing lists work, how to set up one of your own with services such as VP or Coollist, plus general news from the world of mailing lists is Liszt—http://www.liszt.com—also a searchable and browsable database of over 71,000 lists, complete with descriptions.)

Live chat accounts for a full third of the hours users rack up at America Online, and Internet Relay Chat has a rich and venerable history of its own. Popularly associated with flirting, chat can also play an important role during times of crisis, as it did after the Kobe earthquake or during the Gulf War. An important difference between conferencing and chat is that *not* talking in real time can be a genuine advantage. In fact, the very format of most conferencing systems reminds the participants that they aren't talking at all, but writing. Just as there's an art to hosting (see sidebar), there's also an art to posting. Conferencing, in one form or another, has been part-

Member: orbot

SURVEY: INTERNET ADDICTION

The basic misunderstanding, just like the Internet porn routine, is that Internet addiction is a bad thing. It isn't. We don't talk about information addicts when they go for a useless Ph.D. We always understood that the life of the mind is the really important one. Lighten up! How can a society discourage the inquisitiveness of its members? First you complain because we drive around aimlessly, then you complain because we use the elctronic means to move our minds, which are the only part that matters, the defining part of a human. As long as the physical needs are met, there is no problem here. I've always been a magazine subscriber, now I just don't kill trees to read things. I can hardly wait for the next step in this evolution.

member: YCantIBU

SURVEY: ONLINE COMMUNITY

One doesn't pick up all the myriad subtle clues of human interaction behind a computer screen. The end result is it's much easier to get emotional with someone you can't see, be it either falling in love or absolute hatred. Catholics have known this for centuries—that's why you can't see the priest when you go to confession, because you become more emotionally attached to him (and by extention, the Church), and this effect has been documented through several psychology experiments.

ly responsible for a minor renaissance of the written word in the same way that letter writing in the eighteenth century became a literary genre all its own.

It's interesting to note, for example, that the WELL, one of the most famous of all conferencing systems, has now taken to choosing particularly engaging posts to place on its front page on the Web.

> Host Your Own Conference

First, the most practical of concerns. How do you create a conference in the first place?

1. Several existing sites allow you the ability to create a conference for free if you don't mind their ads, their conditions, and sharing their URL. Try Bianca.Com, Community Ware (http://www.communityware.com), GeoCities (http://www.geocities.com), or The Mining Company (http://www.miningco.com) to see which model suits you best. Forum One (see sidebar on page 31) has plenty of tips and pointers here.

2. Start from scratch. No one has lifted the hood and checked out the wealth of conferencing software programs more closely than software designer and writer David Woolley. Woolley's "Conferencing on the Web" page (http://freenet.msp.mn.us/~drwool/webcon2.html) outlines the technical features the ideal conferencing system should have, such as a clear list of topics within broadly defined conference areas, threaded discussions (as opposed to the branching tree free-for-all), and a set of pruning tools for hosts.

Once you've got the house built, you're halfway there. Now, how do you get people to come—and stay?

1. Your most important tool as the host of a conference or even a whole online community is your own intuition. Sure, there are plenty of helpful tips and guidelines, and we'll get to those, but if they were enough, you might as well hire a knowbot. People will be coming to your place to meet and engage with other people, complete with all their idiosyncracies and all those foibles that make us human. They're looking for a bit of warmth in the machine, and the best way you can offer that, as the cliché would have it, is simply to be yourself.

2. A clear yet somewhat flexible vision of what you want to happen in your conference is vital. "Let's just get a bunch of friends together and talk!" isn't going to hack it. That's a sure recipe for bad art and empty topics. Write a mission statement. And if your system allows it, you'll want to place it right up front and make it one of the first things newcomers see as they come in.

3. Make sure there'll be at least some activity going on when the first strangers stroll in. Try to secure commitments, if not ironclad then heartfelt, from friends to help get the conversation going and hang around once things take off. What you don't want your guests to see is, "This is a conference about football," and then your trigger question, "How 'bout them Niners?" just dangling there in empty space.

4. Don't dominate the conference. Your goal is to encourage conversation, not to sound off. Nevertheless, if you have an introductions topic, and you should, be sure to welcome any and everyone who introduces himself.

5. Draw out the shy with compliments (not outright flattery, of course) and questions. That's the easy part, since most will respond. More difficult are the ones who come on too strong. If they're contributing valuable insights or entertaining posts, you might be best off simply letting them go while opening another topic or two to give others a chance to get a word in. But if they're just blabbering

continued on page 29

People on the WELL have long recognized and rewarded (with attention, the real currency of cyberspace) their fellow "WELL beings" who have a talent for crafting the well-made post.

Instead of simply typing extemporaneously (pretty much the chat paradigm), conference participants have a moment or a day to gather their thoughts, form them, take other people's feelings into consideration, weed out possible flame bait, and in their own good time, contribute to the conversation. The result is often — though, of course, not always — a long thread on a particular subject comprised of genuine substance and intelligence.

That's what makes people want to come back. So much so that in the case of some systems like the WELL (located in Sausalito, California) or ECHO (in New York), members are willing to pay for the opportunity to be a part of the proceedings. Besides the potentially fruitful exchange of ideas, it's also those with whom they're exchanging that keeps people returning. When you post in a conference for the first time, you take a chance by investing something of yourself. If someone replies, or even better, if someone picks up on your thought and riffs on it, you may have just made a friend, and eventually, lots of friends. (Okay, and some enemies, too, but that's what makes life interesting, right?)

Exactly what the nature of these bonds is has been the subject of debate for years. For some, the lack of physical presence, geographical proximity, intonation, gesture, and all the other subtle means of communication that go on in "real life" communities means that online conferencing is stringing posts together, no more and no less. For others, such as Howard Rheingold, who popularized the term, these conferences can develop into bona fide "virtual communities."

In 1993, Rheingold's book, *The Virtual Community: Homesteading at the Electronic Frontier*, became one of the best-selling books about online technology, then still a mystery to many in the mainstream. While cyberculture seemed to be teeming with off-putting hackers, geeks, and anarchic digital revolutionaries, here was a book that put a human face on the Internet, arguing that online technology could feed "the hunger for community that grows in the breasts of people around the world as more and more informal public spaces disappear from our real lives."

Member: Dunahein

SURVEY: ONLINE COMMUNITY

Being able to share views and ideas without worrying about appearance, socio-economic conditions, disabilities, or any of the other superficial criteria we judge people by on a daily basis is an incredibly rich experience. I don't ask age, sex, race, or creed when meeting folks online. That is inconsequential, I am far more interested in learning from them, seeing the world through their eyes.

member: Paulson

SURVEY: ONLINE COMMUNITY

A great deal is made of the games people play when online and how people hide behind the anonymity of not being seen. Is this any different from the games people play when going into a bar? Is it unknown for someone to remove his/her wedding ring in a social situation? People play-act in many situations, the Net does not cause it. I have many friends I have met online and they are as real to me as those I have met offline. In some ways they are even more real since so much effort has to be expended in understanding what is being said. Aside from those little smiley characters, there are no hints as to the meaning of statements. You cannot hear the anger or angst in a statement. You cannot see the hurt or glee in eyes. You have to be more careful with what you say and how you intrepret things. In short you have to "think" and in my mind, thinking is not a bad thing.

Not everyone bought that argument, of course. Critics claimed that Rheingold was still hauling around quite a bit of baggage from the '60s, that hunching over a keyboard for hours on end exchanging messages on Usenet or on some local BBS was hardly communicating at all, much less the building block for a real community.

Rheingold heard his critics and in 1996 he set out to put his ideas about online communities to the test by launching a Web site called Electric Minds. Minds was certainly not the first online community on the Web, but it was important in that with all the incum-

> Host Your Own Conference, cont.

harmlessly yet dully, believe it or not, the community will take care of it by ignoring him or her. Without feedback, he or she will cool off sooner than you might think.

6. Worse, of course, are the true jerks. They're out there, and sooner or later, they'll find your place and start trying to cause a ruckus. The main thing is not to blow your top. Take a deep breath before you post anything condemning their actions, and when you do, make it polite. You'll immediately win over the support of the others. But then there are the jerks who feed on this sort of thing. The tragedy of our postmodern times is that we often think self-referentiality is about the smartest thing around. It works for *The Simpsons*, but not in online conferences. One of the deadliest things you can do to a conversation is have it go meta. It's not just off-topic, it's boring and tedious, and your good posters will start to wander off. This is when you'll have to resort to backstage maneuvering. That's right, E-mail. First, E-mail the jerk, and again, be friendly yet firm, stay above the fray, but let him or her know that the conference has a chosen theme and he or she is not it. Second, E-mail your steady participants and let them know you're on the case and that you appreciate their patience. Remind them that all the jerk wants is attention, so the best way they can deal with the situation is to ignore her.

7. You won't want to E-mail too often, however. The conversation should be going on in your conference, not behind closed doors. And some people find E-mail intrusive. But E-mail can be a handy tool for encouraging the quiet ones and suppressing the party poopers.

8. Depending on your software, you might be outfitted with a set of hosting tools—ways of freezing or zapping individual posts, topics, or whole conferences. Use these very sparingly because the overall impression you want to create is that you are one among equals, that all voices should be heard, and all you're doing is gently nudging here and there and only when necessary.

9. Keep an eye out in real life for newsy or intriguing bits with which to spice up the conversation. If you're talking about books, toss in the news of who's just won the Pulitzer or open a topic on a newly released controversial title. But again, you don't want to overdo it. You'll soon get a feel for how much space your group needs.

10. Finally, be there. The last thing you want is for someone to ask a question or venture a risky observation and then have it dangle for days. If you don't have a ready reply, post something, anything, even if it's, "I don't know. Anybody else?" Of course, you can do better than that, but the point is to let the poster know you're there and listening. That's what they've come for.

bent media attention (it was listed as one of the ten best sites of the year by *Time*, for example), it raised public awareness as to the Web's essential flaw: Surfing is lonely.

Rheingold set out to remedy this sense of isolation by creating what he called a "Social Web," putting the conversation up front. By any measure but one, it was a rousing success, with tens of thousands of members talking up an electric storm. But that one missing element—financing—was crucial. With its large budget and staff and its lack of sufficient advertising and sponsorship income, the site was in severe danger of closing down not one year after it had been built.

But the members rallied themselves, setting up conference topics devoted to saving their virtual home. Eventually, Minds members worked out the terms for a deal with Durand Communications, who bought the rights to the name and then packed the server into a van to drive it to the company's headquarters in Santa Barbara. The van bore a sign for the trip: "Wide Load—Community Inside."

Rheingold had succeeded in proving that while people might not display any overwhelming signs of loyalty for one search engine or browser over another, they will for other people they've met via this technology. And for the place(s) where they met.

So what was right about the Net all along has finally been brought to its primary interface, the Web. Some have suggested that once all the technological dust has settled, Net users and the media alike will be less concerned with the features of this or that software program or with which new media company has bought out which other company. Instead, we'll be reading, hearing, and watching stories in the press about what's actually going on in the conferences themselves.

Perhaps. But with the settling of the dust may come the convergence of online technologies with appliances we already know (and love?): television, radio, and the telephone. While that would seem at first glance to point to real-time video chat instead of considered,

member: Traegorn

SURVEY: ONLINE COMMUNITY

When I got on the Web in 1994 through my school I was pretty hyped up. The community on the Web felt a lot more tight-knit than it does now. I met some people on the Web that I got really close to. They were intelligent, funny people. Then, after the school year ended, I lost access and changed schools. It wouldn't be until 1996 that I got back online. Things were different; 90 percent of what I found was a bunch of link pages. I returned to my old haunt to find that only one or two still even used the place. The place, well, dumbed up. The conversations were nothing but Cybersex and a bunch of people who were amazed to see their own text appear on the screen. I ended up searching other chat servers. I found the same thing. I *finally* found an intelligent RPG-based room, but alas, our Internet service bill was too high and I had to limit myself for a while. When I returned to the room I found that yet again, another place had been discovered by the Cybersex morons. More recently I found an RPG game that ran its own room and kicked out nonplayers. I joined. That is the only room out there, and it's not populated lately (they just changed servers). But in there I met people that I found out I knew in RL but had never talked to. I also met some people from other places and have become friends with them. So in a way, the Internet can provide meaningful friendships, but you gotta dig, I mean really dig, to find the people worth befriending.

threaded, text-only discussion, we as a society have persistently held on to allegedly "outdated" media such as the book, the magazine, and the newspaper because they enrich our lives in a way no other medium can. In much the same way, online conferencing may already have proven itself worthy of our continued persistence.

Member: QueenMeow
SURVEY: ONLINE COMMUNITY
There *are* a lot of jerks and phonies out there so everyone should still beware, but if it weren't for the Internet, I would not have found the happiness that I have now. The guy I met on here is fantastic and makes me feel love like I never have before. I know in my heart this is the one I will be with for the rest of my life. I have quite a few friends on the Net that I know I can go to about anything and vice versa. We laugh together, cry together, and I wouldn't trade any of them for anything.

> Conferences to Check Out

FORUM ONE
http://www.ForumOne.com
A fascinating starting point that lists and links to over 100,000 conversations going on all over the Web. It's a handy tool for host wannabes because you can try out a variety of software, see who's already talking about what you'd like to talk about, and measure various hosts' approaches against your own. Search or browse by topic.

SALON'S TABLE TALK
http://www.salonmagazine.com
CAFÉ UTNE
http://www.utne.com
The Big Ones. Interestingly, both systems are located "behind" magazines, so there's a constant influx of new material to talk about. Both have begun to scour their conferences for juicy exchanges, which they link to right from their front pages. And it's no coincidence that both have a team of sharp hosts who are always there without getting overbearing.

THE WELL
http://www.well.com
ECHO
http://www.echonyc.com
The old-timers. Both charge for admission, but if you're serious about conferencing, it may well be worth taking a peak at professionals at work.

CONCRETE MEDIA
http://www.concretemedia.com
http://www.GirlsOnFilm.com
The well-honed conference with a purpose. Dan Pelson of Concrete Media has a great idea. Instead of throwing everything under the sun onto one system, he's created several different systems with their own URLs. At Girls on Film, for example, users, 80 percent of them women, respond to the irreverent and chatty movie reviews by a handful of female writers. A select topic for a select group.

Chat

Perhaps the most popular application on the Net, chat is creating a whole new brand of human interaction.

by Christina Simmons

> Some are tempted to think of life in cyberspace as insignificant . . . It is not. Our experiences there are serious play.
>
> —SHERRY TURKLE, *Life on the Screen: Identity in the Age of the Internet*

Chat is more than the CB radio of the twenty-first century. For starters, chat is one of the most popular applications on the entire Net: As of this writing, one-third of all the hours racked up by America Online users is devoted to chatting. Chat is also fast becoming a key component to the online presence of major corporations. The leading purveyor of chat software, ichat, counts the *Wall Street Journal*, AT&T, and Sony among its clients; companies who promote chat software online find no shortage of users.

But what makes "chat" all that? After all, it's just a group of people (2 or 200) congregating somewhere behind the computer screen, often identified only by pseudonyms. Chatroom illiterates imagine that all these aliased folks are in actuality adolescent males pretending to be older men, mousey young women pretending to be *Playboy* centerfolds because they can't get a date, or social deviants looking to hack, stalk, rape, pillage, or lure the unsuspecting into shady business deals. If the skeptics could paint a picture of Internet chat, it would look like the works of William Gibson crossed with *Penthouse Letters*.

In truth, those who take chat seriously, as a means of meeting other like minds and sharing mutual interests, can suss out who's a cyberfreak and who isn't. Chatroomers do not suffer fools gladly. And intelligent conversationalists don't tend to advertise their presence.

For first-timers, chat is usually inane. Newcomers are not likely to walk into the sort of stimulating, chummy atmosphere true chat addicts thrive on. For newbies, it's like going to a party and not knowing who to talk to. It takes a while for some users to get their "chatting legs," but after some practice, folks start feeling more and more comfortable in these virtual gab fests.

"The need for human communication is ubiquitous," John McAfee, chairman and founder of Tribal Voice, said via E-mail. "In cyberspace it is evolving into chat communities that include many activities beyond chatting." According to McAfee, people using his product have gotten engaged without meeting in the flesh.

Perhaps not everyone who wants to chat is looking for a life mate, but people are clearly looking for something. Devotees of a particular television series, having exhausted the patient ears that surround them on a daily basis, seek other similarly obsessed fans online. Parents chat with their campus-bound offspring without running up astronomical phone bills.

Chat is also the shy person's haven: a chance to initiate relationships minus the usual pressures of a first face-to-face meeting. Many longtime chat acquaintances do eventually agree to meet IRL (In Real Life), by which time the initial awkwardness of meeting is gone—because you're no longer meeting a stranger.

This liberating anonymity also gives rise to one of the darker aspects of online chat. Sherry Turkle, author of *Life on the Screen*, spent months observing online communities and notes:

> Life on the screen makes it very easy to present oneself as other than one is in real life. And although some people think that representing oneself as other than one is is always a deception, many people turn to online life with the intention of playing it exactly this way. They insist

`member: Rachel`

SURVEY: ONLINE COMMUNITY

Online communities have certain advantages—for one thing, it's easy to find others who share your interests, no matter how isolated you are in RL. (For example, I've found a significant community of interfaith couples online, which beats the small town I live in. I think I know two of us in RL here.) On the other hand, RL communities have to do with shared experience, shared space, and necessity of getting along; even if you don't share special interests with the people in your local community, you have something invested in remaining a cohesive community, so you make things work. In the online world we don't have as much invested in staying cohesive or functional, which makes online communities disintegrate and splinter more easily than RL ones do.

`member: MaxGoof`

SURVEY: ONLINE COMMUNITY

I have never been a people person, so to speak. I wanted others to start communicating with me through E-mail, MUCKs, or whatever online chat material there is out there. It is much easier to talk to others when you don't see the person, than when you talk face-to-face. I use that to my advantage, being quite shy.

`member: RbarthJr2`

SURVEY: ONLINE COMMUNITY

I think chat works like psychoanalysis does—it's all projection. In reality, it is essentially *you* that you are talking to!

that a certain amount of shape-shifting is part of the online game. When people become intimate, they are particularly vulnerable; it is easy to get hurt in online relationships.

This prospect is enough to turn some people off chat before they give themselves a chance to find their niche. Learning the ins and outs of chat is an adventure—a quest for real companionship in a virtual world. And as any truly devoted chatter will attest, it's

member: Gonosnexus
SURVEY: ONLINE COMMUNITY
I think that Net relationships are just as valid as any other . . . in fact, I think that there is an advantage to them in that you don't get tripped up on aesthetics from the get-go . . . you are forced to experience the personality first.

> Chat Etiquette

- You'll need a name: a "nick," a "handle," a "screen name." To avoid unwanted romantic advances, pick one that's gender-neutral. For example, "Hunter_Class" is more gender-neutral than "Horse_Girl." Stick with that name. If you're a different person every night, how will people recognize you?

- People who chat in a select number of chatrooms tend to form closer online friendships than people who bounce around a lot. Try out a few different chat forums, then pick the one or two you like best.

- Greet people when you enter a room and say good-bye before you leave—it's amiable.

- There's nothing wrong with keeping quiet during your first visit to a room; it will help you get to know the "house rules."

- DON'T TYPE IN ALL CAPS! IT'S THE SAME THING AS SHOUTING, AND YOUR FELLOW CHATTERS CAN HEAR YOU PERFECTLY ALREADY!

- Avoid questions like, "Anyone want to chat?" (if you have to ask, the answer's already No), "Are you male or female?" (if they wanted you to know, they'd have told you), or "How old is everyone in here?" (that's generally the question of thirteen-year-old boys pretending to be twenty-one or older).

DON'T TALK TO STRANGERS (AND EVERYONE'S A STRANGER)

- Keep a low profile until you're sure of the people in the room—until you know them and they know you. After all, you wouldn't walk into a strange apartment and assume that everyone's your best friend. Hackers and stalkers need to notice you before they bother you—and the quickest way to attract their attention is to walk around making it clear that you're new in the area.

- Don't accept transferred files or programs from someone you don't know well. More than one innocent chatter has downloaded a virus that way, and some nasty folks use chat to spread as many RAM-trashing programs as they can.

- Be *very* careful of the information you reveal in *any* chatroom. Saying, "I'm John from Tulsa" is fine in most cases; saying, "I'm John Smith from Tulsa" is not. Remember, it's too easy for people to find you online as it is. Even if you don't mind perfect strangers turning up on your doorstep, in your mailbox, or on your answering machine, it doesn't mean that your roommate (or parents or spouse) would be as open!

- If someone wants to contact you offline, ask for his or her information first and try to be the initiator.

- Remember, most online psychopaths will appear perfectly normal and friendly until you're alone with them face-to-face! Yes, this is scary, but it's also true; more victims of violent crime are assaulted by a person they know and trust than by a complete stranger.

worth putting up with a cybertroll or three to make really good friends.

Playing in the MUD

No chat article would be complete without some mention of what has become the premiere amusement of choice for chat addicts—MUDs. MUDs (Multi-User Dungeons) have been the backbone of chat ever since some long-forgotten Dungeons and Dragons players decided that it would be fun to bring friends together remotely for an evening of gaming.

To participate in a MUD—or a MOO (Multi-User Object Oriented) or MUSH (Multi-User Shared Hallucination)—or in any of the other variations the phenomenon has spawned, you need a computer with IRC or Telnet connectivity (see sidebar on page 40) and a very active imagination. MUDs in any format rejoice in bringing the fictional to life, whether the dreamworld of choice is Tolkien's Middle Earth, a lonely planet in a galaxy far, far away, or a World War II strategy room. If it's popular and copyrighted, it probably has an unofficial MUD—games based on *Star Trek* and *Star Wars* have become as popular as the more "traditional" pure fantasy MUDs, and MUD-type gaming communities exist for everything from Marvel Comics' *X Men* to the *X-Files*.

It's generally unwise simply to leap into a MUD without first doing some background work. To join these particular chat communities you'll be expected to have a character—an alter ego. Men can be women. Women can be men. In certain settings, players don't even need to be human. Within the various dragon-populated worlds spawned by Anne McCaffery's popular *Dragonriders of Pern* novels, players may opt to be dragon, rider, both, or neither. Confusing? Exactly! And that is precisely why you cannot leap into a MUD unprepared. It's always prudent to lurk around a MUD as a guest before deciding to make a home there.

The first thing necessary to make the MUD enjoyable for you as well as your fellow players is a shift of mindset. Repeat after me: "I am *not* my character! I am *not* my character!" Good. If a potential MUD player has any doubts about the distinction between a fictional character and a real person, he or she might want to check out

member: Ashi_aana

survey: Online Community

Net friends can be more compatible. People tend to open up more on the Net because there is no risk of being embarrassed at times as you are not known physically. Hence people are able to share secrets buried fathoms down in the heart.

Member: meian

survey: Online Community

I haven't quite found a real "community" on the net—Geocities is too big and I feel a little left out in Tripod. I did find an E-mail pal. You might be able to say that I'm part of the Sailormoon and general anime subculture, whatever you want to call it. Every now and then I go look at pages and see what I can find. It's nice to know that there are other people with the same interests.

member: Miranda1

survey: Online Community

I don't participate in IRC, and probably won't ever. It's far too vague and unreal. There's just too much room for dishonesty. I don't believe any online relationship can be compared to real life. That's stupid. It's a totally different dimension, and no matter what people may claim, it's not the same.

member: Twyla

survey: Online Community

There are loons loose in the ether world, and they seem to delight in dragging communities down to the lowest common denominator, but if there is a strong bond in the group, it survives.

these guidelines, drawn from the player manual for the IRC's Office of Paranormal Investigation Simulation Game:

> Obligatory reality check, beginning now. PLAYERS are those flesh-and-blood entities on the business side of the keyboard. CHARACTERS are free-ranging entities within the ether. While characters may possess many of the qualities of their players—as many as said player

> Chatrooms We Love

IRC

True, Internet Relay Chat is entirely text-based—no icon buttons, no silly HTML tricks, no .gif or .jpeg wallpaper for the rooms, no Halloween-mask avatars chatting with one another. But hey, if we want to see pictures, we'll use our browsers and hit our favorite Web sites! IRC is the place to be for back-to-basics chat for chat's sake, available 24/7. You pick the subject: with DALnet, UnderNet, EffNet, and all the other IRC supporters, you've got the widest single-location range of topics to be found online, from the *X-Files* to all things X-rated.

NOTE: You'll need special software to connect to IRC. We recommend PIRCH or mIRC for PCs, and Ircle for the Mac. (Check the section on Shareware and Freeware earlier in this chapter for places to download these programs.)

WEB-BASEDCHAT

ICQ
(http://www.mirabilis.com/)
With sound-it-out humor, "I seek you" becomes ICQ. Search the user's lists to join established discussion groups dealing with specific topics—from great vacations to Great Danes—or create a user list of your own. Set your ICQ to notify you when your friends log on, or place an ICQ pager on your homepage.

TRIBAL VOICE'S POWWOW
(http://www.tribal.com/powwow/)
It's more of a community than simply a chat service and one of our favorite chat places to be. Be sure to check out their twenty-four-hour community rooms with topics ranging from fantasy football to dolphin lovers, and the chat feature that allows you to play tour guide and haul your PowWow friends from URL to URL—slick!

ACTIVE WORLDS
(http://www.activeworlds.com/)
With its 3D interface, this is the next step in online chatting. As a chatter, your animated "avatar" roams a remarkably detailed world, meeting and greeting as it goes along. Do not attempt to use Active Worlds if your computer isn't up to snuff! You'll need to download their software, and you'll need the disk space to run it (if you're already a computer-gaming fiend, you probably have enough)—but it's worth it.

THE PALACE
(http://www.thepalace.com/)
One of the original fully graphic chat sites, and still a classic. When you first join up, you're able to move about with a generic smiley avatar, but once you've decided this is the chat for you, you may choose to pay a nominal fee to upload your own customized avatar.

TALK CITY
(http://www.talkcity.com/)
Friendly to Web TV users, no software required, and three interfaces to choose from. We particularly like the feature that highlights what rooms are open and populated at the time you log on.

YAHOO! CHAT
(http://chat.yahoo.com)
From the original Web directory comes a new chat community that plenty of people are talking about. You'll need to register and download the software, but one of the most convenient things about Yahoo! chat is that there is a virtually endless supply of topics—just run a search on Yahoo! for your favorite subject, and you're bound to find listings for a chat.

TRIPOD CHAT
(http://www.tripod.com/planet/chat/)
Okay, so maybe we're biased . . .

> feels comfortable writing into the profile—they are, for all practical purposes, imaginary. Please, for the sake and sanity of your fellow players, remember that words and actions directed at your character in the course of a [game] do not necessarily reflect that player's attitude towards YOU.

member: Sarashay
SURVEY: ONLINE COMMUNITY
The Internet has done wonders for sustaining all kinds of subcultures. It's not as though these subcultures were entirely new—there have been fanzines and clubs and so forth for years before there were even modems. The Internet is just another tool for people with common interests to communicate with, added on to the postal service, the telephone, and the convention.

Chatting in character can be incredibly liberating, allowing a MUD player to explore different facets of his or her personality without worrying about deceiving others; in a MUD, unlike in "straight" chat, having more than one personality is part of the fun. To a certain extent, the masquerade of a MUD lends itself to a greater depth of honesty when two players decide to extend their

friendship into reality; if you learn that your friend Vlad the Barbarian is actually Phyllis, a secretary for a small packing firm in Detroit, you'd probably be less surprised than if you discovered that the single-and-swinging Charles from Singles Chat is actually a fourteen-year-old kid who invented Charlie with a group of his hormone-addled friends. As with any chat community, the newcomer must expect a certain amount of falsehood or deception; but within a MUD, at least the deception is part of the game and not simply someone playing games.

member: robertcooper

SURVEY: ONLINE COMMUNITY

The difficulty of use when the only Internet access you could get at home was your Netcom shell account, frankly, filtered out a lot of these people who are looking for nothing more than Pamela Anderson pictures and someone to "chat up." Get a life.

member: zeta

SURVEY: INTERNET ADDICTION

My husband and I came > < this close to divorcing in the past month. We've been on the net just over a year now and the online relationships were killing our RL relationship. I honestly don't think I could quit. I have friends who had to pull their modems for a year to save their marriage. They've been an enormous help, but I'm too addicted to quit. I've stayed up all night on many many occasions talking on MUCKs and MUDs. We've spent money we really can't afford on hardware and net connections and we've alienated many of our RL family and friends. I don't know what can be done about it. I think it may just be a fact of life now.

member: czfz

SURVEY: ONLINE COMMUNITY

The Internet is a valuable information/ communications tool in the global economy especially for science writers like me. I located and communicated via E-mail and real-time chat, for example, with a physicist in Russia and a software developer in Albania. This would be virtually impossible otherwise.

Build Your Own Homepage

The personal publishing revolution is upon us in a huge way. And if you haven't built your own outpost in cyberspace, you're really missing the boat.

> The web is the first semi-permanent unlimited worldwide exhibition space. Think of it as a never-ending world's fair, where anyone can set up a booth, and you don't have to be there to see it.
>
> —JUSTIN HALL *(http://www.justin.org)*

by Michele Chihara

It's not explaining your homepage to other people whose REM sleep has already been invaded by Hyper Text Markup Language that's hard (those initiated to the rites of code know what it's like to dream their dreams in tags). It's explaining a homepage addiction to the DGIs—Netspeak for those people who don't get it—that can be tricky. "I just don't get it," they say, ignorant of the call of the nested table. "What's the point?"

Describing the phenomenon of the homepage to a DGI is like explaining a key to an alien life-form who knows no doors. In a new medium, no one metaphor is sufficient. Homepages are another way of expressing ourselves and looking at one another. People use them to magnify, intensify, calcify, stupefy, and elevate themselves at alternating moments. A homepage can be a résumé, a magazine, a portfolio, a poem, an essay, a meeting place, a personal ad, a diary, a gallery, a collection, a business card, a care, an imaginary world. It can be a work of art or absolute drivel, and either way, it pops up on your screen in the same way as a number of well-known Web publications with very deep pockets, like *Salon* or CNET.

In this regard, the Web is the great equalizer, an egalitarian affair where everyone can have a say. Pages put out by individuals are as easy to call up as *Slate*, Microsoft's biggest financial venture into content-providing ("content" being the Web world's word for anything that might pass for editorial material, text or otherwise). Typing in the URL—the Internet address at the top of your browser—for Jane Schmoe's Page About Herself is as easy as typing in http://www.slate.com.

This explains why those of us who have a knee-jerk tendency to doubt the mainstream are so excited about the Web's possibilities. Jane Schmoe gets to have her say, and we bet our chips on the idea that the Jane Schmoes of the world are ultimately more subversive and interesting than any site brought into existence and funded by Bill Gates.

The homepage started out as a way for individuals to have something of a home base in the anarchic cyberfrontier. Even today, as the Web proliferates, a good set of links expresses something very deep about a person's taste. The Web weary will sigh, "Oh, I never surf, it's too frustrating." And granted, there's nothing as frustrating as when you're looking for some solid information about Hanson's past and you just keep getting the same links to the same "What 'MMMBop' Means to Me" sites. At the same time, finding a collection of links by somebody who's really done their surfing is like landing on a gold mine. This is how I found *Plotz*, a zine for the hip Jew in all of us (http://www.flotsam.com/PLOTZ), or the *MIT Guide to lock picking* (http://www.lysator.liu.se/mit-guide/mit-guide.html). Finding one links page authored by a person whose taste you trust can provide you with the starting point for hours, weeks, even months of satisfying surfing. So don't be afraid to collect and publish your own. Think of this as classic homepage building.

Some of these "links" pages eventually morphed into Vanity Central: "This is what I find fascinating" to "Find me fascinating, though you know nothing of me save my favorite band." In other

member: Absynthe

CONFERENCE: How Do You Use the Internet?

I waste a lot of my time online writing long E-mails to people I will never meet in person . . . signing guest books for the pages of people that often I would never want to meet in person . . . improving my Web page, so lots and lots of people (more than I could ever possibly dream of meeting in person) can gape at their screens in collective awe of my HTML prowess . . . I spend too much time online.

member: mrusk

SURVEY: Homepage

I built my homepage because it was fun, basically free, and a way to publish things that I wrote. After the initial excitement wore off I felt I had to add meaningful content. I didn't want to clutter up the Internet with totally self-serving writing. So I decided to create an HTML guide that I felt would be helpful to beginners like myself. Then I found a drawer full of family history that I wanted to make available to other, as yet undiscovered, members of my family tree. It has been a very rewarding experience and I've met many people from around the world.

words, The Me Page, which is still the widely accepted view of the homepage's main purpose. Me pages have an alarming tendency to be boring. But Me pages, in their very self-absorbedness, can also be wild, weird, and wonderful. Some of the most famous homepages are diaries by the likes of online pioneers Justin Hall (www.justin.org) and Carolyn L. Burke, who made headlines by baring their souls online. Collections of online journals like *Archipelago* (http://www.geocities.com/SoHo/Studios/4350/index.html) link groups of people who keep track of

> Killer Homepages & Why They Rock

The Power of the Guest Book

(http://www.fray.com)

The guest book is one of the first things that everybody asks for. You put up a page on the Web and the first thing you want to know is, "Who's out there? Who saw this?"

The Fray is one of the best examples of just how powerful a guest book can be. Many homepages are emblazoned with blinking, font size 5 orders to "Sign My Guest Book." But often, people have no response to these pleas, and we homepagers are left bereft and frustrated. The Fray, on the other hand, by posting strikingly honest stories, creates a strikingly honest atmosphere. Derek Powazek of HotWired created this site in his spare time. Its design is cutting edge, but he has done much more than put his Web expertise from HotWired to use. Every time I visit, I am most impressed not by the layout but by how Fray's visitors' contributions—hundreds and hundreds of posts—are consistently open, eloquent, and trenchant.

A guest book is made of two components: an HTML page with a form that users fill out with input, and a CGI script. CGI gives input from an HTML page to an external program, like a PERL script. If that I-don't-do-that-stuff glaze is starting to come over your eyes let me reassure you that you don't need to learn CGI. The vast majority of page builders never will. Most of us who put pages up never have to learn anything beyond our friendly tag language. There are free, already existing CGI scripts at your disposal, which you can use to do things like put guest books on your page. Tripod provides its members with free guest books: (http://screenlife.tripod.com/lifesupport/burningquestions/htmlcode/index.html). Also, Lpage (http://www.lpage.com/) runs a free site called GuestWorld.

The Importance of Navigation

(http://www.thefinger.com)

Zinester (and Tripod contributor) Sam Pratt put his zine experience and design smarts together to create a site with the ultimate navigation device: the hand. Creating a Web site that's both easy to use and deep (multilayered) at the same time is no small task. The Finger uses the hand as an organizing principle, with each finger representing a day, a section, and a general tenor for whatever gets posted under its banner (the middle finger is the Bird . . . you get the picture).

For a great primer on how to brainstorm an architecture for the layering of your own site, try Crystal Waters's book *Web Concept and Design* (http://www.typo.com/wcd/wcd.html).

Pushing the Boundaries

(http://www.entropy8.com)

With Entropy8, called by its creator a "labor of love and frustration," Auriea Harvey pushes the boundaries of Web design. She calls the site her "outlet and also a playground for experimentation. I am interested in collaborating or freelancing with other artists whose idea of free is to make the unexpected happen." She has gone professional with her design work, but Entropy8 began as a labor of love: a homepage. Watch and learn.

the ins and outs of one another's lives (for more personal pages, The Mining Company has a great "guide" at personal web.miningco.com). For a true taste of someone else's humanity, a good online journal beats out *The Real World* any day.

E-zines are an obvious extension of obsession-with-self pages; they are the obsession-with-something-else pages. People have long been expressing themselves in the punk, DIY-style of the zine, even before the *New York Times* (and everyone else) discovered the trend. A number of great collections of resources exist online geared specifically toward the zine enthusiast. Make sure to check out Chip Rowe's *Book of Zines* homepage (http://thetransom.com/chip/zines)—not to mention Chip's piece on starting your own E-zine in the next chapter—as well as Justin Hall's guide, *Publish Yo Self* (http://www.links.net/ webpub/index.html).

Of course, the salsa of the Web is interactivity. And what everyone from the average homepage builder to the hottest venture capital firm is coming to realize is that people go online to find other people. Contact and correspondence is as much of a reason to surf as information. One of the first additions that people crave when they've built a homepage is a guest book. We put ourselves out there, and then we want to know: "Who's looking? Who has been here?" Homepages might seem like the ultimate expression of stubborn individuality but stumbling upon someone's collection of snow globes, if you share that fanatic love of snow globes, is a grand way to feel connected.

member: Patricia_F

SURVEY: HOMEPAGE

I am a preschool teacher who had problems finding good activities that I could use in the classroom. I figured if I was having a problem, other preschool teachers were too. I took matters into my own hands and started my own page, which provides craft recipes, holiday activities, teacher tips, and more. I have slowly added more and more to my page, and the few people who have visited have said very nice things about it. I love to see a new name in my guest book; especially when they tell me that I have helped them in some way.

member: JDConrad

SURVEY: HOMEPAGE

I figure if I would like to know something, there are probably a few other people who would like to know it too. I don't see the point in simply making a page about yourself. And pages and pages of links without commentary seems redundant.

member: thersites

SURVEY: HOMEPAGE

My six Web pages are used to politcal purpose, to promote a cause, or to campaign against a political development I consider despicable.

Making Some Pages (The Nuts and Bolts)

You've browsed, you've surfed, you've posted. Now you want your own page. Before you can put them on the Web for all to see, you must first make them on your own computer. One phrase: HTML.

HTML—Hyper Text Markup Language—was invented in 1990, by a physicist in Switzerland with a lot of time on his hands. HTML is a simple coded language that your browser reads to display the pages that you see when you surf the World Wide Web. Think of it as the universal language that speaks to all of the different browsers and computers that access the Internet. HTML is basically a word processing language, with some essential differences. Instead of choosing Bold from a menu and then watching

> The Personal Publishing Revolution

As perhaps the first person on the planet to publicly state that video games, computers, and TV remote controls are fundamental building blocks to a healthy adulthood, writer/media analyst Douglas Rushkoff is a rare voice in a world lamenting the demise of the American attention span. Rushkoff believes that new technologies in media and publishing are granting us the power to take conscious control over our media intake. These technologies, he says, not only break the spell of passive media consumption but are actually aiding and abetting what he calls "a global evolution of consciousness" that is breaking down established Western structures faster than you can say, "You've got mail!"

With industry deregulations and the onslaught of personal publishing technologies, the media is no longer dominated by a group of guys in suits instilling group-think into the herds. Instead, Rushkoff believes, it has evolved into a complex interactive and organic system that is an extension of human consciousness. For more from Rushkoff, check out his books, the titles of which include *Cyberia*, *Media Virus!*, *Playing the Future*, and *The Ecstasy Club*.

Tripod: What is behind today's increased interest in the notion of personal publishing?

DR: We're moving into a world where an increasing number of people want to direct their own experience. Personal technology and publishing allow us to do just that. TV can show you a dying baby, but there's nothing you can do. Eventually, the nerve ending goes dead. Interactive media and personal publishing lets you at least say something, and perhaps choose to *do* something, too.

Tripod: What do you see as the role of personal publishing in this media evolution you've written about?

DR: Really, there are two ways to interact with media. Media can either impact your life or you can impact the world through media. If media is exclusively a way for others to impact on you, then the evolution of technology will be a further degradation of your ability to express who you are and to influence the world around you. You'll be programmed that much further and you'll be further victimized by external influences. But if you're able to think of media and technology as a way to express yourself and extend who you are—literally, to extend your nervous system through media in one form or another—then the more technology there is in this world, the more you will feel extended out, reaching out and touching the lives of other people.

Tripod: So you're saying you think it's a necessity.

DR: I don't think it's possible to have one without the other and stay healthy. If a person is going to be a receiver of information and influence other people's thoughts through new technology, then it behooves them to also be a transmitter.

Tripod: Why? What's so potent about the media as it is now?

DR: Once media becomes out of the control of any one select group of people and becomes a more natural system—which I think it has—it becomes part of the mechanism by which society regulates itself. In other words, rather than having Rupert Murdoch or William Randolph Hearst regulating us, it becomes the way we direct ourselves. It's a collective dreamspace where we try out new scenarios. The more people can contribute to the collective dream, the more influence they have over the collective reality. Our media space is the battleground of a many-centuries-old ideological war. Only recently have plain old folks like us had the ability to enter it and change it. This does make a difference.

—*J. Betty Ray*

your letters turn dark on your screen, you have to say "bold" in HTML with a tag:

<bold> These words should be dark</bold>.

Your browser will interpret anything in <tags> as an HTML command and execute it as such.

While it's true that as Web technology gets more and more advanced there is more and more that you can learn, basic HTML will always be easy to learn. Dynamic HTML and cascading style sheets are expanding the possibilities of what you can do with the language, but they are far from necessary for most homepage builders. Bottom line is: If you want to change the size of your font, type <font size=3> and that will be your font size.

The best way to learn HTML is to choose Source or Document Source from the View menu in your browser. This will show you the code for whatever page you're looking at. Studying code that you like is the best, and some say only, way to really perfect HTML skills. Ultimately, every budding HTML whiz just has to be prepared to tinker. Take tables, for example. HTML's way of arranging objects, both text and images, on a page, is to arrange them in a table. You create a table row, and then you create a cell, and then you put data (text or images) in the cell. The hard part is not figuring out how to create a table. Once you know how, the hard part is getting to the point where you can create a table that does exactly what you want it to do on the first try.

member: Miranda1
SURVEY: HOMEPAGE
I have Web counters and so on, but really, the number of visitors doesn't do a lot for inspiration. I suppose that if even one person happens to enjoy the site, I'm glad.

member: Samdo
SURVEY: HOMEPAGE
I am a self-taught artist but find it hard to try to sell my work. I use my homepage as a way to share my work with others and not have to worry about what to charge. And, I have been commissioned to do a painting because of my page.

Pictures and Other Images

HTML can manipulate the size, shape, and placement of your text and images. It cannot create images, however. You've got to get those on your own. Beware of stealing images from other sites, which is as easy as viewing source but not anywhere as laudable or as legal. Tripod has a huge collection of links to sites that give away clip art and other pictures for free. If you're not using art that you know you can use, you're probably depriving some starving artist of his next pack of Ramen. Repent, take the image off your page, and go buy yourself a copy of Photoshop.

Adobe Photoshop (http://www.adobe.com/prodindex/main.

html) is the industry standard for creating and manipulating graphics and photographs. On Steven's page (http://www.echonyc.com/steven/einstein.html), for example, his name is a graphic, not just text and HTML. There is no tag for <cool font>, as of yet, so to change much of anything beyond color and size, you have to create images of the font you want. If you master Photoshop to the point where you can use it to create really good-looking images, you can land yourself a job at a Web design firm. There are, however, smaller packages for the less ambitious, as well as a scaled-down version called Photoshop Deluxe, which is all that you need to monkey around with photographs. Tripod also offers tips, and can point you to free or cheap software for fiddling with your own images (http://screenlife.tripod.com/lifesupport/toolbox/design/webgraphics.html). Photographs, like Steven's photograph of himself, have to be scanned into the computer; scanners are available at most photocopying businesses (like Kinko's) or sometimes at public libraries (try searching Tripod for more information on how to scan images).

member: VixenOne
SURVEY: HOMEPAGE
I find writing HTML allows me to express my creativity. Before I taught myself HTML, I was afraid of it because I thought it was terribly technical. Once I took the plunge, however, and made my first page, I was hooked. I get immense satisfaction from a page well done and never stop looking for just the right backgrounds to keep the look fresh. Content, however, is still the most important thing to me. I review and update content regularly to keep people coming back.

Putting It on the Web

Once you have created your pages, you need them to exist in a place where other Web users can get to them. Doing so means using the File Transfer Protocol or FTP (careful, more acronyms). Some browsers incorporate FTP software, and many computers now come with an FTP client already installed. If not, check Yahoo!'s list of FTP software sites: http://www.yahoo.com/computers_and_internet/software/internet/ftp/index.html.

E-Zines

Publishing your own E-zine is an incredibly low-cost way to reach a potentially huge audience. So make sure you proofread: The world may be reading.

by Chip Rowe

In 1994, faced with increasing printing and postage costs, I took my zine electric. My life has not been the same since. I no longer plant myself in front of a television. Instead, I plant myself in front of a monitor and spend hours fiddling with the *Chip Electric*. It's immensely satisfying and habit-forming, especially if you love the idea that you can change, update, and improve your product twenty-four hours a day. (My wife is less enthusiastic.) I haven't abandoned paper, but I have expanded my audience: In the same year that my print zine reached 800 readers, my Webzine reached 10,000.

Print zines have been around for decades, created (often photocopied) on a shoestring by men and women who had something to say and needed a venue in which to say it. It was the Internet, however, that introduced zines to the masses and organized them with search engines and directories to bring readers, artists, and writers together. Though everyone from *Time* to *Penthouse* has written about the Webzine explosion, focusing on advertising-driven sites such as *Slate* and *Salon*, the majority of E-zines remain in the hands of solitary editors driven by passion rather than profits. There's *bitch dyke whore*, "a super-personal, angry, grrl-powered zine"; *A Call to Cud*, "the official E-zine of the Holy Church of Moo"; *Curriculum Vitae*, "the zine dedicated to mean-spirited intellectual discourse"; and *Come*, "the journal of eclectic journeys," to name a few of the titles included in John Labovitz's online list of E-zines. John began the list in 1993 with 25 entries. It now has close to 2,300 and is admittedly far from complete.

That growth has come as people realize they can create their own magazines and present them to the world at little expense. Many Webzines are incredibly well-designed and written. They are personal and political. They are raw and honest. Some are much better than others. But that's not important: Most Webzines are not created to enlighten surfers or please advertisers, but to satisfy the men and women who felt a need to create them. The goal, in the words of E-zine creator George Myers Jr.: "Have fun, write well, be smart, sound like a human being, entertain yourself as you would have others entertain you."

member: kennyaj

SURVEY: E-ZINES

The main difference between E-zines and online magazines is that E-zine publishers *have* to publish what they've got to say—release through sharing. Who's going to listen to them otherwise? People who write E-zines do it for fun, not profit; people who write online magazines may have other ambitions. It's easier to publish a zine on the Net than by any other means, and anyone can read it, if they know where to look.

Online publishing is a lot like sex. Before your first sexual encounter, your mind may race through the many kinky positions and oddball fetishes you can't wait to try. As you become more experienced, however, you discover simpler pleasures. You realize that it can be very erotic simply to stroke your lover's hair.

In online terms, there are many exciting ways to present your zine. But the equivalent of stroking your lover's hair is the ASCII format. It's nothing more than your words dumped on the page—no bold, italic, underline, graphics, or varying type sizes. It can be read by any personal computer in existence with minimal software. That's an audience you can't ignore.

The simplicity of ASCII can also help the novice zine creator focus on the important things. The format requires that you focus exclusively on the substance of your material, since you can't rely on fancy graphics or spinning Java applets to entertain readers. "E-zines, because of their lack of material presence, need an extra boost in the literary department," explains Alex Swain in his FAQ (Frequently Asked Questions) list on E-zines. Being ultra-descriptive is the only way around not having pictures or drawings. After you write something, go back and pretend that you're an innocent reader of the text. Can you see it? Is it concise? Does it flow?

Though you'll lose some technologically challenged readers, graphics and other more sophisticated geegaws may be the next step for your E-zine. To create an E-zine that can include color, photos, icons, and other gizmos, most editors rely on the Web, with all its linking possibilities as well as its capacity to handle graphics, sound, even video. In order to catch as many readers as possible, some zinesters create two or three versions of each issue, including an ASCII and a paper version. Until graphics technology becomes ubiquitous, I recommend always creating an ASCII version. This way you aren't limiting your audience by creating a version that rubs its belly, blows bubbles, and walks backward at the same time. Remember, there are also many people in the world who do not have Web access but who definitely can receive your ASCII zine by E-mail.

> Words from the Wise

Offer information (as opposed to the ho-hum rant), ease up on the graphics, and try, try, try to write without sarcasm. The reasons and routes to a zine are hairpin and oblique. Once you've got a reader or browser, offer him reasons to stay. Frames are not reasons to stay, long download times aren't reasons to stay, and brassy opinionating doesn't mean a thing. (Lots of people have balls. So?) If you can explain your zine in a sentence you have a fighting chance.

—George Myers Jr., george jr.
(http://www.georgejr.com)

Everyone I know who has done a Webzine has wildly underestimated the time and the hassle involved. Those who promise a daily edition are lucky to last a week or two before slacking off; those who promise weekly updates drift onto a two-week, or month, or two-month plan and begin to resent the "duties" involved in what started as a labor of love.

—David Futrelle, dimFLASH
(http://www.well.com/user/futrelle)

Have a few prolific contributors. Give them a schedule for their columns and have them supply the first two or three. As you publish, always stay one column ahead. That way, when the day comes when someone flakes (and someone will), you'll have enough ammo to get you through.

—Benjamin Serrato, 15 Minutes
(http://www.15minutes.com)

Don't post everything from your paper version online or you're not giving anyone an incentive to seek it out. Leave something for those who enjoy reading on the toilet. If you can get inter active, do it. Whether this be a poll with a simple E-mail response form or a quiz, it makes the site a lot more fun than just pages of text.

— Rod Lott, Hitch
(http://www.ionet.net/-twilken /HITCH)

With my first Webzine, *Traffic*, I followed the model of a print magazine: a "cover" that led to a few articles or a table of contents, six departments, and a navigation scheme that broke articles into pages rather than letting them scroll. Unfortunately, having all those departments made it hard to get a sense of momentum in any one of them. So I created the weekly Soundbitten, which has no graphics, no animations, no sound, no video, no cover page, no departments, just one article that anyone who comes to the site sees as soon as they get there.

—G.Beato, Soundbitten
(http://www.soundbitten.com)

Once you've created your E-zine, test it thoroughly before inviting readers to read it. In the case of an ASCII zine, Phil Agre of the *Network Observer* suggests that you label it "Draft—Do not circulate" and "send it to a dozen friends and a dozen people who already run online newsletters with a low-pressure request for criticism and comment." If you've created a Webzine, test your work on as many machines and with as many browsers as you can. That's how the software developers test new products. It will eliminate a lot of headaches later on.

There are two bits of advice that you will hear repeatedly from other E-zine editors: First, keep it fresh. "Don't put your zine online and abandon it," says Jim Romenesko, editor of *Obscure Publications*. "My visitor count was flat when I let cobwebs grow on my site."

Second, take it slow. Many zine editors start out gung ho, take on more than they can handle, and find themselves bored or frustrated as they try to manage a cornucopia of features and files. John Labovitz of the E-Zine List suggests keeping your ego and early enthusiasm in check. "Like with a paper zine, it's easy to think of all the great things you'd like to publish, all those great designs, fancy graphics," he says. "But when you do that, the zine never gets finished. Keep it simple to start, then build on it."

member: Traegorn

SURVEY: E-ZINES

What I hate are the sites that update once every two years or something. I just saw a site last week that was reporting on the opening of *Star Trek: First Contact*. This of course was *over a freaking year ago*!! Needless to say, most E-zines suck, and you must look really hard to get the good ones, but they exist.

Once you've found your voice and brought something new to the arena, be diligent about getting the word out about your creation. Many editors with ASCII text versions of their zines compile lists of the E-mail addresses of friends and readers and send them each new issue. For privacy's sake, send out copies individually or use a blind cc. It's bad online etiquette to send your E-zine to large numbers of people unsolicited, a practice otherwise known as Spamming. Always include information about how people can sign up to receive each new issue; that way, if your readers pass an issue along, the new reader can contact you to get on the list. Announce new issues of your zine on the Usenet group alt.zines and post your ASCII version to alt.etext.

Getting the word out takes serious promotion, indeed. "The Internet," notes Swain, "is very big no matter how you slice it. It is quite possible to use the Net for ten years and never come across something you would have enjoyed. Because of this you have to viciously plug yourself wherever you can." To that end, register with directories such as Yahoo! and John Labovitz's E-Zine List and search engines such as Lycos. Notify other E-zines and paper zines through alt.zines or personal E-mail messages. Include the URL in your signature file.

You may find, however, after all you've done to put your zine online, that your readers will bring you full circle, pining (as mine were) for a paper version. If you do a paper zine and enjoy it, think of your digital version as a supplement rather than a substitute. That has become my happy medium. A paper version will satisfy your readers' desire to hold the zine in their hands. An E-zine will take you back to the roots of why you publish—to be read.

member: mazdaman
SURVEY: E-ZINES
E-zines save trees!

member:pirate_editor
SURVEY: E-ZINES
E-zines are a mass-media mogul's worst nightmare. Before E-zines we had a choice between believing one of less than a dozen news agencies or ignorance. It is no longer the province of these global corporations to disseminate information, but the actual community of the world. Now, a single person can have the same credence as a large multinational, by producing a damned fine E-zine. Simple, easy, and the height of Democracy, which the Western world has aspired to so often, always pretended to have achieved, and woefully failed without exception.

> E-zine Essentials

Resources

DIY Search
http://www.diysearch.com
Do-It-Yourself central, from E-zines to music to the arts.

How to Publicize Your E-Zine
http://thetransom.com/chip/zines/
Ways to inform the online masses about your work.

Todd Kuiper's E-Mail-Zines List
http://propagandist.com/tkemzl
ASCII zines available via E-mail.

Factsheet Five
http://www.factsheet5.com
Excerpts from the magazine of zine reviews.

The E-Zine Resource Guide
http://www.zinebook.com
Links to more than 100 quality E-zine resources.

John Labovitz's E-Zine List
http://www.meer.net/-johnl/
The one-stop-shopping Webzine directory.

Six Great Webzines

bOING bOING
http://www.members.tripod.com/-boing_boing/index.html
Fringe technology for mutants who bounce.

Bust
http://www.bust.com
The E-zine for women too old for *Sassy*.

Cardhouse
http://www.media.mit.edu/people/dryer
Cultural macros and assorted pranks.

FAT!SO?
http://www.fatso.com
"A waist is a terrible thing to mind."

Inquisitor
http://www.inquisitor.com
Media, art, culture, technology, and 90210.

Kooks
http://www.teleport.com/-dkossy
A report on people who have big ideas and time to work them out.

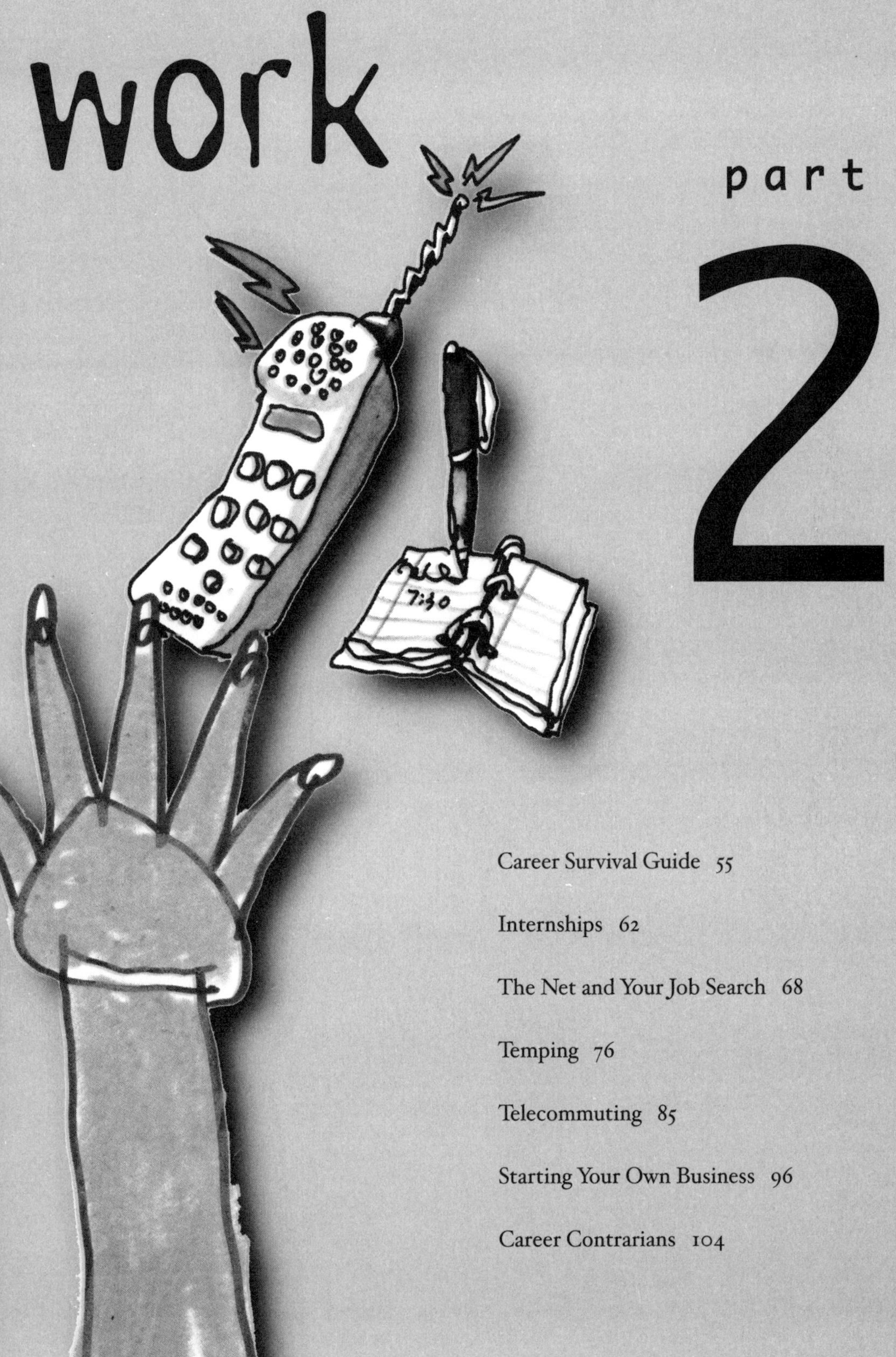

work

part

2

Career Survival Guide

The days of the 25th anniversary gold Rolex are gone for good. In the New World of Work, only you and you alone can make sure your career path isn't leading to a dead end.

by Bruce Tulgan

Thought you'd start on the bottom rung of a big established company's corporate ladder and after a few years of selling ads or writing your boss's dinner speeches you'd be set with a secure long-time gig? Thought you'd get a job when you graduated, one with tasks and responsibilities that stayed pretty much the same from day to day? That you would go to the same building every day, work the same hours, for the same boss, and hope for your boss to get promoted so you could move up, too? And the longer you performed the same tasks day in and day out, the more seniority you'd accumulate, giving you more status, power, and money, right?

Wrong. Dreadfully so, in fact. In today's hypercompetitive business climate, the full-time job as it's traditionally been understood has become a much less stable institution. In the past, companies used to lay off workers when business was slow and rehire when business improved. But now, the constant flow of sudden business shifts has made that start-and-stop ethic obsolete. Employers need to be able to staff a project the moment a market opportunity arises and achieve instant results, and respond to equally abrupt moments of crisis in a similar fashion.

Thus, the rapid growth of more "flexible" employment arrangements—temping, employee leasing, and outsourcing. But even if you are employed full-time, your relationship with your employer is more likely a short-term transaction than a long-term commitment.

member: jbdab

CONFERENCE:
WORKPLACE OF THE FUTURE

I think we definitely need to reevaluate our perceptions and expectations of the American workplace. Employers demonstrate to us every day they cannot be trusted to be guardians of our job security. Security will only be as secure as we make it. While we must continue to be loyal to our employers as long as they sign our paychecks (unless they ask us to do something illegal, immoral, or uneth ical) employers' loyalty *has been* and *will always be* the bottom line. Career commitment? No longer. We're contractors nowadays. We'll be moving from contract to contract instead of progressing up the fictitious "career ladder."

member: Lyn Nelson

CONFERENCE:
WORKPLACE OF THE FUTURE

The future of work is what some are calling "portfolio employment." That's where you work for several different companies at the same time, providing only the services they are willing (or able) to pay you for. You have to decide which employers you want to work for. Under the portfolio scheme the best way to contribute to corporate America "on your own terms" will be as a technical/service consultant/contractor, there to add your talents or experience to a specific project, and then off again to help a different group, or a different company.

These new employee-employer bargains go something like this: Workers contribute their skills, knowledge, time, energy, and creativity to achieve concrete results meeting the immediate needs of an organization, its customers, or its clients. In return, employers offer financial compensation, benefits (sometimes), training and development, work experience, opportunities to build valuable relationships, and more and more control over schedules and work environments.

Now this sounds terrific (especially if you're an employer), but there's a dark side to this alleged New World of Work. Yes, parts of the above-described bargain are valid: Employees are these days more likely to be offered "flex-time" schedules and the possibility to work from home (the ascendancy of the Internet is largely responsible for this development). And some kinds of workers—highly skilled, and often rather young, computer programmers, for example—can indeed skip from project to project, from company to company, pretty much writing their own ticket and getting the best of both worlds, as they say.

But for many people these new workplace arrangements really suck. Or at least are really scary. Because what's happening, essentially, is that employers on the whole are relinquishing responsibility for their employees to an unprecendented extent. Pension plans have gone the way of the great lizards and the Bureau of Labor Statistics predicts that Americans now entering the work world will have five or six different careers over the course of their professional lives. You'll likely change jobs more frequently in your first decade in the job market than your parents have over their whole careers. Again, this is ideal for employers, who have you when they need you but no longer have to hold your hand down the path to a twenty-fifth anniversary gold Rolex. But for you, the worker, all this means that the buck really stops with you.

Whether you're presently employed full time (or want to be) or you're a temp who hasn't worked more than two weeks in the same office for more than a year, no one but you will ultimately look out for your own best interests. This is the real legacy of the corporate re-engineering and technological innovation that's characterized this last decade of the twentieth century. Hence the oft-used phrase,

member: tigerchick
SURVEY: BULLY BOSS
I think that there is a pervasive attitude among employers that human resources are as expendable as old 286 computers. It hurts me to see that companies mistakenly think they are succeeding by downsizing . . . this climate makes it easy for bosses to bully.

member: briansmi
CONFERENCE: YOU, INC.
Humans already run their lives like mini-companies without realizing that they are doing it. They realize that they need to have an income (just like a company). They realize that they have expenditures (just like a company). They realize that any money left over is a profit (just like a company, only people call it savings). And they try to operate their minibusinesses within their means (just like a company does). When you decide to try to get a job out of your career focus, it is like a company entering a new market. If you go for a job that is in your career path, you are expanding your experience in the field just as a company would further a product directed at a certain market. The question shouldn't be "Why don't people run their lives like a company?" and should be "Why don't people realize that they run their lives like a company?"

"You, Inc."—a way of saying that wherever you work, whatever you do, you are in business for yourself, and must learn to be the sole proprietor of your skills and abilities.

Now that you're shaking in your boots, we can acknowledge that something positive (and possibly even liberating) can come out of this. As much as you might be alarmed by the lack of an obvious career path, isn't there at least a part of you that has always dreaded the idea of getting an old-fashioned job? Of getting up at the same time every morning, putting on a suit, going to the same office, answering to the same people, and taking responsibility for the same tasks, for the same eight hours, every single day? Now you have an answer for all those folks who keep asking, "Are you ever going to get a job?" The answer, once and for all, is, "Whatever. I like to think of myself more as an independent contractor: Work hard on a project, cash out, then reassess and renegotiate."

Feeling less anxious? Good. All that's left now is to show you how to be one of the lucky ones. First, a pair of case studies and then, a list of career survival tips.

member: Tacitus
CONFERENCE: STRATEGIES FOR STANDING OUT
One good way to get credit for your ideas it to put them in writing. Each idea could be a letter to your supervisor, and if your idea involves how other departments work with your own, you can address the letter to their supervisors as well as your own. The only danger is if your supervisor would get jealous if you communicated to other supervisors. In some places it is okay, in others, it may be taboo. It probably would not work for a newcomer to an organization.

member: Tripod Josh
CONFERENCE: STRATEGIES FOR STANDING OUT
Some bosses wouldn't acknowledge your efforts even if you printed them on a billboard and hung it over their desk. Other bosses go out of their way to acknowledge even those little things you've done but didn't mention to anybody. I was really frustrated by my boss's inattention to my accomplishments at my last job. I tried everything—sending E-mail updates, mentioning them in staff meetings (I'm sure to the annoyance of other people), but nothing worked. So I started keeping my résumé on my desktop, and every time I did something worth noting, I'd add it to my résumé; I figured, even if my boss doesn't notice this stuff, someone else will. And before too long, someone else did.

How the New World of Work Works

Let's take Mervyn's chain of 274 department stores as a starting point. At first glance, Mervyn's buying program looks like the classic workplace hierarchy: Start at the bottom as an assistant buyer, then pay your dues and climb the ladder one rung at a time, from merchandise planning analyst to senior analyst, then manager, supervisor, buyer, and finally senior buyer (seven rungs on that ladder). But Mervyn's realized that this system was not sufficiently fluid to meet all of their unexpected business needs. Plus, the system was causing them to lose some of their most ambitious young people.

In response, Mervyn's created the SWAT Team. Mervyn's SWAT Team members roam the company halls, filling in wherever there are personnel gaps, helping out when there is an opportunity to seize or a crisis to quell. To join the SWAT Team, members are required to master at least one of the new software packages always being introduced for internal use. The SWAT Team member then serves as an internal consultant on the software, offering training as well as troubleshooting services to other employees. In exchange, the SWAT Team members are freed up from the traditional hierarchy: They work flex-time, flex-place, and chart their own career paths. While the program was created to accommodate a few people requesting more flexible conditions, Mervyn's has discovered that the SWAT Team members are among their most valuable employees—and among the most satisfied.

Since 1996, Eric Hutcherson has been in charge of college recruiting at Lotus Development Corp. and has also managed the recruiting and retaining of both minority and female employees. But Hutcherson started off his career five years earlier, light years from his current position, with a master's degree in sports management and a public relations job with the Boston Celtics.

After two years with the Celtics, Hutcherson went to work for the Kinney Shoe Corporation doing marketing and promotions, a job that lasted a little under a year and a half. Then he spent about the same amount of time working for Inroads, a career development organization that facilitates corporate internships for minority college students. The experience at Inroads led to Hutcherson's current responsibilities at Lotus.

"To succeed at Lotus, you need the ability to pick up new information in a hurry, especially technical information, and put it into practice," Hutcherson says. "You need to be able to shift directions in midstream. You need to be able to market yourself and make your own opportunities.

"It is incredible how quickly you can move here, laterally and vertically," Hutcherson continues. "It's not like an old guard company where your moves are scripted; everything about Lotus is that the individual determines his or her own future."

Survival Tips for the Post-Jobs Era

1. Keep your skills and knowledge ahead of the obsolescence curve. Much of what you will need to know in five years hasn't even been discovered or invented yet. That's why it's so important in today's world to be a voracious learner. The number-one challenge we all face is keeping track of the endless amount of information being produced every day, from an overwhelming number of sources, on every conceivable subject (and plenty of inconceivable sub-

`member: marnster`

CONFERENCE: STRATEGIES FOR STANDING OUT

Bosses, generally—and specifically middle-level managers—don't want to see their subordinates shine or excel or be acknowledged for doing good work. It fucks up the flow of the hierarchy when some peon is a stellar worker, and obviously ambitious. I've had several bosses that were actively, vocally pissed when I took on extra tasks or, God forbid, went to other people on their level to network, ask questions—even when it meant that I was more effective at my job. They found that threatening. Maybe that's just my bad luck for working at dysfunctional, rigidly structured companies, or maybe it was my approach—my ambition was too obvious—but I don't think I'm alone in this complaint. One stands out at one's peril.

`member: brianog`

CONFERENCE: YOU, INC.

When I worked in Microsoft I used to read the internal BBS and got to know some very interesting and outspoken people. I remember once when I met one of them (she'll remain nameless), she told me that she hated her job and that she'd stopped making any effort whatsoever. She then said that in MS at that time it took about a year for all the machinery to eventually get around to firing you. You got sent to courses, you got put on probation, but it took a year to actually get fired. So she said, you've always got that year to coast at Bill's expense. I never took up the offer myself, but it was a nice thought.

jects). So how do you decide what to learn? Trust that anything you learn is marketable and focus on learning what you love because then you will learn most voraciously.

2. Build loyalties with individuals instead of institutions. As you pass through various organizations, schools, companies, and other institutions, latch on to mentors, students, coworkers, managers, subordinates, customers, clients, vendors, and suppliers. But don't just let these relationships happen to you. Shape meaningful and gratifying roles for yourself in the lives of others and take responsibility for maintaining these relationships. Together, the individuals with whom you connect and maintain contact over time will become the most reliable institution in your professional life—perhaps the only one.

3. Be prepared to sell your added value on the open market. Look at every person as a potential customer and every unmet need as an opportunity. Match your skills and knowledge with unmet needs to add value:
    a. identify a problem that others have not yet identified
    b. solve a problem that others have not yet solved
    c. invent a brand-new service or product
    d. take an existing service or product and make it faster, easier, more efficient, more effective, more attractive, less expensive
    e. deliver an exising service or product in a more timely, more competent manner

4. Keep your working and nonworking life in balance. Go home and don't take work with you. Go for a long walk without a destination in mind. These are the moments where energy and sanity are regained; you will inevitably do better work if you are not completely consumed by your job.

5. Set concrete goals and deadlines and plan your time effectively. Spend some time at the beginning of each week reviewing all of your upcoming deadlines and brainstorm all the daily actions

member: Tacitus

CONFERENCE: BULLY BOSS

In my office there was a signout sheet and any time an employee had to leave the room for any reason he had to write the time and an explanation of where he was going. So the employees started to sheepishly sign in, "Went to Department X" or "Bathroom" or "Lunch" or whatever. Most of these people were professionals in their thirties to fifties and finally they had enough of being treated like children. One fine day an employee they really couldn't afford to fire started writing in the signout book about his trips to the bathroom in a very detailed way. When nature called, he described the event in some indelicate detail, using all the Anglo-Saxon words at his disposal. Some other adventurous employees quickly followed suit. The signout list immediately became a company-wide joke (as did the department manager whose idea the list was) and within a week or so everyone had stopped signing out and the list was forgotten. Petty tyrants can be fought. It requires people who would be inconvenient to fire to get the ball rolling, and then it is safer for all the lesser pee-ons, oops, I mean peons, to rebel also.

you'll need to take to achieve your goals. Monitor what is working and what isn't and make the necessary adjustments every step of the way.

6. Wherever you are working, learn to manage your boss. Insist on concrete goals and clear deadlines for every assignment. Circulate memos detailing what you are working on at any given time and circulate copies of your finished products.

7. As long as you want to keep working in any one organization, be prepared to reinvent yourself and your role constantly. Be on the lookout for multiple clients in any organization—do not be content to work for one boss. Be able to define problems and come up with innovative solutions. When one project is running out, start looking around for what needs to be done next and design a proposal for the next project you'd like to work on.

8. Remember that no job is "just a job," unless you decide it's going to be. Transform your time at work into a fulfilling, self-building opportunity: Brainstorm ideas about how you can maximize the potential of your situation and use it to add value to yourself.

9. Master the art of negotiation. Practicing these six techniques will make you a better negotiator:
    a. identify the decision maker
    b. find the common ground
    c. identify each party's bottom line, especially your own
    d. get clear on who has the "walk-away power" (if you can walk away with minimal ultimate loss, you are in a very strong position)
    e. move the conversation to specific terms—time, place, and money
    f. shut up: sometimes the best negotiating tactic is to state a position then sit still for excruciating periods of time

member: barrya

CONFERENCE: YOU, INC.

Over the years, there has been a decay of the "corporate family" attitude in the workplace. My grandparents often spoke of their employers more than they spoke of their own parents or "real" family. I think they perhaps came from a time when loyalty was a two-way street, and as a result, often their best interests were looked out for by the "boss." Not so today! For whatever reasons, corporate relationships have changed and no longer can provide the level of security that they once did. Now this doesn't mean that employees should "screw the company." It simply means that if I want someone to be watching my best interests, it had better be me.

member: johncar

SURVEY: BULLY BOSS

You're not going to change a bullying boss. Do what I did—quit. The boss has the advantage of knowing he can fire you. If you want to go toe-to-toe with a person like that, you had better keep your wits about you at all times and *know* you have evidence to take with you to court. You cannot rely on fellow employees to back you up—no matter what they tell you in private.

member: R A Rumpf

CONFERENCE: BULLY BOSS

The law, in most states, indicates that for every four hours of work, fifteen-minute lunch breaks are allowed.

10. Leverage your uniqueness. Identify the factors in your background that set you apart from the crowd and qualify you to help an organization better understand, connect with, or maximize a particular market.

member: hash07

CONFERENCE: BULLY BOSS

In my humble opinion, a bad boss just isn't worth the hassle. Why spend most of your life (at work) dealing with insane and/or corrupted personalities? I can easily think of more enjoyable torture. I tried surviving a bad boss and even went into therapy in an effort to manage the situation. Instead of managing the situation my personality began to change. I started behaving and responding to others as I would my manager. You can imagine the disaster that ensued. My advice to anyone trying to survive a miserable job situation is to leave, but on your *own* terms. Take an action every day to get a new job. A step forward, no matter how small, does wonders for your damaged self-confidence.

Internships

For better or worse, internships have become the new bottom rung on the corporate ladder. Unfair? Maybe. But unless you're sitting on a trust fund, you may have to suck it up and play the game.

by Emma J. Taylor

Critics of internship culture complain that these near-mandatory apprenticeships are nothing more than a chance for rich kids to play at slavery before ascending to their master status. In a 1997 issue of the lefty über-zine *The Baffler*, Jim Frederick wrote of the problem with internships: "You can't take an internship unless you can be supported by Daddy for a couple months [thus] the system guarantees an applicant pool that is decidedly privileged." Why is this so? Because the internship system is driven by two things: its constituents, who are willing and able to work for free, and the '90s necessity of listing at least one internship on your C.V. when you apply for a "real job." An annual hiring survey at Michigan State University found that more than half of last year's new hires had completed career-related internships prior to their first paid job. In some industries, it may be the only way in. Patrick Scheetz, who conducts that yearly hiring survey, notes that prior career-related experience is often rewarded with extra compensation, too.

Of course there are other forms of "payment" available for interns. You might receive school credit, or the internship may offer what Dan Golden, dean for Work and Service-Learning at Wheaton

member: shazya

SURVEY: INTERNSHIPS

My first internship was with a company that hired me as a technical assistant. The unfortunate part was that the gentleman I was assigned to was very paranoid that if anyone learned anything, he or she would take over his job. So my "assisting" duties were to take computers into this back room, take them apart, and vacuum the dust out of them. To top that off, I was encouraged by this fellow to "take my time" doing things, so he didn't have to invent something new and trivial for me to do. He was even going to have me clean his office (by then I could see how office cleaning was going to spruce up my résumé for computer science). When I brought these issues to both my college adviser and my supervisor's manager, the whole thing ended up in finger pointing and it went down in flames (because of course the manager was going to support his supervisor).

College calls "psychic dollars," the value of contacts and skills you pick up during an unpaid internship that will allow you to get a leg up on the competition when it comes time to do battle for precious entry-level jobs.

The Fair Labor Standards Act of 1938 was enacted to prevent employers from abusing workers, which includes not paying them. Companies are exempt from the FLSA when they hire "student learners," but in some states it is illegal for a company to pay anything below minimum wage unless the employee is receiving school credit. Unfortunately, the FLSA is not strictly enforced. The internship market is so competitive that there are usually plenty of applicants lined up behind you who are prepared to work for free.

But, as Jim Frederick writes, "by giving away work, interns reduce the value of everybody's labor." Dean Golden takes a more optimistic tack: "If I could get a résumé plum of an internship at a hot organization, I'd swallow any resentment about being unpaid and take three night jobs with a smile. Today's unpaid internship is tomorrow's summer job or real position after graduating!"

Let's assume that despite the unfairness of the system, you realize you've got to play along as Golden says and "swallow any resentment." And you want to play along well.

member: rwilde

SURVEY: INTERNSHIPS

The best internship I ever had was when I was spending a semester in London during college. I had interned for some local TV news stations back home in the United States in previous summers and really wanted to get hooked up with a U.S. network news bureau in London, the "hub" of international coverage. After weeks and weeks and weeks of calling, writing, and visiting the NBC News Bureau in London, the bureau chief finally, grudgingly, relented and allowed me to come in and intern there. My first assignment? Removing and cleaning the floor-to-ceiling window panels. It worked out great though—after a number of months they ended up hiring me to work on the assignment desk and at Wimbledon, and my contacts there led to a great job at ABC News in Washington after I graduated. Moral of the story: Fight your way into the place you want to work—it often leads to great things!

Ten Tips for Attaining Internship Nirvana

1. Don't panic if you weren't focused on your résumé back in high school. Work experience is valid whenever you start, be it high school or post-college.

2. If you know a place you think you'd like to intern, seek out former interns—they're usually prepared to dish. Ask them if the exposure is worth the drudge work. Ask them if they were allowed to initiate projects. Ask them about hours, pay, and how potential employers have viewed this particular entry on their résumé. And ask them how much coffee and how many photocopies they made that summer.

3. If you haven't a clue about where to find an internship, you need to get one. You'll find internship lists and advice in countless

books and Web sites (see sidebar on page 66). Ask anyone who might have a lead for you. If you can't find a bearable internship, consider approaching employers and offering your services as an intern.

4. Once you're in, figure out who's important in the office and try to get on a project working with him or her. If you're not given a mentor or supervisor, seek one out. Initiate, and prove you're not just out to pad your résumé. Let them know you want responsibility and then run with it.

5. If you're bored out of your mind with nothing to do, work up a list of projects you'd like to work on, and ask permission to go ahead with one of them. As Albert Oh, who interned at Samsung in Korea, puts it: "Try to think like a consultant: Create a need for work."

member: Geenius

SURVEY: INTERNSHIPS

The intern system is the culmination of an unofficial corporate crusade to foist the cost of training new employees off on the taxpayer. The business gets free labor with no long-term obligation to the intern. The intern suffers because it is now the only way to gain entry-level experience. It's part of the great machinery in which people are forced to pay $10,000–$20,000 for the privilege of becoming employable, because a high school education is no longer considered proof of functional literacy, even though the whole point of having a public school system is to guarantee functional literacy to everyone who goes through it. Nobody thinks to question this arrangement.

> Internship Cheat Sheet

There are ten questions you should ask about any internship. Some you can ask at your interview, some may take a little homework (use the Internship Resources and ask former interns), and some involve decisions you'll have to make yourself. The difference between a "busy work" summer and real responsibility and exposure is important enough to warrant the extra effort.

1. Does the company have a formal internship program? It's not the end of the world if one is not in place, but it's a good sign if there is one, especially at a glam company where grunt work abounds. Eric Furie interned at Industrial Light & Magic, the visual effects firm owned by George Lucas. It had fluff potential, but the internship program led to a rewarding experience.

2. Will you have a mentor or supervisor?

3. Will they pay you? If not, will you get credit? If not, is this legal? And will you be able to survive?

4. What are the fringe benefits, if any? Free housing? Free T-shirts? Free meals? Travel compensation?

5. Will they have real work for you, or will you be making coffee all summer?

6. Just in case you end up making coffee all summer, what's the industry exposure like?

7. What are the networking prospects?

8. What is the company's rehire rate (how many interns are offered full-time employment at some point)?

9. Considering your plans for the future, is this a smart addition to your résumé?

10. Will you have fun? Especially important if (a) this is your summer, and (b) you're not getting paid!

6. Don't just snooze in front of your computer. Network! Stacey Irizarry, who did a post-grad internship at the White House's General Counsel's office, says: "There is no reason not to talk to the tons of interesting people around who are dying to tell their stories—how they got there, what they do, advice on how to make a career path for yourself." And if they're not "interesting," (and many of them won't be) pretend that they are and start flapping your gums.

7. You're shy so you're not schmoozing and instead you're stuck in front of that computer? Learn the software: Surf the Web; teach yourself Photoshop or Quark or HTML—computer skills will never go to waste on your résumé.

8. Recite the Zen of interning with me: Every pot of coffee and every hour at the photocopier teaches you something. Patience. Endurance. Whether the guy who got to interview Jakob Dylan prefers regular or decaf.

9. If you're going to do more than one internship, make sure you don't end up doing the same thing every time. If you do a sexy internship one summer, try one that actually teaches you something the following year.

10. If you eventually want to be taken on full-time by the company where you're interning, first make sure that it's a possibility. Besides, the longer you work (hard) for free, the less incentive they have to pay you. Some companies use interns for grunt work alone and would never consider hiring permanent staff from such lowly ranks. Just make sure this situation isn't the case before you start your "hire me" campaign.

nightdriver

SURVEY: INTERNSHIPS

I dressed up in a suit and drove out to a hotel three days a week to serve as intern for an inhouse audio/video company. I didn't make a red cent. There was not even a hint about the possibility of being hired on after my internship was finished. I did learn a few things there, but overall the experience was a waste of my time. The audio/video company just used me to fill a position without compensation.

member: DIMOV

SURVEY: INTERNSHIPS

Interning is a form of corporate slavery for the middle classes that discriminates against those who can't afford to work for free.

INTERN EXEMPLARS

Heather Irwin, now a producer and graphic designer for *New York Times* electronic media, was a stringer for the *New York Times* in college and then an intern for the national bureau of Newhouse

News Service in Washington, D.C. "I always tended to go for the glamour jobs if I could. No one really cares what you did as an intern, so I figured being able to put a big name on my résumé would help me get in the door," Irwin says. This strategy led to a post-internship bidding war for Irwin's services so it's something to keep in mind.

William Georgantas spent a miserable summer interning at *Spin* magazine as an unpaid errand boy. The following summer, he worked in the production department of the *Austin Chronicle*. Not quite as sexy, perhaps; he certainly didn't glimpse any rock stars in the hallway, but he was given responsibility and real reporting experience.

> Internship Resources

1. *America's Top Internships*, by Mark Oldman and Samer Hamadeh. *Princeton Review*'s Oldman and Hamadeh interviewed hundreds of interns to find out the best internships, based on busy work quotient, sexiness factor (David Letterman equals sexy), and pay scale.

2. *Peterson's Internships*
More internships, less thorough and personal research than the Oldman–Hamadeh book. Includes international offerings.

3. National Society of Experiential Education (http://www.nsee.org)
Order their internships directory—as Golden notes, "NSEE is at ground zero of internship movement and related out-of-class learning innovations."

4. Good Works (http://www.tripod.com/work/goodworks/)
Opportunities at social change organizations.

5. Rising Star Internships (http://www.rsinternships.com)
Post your résumé here for a chance at an internship and search their database of internships—it's well-organized, thorough, and up-to-date.

6. Washington Intern Foundation (http://interns.org)
A nonprofit organization that helps you find internships on Capitol Hill and in the D.C. area. Includes advice on being a successful intern, help finding housing, and stories from former interns.

7. Student Center's Guide to Internships (http://www.studentcenter.com/where/intern/intern.htm)
How to research intern opportunities and find the one that's right for you.

8. Wet Feet (http://www.wetfeet.com) Great for pre-internship company research.

9. Tripod's Résumé Builder, (http://www.tripod.com/work/résumé)
Tips on building an outstanding résumé, plus a step-by-step guide to building and posting your résumé on the Web.

10. Know your legal rights: Department of Labor (http://www.dol.gov) and Thomas (http://thomas.loc.gov), a resource for legislative information on the Internet.
In January '97, Republican Rep. Joe Knollenberf introduced an amendment to the FLSA—"The Job Skills Development Act"—that would make it easier for companies to get away with not paying interns. It hasn't been passed into law yet; check on its progress at these sites.

Molly Steenson took an editorial internship at Coffee House Press, a small book publisher in Minneapolis. "It helped me discover things I liked to do and things I didn't want to do," Steenson says. "Surprisingly, I discovered I enjoyed promoting books and setting up book tours." Would she have learned this much at a bigger publishing company? Probably not, she says. "In the end, I think it's more important to learn something meaningful in an internship than to get a good name on your résumé."

The Net and Your Job Search

The Internet may be the biggest boon to job searchers since the invention of the firm handshake. Assuming, of course, you know how to use it.

by Randy Williams

> I've had my résumé posted on five different employment sites on the Web for over three months and haven't heard a thing! Do employers actually check these highly publicized sites?
>
> — *Tripod member TK4BILL_2*

> I just sent E-mail to a potential employer today! It was amazingly easy. I wrote a brief cover letter, and then included a link to my résumé on the WWW. Amazingly, incredibly easy. Of course, I'll bet there are many others who were thinking the same thing.
>
> — *Tripod Member SpittingLlama*

These two comments pinpoint everything that is wrong with looking to the Internet, particularly the World Wide Web, as a foolproof push-button device for landing the job of your dreams. But given the constant hype about online job sites, who could blame these folks for expecting the Net to be the electronic equivalent of a handful of magic beans, capable of instantly sprouting a miraculous bean stalk reaching toward the land of milk and honey?

The bottom line is that these "online employment services" are all about commerce, just as "scientific breakthroughs" like fat-substitute Olestra owe more to the desire for filthy lucre than empathy for your inability to squeeze into a bathing suit in time for summer. The people who run these sites are more than happy to keep you coming back, whether or not you have any real hope of finding a job, so they can get more hits and sell more ads. Oh sure, a few people—those with highly specialized and hotly sought-after skills—may jump-start their careers by casually posting a résumé alongside the millions of others cluttering the Web, but somebody's going to win the lottery, too, right?

If you decide to toss your own employment history and credentials up on the Net, don't fool yourself into thinking that your grueling search for work is over. The truth is that you'd probably have just as much luck renting a plane and carpet bombing major metropolitan areas with your résumé. There are very few reliable shortcuts available for changing any aspect of your life, and that includes your employment situation. If you really want to make it better, you've got to roll up your sleeves and work at it. Hard.

member: hardpack

Survey: Internet Job Search

All I did was go to sites I thought were cool and click around until I found a "jobs" page. and even if they weren't looking to hire, I just sent off a résumé and cover letter to the Web master or whomever. Through this method, I received a lot of "your résumé is on file" responses, but I finally landed a job at amazon.com, for a spot they hadn't even advertised! I just sent in my creds, and they called me up, and the rest is history. There's no real "push" technology when it comes to finding jobs.

At this point, you may be feeling like a nimrod for blowing two grand on a shiny new computer in the hopes that it would transform you into a lean, mean job-finding machine. Therefore, a confession is in order: I found my job online. Before you start calling me a hypocrite, consider that two things differentiated my situation from the one the hapless job seekers at the beginning of this chapter find themselves in. First, I found a position only after months of diligent effort that incorporated both the Internet and more traditional means of job scouting. Second, my job *is* online, working as an editor for Tripod, a company whose flagship product is a Web site. It's hardly surprising that such a company would advertise job openings on the Web, or expect a certain amount of Internet savvy from its applicants. I might also add that my position was not advertised on one of those big job bank hype-o-ramas. So, if used with a little imagination, that expensive hunk of hardware could still be the key that opens the door to your groovy new gig.

But where to look? For what? And how? There are now more

> The Truth About Résumés

In one corner of a computer room at a certain prestigious business school stands a lone laser printer. THIS PRINTER IS EXCLUSIVELY FOR PRINTING RÉSUMÉS. It is a sacred device, a machine for communicating with the gods, and it is treated with a reverence appropriate to its exalted status.

At photocopy shops and graduate seminars around the country related rituals take place every day, rituals in which students and job seekers are taught how to approach the inscrutable corporate beings who will admit—or deny—them entry into the ranks of the middle class. They are being instructed in the fine points of a strangely American, strangely religious literary form: how to best compose what is probably the most intensely wrought piece of writing they will ever do in their lives. They are writing résumés.

The résumé is never studied as a literary artifact. And yet in the various seminars, advice books, and how-to manuals that surround the form, résumés are as closely contrived as sonnets, as meaningful as epic poems. Martin Yate, the author of *Résumés That Knock 'Em Dead*, goes so far as to compare résumé writing to sculpting: Your life's accomplishments are "like a block of stone, at which you chip away to reveal the masterwork that has been hiding there all along."

In the rationalist version of the job-finding story, we inhabit a perfect meritocracy in which the most qualified individual will always, given a modicum of ingenuity and effort, win the appropriate position. But as nearly everyone over the age of six knows, this is hogwash. The gods of capitalism are inscrutable gods indeed, with all manner of strange whims and tastes that are largely incomprehensible to the lowly job seeker. Who knows why one person is hired and another ignored? Enter the vast and ever-growing résumé industry, which exists to explain, as did Milton, the strange ways of the gods to man.

But what is the correct path to heaven? Alas, the holy texts do not agree. While it offers hope to the forlorn, the résumé-writing process is also fraught with mystery and fear. At its dark center stands a terrifying but invisible demiurge, the corporate personnel manager who, we are repeatedly warned, needs but a few seconds to cast us into the oblivion of his trusty trash can if our life's work fails to meet his exact criteria. Like capitalism itself, the Zeus-like company man on the other end of the résumé process may be a poor judge of men, a tyrant even, but from his decisions there is simply no appeal.

To mollify this deity, the literature asserts, a résumé must be exactly right. Certain styles work and others do not. Make one error and he will banish you without a second thought. Some say photocopying is okay; others counsel against it. Some insist that personal data like salary, health, and place of birth are essential; others strongly advise that they be omitted. Some texts offer lists of magic words guaranteed to make your prayer to the gods of capitalism more effective, either in the form of "key words" that their computers will notice, or in lengthy compilations like *Knock 'Em Dead*'s list of 180 "action verbs" that are sure to mark you as a self-starting ass kicker.

As a self-policing enforcer of capitalist discipline, the résumé has its moralistic elements as well. All authorities agree, for example, that you must have always been employed. If your résumé has "holes," you can forget it. It doesn't matter whether you were taking care of your ailing aunt or living with the Zapatistas during those six months between IBM and AT&T, you'd better have some proper corporate reference for that period or they'll naturally assume the worst.

Finally, in what is perhaps the oddest feature of this utterly self-interested literary style, your motives must not derive from personal ambition. You must be a dedicated servant of the greater corporate good. This is most painfully obvious in the "objective" section of the résumé, where the writer sets forth his or her career plans. However desperate you may be, the standard form is not to declare your desire to have a job or earn a lot of money, but to speak selflessly about how much you want to "contribute to the advancement of my field," "to be a key individual on the management team," or to find a position "where my experience and training can be fully utilized."

Résumés may get us jobs, if we send out enough of them, but they're hardly as effective as all the energy devoted to them would indicate. Their true function is as a sort of prayer, a capitalist loyalty oath, a miraculous device through which the gods who rule our society exact our groveling fealty. Even when we're angriest at and most disillusioned with the world they have created, we sit down and, sometimes at great expense, write homages to them, declaring ourselves selflessly for whatever management team will take us on. At our time of greatest doubt toward capitalism, through the résumé we proclaim our unquestioning faith in the justice of the marketplace, in the inevitability of every product finding its special niche.

— *Thomas Frank*

than 10,000 career-related sites on the Web. A cynic would say that the seemingly endless barrage of these sites proves their lack of efficacy, which is not quite fair since not all sites list the same openings. But the fact remains that most openings listed in job banks are also listed in newspapers; just because you found a job description on the Internet doesn't necessarily mean your odds of landing the gig are any better than if you had stumbled across it in the want ads section of the local paper. And want ads have never been a great way to land a job; moreover, the availability of those same few job postings to anyone with computer access only means there will be that many more eyeballs scoping them out. In fact, most job experts believe that looking at job listings and sending out résumés electronically is unlikely to pay off more than 1 or 2 percent of the time.

Not much more fruitful are the online résumé banks, which are simply searchable databases of résumés sent by job seekers. Recruiters subscribe to the service and key in specific criteria for jobs they need to fill. If your résumé is flagged for meeting the required criteria, you may be contacted by the employer. Or, you may not. For the individual user, these are passive services: point, click, type, send, and wait. And wait and wait and wait—because the truth is that these services are most often used by recruiters who need very specific skills or the kind of experience that only comes from years of executive or governmental work. The types of jobs that are most often landed through résumé banks include those in such professions as computer programming and systems administration, engineering, chemistry, physics, mathematics, finance, management, accounting, marketing, and human resources. For the huge number of applicants who earned a liberal arts degree fairly recently, the odds of finding a good job in such a passive manner are ridiculously low—and the competition for the few relevant openings at these sites alarmingly high.

member: Richard_Bulger

SURVEY: INTERNET JOB SEARCH

A long lost colleague found a posting of mine in a newsgroup, E-mailed me to confirm my identity, and asked if I'd write an article for a publication he currently edits. A freelance assignment without me ever saying hello!

A much more realistic way to integrate the info-laden world of the Net into your job search is to harness the Web's capacity for serious research about the places you might like to work. Rather than waste your time with "company profiles" at job banks (usually the only companies profiled are sponsors of and/or subscribers to the database service), start scouting the Web for individual companies.

Many corporate Web sites will list current job openings (that's how I found out about the job at Tripod), but even those that don't can be informative. By meticulously combing through a company's Web site, you can learn about its mission and corporate style, the kinds of openings it typically has, its needs and expected growth, and projects to which you can apply your skills. Most important, you can fish around for the names and contact information of key players (most large corporate sites include a "staff page").

Be aware, though, that corporate Web sites generally consist of prettified PR and sanitized "versions of the truth" approved by the Powers that Be for public consumption. I recommend going to a search engine and entering your target company's name. More often than not, this will retrieve dozens of pages of links pertaining to the company—the good, the bad, and the ugly—from news reports and other media coverage.

Another excellent Internet tool is Hoover's Online (www.hoovers.com), a site claiming to be the ultimate source for company information. For once, this isn't hyperbole—one can look deeply into an organization's financial stability, its standing within its industry, and its corporate structure (for starters) by simply entering the company's name into Hoover's searchable database. Two caveats: (1) Some of Hoover's advanced options are available by subscription only (in other words, you've got to pay to play) and (2) you could probably dig up much of that same information yourself with a search engine if you had unlimited time and a fair amount of expertise in knowing which key words to enter. Still, if you need to research several potential employers at a time (you weren't going to apply to just one company, were you?) and are pressed for free hours in the day, Hoover's can be a godsend well worth the small investment.

Perhaps the most signififcant way in which the Net can help you in your quest for employment is as a Rolodex builder. Compiling a list of contacts is the most time-honored method of insinuating your way into rewarding work. Companies do recruit through conventional means, but one of the dirty little secrets of the human resources game is that some of the sweetest jobs are never advertised and are unplanned—such as openings resulting

member: kaelyn

SURVEY: INTERNET JOB SEARCH

I'm an eighth-grade student, and it's always been my dream to be a writer. Not only did the Internet open up tons of new openings for my work on Web sites, but I also began corresponding with an editor of my favorite magazine through E-mail. Now I might be writing a monthly column for them!

member: ohiskool

SURVEY: INTERNET JOB SEARCH

I put my résumé online—placed a link on my homepage, registered all over the place my homepage, and contacted job services too . . . have had E-mail responses however not anywhere I'd want to live. Oh well still no job off the Net . . . all glitz and glitter, no substance . . .

from a firing, resignation, or unexpected growth opportunity. If you've already been in contact with key people at such a company, they may just remember you when an opportunity presents itself.

Among the best tools for making contacts is an online bulletin board (BBS). Two of the very best BBS systems—the West Coast service known as the WELL (www.well.com) and the New York City–based Echo (www.echonyc.com)—have grown and evolved to become Web-centric services with extremely lively conferences and thousands of active members from around the globe. These are the powerhouses against which all other online meeting places are measured, both in terms of potential contacts and user loyalty (to take advantage of everything these services have to offer, you will have to pay a subscriber's fee). Remember, as you begin to network online, to be a good Netizen—be friendly in your regular dealings with other users and members, be willing to show your usefulness by helping others and giving advice, and keep your eyes open for the chance to discuss careers with new online friends who are on similar career paths. Any BBS worth its salt will also have specific job and career areas.

Other sources for potential contacts—and these are free—include USENET newsgroups and E-mailing lists (also known as listservs). USENET's newsgroups are accessible on the Web through DejaNews (www.dejanews.com). Such newsgroups function much like the conferences at the WELL and Echo, although posting to them may be more sporadic and have less of a community feel. Each user leaves a message for the others on message boards, many of which are related to jobs in specific areas or career categories.

E-mailing lists are discussion groups much like those on USENET, except that each of the "posts" comes directly to you in the form of an E-mail (many of the better listservs offer a "digest" version that collects all of a day's posts and sends them in a single E-mail). You can find newsgroups and E-mailing lists relevant to your job needs by searching the Synapse Web site (www.synapse.net/-radio/finding.htm). Neosoft's site offers an even more thorough list of publicly accessible mailing lists (www.neosoft.com/internet/paml).

The Net can also help you ace the interview after you've gotten

member: MonicaD

Survey: Internet Job Search

The Internet was practically the sole research tool I used for finding my last two jobs, including my current one, as both times I was relocating to a different city/country. For my job in London, the Net proved to be the best way for me to explore the local business scene—checking out UK papers, online media, newsgroups, and company sites that gave me leads to send my résumé. Then, when I decided to move to Philadelphia, I again used the Internet as really my only research tool for leads and to explore my field in the area. Bottom line: There is a great wealth of information on companies if you're prepared to search long and hard, and it's a relatively inexpensive way to do a long-distance job hunt. Best if you're looking for a job that is in some way related to technology. Of course a generous dose of luck and timing, along with a good résumé helps!

your foot in the door. One former Tripodian has become something of a legend at headquarters due to the savvy way he prepared for his job interview. This fellow not only read every bit of Tripod content he could get his mouse on, he also looked closely at our online staff pages and made copious mental notes. Since those pages contain pictures and bios of all the staff members, he was able to put names and faces together the second he met the cast of characters here in Williamstown. He knew which of us played sports, pursued artistic endeavors, or just watched a lot of TV. He knew what we all do for the company and, wherever applicable, had read some of our writing both at Tripod and elsewhere. We were all blown away by his efforts to transcend the stiff awkwardness that typically characterizes initial introductions and/or long rounds of interviews.

member: WendieS

SURVEY: INTERNET JOB SEARCH

So far, all I've received from all the E-mailed résumés I've sent are some confirmations and a few company applications. But, I cover a lot of territory for only my $19.95 a month Net charges . . . no stamps, envelopes, paper, faxing, etc. This really helps out on the budget crunch when you're unemployed.

Whenever possible, call or E-mail to find out the name of the person who will be interviewing you—and use that information as a starting point for preparing a face-to-face strategy. If the company to which you are applying doesn't have detailed online staff pages, dig through their site to find press releases or other documents that may help you to understand your interviewer's role in the company hierarchy. Run this person's name through a search engine: Was he ever quoted in the local paper? Did she write an article for a trade magazine? Is he involved in any community activities? Does she have a personal homepage tucked away somewhere on the Web? (Building just such a page to highlight your own achievements and abilities is not a bad idea at all—think of it as a twenty-first century business card.)

By now I hope I've convinced you that successfully using the Net as part of your job hunt is a bit more involved than slinging a document into the abyss of a résumé bank and playing Quake until those megabucks offers start coming in. That said, it's probably still worth poking through some of the better heavily hyped mondo sites. Three of the biggest and most successful are Monster Board (www.monster.com), HeadHunter (www.HeadHunter.net), and CareerPath (www.careerpath.com).

Rather than being a cure-all for your job troubles, the Internet should be treated as a valuable tool—but only one of many arrows in your quiver. Don't forsake traditional means of job searching and networking just because you have a shiny new PC on your desk. If you E-mail or fax a résumé, it'll likely look like hell when it gets there; it's a good idea to follow up by mailing a nicely formatted "hard copy" on good quality heavy bond whenever possible. A little research should turn up a mailing address for your target company, even if one is not posted on its Web site. For example, WorldPages (www.worldpages.com) and Switchboard (www.switchboard.com) will give you the mailing addresses and phone numbers (even a map with directions) of virtually any company in the world.

No matter how much technology has transformed the way we look for work, how much different—and better—you look to a perspective employer is still largely up to you.

Temping

Between 2 and 6 million Americans work a temp job on any given day. Next thing you know, that temp scurrying down the hall loaded down with copy paper could be you. Here's how to make sure you stay in control.

by Harry Goldstein

This country's largest private employer in 1997 was Manpower, Inc., a multinational temporary employment agency. What does that say about the rest of the '90s and the decade to come? It signals a volte-face in American business: the much-discussed shift from a permanent to a transitional labor economy, a shift that promises to be hard on American labor. From 1991 to 1996, the number of people employed by temp agencies climbed 50 percent, from 1.15 million to 2.31 million. Currently, between 2 and 6 million people work a temp job in the United States on any given day.

Manpower, Inc., is also the world's largest temp agency. It operates hand in glove with the phenomenal number of corporations that now depend on temporary workers. In 1996, Manpower employed more than 800,000 people over the course of the year, with worldwide revenues at $6 billion and net profits up 18 percent from 1995.

The reasons for the growth of temp work can be found on corporate America's bottom line. Companies save a lot of money by not paying full-time workers' health benefits, or giving them vacation time or sick days. A brochure from the National Association of

Temporary and Staffing Services (NATSS) explains that "the proper and appropriate use of temporary employees as a supplement to full-time employees can help a company maintain a strong bottom line by reducing expenses in recruiting, testing, training, and turnover . . . each full-time employee salary costs the company an additional 38 percent in 'hidden' expenses . . . [while] another 5-20 percent is spent on recruitment and hiring."

Corporations may avoid these added expenses by turning to temps, but many of the advantages they enjoy turn out to be major disadvantages from the employee's side. There's little stability for the temp and no guarantees. If the boss doesn't like you, you're just a bad memory. There's no ugly scene to deal with; they just call your agency and unload you. There's no resolution of tensions, no grievance procedures. The agency acts as a buffer between the temp and the company.

On the other hand, if you don't like working for a particular company, you have to decide whether the situation is bad enough to warrant action on your part. You could just suck it up until the job ends or something better comes along. In the temp world, appearance is everything. If I ask to be reassigned, will my agency think that I just couldn't hack it? If I don't get along with my supervisor and I leave the job, will it stain my reputation, making it harder to get work through this agency? Basically, agencies make it easy for companies to sever employment relationships, but for the unhappy temp worker the situation is always more complicated.

As a temp, it's easy to get stuck in a rut. Maybe you decided to temp just to get by until you find other work. So you take a job as a word processor making $12 an hour without benefits. You're going to look for that dream job, but there's really not much time during the day—you have quotas to make or an assignment to finish, so you put off making those phone calls. Maybe you start thinking that one in the hand is worth two in the bush.

Maybe you feel grateful to have any kind of job at all.

Remember, you may be filling a company's short-term staffing needs, but in the process, you're short-changing yourself. It's an insidious trap. In a few months, you'll look up from the document you're formatting and remember that this is actually your life that's

member: sfshan

SURVEY: TEMPING

I moved to San Francisco without much money and without a job. But I did have some work experience and good skills. I went to three temp agencies, and I never had a day off once I started. In less than two months I was at a company that wanted to hire me permanently, and I accepted their offer. (I've now been working there for two years!) While you can feel slightly objectified by the temp agencies, there are good things about it too, like freedom to pick a new job if you don't like the one you have. And it is a good springboard toward permanent employment.

passing between the bullet points. Day to day, temping can be frustrating. Coworker camaraderie is hard to come by. A temp is expendable and consequently always the outsider. No one wants to be pals with someone who could be gone tomorrow or next week.

In the most innocuous circumstances, temping is Zen-like. You are the action: an envelope stuffer, mail sorter, message taker, or copy maker. At worst, you're trapped in a competitive workplace surrounded by backstabbing weasels intent on using you for their own special projects. At best, people make friendly chitchat, maybe ask what it is you really want to do, smile politely when they tell you they're going out to lunch.

The upside to all of this occupational angst? Now that you know the score, you can make the most out of a marginal situation, one in which you know you're going to be exploited.

Since the vast majority of large companies use temporary agencies to satisfy their craving for fresh flesh, you'll want to sign on with agencies that are going to give you the most for your time and labor. Be demanding: You can tell which agencies care about their temps by the quality of the benefits they offer. For instance, Worknow.com, an agency that specializes in high-tech temps, offers medical benefits—but only if you work 450 hours within four months (roughly twenty-eight hours per week). In addition, the benefits stipulate the worker must put in 110 hours per month to remain eligible. The cost to the temp worker is approximately $90 per month. Vacation pay is available if you complete 1,500 hours in a calendar year. (That's a little over thirty-one hours per week.)

If you're planning on temping, ask the agency recruiter about the agency's benefits policy first. Then ask: What's their temp-to-perm policy? Does the company have seniority bonuses? Do you get a bonus for referring other workers? How often are you paid? Can they guarantee to keep you busy? Whatever their answers, always register with other temp agencies simultaneously. The worst thing that can happen is that you're offered so much work that you have to turn down some. Don't worry too much about this aspect of your relationship with your temp employment agent—they'll understand, and they've got plenty of other bodies they can put in the same position.

Once you've registered with as many temp agencies as possible, start calling them every day. Be a pest. Ring them as soon as they open for business. Call again around 9:15, right after people have called in sick and companies are looking to fill day-long slots. If nothing comes through in the morning, get working on whatever it is with which you occupy your time. If you don't have a beeper, get one; it's a necessity. If you haven't heard from your agents during the afternoon, give them a buzz around 4:00 to let them know you're available for the next day. Then start over again the next morning. Within a month you'll most likely be working as much as you want.

The Varieties of the Temping Experience

The most important question to ask is the one only you can answer: Why do you want to temp? Often people temp because they're between jobs. According to NATSS, 59 percent of temp workers do it to make ends meet while they are between full-time jobs. The others—those who can make temping work to their advantage—fall into three categories.

member: charPEF

SURVEY: TEMPING

Temping wasn't such a bad job—it kept my interest since I never knew where I'd be working, and I learned several different kinds of skills I'd probably not have if I hadn't. Temping also let me sample jobs and let me see if I could conceive of myself working there the rest of my life (most of the time I knew I couldn't).

The Free Agent

The free agent temps because she needs the flexibility. If your avocation doesn't pay very well—sculptors, for instance, aren't exactly in demand—but you want to devote a major amount of time to it, the flexible scheduling that temporary work affords you might be the way to go. The majority of temps—63 percent—like the job precisely because it lets them work when they want to. In fact, 39 percent of temps plan to temp indefinitely.

The key to happiness for people who temp to accommodate their lifestyles is money. Ninety percent of all temp jobs pay less than $11 an hour. One in five temps is fortunate enough to be employed in the technical, professional, marketing, and medical arenas; this includes engineers, computer specialists, and illustrators. As companies increasingly outsource these kinds of positions in an effort to shave expenses, more of these jobs will become available. Pay varies according to experience and geographical location but according to NATSS, average hourly wages for graphic artists are $17.63, computer system analysts $28.75, technical writers $22.71, computer programmers $25.40, and so on. The bad news is that two out of every five temps makes substantially less, with data entry operators, customer service workers, general office clerks, receptionists, secretaries, and word processors pulling down a paltry $7 to $10 per hour.

So how do you get a high-paying temp gig? Skills. If you don't know anything about computers, it's time to learn all you can about personal computers, printers, local area networks, and various operating systems. Even more important than the hardware, though, is the software. If you know Word Perfect, great. But if you know WP, Microsoft Word, PowerPoint, Excel, File Maker Pro, Lotus Notes, and a couple of E-mail programs, you can probably earn upwards of $15 an hour. If you want the really high-paying jobs, you'll need to pick a specialty. If you're artsy, learn one or several desktop publishing programs, like Quark Xpress and PageMaker, or Web publishing software like Hot Dog Pro. If you know Photoshop, you've just boosted your pay range and employability for temp jobs at places like ad firms and magazines. If you can use the same software on different platforms, say PC and Macintosh, you're that much easier to place.

Often temp agencies will throw you into a job working software you don't know—sink or swim. If you want to earn the big bucks and make your own hours to boot, you need to do the backstroke and breaststroke and excel at the freestyle. If you want flexibility in your life, then flexibility in skills is essential.

The Stone Stepper

The stone stepper wants to check out what different careers and companies have to offer and to improve her skills. In a recent Georgia State University survey of former temporary workers, 56 percent said they learned new skills while working as a temporary employee and 29 percent found permanent work as a direct result of their temporary assignment (many through explicit "temp-to-perm" arrangements).

Temping at different jobs gives you an insight into different careers at no risk. Transitory work can also boost your starting salary at a permanent job. The Georgia State study found that people ultimately obtained a higher-paying job after working as a temporary. The study concluded that such workers may be better off in the long run because "a transitional job will relieve enough financial pressure to give them the bargaining power to hold out for higher wages or a better job."

Obviously, temp agencies ply both employer and employee with the same message: Try each other out. The agency's subliminal rap goes something like this: "If it doesn't work, there will be another job for you, Mr. Temp and another body for you, Ms. Client."

Of course, it's not that cut-and-dried. When you sign up with an agency, you need to be very clear on the terms of temp-to-perm employment. In many cases, temp agencies charge clients substantial fees to take on a valuable temp full time. On one hand, a substantial agency fee might discourage a potential employer from snatching you up (of course, if they do pay the fee, then you know how much they value you and you can squeeze them during salary negotiations).

On the other hand, saving your potential employer the agency fee by going behind the agency's back to strike a deal on your own will endear you to your new boss. But what about burned bridges? If you're getting a full-time job with a company you like enough and trust enough to screw over the temp agency altogether, then why worry if you're burning that temp bridge? How is the agency going to find out, anyway? The company sure isn't going to tell them. You certainly won't. If a bridge burns and no one realizes it, is it really burning? If you want a full-time job, do whatever it takes to get one (within reason, of course). Remember, temp agents are basically pimps. You owe yourself a chance at occupational bliss; you don't owe the agency a thing.

If you're using temping as a way to find a long-term job, and you know of a few companies for whom you'd like to work, call their human resources departments and ask them what temp agency they use. Then register with it; if you slog through some random temp gigs and prove your worth, after a short time you should be able to request assignments at particular firms.

So let's say you researched the entertainment megaconglomerate you love best, registered with their temp agency and, a few months down the line, are temping there on a regular basis. And lo and behold, you find yourself spending two weeks at a desk behind

member: Raer

SURVEY: TEMPING

Temping requires you to always be "on." The constant moving around becomes dreary. Don't expect challenging work. Although you may land a temp position in your dream field/company—you'll probably be answering their phone or reorganizing their filing system.

member: Woodland_Spryte

SURVEY: TEMPING

Temping was the only way I could get a paying job as the surrounding area was so depressed you couldn't even find a job flipping burgers. Later, I found that I could learn something at each job and gradually developed skills and a "track record" with my temp agency that had them calling me for "first-time customers" as they had confidence in me. The job I have now, and have worked for the past ten years, I got after filling in over the years for the lady who held it before me. When she retired, rather than go through tons of applicants, they called me and offered the job, as I already knew the basics.

which you know you were born to sit. Now's the time to grab the ring. If you think you've found your dream job, here are some commonsense ways to do your part in getting it to go from temp to perm:

> Talk with your supervisor. Is she looking to fill the position full time? If that's the case, let her know you're interested and that you're serious. If the discussion goes well and she seems receptive, have a résumé ready.
>
> Have a frank discussion with someone from the company's HR department to see if they are looking to make the job permanent.
>
> Check internal job postings. Most companies do this a week to a month before they place a classified ad.
>
> Talk to your perm coworkers. Frank conversations about the workplace will help you decide if this is the place to jam the door open.
>
> If you really enjoy working there, you're probably already doing a good job. If it seems like there's a chance that the company wants you to go from temp to perm, treat work like an audition. If you want to make the team, you're going to have to impress. Feed off the confidence that comes with being on the inside track.

member: jngamble
SURVEY: TEMPING
Temp means just that, *temporary*. You don't get anywhere and you're always starting over.

The Guerrilla Temp

Some people temp to gain access to office equipment and supplies to further their own projects. French philosopher Michel de Certeau identified a trend in French factories and offices called *la perruque*, which, in the tradition of French philosophical obliqueness, means "the wig." It's a subversive act in which the worker offsets alienation by disguising his own work as work for his employer. "It differs from pilfering in that nothing of material value is stolen," de Certeau wrote. "It differs from absenteeism in that the worker is officially on the job. *La perruque* may be as simple a matter as a secretary's writing a love letter on 'company time' or as complex as a cabinet maker's 'borrowing' a lathe to make a piece of furniture . . . the worker who indulges in *la perruque* actually diverts time (not goods, since he only uses scraps) from the factory for work that is free, creative, and precisely not directed toward profit."

A lot of temps wear wigs, too: We pretend to be one thing, when in fact we are something quite different. The eager temp slave needs to collate that stack of reports as efficiently as possible, but when the job's done she runs off a hundred issues of her zine on the copier. She's using an oppressive system to her own advantage.

American offices are chock-full of tempting supplies and equipment. And though appropriating machines and supplies for your own purposes seems like stealing and the act of stealing seems like a subversive move that undermines the very material foundations of the company—nay, the entire Capitalist System!—it's not. You may think you're putting one over on The Man. He's more than happy to let you keep thinking that. Go ahead and imagine that you're a badass because you scammed a box of paper clips. But who's the

sucker making less than ten bucks an hour? De Certeau's *perruque* sounds so familiar because it's as obvious as your boss's toupee, so ubiquitous and tolerated is it in everyday corporate life.

If you're going to pilfer, you should at least be subtle. Use only what can't be traced, like the office fax everyone uses or a copier that doesn't need a code. Stay away from stuff like FedEx, which your employer can trace directly to you and is an instantly quantifiable expense. A FedEx letter costs $11—who knows how much 500 copies cost?

If there is a code on a copier, then don't make so many copies that people might say, "Wow, who's burning all the paper?" or worse, "I only asked you to make ten copies this whole week—why did we make ten thousand?" Of course, if you know that your days on the job are numbered and you don't care about the employer giving your agent a bad report, then by all means, go for it.

If you're using a computer for a project, keep all your work on your own disk. Leave nothing on the computer's hard drive. Use the copier in the middle of day, during lunch, when most people are gone. Don't wait until the end of the day when some executive with a looming deadline is going to storm into the copy room and demand that his project be pushed to the front of the pile. He might not be too supportive if he sees you running off a dozen copies of your screenplay—of course, he may be doing the same thing.

If you're blessed with access to long distance and you don't need a code give Mom a call. Have a long distance lunch at your desk. Just have a plausible cut line if the boss comes into the cubicle, preferable something that sounds like you're talking to your temp agency. Something like, "I think I'm going to be back here tomorrow, Mr. Temp Pimp. Keep me in mind for that other job though."

Telecommuting

Tired of long commutes and workdays spent in cubicles, many former office workers have lobbied hard for the privilege to work from home. But are they better off?

by Randy Williams

As a gospel choir sings of the joys of living in our wondrous age, clapping to the beat for emphasis, a popular television personality purrs over their hallelujah bedrock, his honeyed voice enticing the viewer to use modern gadgetry to simultaneously increase productivity and simplify life. A quick succession of images flashes across the screen: a mother clicks a button and sends a report to her employer by modem as her infant child peacefully rests nearby; a rather hip-looking businessperson quickly checks a personal digital assistant for voice messages and electronic mail while sipping a frothy coffee concoction at a sidewalk café; a middle-manager type receives a fax while sitting in a lounge chair on a glistening white sand beach.

The first few times I saw these TV commercials for a telecom giant, I was buoyantly swept along by the sea of smiling faces and lifted up by their air of global village capitalism and spiritual bonding. Then I began to notice that none of the people in this electronic utopia ever seemed to be off-duty; in particular, I wondered why that poor schmuck had to read a fax on the beach at Aruba. If I were ever to get my happy ass on some of that tropical white sand, you can bet I'd be wanting to harvest sea shells, not information.

Make no mistake: Big businesses are pushing a shiny happy image of teleconferencing and virtual offices with every slick weapon in their advertising arsenals. The very same businesses that want to sell the technology that makes telecommuting possible (and thereby reap enormous corporate profits) often have huge telework programs themselves (resulting in enormous corporate savings). Telecommuting can also have distinct advantages for many workers—but not all, and that's where problems with the song and dance routine we're being sold begin to appear.

First off, one needs to question whether there is in fact a telecommuting revolution, and if so, if it is a beneficial change for employees or a scheme by which employers seek to squeeze more out of workers while saving in overhead costs. In a 1994 report by the Congressional Office of Technology Assessment, the Department of Transportation predicted that there would be 15 million telecommuters by the year 2000. This figure represents nearly 11 percent of the U.S. workforce. The advocacy group Telecommute America estimates that there are currently more than 11 million telecommuters, 75 percent of whom use personal computers (up from 59 percent in 1995) and 31 percent of whom use the Internet (which is more than double the normal home-usage rate).

Before we jump to conclusions about this trend signaling a "revolution" in which rebellious cubicle soldiers are winning a heartening victory over their dark corporate overlords, let us take a clear-eyed look at the major players in the border skirmish between the home and the traditional office. For starters, there are corporations such as AT&T (which boasts more than 47,000 telecommuters), Pacific Bell, and IBM, all of whom have implemented highly successful telecommuting programs. Advertising giant TBWA Chiat/Day made national headlines by turning most of their staff loose to telecommute and radically altering their office concept to create vast shared spaces with remarkably few assigned desks or rooms, favoring instead a sort of corporate rumpus room where employees can plug in their laptops, cell phones, and other toys when they drop by for meetings or presentations. Considering that

member: jj

SURVEY: TELECOMMUTING

Telecommuting is the greatest thing since, well, ice cream! I can get up when I want, go to bed when I want, and hang out all day in the comfort of my fuzzy slippers and terrycloth robe. I can let out the dog, do laundry, listen to music, have a nice home-cooked meal—all the stuff one normally has to rush home from work to do before collapsing on the sofa in front of the tube. Being a "second shift" person by nature (4:00 P.M. to midnight), I've produced some of my most brilliant work during hours when the rest of the world is sound asleep. Since telecommuting allows me to set up my own "core hours," I get much more accomplished than I would if I had to drag myself to an office by 9:00 A.M. and waste three or four hours of my scheduled workday just trying to wake up. Rain? Snow? Feeling a little "under the weather"? These primary reasons for absence from the workplace become a nonissue when telecommuting. I haven't missed a day in over two years!

this list of "revolutionaries" includes giants of the telecommunications, computer, and advertising worlds, the shift to telework can seem less a subversive coup than a slick PR campaign.

But it's not just big business tooting its own telecommuting horn: The government is humming the work-from-home tune as well. The U.S. federal government recently announced ambitious plans to convert 60–70,000 federal workers (upward of 3 percent of the federal workforce) into telecommuters over a three-year period, with many more expected to follow. In Southern California, where traffic congestion and smog have long been health-threatening if colorful epidemics, the state government offers companies huge tax incentives to increase the number of telecommuters in their employ.

Start-up companies—especially those related to computers and the Internet—have also been early adopters of these same trends. Many such companies come and go and they often offer spotty benefits and dubious job security in exchange for brutal deadlines and long hours, but the appeal of being able to work from home (or in informal offices that are utilized primarily for group meetings and strategy sessions) has proven to be an effective lure for young talent. Some estimates of the number of employees who telecommute at least part-time in the prominent locales for such fledgling companies—California's Silicon Valley, New York City's Silicon Alley, and San Francisco's tight concentration of "new media" companies—have the figure hovering near 50 percent.

member: AlexisMarie

SURVEY: TELECOMMUTING

Where am I most productive? Working in the family house (now magically transformed into my office), telecommuting from Montana to places like Boston, New York, and San Francisco. I'm self-employed, a freelance writer, and I write about the Internet. I love my work, and I actually make a fair wage in a town where most earn substantially less than the average per capita income. I set my own hours and best of all I get to live in this beautiful place nestled against the state's highest mountains and do the kind of work I enjoy.

Last, employees themselves have in many cases embraced the move toward telecommuting. Tired of long commutes and demoralizing workdays spent in cubicles while supervisors hover over their shoulders, many former office workers have lobbied hard for the privilege to work from home on a flexible schedule. Membership in employee-led telecommuting advocacy groups such as the International Homeworkers Association, the International Telework Association, and the Home Office Association of America is sharply on the rise. But as we shall see, for every distinct advantage of being a telework employee from the privacy of one's home there can be an equal and opposite disadvantage.

The Good

PacBell, one of the largest employers of telecommuters in the United States, warns new teleworkers to "expect a thirty- to ninety-day acclimatization period when you start telecommuting" because "it takes a while for even the most organized to figure out how to manage time, space, communication systems, and projects while working in two locations."

Once the period of adjustment is over, many teleworkers find themselves happier than pigs in slop. Working from home can provide a more satisfying balance between work and life than can be achieved by those who must put in a required number of rigidly scheduled "face time" hours at the office and scramble to tend to their personal lives in whatever time is left after the commute home. It can provide an environment that fosters time for mentally intensive or creative work, or it may be an opportunity to reduce stress and increase productivity.

Such high-minded reasoning aside, the creature comforts of working from home can be awfully tempting. Responding to Telecommute America's 1997 survey, 51 percent of telecommuters said they wear shoes in their home office only occasionally, while 32 percent said they never bother with footwear at all. A whopping 38 percent of those surveyed said that they are able to spend more time with family and friends now that they have eliminated the physical commute to and from a traditional office. Asked what it would take to make them give up telecommuting, 39 percent of respondents said their employer would have to double salaries and 36 percent claimed that *nothing* would make them change the way they work.

I spend about a third of my considerable working hours at my home computer. I can sip hot cocoa from my vintage '60s Adam West *Batman* mug, cue up some Elvis Costello or John Coltrane on the CD player, and write in a nurturing atmosphere, surrounded by the things that give me pleasure. Because I live alone, there are rarely interruptions of any sort, and I find that I am able to complete more work, most of it of a higher caliber than anything I could produce in our warehouselike office with its constant noise and activity.

member: Maryvonne

SURVEY: TELECOMMUTING

Having been a telecommuting editor and writer for over twenty years, I can tell you that as far as I am concerned, telecommuting is fantastic! Distance is of no consequence; my work is faxed or E-mailed. I have no office overhead expenses and my work environment is peaceful and pleasant. No interruptions. What more can a person ask for? If I am tired and my eyes start to see double letters, I take a break, have a cup of coffee, take a nap. Whatever, as long as *all* my deadlines are met.

Speaking of pleasure, for all you know I could be wearing nothing but a pair of fuzzy sheepskin chaps as these words are being composed. The majority of teleworkers polled in national surveys say that they typically work in jeans, sweatpants, bathrobes, shorts, or whatever allows them to feel most comfortable. The hours one saves by not "dressing for the part," along with the time saved by eliminating a physical commute, can easily add an hour or two to the truly productive part of the working day.

Working from home also allows telecommuters to run personal errands on breaks during the day (you know, when businesses and government offices are actually open), help get the kids off to school and be there to greet them when they return, or spend a few more minutes or hours with a spouse or loved one. While it may be necessary to make yourself available to clients or colleagues during

> Home Office Setup

Think you can jump into telework with your battle-scarred old 386 PC or Mac Classic? Think again. In a 1997 survey conducted by the telework advocacy group Telecommute America, 64 percent of the respondents defined their home offices as "high-tech" (Pentium or PowerPC processor, CD-ROM) and another 13 percent deemed their setups as "cutting edge" (including videoconferencing and the works). That teleworkers seem to take pride in their home offices is important; such employees must be intimately familiar with both software and hardware: applications, machines, troubleshooting techniques and maintenance requirements. Quite simply, they will not have the luxury of summoning a friendly IS department worker over to figure out what went boom.

A realistic list of the minimum equipment required for an effective home office would look something like this:

- A reasonably high-end CPU (Pentium or PowerPC)
- 16+ MB of RAM, 32 MB or more if the teleworker expects to do conferencing or memory-intensive graphics, video, or number crunching
- No less than a 28.8 modem
- An up-to-date Web browser (Netscape or Internet Explorer)
- Networking software, including PPP, FTP, and Telnet
- 1.5 gigabytes of hard-disk storage (more is better, and file sizes are getting enormous)
- A reliable Internet connection
- A work-only phone line for voice transmissions, preferably with three-way calling and call waiting
- A dedicated phone line for data
- An answering machine (or access to company voice mail)
- PC fax capability or a separate fax machine (a separate machine may require a third line if you wish to receive faxes while tying up your primary data line with the modem)
- A fairly high-speed ink-jet or laser printer

Obviously, an effective teleworker needs a lot more than two tin cans and a length of string to get the job done. Such a worker also needs a home with plenty of space for equipment and other supplies, whether all of this paraphernalia is installed in a separate "office" or in a vacant corner of a living room or bedroom. If there are to be children, spouses, domestic partners, or roommates wandering through the home while work is being conducted, it is probably foolhardy to expect that anything less than an entire spare room—with a door that can be closed for privacy—will do the trick.

traditional office hours via phone or E-mail, the meat of one's workload can be accomplished at one's own pace and on one's preferred schedule. Not all of us are "morning people" and many find that inspiration can strike at odd times.

The Bad

Isn't it sweet of our dear employers to provide this option for us? Hardly. Employers are not by nature altruistic and the opportunity to telecommute would not exist were there not considerable bottom-line advantages behind the push to move workers off-site. Telecommuters save firms huge amounts of money in overhead—you know, pesky things like office space, electricity, furniture, and coffee and doughnuts. Therefore, more and more people are being expected to have a home office from which they can work, and that can cause several problems—not the least of which is the realization that one can't relax at home and leave the pressures of the office behind if the office *is* the home.

There are also financial considerations for the employee who's about to give teleworking a shot. Equipping an off-site employee with a suitable home office costs most companies between $4,000 and $6,000. While that's a drop in the bucket to a Hewlett-Packard or AT&T, it can be a pretty daunting figure for many individuals, particularly if they have no way of knowing whether telecommuting will dovetail with their own work habits until they've tried it. And the unfortunate truth is that not all companies are willing to lay out the cash.

In their book *The Telecommuter's Handbook*, authors Brad and Debra Schepp present a survey of one hundred companies that employ teleworkers. They found that more than half of the telecommuters in the workforce are having to cover some or all of their own equipment costs. Will you be responsible for the costs of repairing or upgrading equipment? Will you have to buy new software on a regular basis? Will you be able to continue working if you have a major computer meltdown?

These personal expenses and headaches might be more tolerable if telecommuters got an appropriate tax break in exchange for converting part of their home into a remote office for their employ-

member: Soppie

SURVEY: TELECOMMUTING

Telework saves on child-care costs and enables me to get things done that I wouldn't normally have the time to do. Also, not having someone constantly looking over my shoulder or handing me new projects every five minutes helps me to think better and be more productive.

member: JuliH

SURVEY: TELECOMMUTING

I honestly believe telecommuting helps us in striving toward a more humane balance between work and home. For those of us with families, it's a blessing. It allows us to be there with our kids a little longer before school—and be home in the afternoon when they return. It helps reduce the number of latchkey kids in the world. On the productivity side, the vast majority of people say they get more done when they telecommute due to fewer interruptions and the availability of quiet space to think deeply about solutions for tough situations.

ers, but logic has never been the strong suit of the IRS. In particular, telecommuters should not make the mistake of assuming that the few available loopholes for home-based businesses apply equally to off-site employees. Eva Rosenberg, an Enrolled Agent and tax columnist for Tripod and other media outlets, warns that taking the "Office in Home Deduction" on tax forms "can be like waving a red flag in front of a bull—if you can avoid it, don't use it."

But what of the work itself? While it would be nice to report that all workers adapt well to telecommuting, there are in fact several distinct traps into which teleworkers are prone to fall. The first of these has to do with a lack of self-discipline. Even though the flexibility to establish one's own schedule is one of the primary perks of telecommuting, the self-management required to make it work is not to be underestimated.

Though it's nice to escape the distractions (and occasional sterility) of the office and work among creature comforts, easy access to all your cool stuff can sometimes be just as distracting as workplace hurly-burly. At the office, it's fairly easy to summon the discipline to get back to work after a break—after all, you can see everyone else doing it. At home it can be tricky to chain yourself to the desk again after taking leisure time, especially if you've taken so much leisure time that your energy and concentration levels have plummeted. If you're one of those easily distracted types who can't stay away from the coffee pot or office gossip about that new hottie over in accounting, just wait until you have twenty-four-hour-a-day access to the telephone, TV, stereo, and refrigerator.

member: jemstone

SURVEY: TELECOMMUTING

The only problem with telecommuting is the isolation . . . interactive media is a collaborative endeavor and working alone all the time harms the final product. There has to be a little bit of face-to-face in order to take advantage of all the team members and their input.

If you have trouble with motivation without a supervisor hovering nearby, try using a reward system. One such system that I find helpful when telecommuting is to take short breaks of a predetermined length at regular intervals; these can include coffee breaks, exercise breaks, phone breaks, work-related reading time, and meal breaks. For others the best rewards might be time with the kids, the pets, or a short visit with one of the neighbors. Use these rewards wisely to avoid burnout and cabin fever.

Off-site employees should also strive to be organized by creating realistic to-do lists and setting clearly defined goals for each day. While the same rules apply to deadlines at home as at the office, being organized will help you to accomplish your tasks while still leaving time for those "lifestyle improvements" that are supposed to be part of the telecommuting package.

Many teleworkers, however, have no problem producing while working from home. And it's just these highly disciplined, self-starting employees who genuinely enjoy their work and want to give it all they've got who are most susceptible to the nasty problem of overwork. Once they start telecommuting, such workers will have twenty-four-hour-a-day access to tasks and projects. The simple presence of the computer at dawn, or midnight, or on weekends and holidays, can become an irresistible temptation for these super-driven types.

The previously referenced 1997 Telecommute America survey that found a majority of telecommuters happily working barefoot, and unwilling to trade that privilege for anything, also hinted at the problem of creeping workaholism. When asked what they do with the time saved by avoiding the physical commute, a popular answer (39 percent) was that they work more hours. When asked how many days a week they telecommute, 21 percent said six to seven. That this was the second highest-ranking response seems troubling in light of telework's purported "lifestyle advantages."

Pacific Bell's excellent telecommuting guide cautions potential teleworkers that "working too hard causes stress-related illness, burnout, and reduced productivity . . . The quality and effectiveness of your work are related to factors far more complex than clock hours." That the guide goes on to suggest that "knowing when to stop is essential to good job performance" is encouraging, but the truth is that some managers are *counting on* precisely this sort of overwork to squeeze every possible nickel's worth of effort from their employees. Scott Kendrick, a computer programmer at a nationally respected software firm in Alabama, had exactly this problem. "After my wife and I had our first child a few years ago, I put in a home office," says Kendrick. "My wife owns her own business, and she keeps her shop open late one night a week. Because she's not able to pick our daughter up at daycare that night, I talked my boss into letting me leave early in exchange for agreeing to telecommute a couple hours later that same evening. He reluctantly

member: Matt Hauser

SURVEY: TELECOMMUTING

The interesting thing about telecommuting is that it blurs the workday. You start when you get up . . . wake up, turn on the computer, shower, get E-mail, coffee, respond to E-mail . . . start lunch, keep working, eat while you read, work, or make notes. And you don't stop working at 5:00 sharp. I found that I work more time at home instead of watching the clock.

member: M_Finn

SURVEY: TELECOMMUTING

The biggest problem for me is that I have always been a type-A personality who wants to continue to work and work and take on even more work. Not firmly defining "office hours" can lead to overwork, exhaustion, and burn-out.

agreed, but once he got used to the idea of me being able to dial in from home, he acted like my computer was some kind of beeper. Now this chucklehead sends E-mails with all sorts of questions and requests on nights and weekends—and gets ticked off if I don't respond right away."

Joan Greenbaum, author of *Windows on the Workplace*, suggests that high-pressure management tactics will inevitably increase as information technology allows bosses to cut costs and staff members. "Business school theories and management techniques are about getting more work out of workers, or getting workers to work more cheaply," says Greenbaum. "Today the most effective management technique is to rely on the 'professionalism' of office workers, whether on- or off-site, encouraging them to get more done in the name of their professional reputation. Of course, it isn't a matter of choice. People know that if they don't work harder, longer, and more intensely, someone else will be there ready to do their job."

Your Working Future?

In my own life, despite finding occasional telecommuting to be useful, I have worked hard (and thus far successfully) to draw a line between working from home (or any other remote location) and the

> Telecommuting Web Sites

Learn more about telecommuting and the virtual office at these outstanding Web sites:

Organizations

International
Homeworkers Association
http://www.homeworkers.org/iha.htm

International
Telework Association
http://www.telecommute.org

Home Office
Association of America
http://www.hoaa.com

Telecommute America
http://www.att.com/Telecommute_America/

Resources

Business @Home
http://www.gohome.com/

The Smart Valley
Telecommuting Guide
http://smartone.svi.org/PROJECTS/TCOMMUTE/TCGUIDE/

PacBell Telecommuting Guide
http://www.pacbell.com/products/business/general/telecommuting/tcguide/index.html

Office Plus
http://www.officeplus.com/Services/

idea of constant electronic access. Cell phones, beepers, digital pagers, laptop computers—I've resisted becoming too dependent upon these gizmos for many years. As I said, it's not that I don't get off on gadgetry and convenience as much as the next inquisitive land mammal—it's just that I think they have their place. And those rare times when I'm able to get away to enjoy nature or the theatre or an art exhibition or the company of good friends—well, that is not an acceptable time or place to interrupt my hard-won serenity. Very few emergencies can't wait a couple of hours until I'm back in work mode. I am constantly amazed to see people all around me, hunched over their PowerBooks and ThinkPads, functioning like empty vessels awaiting information, always more information. Whenever I fly these days I see folks plugging their laptop computers into phone jacks on the seat in front of them and computing away, oblivious of their surroundings.

Other times, walking around New York City, among the bums, winos, and downtown hipsters, I am reminded that most Americans still aren't living exclusively in the digital domain. A loud and pungent wave of women and men from all walks of life refuses to be confined to the world visible on a monitor. In such surroundings, one has to step lively and remain alert and aware of the physical surroundings at every moment. And quite frankly, despite the jokes and eye-rolling about the dangers of the city, I find its challenges preferable to being in the company of zombies who can't pry their eyes away from the computer screen for fear of losing their supposed edge.

If you find yourself in the position to telecommute, make sure you fully understand what you're getting into and take steps to ensure that you not only work smart but work sane. While those hired specifically as teleworkers will have fewer options, many pilot programs designed to encourage telecommuting include provisions for the employee to return to on-site work if either the employer or employee feels the arrangement is not advantageous. There should be a system of checks and balances to ensure that certain performance levels are met *and* that the teleworker does not become a glorified indentured servant.

In an ideal world, the time we spend working would be propor-

Member: TheWriter
SURVEY: TELECOMMUTING
Because I work for myself, with an office in my home, many people think this is the life of Riley. That I can work when "I feel like it." Ha! My typical day runs from 6 A.M. to midnight. From making calls and E-mail around the world to editing manuscripts into the wee hours of the morning, my life is just one bloody adventure after another. The best part is that I can pick up the kids after school and sit down to a family dinner without the workload suffering. The worst part is that I never leave work! If you are considering starting a business in your home, make sure you have a door you can close "after hours!"

member: Polymath
SURVEY: TELECOMMUTING
When two telephones ring or passing children throw stones at the dogs or a courier arrives, it is impossible not to be distracted. On occasion I have taken a train to town to do my work in the local library or a coffee shop where I cannot be disturbed. The other drawback of living in one's office is that one is not permitted to be ill. The last time I *tried* to be ill, I was called out of bed so many times that I eventually had to pretend I wasn't feeling sick in order to conduct business as usual.

member: JHM42
survey: Telecommuting
I enjoy going to the office and seeing my co-workers, having lunch with them, and then going home at night. I feel I would probably begin to go stir crazy after only a short time if I worked at home.

tional to how efficiently we can do our jobs—the less time it takes for us to do our jobs, the more time we should have for leisure activities and family. Perhaps the best way to actively move toward making that ideal a reality is to become active in one of the fast-growing telework advocacy groups (see sidebar). But for employees working in the home without direct supervision, the real responsibility for striking the right balance between work and private life belongs to the individual. When you become a telecommuter, you are becoming a pioneer on a new frontier, the parameters of which are still being defined. Make sure you understand what you're surrendering as well as what you stand to gain.

Starting Your Own Business

With a great idea, the willingness to work your butt off, and impeccable timing, you might just get a shot at spending your professional life chasing your own rainbows instead of somebody else's.

by Michael Kaplan

When you discover that 64 percent of Americans between the ages of eighteen and thirty-four either have started or plan on starting their own companies, or that 600 U.S. colleges offer courses of study specifically geared toward would-be entrepreneurs, the allure of going out on your own can be irresistable. Start-up companies have become such a ubiquitous feature of the late '90s business landscape that Richard Bright of the Young Entrepreneurs Association has taken to labeling today's wannabe presidents and CEOs "Generation E."

Many eventual entrepreneurs catch the bug while working for someone else's high-tech start-up. "They see how someone else does it," Bright says, "and get inspired to start their own companies, work hard, and have a great life."

Unfortunately, many of them fall flat on their faces. After hitting the age of thirty-five, nearly 30 percent of these budding entrepeneurs will switch lanes and opt for the more staid corporate route. "It's just not as easy to make it on your own as it may look," cautions Meredith Oppenheim, who's employed by CNN/*Sports Illustrated* to hunt for entrepreneurial companies with which to partner up. "The start-ups that make millions of dollars are way in the minority."

To increase the chances you'll be a member of this fortuitous minority, Bright says you've got to follow the gospel of early planning. "Not going through the business plan process and failing to analyze the costs hurts a lot of people," he says. "You need to look at the worst possible scenarios and be brutally honest about the amount of money you can conceivably raise. A lot of people have an idea, but that is all they have. They fail to truly realize whether or not the marketplace needs what they are selling."

Demoralized? Don't search out a headhunter just yet. With a great idea, the willingness to work your butt off, and impeccable timing, you might just get a shot at spending your professional life chasing your own rainbows instead of somebody else's. To that end, we offer a group of case studies of entrepreneurs who've been where you might want to go. Using their experiential toeholds as a guide, you will increase the likelihood of trekking to the top of Mount Independence without tumbling.

member: DKEMERY
SURVEY: ENTREPRENEUR
I know from my own experience that DIYs can be successful. A few ground rules should be taken into consideration to help assure success. First, gain a clear understanding of the environment in which you hope to operate. Second, become well acquainted with the needs and expectations of your core customer base. Third, have enough capital in reserve so that you can take no cash draws from business proceeds for a minimum of the first six months of operation—preferably the first year. Any income for this period should be reinvested in your business.

Catching a Buzz

You've come up with an ingenious idea and have the potential to corner a tiny little triangle of the market that nobody has even thought about yet.

Now you just need to make sure the rest of the world knows how smart your idea is. It's called creating a buzz, and it can be done for a lot of money (through a spiffy national advertising campaign on television) or for hardly any money at all (generating media attention and allowing word to spread on a more grass-roots level). Like most cash-strapped entrepreneurs, Rick Tyler and Andrew Dreskin employed the latter approach to inform the world about TicketWeb, their San Francisco–based company that sells tickets to sporting events and concerts via the Internet at a lower cost and in a more expedient manner than its deeply entrenched competitor, TicketMaster.

lmember: alato
SURVEY: ENTREPRENEUR
DIY doesn't always have to be about making money. I run a very small business for the fun of it. I sell comic books and collectibles to local collectors and friends. It all started when I couldn't get the comics I wanted from local stores. So I decided to start my own business. I'm not trying to make any money (that's not to say that I couldn't), but it really doesn't interest me. I really enjoy playing at business. I would pull my hair out if I had to survive on it. The only problem I have is the taxes. I had a hell of a time trying to figure out what to deduct.

Dreskin began by chatting up the local print media. First he sent out a mailing of eye-catching postcards that announced the company's mission and planted the seed for a David-and-Goliath story about little guys going up against the corporate behemoth TicketMaster. Then Dreskin let his fingers do the walking. "I called reporters and told them that we had a great story: a low cost alternative to TicketMaster that is also the only way to get tickets to a lot of the hip, alternative rock clubs," he says. After several solicitous calls, which were timed to his company's alignment with a few large clubs, the *San Francisco Chronicle* finally came around. "They did a lead story on us in the Sunday entertainment section. Business improved and we established more credibility with the venues."

National press in *Rolling Stone* and *PC* magazine followed and Dreskin developed a sure-fire technique for convincing reporters to meet with him: He makes it clear up front that he loves buying drinks and dinner. "It's a small investment that really pays off," he says. Rather than buying ads, Dreskin and his partner have put their meager advertising budget into mounting sticker and poster campaigns around San Francisco, Berkeley, and Palo Alto.

Now that TicketWeb has pulled down $1 million in revenues in its second year of operation, Dreskin and Tyler can afford to do more traditional buzz-building, but they don't see a need for it. "It's always more effective to have other people talking about us," he says. "We manufacture buzz very inexpensively through grass-roots marketing. Throwing money at something is not necessarily the way to go. Companies stay around longer when they stay low budget and don't hemorrhage cash. Even when we get more capital, we'll still pretend to be broke."

member: HHarrison

SURVEY: ENTREPRENEUR

I've had a number of businesses over the years, some of which I've run as a sole proprietory and others as partnerships. In each case, with the partnerships, I lost out in the end to the more unscrupulous nature of my partners (who were inevitably putting in money versus ideas and energy). I'm now back working for myself again, which is always the most satisfying. My recommendation to anyone considering a partnership is to avoid gentlemen's agreements and make sure that every contract, every legal aspect of the partnership, is self-protective and watertight. You must have your own lawyer, your partner should have his or her own. The only sturdy foundation for a business partnership is a strong legally defined relationship.

Action Items

- Create a look for your company through interestingly designed posters, then plaster them all over town.
- Concentrate on generating free publicity rather than paying for costly ads.
- Devise compelling news stories about yourself, then schmooze journalists (especially local ones) who can get them published.

PLANTING ROOTS AND GETTING NOTICED

Ted Gottfried sold his share of a record store in Miami and moved to Manhattan's East Village with the intention of getting into a similar retail business there. Then he got an eyeful of how many record shops were scattered around that neighborhood and thought better of it. Instead, he decided to concoct a retail operation that would be unique enough to get noticed at street level without having to compete against established businesses.

Gottfried did casual market research and brainstormed an idea for a business that could actually benefit from the density of record stores. "I looked at specialized bookstores like Forbidden Planet—which keys in on horror, sci fi, and comics—and figured that I could do well with a store specializing in music books since none of the record stores were selling them at the time," he says. His plan was to keep things simple and cater to a base of fervent consumers whom he knew would go out of their way to find books about their favorite bands.

He christened the store See Hear and began making money from day one. "There are a lot of music fanzines, and, trying to be as complete as possible, we carried a bunch of those as well. Then my customers began asking for other kinds of zines and they decided for me that we were a fanzine shop." Soon after he opened, Gottfried became the first retailer in America to specialize in selling independently produced titles like *McJob* (a work journal for slackers), *Hair to Stay* (aimed at those who love hirsute women), and *Motorbooty* (an irreverent culture zine). He has underscored his commitment to cult-audience literature by hosting book signings for indie authors.

The image that Gottfried has established for his shop is friendly and gimmick-free. It's what seems appropriate for an establishment where the decor should not detract from the eye-catching covers on the shelves. He designed a comfortable, well-lit place, where cooler-than-thou salespeople are quickly dismissed and customers are never discouraged from thumbing through the 2,000 titles that fill the recently enlarged store, located right in the center of the East Village. "I couldn't see spending a lot of money on furnishings," he says. "I figured that the magazines and books were what you would see so it didn't matter that the shelves were made of plywood."

member: esotericvideo

SURVEY: ENTREPRENEUR

If at all possible, start part-time. Many years ago I did it the dumb way and went full-time right out of the gate. Within nine months I was mired in debt and had to go get a "real" job. Now I am doing it what I consider to be the smart way.

member: SandysWorld

SURVEY: ENTREPRENEUR

I know that traditionally small businesses fail within the first three years, but that is because many people do not plan properly. I do have my own home-based business. It's a gift basket business and I definitely see growth potential in this industry. Many people are starting to put more care, thought, and effort into gift-giving. This creates a definite niche for people like me.

Action Items

- Develop a strong business idea that can feed off of nearby establishments without competing with them.
- Design your store or office so that the product you are selling is emphasized.
- Create an environment that stimulates sales and participate in community-oriented events—like Gottfried's book signings—in order to establish credibility.

member: KOOL
SURVEY: ENTREPRENEUR
Although the possibilities are endless in becoming part of a small business, it is still risky. Starting out with an idea and building on it sounds great. Many small businesses, though, don't think about growth (hiring new employees), health plans, salaries, a place that can be called an office, money to cover losses in the first few years, and insurance in case of loss or lawsuits.

DIGGING FOR TREASURE

In their quest to take on AOL, Todd Krizelman and Stephan Paternot had exhausted the million or so dollars they'd raised from their initial flight of outside investors. They needed some big-time money to keep expanding their company, theglobe.com, a Web site devoted to creating and fostering Internet communities.

The Cornell graduates had already put together an impressive board of directors that included high-flying investors Bob Halperin

> Entrepreneur's Toolkit

You might want to check out these Web sites and books before launching your own business:

YOUNG ENTREPRENEURS NETWORK
(http://www.idye.com)
A resource center for budding and growing entrepreneurs, this site contains enough links to keep your modem humming for hours.

SMALL BUSINESS ADMINISTRATION
(http://www.sbaonline.sba.gov/)
This government organization caters to the needs of entrepreneurs. Its Web site contains information on everything from disaster assistance to raising money for financing your business.

VENTUREPRENEURS NETWORK
(http://www.venturepreneurs.com)
Entrepreneurs looking for funding can seek out investors with capital (and vice versa) at this site.

EDGE ONLINE
(http://www.edgeonline.com)
The most interesting aspects of this site include resources for interacting with other small business owners and a database that contains 5,000 documents which pertain to entrepreneurship.

BUILT TO LAST (Harperbusiness)
by James C. Collins and Jerry I. Porras
A survey of the business world's most enduring companies, this book takes a long and hard look at what made them successful.

START UP (Penguin)
by Jerry Kaplan
Kaplan's a pioneer of pen-based technology, and this book chronicles how he helped turn his Go Corporation into one of Silicon Valley's hottest players.

ENTREPRENEUR MAGAZINE'S SMALL BUSINESS ADVISOR
(Wiley)
Everything you always wanted to know about running a small business is in this encyclopedic tome.

and David Horowitz (formerly the presidents of Rayco and MTV respectively), but the biggest impact on their incipient company came from a cash infusion of $20 million (the largest single investment made to a privately held site on the Web) from financier Michael Egan. Tipped off by the president of Cornell University, Egan had flown up to meet with them on short notice and agreed to buy in after only four hours. That Krizelman and Paternot can explain their company in under thirty seconds (a must-do for raising capital) and maintain an up-to-date business plan at all times contributed greatly to the positive outcome of their meeting with Egan.

On the path to that precedent-setting investment, Krizelman and Paternot learned a few things about raising money. While venture capitalists may be the people most eager to seed your business with cash, Paternot explains, they may not be a great first choice for providing funds. "Venture capitalists typically try to get in early enough to eat up 80 percent of the equity so they can go public and sell out," he explains. "We were looking for investors who wanted a longer-term commitment and wanted to grow the company. Mike Egan had been with Alamo for twenty years, and he sees this as a long-term commitment."

While it can be more difficult to find the perfect fit, Paternot suggests seeking investors who bring more than cash to the table; for example, Egan came in with a high level of marketing savvy and Horowitz is an expert in entertainment. Look for people who will help grow the company and can help you network. "Just getting money can be enough," says Paternot, "but it's much better to have a brain as well."

Action Items

- Learn to describe your company in thirty seconds or less.
- Update your business plan every six months to account for shifts in your industry.
- Avoid getting financing only from venture capitalists whose goal is to take your company away from you and bring it public too quickly.

member: SolutionsEBS

SURVEY: ENTREPRENEUR

Don't burn your bridges, you never know when an old boss can give you a good reference. Budget, budget, budget. Don't go overboard until you can afford to do so. Any business a person is planning to start must be researched throughly. Make sure the industry isn't already saturated. It feels so *great* to be in charge of my own destiny. It's also easier to get up in the morning knowing that If I don't get out of bed, I might be missing an opportunity to go farther.

member: Samdo

SURVEY: ENTREPRENEUR

My husband and I are going to raise donkeys. We live in South Texas, which is cattle country. Donkeys have an inbred hatred for coyotes, and a lot of ranchers run a donkey or two with their herd to keep the coyotes from killing the calves. So far it has been a lot of fun because they behave more like dogs than equines. We've taken great pleasure in them . . . stubborness and all!

Setting Up Shop

Five years after falling in love with the game of roller hockey, Brad Shook and his partner David Walsh decided to make the game their livelihood, opening up facilities for the sport in Denver and San Francisco. For a business where the physical space is the commodity, they've learned that setting up shop is anything but a game. "I'm still paying off lawyers," Shook gripes, explaining that they required an attorney for lease negotiating. "Legal fees came to ten thousand dollars, but lawyers are notorious for running up bills, so you have to set limits."

While in most instances location is a primary element for the success of a business, Shook and his partner required so much space for Bladium that they had to be flexible. "We saw a place in Oakland that we turned down because it was just too rough there." They settled on a 27,000-square-foot metal building in a slightly more upscale section of San Francisco.

The building, however, was a mess and required $500,000 of renovations. Shook kept costs down by rolling up his sleeves and becoming his own general contractor. "I leveled walls, laid the floors, and put in showers," he says, explaining that he had some house remodeling experience but largely learned as he went along. "And we minimized our costs by putting in only the bare basics at first: a used carpet on the floor and no pro shop or bar. We figured we'd put those in after we turned a profit."

At least as arduous as the physical labor was the mental strain of negotiating decent leasing terms. "The landlord wanted us to sign our lives away; I signed away only half of our lives," Shook says with the kind of chuckle that tells you he's not kidding. "The big thing to look out for is the guarantee on the lease. You want to be excused from any liability. They wanted us to guarantee a full five years on the property. I got it down to a portion of that, a portion that I thought was fair."

Where Shook knew not to cut corners was on staffing, insurance, and equipment. He also kept his love for the game from getting in the way of the business's reality. "Before signing a lease, we did a feasibility study, which questioned every aspect of our business plan," explains Shook. "We figured out whether or not the market

member: Scodak
SURVEY: ENTREPRENEUR
I recently started my first home-based mail order business selling personal protection products. At first it was very disappointing, as I really had no money for serious advertising. Now I have turned enough profit to expand into personalized children's books (with a national company). I would say that if you're going to start any type of business, stick with it! You may feel broke at first, but the rewards are wonderful.

member: robertkaron
SURVEY: ENTREPRENEUR
I own and operate a home-based computer consulting/network installation company. It took about three years before it was able to support me. Now, five years after I started, it's a decent income and I know I will never work for anyone again ... ever. Although I now know how to run a business—dealing with clients, suppliers, taxes—my problem is how to expand. I can't afford to hire full-time people, advertising does not work in my business. Referrals and direct mailings are all that ever worked.

was big enough, if it could generate an acceptable amount of money, how much all of this would cost to do. And of course we had a contingency plan in case this business didn't work out." He hesitates for a beat before adding, in a funereal tone, "You have to prepare yourself."

Action Items

- Remember that the importance of location is in direct proportion to the uniqueness of your space.
- Negotiate as much liability out of your lease as possible; before sinking too much money into your business, ensure that it can turn a profit after you make your investment.
- Do as much of the physical construction labor by yourself as possible and hold off on any unnecessary fixtures until you see the business bringing in money.

Career Contrarians

Believe it or not, there actually are people out there whose identities aren't necessarily tied to their jobs. And they're not starving, either.

by Candi Strecker

Once upon a time, you'd graduate after four years of college and then work for the next thirty or forty years with no breaks except for weekends and tiny slices of vacation time. But today there are other ways to play the game. Instead of traveling the traditional road of continuous, linear employment, many people map out a start-and-stop path that alternates periods of paid work with time spent pursuing their own interests.

Who are these people? Call them career contrarians. Quite simply, they're people whose identities aren't tied up with the jobs they sometimes fill. They understand that in life, there's always a trade-off between two scarce commodities: time and money. Career contrarians rethink their relationship with money in order to gain control of their time. And they're among the millions of Americans who are voluntarily "downshifting" out of the career fast track. Twenty-eight percent of those polled by the Merck Family Fund in 1995 said they'd made choices in the last few years that lowered their income—working fewer hours, turning down promotions, or switching to lower-paying jobs—in order to find more time for themselves and reduce stress.

A crucial strategy for the successful contrarian is frugality. You can lower the amount of money you need to earn through practices

member: rois

SURVEY: CAREER CONTRARIANS

I think that if you don't spend time pursuing interests other than what puts bread on the table, you're already dead. All of my skills lie outside of the realm of things I can be paid to do, and if I didn't have them, I'd be miserable. You can turn into a real jerk if you have no fun in your life.

member: marmar

SURVEY: CAREER CONTRARIANS

I am not a career person, never have been, and resent being lumped into a category when asked what I do for a living. Thankfully, my identity is not and never will be wrapped up in how I earn money.

member: andavall

SURVEY: CAREER CONTRARIANS

As a street artist, I see many folks like myself who have given up the corporate climb and security for that of a self-sustaining, self-made craftsperson. We may not get rich, but we pay our bills and don't have a boss. It's not nine-to-five but our own labor and our own fruits to harvest.

member: shaikh

SURVEY: CAREER CONTRARIANS

My biggest worry is how to cope with the health insurance coverage. I am paying COBRA to my previous employer and it is about $500 per month (there goes the $1,250 per month living standard!!!).

like thrift-shopping, clipping coupons, avoiding credit card debt, repairing things instead of replacing them, and renting or borrowing things instead of buying them. Being frugal also means separating your true needs from socially constructed desires: i.e., choosing ten dollars' worth of function instead of one hundred dollars' worth of status. As Stewart Brand, founder of the *Whole Earth Catalog*, puts it, "Living below your means is the only easy way to be rich." The money you save by living frugally can be used to buy time for yourself. By pinching pennies, keeping out of debt, and buying smart, most single people can save enough from several years' work to cover their expenses for a year off. When you alternate periods of employment with time off, you can structure your working life like a series of sprints, instead of a single forty-year endurance marathon.

Just think of the things you might do with a year of your own: Go on the road with your band; start a zine; work on an archaeological dig; write a book; read a book; go back to school and this time do it right; start a business; get a life.

You'll need to estimate your expenses for the time you plan to take off from working. Besides the obvious survival needs—food, clothing, shelter, and transportation—don't forget to budget for the cost of health insurance. Estimate your future needs by looking closely at your present expenditures. The classic way to do this is to carry a pen and notebook everywhere you go and jot down every single dollar made and spent each day for several months. It may seem compulsive and nerdy, but it really works.

The career you've chosen may determine how easy it is for you to pursue an on-again, off-again worklife. If your skills are in demand, it will be easier for you to return to work after taking time off. There are always "help wanted" ads for waitresses—but there are always ads for nurses and computer programmers, too.

Or consider jobs with built-in seasonality. Schoolteachers typically work ten months and get two months off. Tax preparers and tax accountants have an intense work season leading up to April 15, but aren't in big demand during the rest of the year. The tourism industry is full of seasonal workers: ski instructors, lifeguards, campground managers, wilderness guides. I know a sculptor who sup-

member: web mystress

SURVEY: CAREER CONTRARIANS

I watched my parents pour themselves into their jobs and come home tired and unfulfilled, and I won't do the same.

member: Lorissa

CONFERENCE: WORK AND PERSONAL GRATIFICATION

For me personal success is having a job that I enjoy. Yes, money is important, but not if you are unhappy at the job that you have. I worked in industry for several years and made lots of money, but I was not happy. I decided to go back to my first love, teaching. I love my job now. The pay is not as much as it was before, but I enjoy it. I look forward to going to work. So, for me personal satisfaction is better than having the wealth.

member: patlewis

SURVEY: CAREER CONTRARIANS

I feel that being free is worth more than money. Unfortunately, having an income (no matter what level) is almost as essential as oxygen in today's world.

member: AlMiller

CONFERENCE: WORK AND PERSONAL GRATIFICATION

When I wake up and see Lake Tahoe out my window, breathe fresh air, have drinkable tap water, and can go skiing or hiking or do anything else almost every day, I feel successful. In fact I feel sorry for the "successful" person who must rise at 5 A.M.; put on an uncomfortable three-piece suit; swill down Maalox; commute three hours per day through agonizing rush-hour traffic; and spend forty hours per week under fluorescent lights.

ports himself by working as a carny—a carnival worker on the county-fair circuit—every summer.

Maybe you don't need big chunks of time off, just a few more hours each week to pursue your dreams. In that case, try rearranging your work life on a smaller scale. If you can live on the income from four days of work per week instead of five, you gain an entire day to use as you see fit. Or consider a flex-time arrangement of four ten-hour days per week instead of five eight-hour ones.

Not all workplaces are open to this kind of flexibility. You're not going to get much sympathy in an office where there's an unspoken competition to see who can stay at their desk the longest. This behavior is especially prevalent in "younger" organizations; people with no families to go home to are the ones most likely to say "Hey, let's pull an all-nighter!" You may need to look for a job where there's

member: agger

CONFERENCE: WORK AND PERSONAL GRATIFICATION

Money is the true measure of personal success. It allows one to control time, and time is the ultimate luxury. Think back to the root of most of your problems in life and I bet money would play a substantial factor in either the cause or the solution. Whenever I hear people parrot the disgusting platitude, "I don't care if I have money, I just want to be happy," I bristle at their incorrect assumption that money and happiness are mutually exclusive. Guess what, they are the same thing.

> Profile: Stephanie Rudloe

Stephanie Rudloe saw henna for the first time in Belgium two years ago on the hands of an Arabian woman. Since then, Rudloe, 29, has been a professional henna body painter, covering people's epidermis in leafy tangerine-colored designs.

Using dye extracted from henna plants from the Sahara desert, Rudloe paints intricate images that last for two to three weeks. Henna is traditionally applied to the hands and feet, but kids today have it applied to any clean epidermal surface whatsoever. These new henna-heads are into the designs as an alternative to conventional and, in some cases permanent, body markings.

"There are a lot of young people looking for something to mark their individuality, like piercings or tattoos" says Rudloe. "With henna, you can have that mark and then change it; it's one thing you can do for beauty that isn't destructive." To supplement her income, Rudloe designs and sells beaded bustiers, designs theatrical costumes, and "freelance" embroiders. But her passion is the art of henna painting.

She works nearly full-time running New York City's Mehndi Project, a cooperative of henna artists from India, Morocco, and the United States. Raised in Maine, Rudloe's parents instilled in her some of the countercultural convictions she lives with today. Her family owns a yurt colony, a collection of circular wooden dwellings. "The idea of the yurts," says Rudloe, "was to be an alternative living space for people to pursue their art."

As an adult, she traveled constantly between Maine and New York and then New York and Brussels, Belgium. "Through my twenties, I didn't really settle in one place," she says. "Because of my interest in art, I definitely chose not to have a regular job. I wanted the time. "

She runs her fingers over the fading henna design on her wrist. "I'm finally able to support myself doing something I'm passionate about," she says.

For Rudloe, affluence is a hindrance rather than a help. "It's better not to be too comfortable," she cautions. "When you have money, you're less likely to push yourself." Her own experience has borne this out. "In '96, I survived on not much," she recalls. "I was able to stay at my friend's apartment for free."

She is adamant about not lumping what she does in with professional, gray-suited, 401k plan activities. "Henna painting falls between art and fashion. But I don't think art is a career," she says. "It's a way of life." *—Adam Fifield*

a blend of workers of all ages with a corporate culture that encourages a balance between work and home life.

If you want a nontraditional or flexible schedule, the best time to arrange it is "when your stock is highest—on the day you're offered a job," says career counselor Marty Nemko. "That's the moment when an employer sees you at your very best, and will be most willing to make compromises if that's what it takes to get you to take the job," he says. While you and your potential employer are coming to terms on the job's salary and benefits, you can also negotiate to get the working hours that suit you best.

Can you make your existing job more flexible? It's possible—although Nemko suggests that timing can be crucial. The strategic moment to ask for an alternative work schedule is after some significant accomplishment, for example, when you've completed a major

member: Sawmill

SURVEY: CAREER CONTRARIANS

I'm a freelance artist, studio at home. Wouldn't trade it for all the Fortune 500 jobs out there. True luxury is being able to set my own hours, watch *Oprah* while I work or listen to a good CD, not the elevator music some companies choose! No problems with transportation and no pantyhose! I can set my own dress code. I don't envy the bird in the cage with plenty of seed and water . . . I've got the whole sky to fly in.

> Profile: John Anderson

On top of a Green Mountain foothill in Lincoln, Vermont, sits a modest farmhouse loosely flanked by a few barns and sheds. Two stoical draft horses stand outside one of the barns. The stillness is ruptured by the buzz of a chainsaw. After a minute or two there is the awesome sound of an ancient tree crashing to the ground and twenty-five-year-old John Anderson comes out of the woods, brushing wood chips off his sweater. He greets his horses, Bud and Ted, heartily, like a high school coach about to launch into a pep talk. Anderson uses a team of workhorses instead of the mountain-gnawing machinery of conventional loggers. After felling trees, he measures them and cuts them into logs. Each log is clamped into the hauler, and Bud and Ted do the rest, transporting the timber log by log to a collection site. He cuts and then sells the timber to pulp mills, local residents, and self-employed carpenters.

Anderson resides in nearby Ripton, in a house a mile or so from what was once Robert Frost's cabin. He is single. "All I need to do is keep these guys fed," he says, pointing to his horses.

But Anderson's background is not so humble. In 1994 he graduated from Middlebury College with a B.A. in art history. When he moved to Wyoming for a post-collegiate stint as a hiking and fly-fishing excursion guide, he met a German family who invited him to work on their organic farm in southern Bavaria. "They used horses instead of tractors," he says, "so that's how I started using horses."

After about a year in Bavaria, Anderson was back in the United States. He returned to Vermont, bought Bud and Ted, and started up his business.

Anderson is "entirely independent" and subscribes to an old-fashioned New England work ethic. He became a woodsman, he says, because it is a job with very few illusions. "It's all based on production," he says. "You get paid by exactly how much you put out. No bullshit."

Anderson is one of the best varieties of career contrarians. He is critical of conventional work trajectories, saying, "The term 'career' reminds me of the fifties. A careerist does something for forty hours that he doesn't particularly enjoy, but he does it to support his family. It's only a title. It never really made much sense to me." He simply has no desire to sign up with a larger logging company, even if it would be more monetarily rewarding. On the subject, Anderson says curtly: "Nope. Companies, unions—that stuff's for the birds."

—Adam Fifield

project or received a stellar performance review. Emphasize that your productivity is what really matters, not how much "face time" you provide in the workplace.

If you really want flexibility in your working arrangements, the best option is to be your own boss. But remember that in the long run, you are your own boss, whether you're an employee drone or a CEO. Just because most people pursue their careers one way doesn't mean you have to. A contrarian path may be your road to personal success.

> Profile: Kyle Davies

To hear twenty-five-year-old Kyle Davies talk, you'd think he was possessed by a Luddite octogenarian with frontier nostalgia.

"What do a lot of Americans suffer from?" muses the native of Oneida, New York, who spent much of his adolescence working on farms. "I think it's comfort."

That's why in October 1994, four months after graduating from Bates College in Lewiston, Maine, Davies packed up his 1986 Chevy Suburban with two dozen cans of corned beef hash, a few padded flannels, and about $4,000 worth of diving gear, and hit the highway going west. His destination: Friday Harbor, Washington, a town of 1,800 people on Puget Sound's San Juan Island. It was a place, he thought, where the tendrils of technology would have a hard time reaching and where human interaction would therefore have to be abundant.

What also lured him to this tiny island village rather than some mining town in Montana or Alaska was the water. After two years of combing swaths of marsh and rock in central Maine, he decided the most intriguing place for him to explore was beneath the water's surface. After a few months of cleaning hotel rooms on San Juan Island, he obtained his professional diving certification and landed a job as a research diver. Soon after, he became a member of the county's volunteer search and rescue diving team.

As he settled into island life, Davies became a renaissance rescuer of sorts. He joined the local volunteer fire department, began working part-time as a dispatcher for the county sheriff's office, and volunteered for a local group striving to protect whales in the Puget Sound. One evening, on the way home from a fire, Davies got paged for a dive mission. Luckily his wet suit was right next to his fire gear in the back of his truck.

These varied volunteer activities demanded the majority of his time and energy, so his income never grew to match them. But financial stability was always secondary, he says, to living out a life he had previously thought unrealistic and anachronistic.

In part for financial reasons, Davies eventually moved out of his "downtown" apartment and onto a houseboat that was moored along a chain of floating homes in the harbor. His eccentric neighbors were hardcore Luddites, Libertarians, and San Juan Island "expats"—all of whom would refer to the mainland as "America." On many an evening, he would set up his hibachi on a nearby dock to have a neighborhood oyster bake and would end up swapping diving and other seafaring stories with the gathered company.

Davies admits that when he first moved to the island he couldn't help comparing himself to his peers. "I never thought I was cheating myself," he says. "But part of me said, shouldn't you be more responsible and look for a job in Chicago or Boston or whatever?"

But doubts like that linger no longer. "I don't ever see myself as having a 'career,'" he predicts, pronouncing "career" as if it were two words. "There are too many things I want to do. If you can support yourself or your family, or even your drug habit, who's to say you gotta have one job?"

— Adam Fifield

Not long ago, I found myself in an odd predicament. Although I was a contributing editor to *The Idler*, a British journal devoted to my favorite pastime, I was too busy to write an article on slacking. Ironically, my pursuit of the creative life—publishing a zine, studying philosophy on my own—had landed me a media job so demanding that I now had little time to do the things I truly enjoyed. I missed idling: reading and writing for pleasure, hanging out with my wife and friends, or just lying on the couch staring at the ceiling. I realized at that moment that I was no longer an idler. I was a hypocrite, a hyped-up squirrel in sloth's clothing.

So I quit my job, imagining—as so many others have—that unemployment would give me all the free time in the world to be creatively idle (or idly creative). But all too soon my days filled themselves with chores, obligations, and distractions; again I became chronically un-idle. Work, I soon came to see, is not the opposite of idling. In fact, most idlers hold jobs, and many of them even enjoy doing so. Joining the ranks of the workless allowed me to realize that my frenetic former job was not the sole culprit in my life of unchecked busyness. Whirligigging hysteria infects even our simplest tasks in the contemporary world. I recognized that the accelerated pace of life itself was, in fact, the real enemy.

I had a new job by the time I learned about an upcoming design conference in Amsterdam centering around my new animus: Speed. Written in the Speed conference's brochure were the lines: "Is faster always better, or is there a price to be paid for the constant acceleration of production, information, and daily life? . . . Is it time to build 'selective slowness' into the design of our lives?" Fantasizing about cities, homes, offices, and transportation, all redesigned to move more slowly, I bought myself a plane ticket.

At the conference, dozens of historians, environmentalists, architects, scientists, tech workers, and trend watchers outlined their design solutions to the problem of "the cultural power of acceleration." But after two days of this, I just wasn't convinced that the professional experts had an answer for me; their solutions smacked too much of the traffic cop, whose concern is not to slow down traffic, but to decrease congestion—so that traffic can continue to move swiftly. That's when Ivan Illich stepped up to the podium.

Illich, a social critic who in the '60s and early '70s had inspired an entire generation of progressive Baby Boomers to seek alternatives to professionalized systems of mass education, mass medicalization, and mass mobility, was something of a patron saint to these conference organizers. Speaker after speaker quoted Illich's seminal argument (from his book *Tools for Conviviality*) that "tools" (systems)—even those used by benevolent service providers—which develop beyond a certain intensity inevitably become counterproductive, and thus detract from a community's "conviviality." Although we imagine that moving faster and faster saves us time, Illich suggested, this is just a superstitious "rain dance of time-consuming acceleration": Thanks in part to high-speed highways (which are inevitably not so high speed), for example, we now live so far away from the places where we work and shop that we spend half of our days in transit!

However, standing behind the podium now, in his old-fashioned buckle shoes and cardigan sweater, a more philosophical Illich offered the assembled designers a way out of their own personal speed traps. Advocates of conviviality should abandon the very idea (which he himself had once helped promote) that speed was something to be opposed with slowness. "Perhaps we have already moved beyond the age of speed," he proclaimed hopefully, "and are now in the age of—and I tremble when I say these words—'real time.' Real time is being here, being now; even, in the midwife's use of the word, 'quickening'—that is to say, coming alive."

Flying home, back to the congested traffic of my life, I thought I understood what Illich's Zen-like pronouncement meant. The blessed state of idleness can't be chased; that would be an oxymoron. And slowing down, doing less, while worthy goals, in my own experience do not automatically an idler make. However, by being "quick" as Illich defines the word—being alive to the moment no matter how hard we're working, striving to do everything we do in life for it's own sake—we may find that time itself slows down to the point where we are, in some new and unexpected way, free to be idle again.

—*Josh Glenn*

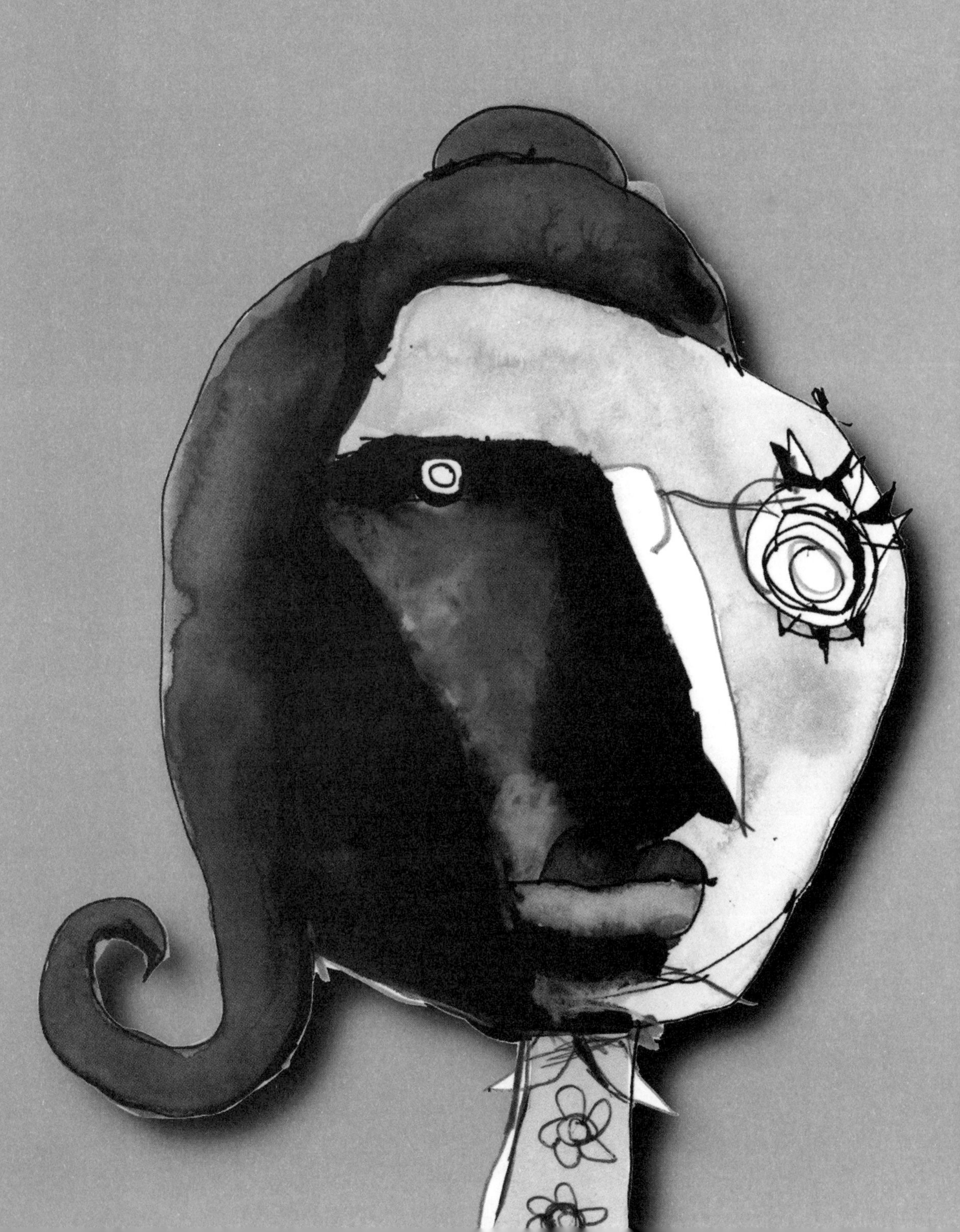

part 3 home

Apartment Hunting

For most people, searching for an apartment is a full-time job and a tremendous headache. But by being realistic and ready to compromise, you can manage to find a great place to live.

by Jim Adams

> I live in my house as I live inside my skin: I know more beautiful, more ample, more sturdy, and more picturesque skins: but it would seem unnatural to exchange them for mine.
>
> —*Primo Levi*

It's easy to despair when you have nowhere to hang your hat, no place to call home. But you can find your first apartment, your dream home, or just a room of your own more easily than you think. By breaking the process into four small steps—selecting a neighborhood, locating available rentals, sizing up apartments, and signing a lease—you can find a home that suits you like a skin.

First, know the lay of the land. Know the map of your city and know what different neighborhoods have to offer. Second, even if you were never a Boy Scout, heed Lord Baden-Powell's advice: "Be prepared." Do some research; then decide what you want, where you want to look, and what you can afford.

member: MsThing

CONFERENCE: LIVABLE CITY

For me, intellectual stimulation and living among like-minded people is a top priority. It's no coincidence that many new media companies are located in San Francisco, or that Silicon Valley is (was?) a hotbed for computing innovation—like minds congregate together and new ideas result. I fear that I'd stagnate in Backwater, U.S.A.

member: rwilde

CONFERENCE: LIVABLE CITY

For the first time since graduating college, I recently moved back to the country for a job. I guess I never appreciated just how good it is to be a part of a small-town community. Maybe this means I'm getting older, or maybe I am just learning how shallow my preconceptions about rural living really were. Don't knock it till you try it. Regular coffee can taste pretty good too, even without biscotti.

Hi, Neighbor: Scoping Out the Area

In most cities, neighborhoods vary widely in terms of residents, available services, and size and price of apartments. Finding out which areas have available and affordable rentals is as easy as looking at the classified ads in the local paper. Take a neighborhood for a test drive. Spend a day pretending to live there and check out what it offers. Does the neighborhood have a bank and post office? How about supermarkets, restaurants, and parking? Is it close to the highways or to public transportation? Consider your safety. Do you feel safe walking home from work or to the drugstore at night? When you're trying out a neighborhood, you'll soon find out if people there are generally friendly. If they're not, do you still want to live there?

The key question to keep asking yourself as you're scouting out a neighborhood is, "Will I be happy here?" Is the area quiet morning, noon, night, or never? Can you survive next to the projects, yuppie suburbs, or a deserted downtown? Make sure you could stand the neighborhood for at least a year, since that's how long most leases last. After you've seen a few different areas, start to weigh your priorities. Is a shorter commute worth fewer restaurants? Can you live without a local bar to be near a bus stop? Establish a set of criteria and rule out all but a couple of neighborhoods. Now that you've narrowed your search, it's time to see some apartments.

member: lscholes

CONFERENCE: LIVABLE CITY

I lived in the place that is closest to my heart—Oxford, Mississippi—for two years after graduating (and quite a few people I went to school with still live there ten years later); then moved to NYC for "the career"; then moved to New Orleans for "the man"; and am now moving back to NYC in the fall for "the career" again. I love New York, I love my friends there, I love the fact that I can get a falafel at 2 A.M. But . . . I work in publishing and I hate that the life that the people in Woody Allen movies live is virtually unobtainable for me. I dream of quiet streets and a cool house and good food and great wine shared with intelligent friends who know me (kind of) and where I can walk to a seductive bookstore and an outstanding restaurant without breaking a sweat.

Finders Keepers: Locating Available Rentals

The next step is figuring out who owns the places on the market and how you can get to see them. In many cases, the classified ads can be your first and last stop. A second straightforward strategy is to simply walk through a neighborhood, noting the phone numbers of buildings with apartments for rent—or of their management companies. You can often get the low-down on management companies and landlords by going into a building and speaking to the super. In addition to giving you the owner's number, a friendly super can tell you about the apartments and how often they become vacant. He might even show you an empty one. But if the super doesn't seem interested in helping you, simply get the owner's number and go through more official channels. Never bribe a super: If you end up living in the building you won't want to pay him every time you need something fixed.

Seeing an apartment by contacting the landlord is simple: Call him or her up and arrange a time to look at the place. The landlord should be able, if not willing, to answer all of your questions about it. A landlord who owns a lot of apartments may be too busy to talk directly to you. Instead, he may send you to his broker, agent, or management company.

Theoretically, a broker serves a useful function: She can show you a seemingly unlimited number of apartments in your desired area and price range minutes after you've stepped into her office. However, in reality, most brokers are leeches whose sole purpose is to strip you of your money and infantilize you in the process. They protect the landlords by running a screening process to find suitable (i.e., reliable, rent-paying) tenants in exchange for a handsome fee, anywhere from a month's rent to 30 percent of the annual rent. Unfortunately, in most cities, you're the one who will be paying the price for this protection. But if you do have to deal with a broker, don't freak out. Be cordial yet firm; don't pay anything in advance (like a one-time service fee) and don't let them pressure you into signing anything you don't understand or taking an apartment you don't love.

member: DigitalCrayon
CONFERENCE: LIVABLE CITY
Being able to grill in the front yard while wearing your underwear is my chief issue for livability. The deer don't seem to mind a bit.

member: paytonc
CONFERENCE: LIVABLE CITY
We use cities to get in touch with our fellow humans; country to connect the primal spirit within to nature. Suburbia offers relative quiet and safety, but is not far enough removed to eliminate the hassle, congestion, and pollution of the city. Suburbs are as boring as the country, but without the option of enjoying untrammeled wilderness. Indeed, suburbs suck the very lifeblood out of our cities.

The Fit: Sizing Up an Apartment

When looking at individual apartments, ask yourself the questions you would ask about any other purchase: Does it look good? Does it go with what you already have? And, of course, can you afford it? Unless a friend is hooking you up with the deal of the century, make sure to look at more than one place. You need to see a few to ensure that you're not paying an inflated price for substandard goods.

Here are a few key factors to help you size up the value of an apartment.

- Is the space livable? Are the rooms large enough? Are common areas, like the living room, kitchen, and dining room, big enough for you to hang out in?

- Will all your stuff fit? If you've got a gigantic sofa or a dresser you can't live without, bring a tape measure to make sure there's enough space for it.
- Figure out which direction each room faces: Southern exposures get sunlight all day long, while eastern and western ones have sun in the morning and afternoon, respectively. If you're facing north, you get a whole lot of nothing, except maybe moss. Count the windows: If they are few and far between, you won't get much of a cross breeze.
- Turn on the stove, flick all the light switches, flush the toilet, run the shower for a few seconds, open the closets, and look in the cabinets. Poking around will help you get a sense of how well the place has been maintained over the past few years.
- If an apartment needs repainting, if there are scratches in the walls, or anything major is broken, ask that these problems be fixed before you move in. If the apartment has any glaring flaws, you can try to haggle for a better rental rate or you can offer to fix them yourself in exchange for a rent reduction.
- If the landlord agrees to any deal, get it in writing and agree on a date when it will be done. Remember, when a landlord has an "as is" policy, you're going to have to live with these problems or pay to repair them yourself.
- "Nice-guy" landlords may throw in utility charges as part of the rent, saving you anywhere from $30 to a $100 dollars a month. If your landlord makes such a promise, make sure it's written into the lease.
- The floor you live on can have a huge effect on your quality of life. Moving into a ground-level apartment is a breeze, but you'll then have to live with street traffic and other tenants walking past your door every day. Living on a middle floor, you'll have a short climb home, but you'll have to contend with noises from above and below. While it may be a pain to lug your possessions—and yourself—to the top floor of a building without an elevator, you'll never have to hear someone dancing above your bed.
- Ask about the kind of people who live in the building and whether they have kids, dogs, cats, or high-decibel hobbies. Ask how clearly you can hear other tenants; when the floors are thin

member: CSproat

CONFERENCE: LIVABLE CITY

Swimming pools vs. orange juice: I narrowed it down to that a couple of years ago. Columbus (where I grew up) had great swimming pools, but NYC has the best orange juice in the world. I admit I grew tired of NYC after a while—spending every dime I had on rent and transportation, and vigilantly defending my garbage bags from the legions of trash-pickers who would drape it up and down the block. But I look back on my years in NYC fondly now that I am in Philadelphia where I have to drive to another state to find tortillas and pita bread and I am still defending my garbage bags at three in the morning.

or uncarpeted, even a downstairs neighbor's late-night TV watching can be disruptive. Finally, ask about the history of people who have lived in the apartment. If the landlord says the previous renters lived in the place for five years, that's a good sign. If four people have moved out in the last eighteen months, that's a red flag and the landlord should have a good explanation.

- To determine what you can afford to pay for an apartment, think of your rent as approximately one-fourth of your monthly income. If you're looking at a place that runs $400 a month, to be able to live comfortably you should earn about $1600 in that same period. Make sure to factor in other costs, like gas, electric, and phone bills. If you're dying to take a place and the rent comes out to a third of your salary, that's livable. But be careful: If you end up paying too much of your salary in rent, you'll be eating beans and rice until you get a raise.

member: Teri P

CONFERENCE: LIVABLE CITY

There is nothing that can make a city livable. I've spent most of my life scraping by so that I didn't have to live in cities. You can't have the sense of community in a city that you get in a small town. In a small town, you belong just because people see your face in the local market every day. How can anything in the city compare to seeing deer outside your door or having racoons stop by for dinner every night? The only thing I wish for are decent paying, full-time jobs, so that those of us who live here wouldn't have to drive into cities to be able to live.

The Dotted Line: Signing a Lease

If a place meets your logistical and economic needs—and you can imagine being happy there—you're ready to sign on the dotted line. You and the landlord should already agree about how much you're going to pay, what is and is not included with your rent, and how long the lease will last. To make sure this is the case, *read everything* before you sign. It might be boring and the realtor might make jokes about you becoming a lawyer right before her eyes, but protect yourself and read the whole damn thing. Make sure you understand what the language means (ask if you're uncertain) and make sure all your terms are included. If something is missing, get the landlord or broker to retype the lease or put in an attachment (a rider) that both you and the landlord sign. And don't leave the office without a copy of everything you sign.

member: Geenius

CONFERENCE: LIVABLE CITY

Poverty and economic stagnation can kill a place, but so can too much affluence, at least when it results in the replacement of real places and real personal interaction with insularity and homogenized mall culture. When people spend their evenings out in the streets, rubbing shoulders with their neighbors, seeing them face to face instead of through auto glass, then a place becomes a place to live and not merely a place to exist.

Before you get to the table, some brokers and landlords will check your credit history to make sure you can cover the rent. It might seem intrusive, but it's perfectly legal for them to ask to see your bank statements, tax forms, and pay stubs, and you may even have to pay a nominal fee ($20 or so) for them to check your credit with a security agency. You can always refuse to let a broker look at your credit history or your bank balance, but if you do that, he doesn't have to give you an apartment. If your landlord is worried that you can't cover the rent, he may require that you get a guarantor, and some landlords will demand that your guarantor be in-state. Usually your parents or guardian, the guarantor simply adds his name to the bottom of the lease, agreeing to pay the rent if you default. This is not a big deal, unless you plan on burning a landlord or are living somewhere against your family's wishes.

After you sign a lease, you will have to hand over a large lump of cash. Typically, it's the first month's rent and some kind of security deposit, often equal to a month's rent. Including a broker's fee (paid separately), this should be the upper limit of the payments you make before moving into an apartment.

If you're worried about not being competitive in a tight market or if you don't have the best credit history, you can easily make yourself a more attractive tenant. Dress up a little, as if you were going to a job interview and bring your checkbook and a printed list of references to your first meeting with the landlord or broker. Treat finding an apartment as a business deal—always be polite and professional. Don't lie to the landlord, don't bend over backward to please him, and don't make promises you don't intend to keep.

For most people, hunting for an apartment is a full-time job and a tremendous headache. But by being realistic and ready to compromise, you can manage to find a great place to live. Don't set your sights too high and don't be greedy. If you're organized, committed, and conscientious, you could wind up with the deed to your own Playboy Mansion, ready and willing to live up to the words of Hef himself: "The house is so suited to my living habits that it's a world unto itself, and in most respects, far better than the world outside."

Renting vs. Buying and Tenants' Rights

Whether you're buying or renting, there's quite a bit you can do to make certain that you don't dig for yourself an incredibly deep hole from which there is no easy escape.

by Kathleen McGowan

On Renting vs. Buying

Buy a house? Me?

Well, actually, probably not you. Not that many young people can really afford to buy houses—a little more than a third, according to the government. Lots of organizations offer income calculators to help you decide, but many of them have an agenda. Check out the Fannie Mae Web site (www.fanniemae.com) for one of the better ones.

But what about the American split-level-townhouse-picket-fence-two-car-garage-equity thing?

Welcome to the 1990s. According to the National Association of Home Builders, house prices have swamped incomes in the last twenty years. Nearly half of American families could afford to buy a new house in 1976. Now, only 36 percent can—NAHB estimates you need to make over $44,000 a year. The average new house costs $136,000; the average monthly payment, with mortgage, tax, and insurance is $1,033.

member: alphadoubleplus

CONFERENCE:

Rent or Buy a Home?

The *frustrating* thing is trying to figure out how to save up the 10–20 percent down payment while you're burning all your money away on rent. And for those of us (the *majority* of Americans) who have really screwed up our credit, the situation is only that much worse—pretty bleak!

member: mec9

CONFERENCE:

Rent or Buy a Home?

I was a vagabond for years, never believing I would own. Now that I do, I love it. In addition to the financial benefits, there is absolutely nothing that equals the feeling I get coming home to my "own" home. A day doesn't go by that I'm not glad I bought. However, I also believe I was a smart buyer. I didn't go for the dream house right off the bat. My mortgage payments are considerably less than rent payments for something comparable. I also put a lot of sweat equity in my home—did my own landscaping, repairs, etc.

Equity still sounds good to me

There is definitely something to be said for sinking your cash into property rather than into the loan payments on your landlord's Jeep Cherokee. You don't feel like such a loser, for one thing. And, in the eyes of the money world, you get clout. It's sort of like this: Banks see that you're willing to go into hock for a big wad of money, and that you will actually give that money back to the bank, with vigor. They like that. They're much more likely to give you other loans, credit cards with absurd limits, even financing for that ostrich farming franchise you've been dreaming about.

But I don't make $44,627

That's where foreclosures and fixer-uppers come in. Houses you get on the cheap and invest with *sweat equity* can be great assets. You'll certainly learn a lot about construction and a lot about swearing, as well. Just remember to count your labor time as part of the investment in the house and pay yourself fairly. If it's selling for a few thousand, but it'll take you three months and $10,000 to be livable, it's not really selling for a few thousand.

Do-it-yourself housing is really only fun if:

- you know a gable roof from a hip roof and a worthless money vortex from a diamond in the rough;
- you know enough carpentry to take on a major structural overhaul;
- you have someplace else to live (not a tent) in the meantime.

member: sneeboo
CONFERENCE:
RENT OR BUY A HOME?
Not only is buying a house completely out of my realm of financial possibility right now, but I wouldn't like the idea of being tied down to a property, even if it were possible. Job opportunities in my field can appear (and, alas, disappear) at a moment's notice, and it behooves me to be able to become mobile fairly quickly. Further, I am more comfortable in big cities—I need stimulation that strip malls and manicured lawns just can't give me. As an urban-centric mammal, apartments are part of my preferred natural environment. And, for the foreseeable future, that means renting.

In sum, you should probably rent unless:

- You know you'll have a stable income and a steady lifestyle for the next five or so years. No point in paying out all that money up front (closing costs alone can total up to 6 percent of the price of the house) if you're going to have to bail out soon.
- You have a hunk of money lying around, allowing you to put down enough principal to keep your mortgage payments tractable. Average minimum down payment these days is 10 percent, cash, average home price around $88,000 in 1996—cheaper in the south, much more in the west.

- You're not depending on getting a good return on your investment. House prices have increased, on average, 3.9 percent a year in the last ten years—but there were two years when prices actually fell. Compare that to the 12.3 percent return on bonds in the 1990s (never mind the rabid stock market), and you realize that people don't buy houses for purely economic reasons.

Actually, I'd like to become that Jeep Cherokee–driving guy

Settle down there. Very few young people (actually, only 3 percent of the people under thirty-four) are landlords (and about 80 percent of all landlords are men, which is why, for the purposes of this chapter, landlords are generally referred to as "him"). You need to have money to make money and being a landlord is a lousy primary source of income. Most landlords make less than 10 percent of their total income from their buildings; fully half claim to lose money.

Only consider being a landlord if:

- you already are a great businessperson, good with both accounts and personalities;
- you can do a lot of minor to moderate fixing yourself, or know somebody who is a crackerjack handyman. Because repair costs are unpredictable, especially if you have flighty tenants;
- most important, you have a significant source of income elsewhere and can afford to lose some money in the beginning.

member: Marcel

SURVEY: THIS OLE HOUSE (LANDLORD HORROR STORIES)

Most landlords are faced with mortgage payments and property taxes that come due every month, whether or not their tenants make the rental payment on time. And some landlords rely on the (usually small) difference between the rent and expenses to put bread on the table and feed the kids. Rent is their primary source of income—and yet there seems to be a prevailing notion that landlords are bottomless pockets or charities and it's okay to not pay the rent when times get tough. I could tell *numerous* horror stories—about *tenants*! Landlords are not charities—they provide a valuable service—and they need to be paid for it. When a tenant doesn't pay rent, or doesn't pay it on time—to the landlord, it's the same as if the tenant's employer paid them late—or not at all! We're all in this together, folks. Pay your rent!

Sample Monthly Payments for Homeowners

Keep in mind that owning a house can be a millstone around your neck and could turn you into a swirly-eyed, fire-breathing libertarian once you start paying all those taxes and fees. Here's a little sample equation—it's only an average, but it gives you some idea of monthly expenses.

Principal and interest payment	$499
Real estate taxes	79
Routine maintenance	25
Property insurance	30
Water	23
Trash	14
Total	$670

Compare that to an average rent of $431, and you see how the immediate costs work out.

member: Encounter
SURVEY: THIS OLE HOUSE (LANDLORD HORROR STORIES)
My family and I got a great price on our home. But the landlord had forgotten to mention one thing . . . the plumbing systems to the bathrooms were badly in need of repairs. My father found this out the first time he came to visit. Soon we had an overflow into the living room, and the estimated cost of repair to the plumbing *and* the carpet is $2,000. We have talked to the landlord about this and he refuses to do anything about it because, "We should have made a thorough check." This gets me angry because there is no way we could have seen this coming.

Tenants' Rights or, How Not to Fight with Your Landlord

Renting isn't so bad. It basically means you have nearly unlimited license to do anything legal on your landlord's property. But that works both ways: Tenant law is a state-by-state thing, and some states don't go very far to protect their renters from arbitrary or dishonest landlords. Outside of a few major cities (New York, San Francisco, Boston among them) with near-socialist tenant/landlord laws, few judges and lawyers know the rules that well.

member: John_Skyn
SURVEY: THIS OLE HOUSE (LANDLORD HORROR STORIES)
Ever have your power shut off in the middle of winter? Fight the eviction notice when you stop paying rent. It'll be summer before it's finished going through, and you can invest the extra money in sweaters and blankets.

If you wind up in court, you'll probably waste a lot of time and money in your search for justice. Really winning the game means staying out of court. One of the keys to happy tenant/landlord relations is demonstrating right from the start that you understand your rights and intend to exercise them. This section will show you how to do just that. For more information, check TenantNet (www.tenant.net).

DISCLAIMER: This is not legal advice, but common sense culled from lawyers and tenant advocates. Many of the latter are living saints with absolute knowledge and a burning desire to help you. For details on your state's laws and regulations (and the skinny on how they really work), please, please, please consult one of them.

The tenant's commandments are obvious, but constantly broken:

- Keep it clean. Don't break things. Prevent your guests from behaving like jerks: i.e., doing donuts on the lawn.
- Your landlord, in most cases, has the right to show the apartment with reasonable notice (usually one to two days), with reasonable frequency. Believe it or not, your landlord can also decide how many people can live together and can refuse to let you to change roommates.
- Most of all, be clear, consistent, and honest with your landlord. If you end up in court, you'll look better.

member: Kathy7

SURVEY: THIS OLE HOUSE (LANDLORD HORROR STORIES)

A friend and I moved into what appeared to be a very cute 1940s-era duplex. Hardwood floors, stuccoed walls, built-in shelves, lots of personality, etc. We had the bottom floor, and were quite dismayed when our upstairs neighbor's hot water heater broke and flooded the ceiling of our pantry. Though our ceiling was repaired about two months later, they never fixed the wiring that was flooded out, nor did they do anything to the wall that was so drenched that it had yellow water stains. Sadly, yellow did not match our decor. The place was quite damp, too. We had mold growing on our bedroom walls, slugs who would appear now and again, and strange yellow mushrooms growing in the soil of our ficus plant.

In the Beginning

Fees? In many states, only licensed brokers can collect a finder's fee. In any case, the landlord himself almost always can't.

Lease or no? Your options are oral arrangements, month-to-month tenancy, or formal leases.

Sometimes you may make an oral agreement, which leaves a lot of room for (mis)interpretation. If you go this route, send your landlord a letter with your first month's rent, explaining the arrangement as you understand it, and noting that his cashing your check means he accepts those terms.

Month-to-month ("tenancy-at-will") usually means that the landlord must give only thirty days' notice before raising the rent or ending the lease. (The thirty days' notice also applies to you if you want to move out.)

Most people get annual leases, often just boilerplate documents from the stationery store—but they protect you. The landlord can't, for example, raise your rent during the term of the lease, unless you were dumb enough to sign a lease that explicitly permits it. Leases do lock you in, however. But, unless you know you'll want to move before the year's up, it's probably worth it to sign the lease—in which case, *read it first*. Don't leave blanks. Look for clauses about late fees, who pays utility bills, whether or not you can change roommates or bring in pets. Remember that it is a negotiable document, and the landlord may be willing to modify it—just cross out or write in changes, and make sure you both initial them. Specifically, you might want to add a clause controlling what happens if you leave midlease. Don't put up with any crap like this:

- Clauses that indemnify the landlord. That means if anybody gets hurt on the premises—including little old ladies that slip and fall on the icy sidewalk—you can be held accountable.
- "Acceleration" clauses. That means if you decide to leave midlease, all the money for the rest of the year is immediately due.
- Clauses that give the landlord permission to enter the premises at any time or permission to raise the rent if his expenses go up—so-called escalator clauses.
- Clauses that ask you to waive your legal rights or require you to pay any court fees for the landlord, even if he loses.

Some of these, like the last, may be illegal and therefore unenforceable anyway. But you don't want to have to go to court just to get your rights. Ask—nicely—for them to be removed right up front, if possible mentioning—nicely—that you know they are not standard. Then, get a copy of the lease right then and there. If things get sticky later, your landlord might misplace it.

Pets: Domestic animals cause lots of fights between tenants and landlords. Try this: Offer to put down an additional pet deposit of $100 or $200, with conditions clearly spelled out on paper.

Member: CJaneway

SURVEY: THIS OLE HOUSE (LANDLORD HORROR STORIES)

I've found that using some common sense and caution in your transactions will go a long way toward preventing problems. First and foremost, make sure *everything* is in writing. Don't take anyone's word for anything. It may sound paranoid but it is good legal sense. When you first move in write down *every* flaw in the apartment—nail holes, scratched counter, dirty face plates, cracked veneer or tile, even the stains and wear on the carpet, and send a copy to your landlord via certified mail. Keep the other copy with your lease. You're creating a paper trail and evidence should you end up in court. At first the thought of a major lawsuit scared and even intimidated me because I couldn't afford a lawyer. Two roommates got a lawyer and were talking about settling. Well, I knew that wasn't right so I called the local law school and found someone who would talk with me. She pointed out that since the landlord was even partially responsible there was no way he could collect and sent me to their law library to dig in the code book. I wrote my own "answer" to the allegations and I included in it every single code, violation, or piece of applicable legislation that I could find. It does pay to fight back if it's done intelligently and at least one gets the satisfaction of trying rather than feeling totally victimized.

Danger Signs (How to Spot a Demon Landlord)

- Look at the apartment with your landlord and discuss any problems before you sign the lease. Does your landlord brush you off? Is he willing to sign a letter promising to fix them?
- Collar the neighbors and ask them about their experiences with repairs and security.
- Is the landlord weird about giving you a daytime and emergency contact number? A beeper's not good enough. Many states require the owner's name and address to be on the lease.

Aside from a credit check fee, don't give the landlord a dime until you've signed the lease or made the agreement. (Credit check fees should be less than $20, and you should get it back if your credit check clears and he turns you down for other reasons. If you back out, you forfeit that fee.) Nonrefundable cleaning deposits are illegal in some states, and many states limit the amount of up-front money to security deposit, first month's rent, and last month's rent.

Here comes the really fun part, now that you're totally paranoid about the place. Before you move in, photograph or videotape (with date-time stamp development, if possible) any scratches, dents, sags, or holes.

member: Missey

SURVEY: THIS OLE HOUSE (LANDLORD HORROR STORIES)

When my husband and I were first married we lived in apartments until we bought our first house. The last apartment we lived in was less than a year old at the time and the landlords were friends of my in-laws. When they found out we were buying a house, they accused us of destroying the apartment (which was a lie), and told us we would not get our security deposit back. So, my husband and I went back to the apartment after we'd moved out and dumped a big pile of garbage in the middle of the floor of each room. They had to use our security deposit to clean up the mess and vacuum and shampoo the carpets.

Living in Harmony

Documentation shows your landlord that you're no fool. Write letters about everything. Use certified mail to your advantage. If you do end up in court, your papers will defend you, and your landlord probably knows that. If you look well-prepared, he won't try anything funny. Solidarity with other tenants also works. Landlords live in fear of rent strikes.

Your Basic Rights

Quiet enjoyment means your landlord can't bust in whenever he wants, unless there's an emergency. Some states don't even give the landlord the right to your keys. One tenant counseled by Cleveland tenant adviser Rich Felton was plagued by an invasive landlady, who would let herself into the apartment, answer the phone before the machine could pick up, and even take messages for her tenant. Don't put up with that.

Implied warranty of habitability holds in almost every state, but varies. Usually, it means that the landlord must provide running water, functional plumbing and lights, access to gas and electric services, four walls, a floor, and a ceiling. He's got to keep appliances working if he supplies them, and he may also be responsible for removing lead paint and snow on the walks. He's also got to get rid of garbage, rats, and roaches. If the warranty is breached, that may be a "constructive eviction"—and you have the right to break the lease.

Late rent? The state may restrict late fees to what is "reasonable." But the landlord may be allowed to start eviction proceedings on the very first day rent is overdue, unless he has consistently accepted your rent late.

If you have repair problems, call your landlord. If you get no reply, write a firm letter and give him a few weeks to fix the problem (unless it's an emergency). Get other tenants involved, if possible, or at least get them to sign your letter. Call a tenant advocate for advice, then mention in the letter, politely, that you've done so.

If he doesn't respond, try the housing inspectors—usually reachable through your mayor's office. They may not respond so well to less-than-extreme situations. But if they can come out, have a list of problems to review with them, ask for a copy of their report, and send it to the landlord. Sometimes you can get the cops to document emergencies—like having no heat in the middle of winter—but don't count on it.

Repair and deduct is the next step, and this isn't legal in all states. Give your landlord two weeks written notice before the rent due date, and let him know how much you plan to deduct and why. If you get no response, get the problem fixed yourself and send him a copy of the bill with your reduced rent check.

Withholding rent is legal in about half the states, and should really only be used as a last-ditch effort. Give written fourteen-day notice that you plan to withhold part of your rent. That should wake your landlord up—again, the point is to get your services delivered and avoid court. Start an escrow account and deposit part of your

member: Dan

SURVEY: THIS OLE HOUSE (LANDLORD HORROR STORIES)

Andy, our fifty-year-old paranoid schizophrenic landlord (diagnosis was clinical, not just my own), lived above the garage and had a habit of knocking on our windows in the middle of the night to warn us of the evils of drugs—or to offer us drugs, depending on the night. He used to tell us about how he and Ernest Hemingway were friends as children (Andy was born in 1942), and about Robin Williams talking to him through the television on *The Tonight Show*. And when the plumbing backed up, he blamed it on the Roto-Rooter guy, who Andy claimed he had seen at some political rally in San Francisco and "now it's my turn," whatever that meant. Andy honestly believed that the anarchy symbol (an A with a circle around it) was being spray-painted on stop signs around town by his friends as a coded message to him. It would have just been sad, all this hell Andy went through—except he was putting us through hell too. He had an evil temper, and when something would set him off he would cock his shotgun and shoot indiscriminately into the forest in the backyard. We never did get our deposit back when we moved out—he claimed all $1,350 for "cleaning costs" even though we left the place spotless—but we didn't care. We were just happy to be out of there alive.

rent money there, giving him the rest. It is extremely important to put your money in that account and maintain clear records. Withholding all your rent basically ensures your landlord will start an eviction proceeding.

Eviction. This process usually starts with a notice of intent to evict, followed by a summons that requires you to file an answer in court. If you haven't already, definitely contact a lawyer or tenant advocate now. Courts can have surprising and ruthless rules. Remember that your landlord must go to court to evict you.

Try mediation. As one good rabble-rouser of a tenant advocate said: "Tenants get totally ripped off by this process." But if you want to avoid moving at all costs and are willing to negotiate, you might give it a shot. Unlike court, it's private, cheap, and fast.

So you ended up in court anyway. Get some real legal advice. If you can't, check out legal guides (Nolo Press puts out some good ones) and try to find your state's tenant/landlord law—many are on the Web. Make sure to show up early, bring extra copies of all papers, dress nice, and be servile.

Leaving, or how to break a lease (and get away with it) if you've signed an annual lease. You've promised to pay each month for a year. You change your mind, tough luck. As tenant adviser Felton says, under contract law, even if you're dead you still owe.

But there is hope. First, you can offer to find a suitable replacement. Even if the landlord won't go for that, you have some protection. The landlord must make a good faith effort to replace you should you skip out midlease. If he doesn't, the court probably won't let him collect the full year's rent from you—chances are he'll keep your security deposit and be done with you.

How to keep your security deposit. Close to half the states require the landlord to put your deposit in an interest-bearing checking account and in many states the landlord must, within two weeks of occupancy, give the tenant the name of the bank where the deposit is being held, as well as the bank account number. You get the deposit and the interest when you move out, unless you've trashed the place or left a real mess, in which case the landlord can keep the deposit—and even sue you for more money besides. You must leave a forwarding address in writing when you move out, and then your

member: kzentek

SURVEY: THIS OLE HOUSE (LANDLORD HORROR STORIES)

I am the tenant nightmare turned around. Our first tenants left our house without letting us know because they bought a new house. They screwed pegs into our precious chestnut paneling, their son punched a hole into one of our doors. They had the electricity shut off, without our knowledge. They never paid the last month's rent. They wrote us a letter to let us know that they had moved out and told us we could use the security deposit as the last month's rent. Even though they left our house damaged and did not have the carpets cleaned upon departure, as was in the lease, we let it all go. We repainted the walls, cleaned the rugs, accepted that our chestnut paneling cannot be fixed and repaired the door. We could have been a landlord from hell, but we are not that way. We licked our wounds and prayed that our new tenants would be more responsible. And they are!

landlord has a limited amount of time (two to six weeks, depending) to contact you explaining why he is keeping your deposit. If he doesn't, you should be able to get it back. Usually the problem that comes up is cleaning. Get somebody to help you clean when you leave. It's easier, and they'll make a good witness if there is a problem. Take pictures if you think your landlord will later try to hold something against you that wasn't your fault.

The difference between damages and reasonable use is a matter of interpretation. Painting your bedroom black counts as the former. So does breaking windows or gouging the hardwood floor. Scuff marks, small scratches, sagging hinges, and the like should pass as reasonable use.

You do not, unless specifically stated in the lease, have the right to use the security deposit as the last month's rent. If you do, and your landlord finds damages when you leave, he could sue you. You might just ask him, when your last month's rent comes due, if he'd mind. Most landlords do.

member: kebara

SURVEY: THIS OLE HOUSE (LANDLORD HORROR STORIES)

I had an "apartment manager from hell," who complained about my cat. The reason he complained about my cat was that the cat objected to being grabbed by a four-year-old who wasn't properly trained to interact with nonhuman creatures. Unfortunately, the apartment manager was the kind who used foul language and unprintable words when he objected to something (my cat was a lot politer). Strangely, my cat disappeared about a week later, along with several other cats that lived with their humans in the complex I inhabited at the time.

When the Going Gets Tough

Self-help eviction is the law's beautiful term for the old heave-ho—when the landlord simply changes the locks, shuts off your services, or throws your belongings out the window. It's illegal almost everywhere: The landlord must get court permission to evict you, and the sheriff will come throw you out instead (then, usually, bill you for it). The law may require them to store your stuff (at your expense), but they may be allowed to dump it on the street.

Retaliatory evictions are usually prohibited, but hard to prove. Some states say that the landlord can't evict a tenant, or even raise his rent, within three to six months after the tenant has complained about service to the landlord or government. That's why it's in your interest to complain proactively and document your complaints.

Housing discrimination is extremely difficult to prove. Federal law prevents the landlord from discriminating on the basis of race, national origin, religion, sex, marital or familial status, and handicap. Complain to the feds—Housing & Urban Development (800-669-9777) and local fair-housing organizers.

Moving

Moving's become a frequent rite of passage for members of a generation less likely to settle where they were raised than any of their forebears. And whether you hire professionals or do-it-yourself, there are a lot of ways to screw it up big time.

by Marni Davis

In the past ten years, I've put all my belongings in boxes and bags and brought them to new digs nine times. Seems like a lot, but considering that two-thirds of those moves have been within the same city, it could have been a lot worse. Schlepping your worldly objects twenty blocks is child's play compared to U-Hauling your life from one side of the Rocky Mountains to the other, and I know people who've done that numerous times. I can't help but wonder if the wandering life is a sound one. First-century stoic philosopher Seneca wrote, "a plant which is frequently moved never grows strong." Can a flower blossom without roots?

A melodramatic question, perhaps. But seeing as I'm part of an American generation less likely than any previous to settle where we were raised, a most pertinent one. Surely this has something to do with the nature of the suburbs, where so many of us spent our childhoods. Suburbia is where our parents moved so they could enjoy tract houses on quarter-acre plots, decent schools, and shopping malls. Despite the convenience—and a lawn of one's own—we don't feel emotionally tied to these communities. After all, our parents had most likely moved away from their parents' neighborhoods. So with neither a tradition worth defending nor a compelling job market—and thus without the dosh to afford what for our parents had

member: Nestore

CONFERENCE: LIVABLE CITY

I moved many times in the last six years between cities. Rome, London, New York, Ottawa, Wales, and Paris . . . they are all the same . . . at the end of the day it is just another move. No matter where you are going the problems will still be the same, just in a different context (not knowing where the nearest post office is and feeling totally lonely because you don't know anybody *sigh*). I just took the plunge and did it because I get excited (and freaked; I guess the two go together) at the idea of starting all over again.

member: Dark_side_of_Genius

SURVEY: MOVING

As I was preparing to move out of my apartment, the managers of the property informed me that the walls needed painting, the carpets needed shampooing, and the curtains needed cleaning. So we would not get any of our deposit back. The last thing I did before turning over the keys was to put my initials on the wall by the door behind the curtains. On the first of the month I noticed a new tenant moving in (I delivered pizza in the area) and asked her if I could look behind the curtain. My initials were still there. I contacted the property manager the next day and demanded my refund.

been so reasonably priced—one might as well split. And so we did.

More recently I split from an apartment I inhabited for three settled years before the landlord jacked the rent up 30 percent (the bastard). Strapped for cash, I opted for a DIY move.

My indie move took place in December, a big moving month. I got started a month in advance and reserved a rental truck for an extremely reasonable price: $39.95 for four hours, plus another $12.50 for insurance. (And remember, these are NYC prices and therefore exorbitant compared with most everywhere else. The only way to make sure you're getting the best deal is to call around and comparison shop.) I lined up ten friends to help me haul my life into and out of the truck. Then I started scavenging boxes from local shops, the corner liquor store, and, most fruitfully, an old boss who donated the boxes in which his office computers had arrived. I packed at a leisurely pace, leaving a few loose pieces, like lamps and big mirrors, that I knew I could trust my friends to carry.

The goal when packing a truck is to organize everything so there is as little chance of major shifting as possible. As an amateur, you won't be able to fit it all together like a jigsaw puzzle, but generally, it's a good idea to keep things low and level: Don't pile things so they're teetering precariously, and if you do have to stack high, be consistent so there's balance.

For me, the bed was a trouble spot, as it invariably is. Usually, one props the mattress and boxspring up against the back wall of the truck, since they're big and flat. But upon arrival at the new home, what's the first thing you want to put in its place? The bed, of course, not only because of its bigness but because it's a declaration of territorial permanence. But how can you put the bed in its place if everything else you own is piled against it? (A major conundrum of the unpack and worth considering before you start loading the truck.)

After an extremely smooth four hours—nothing was broken, or even scratched—we were done. That evening I took my friends out drinking. Unfortunately, we had a pretty wild night and the bar tab whacked out my margin. But it turned out to be the most low-maintenance move I've ever experienced, overall.

By May I was mobile again, and, as I didn't want to become a

member: BlueHalo

SURVEY: MOVING

I had a very valuable record collection and when I moved I made sure to tell my friend how much it meant to me. We kept the crate aside until everything else was packed. My friend took special care to load the crate onto the back of his pickup truck and carefully tie it down. When we got to my new house, all that remained of my $5,000 record collection was a piece of broken rope. Well, we searched high and low for the crate and finally found the intersection where the crate fell off. Of course, there was no crate and only about ten records scattered about. The rest were nowhere in sight. After placing numerous advertisements in the local papers, I had to abandon my search for my precious record collection. In case anyone is wondering, my insurance company refused to pay my claim because I could not furnish any proof of purchase. I learned a very costly lesson about packing valuables.

member: stroud1

SURVEY: MOVING

Don't trust the packers. Don't assume that your emphasizing the importance of an antique's value will ensure their proper packaging of it.

member: SWORDLORD

SURVEY: MOVING

Moving men are dumb! They do not have the slightest fucking clue how to carry a computer up fourteen steps! U-Haul would beat a moving man any day.

nuisance to my friends, I decided to call a moving company. I got estimates from about eight companies; since I wasn't moving heirloom china or anything, I was only calling to get the price differences. That's not the only factor you might want to take into consideration, however. Besides making sure as you interview movers that the company you hire is indeed operating legally (see sidebar on page 134), there are a variety of specialty moving companies available. There are companies that specialize in shipping fragile items or pianos or that claim expertise with small residential moves or overseas shipments. You might also go the identity politics route; I've heard of all-gay moving companies, and in the past I'd hired an all-woman company. This time, I contemplated hiring "Nice Jewish Boy Moving Company"—my mom would've been so proud—but in the end, I went with the company most amenable to my request for some free packing materials.

The next day, fifteen book boxes were delivered to my apartment, gratis. But, for my purposes, fifteen boxes was only a start. The downside of using movers is that you can't leave anything loose; if you do, they will put it in a box, cushion it on all sides with wadded-up packing paper, and then charge you for the box *and* the paper—and you can bet that it would have cost you less if you'd done it yourself. The only situation in which this might not be the best approach is if you're moving expensive or especially fragile items. If

member: Barbara_ Robertson
SURVEY: MOVING
My husband and I were set to move from our apartment near Harvard Square in Cambridge, Mass., to Minneapolis. We'd decided to go with movers, given the scale of our move, and had chosen the company that gave us the most favorable estimate. The movers arrived, checked out our stuff (all boxed and ready to go), smirked, and said that the weight of our load was much more than the estimate indicated. We would have to pay $1,000 more than our estimate if we wanted to be moved. We had nearly maxed-out our credit cards and spent everything else to meet the initial estimate, and other people were about to move into our apartment. I called Cambridge City Hall, to see if anyone over there could help me. I was referred to a consumer advocate, who worked aggressively on the phone to find out what could be done. By the time she was done, we were talking on the phone with the president of this (national) moving company. We got our movers, and the company president (not anxious to get more phone calls from consumer advocates) personally tracked our move.

> Moving Don'ts

- Don't leave everything until the last minute. As a matter of fact, don't leave *anything* until the last minute. Start packing a month in advance, if possible. Arrange for a truck or a moving company as soon as you know you'll need one. Don't be silly about it—don't pack up your entire kitchen a week before your move and leave yourself nothing to cook on or eat with—but the worst thing you can do is wake up that morning and realize that you haven't even acquired boxes yet.
- Don't assume that anything is free—or, rather, assume that everything will cost you extra. If you're renting a truck, determine up front if they offer a flat rate or if they will charge you per mile; this is increasingly important the farther you're moving away, of course.
- If you're hiring a moving company, be aware that if your men are on the job for seven hours and ten minutes, you will be charged for eight hours. Little things like this can sneak past you and totally blow your budget, so be alert.
- Don't forget to inform your utility companies that you're moving. Arrange to have your phone turned off or to have the account moved (if geography allows) on the day of your relocation. Same with gas, electric, cable, renter's insuranc—everyone who bills you monthly.

you pack it and it breaks during the move, your movers are not liable; if you let them pack it for you and it breaks, they are responsible for damages. Of course, value of said items should be worked out with your movers beforehand.

Which brings us to the important matter of insurance. Policy options (and costs) vary from company to company, but, generally, there are two different scenarios: insurance and valuation. Valuation merely defines the limit for which the mover is liable, and, by and large, is an assumption that nothing is going to go terribly, horribly wrong with your move. Valuation costs less than insurance, but it means that you are only partially protected against loss. But if you're not moving anything particularly precious, valuation is your smarter option. If, on the other hand, you are shipping irreplaceable stuff, spending a little extra on insurance might be worth your while; if you're insured, there's no liability limit, and, if something is lost or broken, you stand to collect full replacement value. First, however,

member: nsrosenthal

SURVEY: MOVING

Our only move was from one apartment house to another, which happened to be right next door. Imagine our surprise when we saw the moving van take off in the opposite direction and drive down the street with all our things loaded into it. Instead of backing the van up to the new apartment building, they decided to drive a half-mile away to turn the truck around and come back to park in front of the new building. Needless to say they demanded that we pay them for the one mile of driving. After several phone calls to the president of the company, they finally dropped the charges and proceeded to unload all of our things.

member: Tillie_2

SURVEY: MOVING

Having annointed myself "the most organized person in the state of New York," I carefully planned my move to Arizona down to the most minute detail. The Ryder truck had been ordered, the friends who "volunteered" were standing by on call, and the pizza shop knew where and when to deliver the half-pepperoni, half-sausage pies! As the day approached, all was progressing nicely. As the boxes were being packed, each received a number corresponding to a page in the wire-bound notebook where the box's contents were meticulously listed. Finally moving day arrived. Everyone who promised to help showed up, the truck was packed, and the pizza arrived just as planned. Hurray! Another successful plan completed.

> Moving Nightmares

You found your moving company via a flyer on your windshield and when you called them, they gave you an extremely reasonable price: $50 per hour for three men, and the move shouldn't take more than four hours. Now it's the big day, and you just watched your moving guys mummify your belongings in miles of bubble wrap and packing tape—even the pillows—but how much can bubble wrap cost? And isn't it most important that everything will be safe?

Soon enough it's all out in the truck, waiting to be brought to your new home. But before everyone gets going, they just want you to sign, as a guarantee that you'll pay them when the job is done. When you skim over the form, you realize that the packing material has more than doubled the cost of your move; you thought you were paying them $200, but the bill now comes to $500. When you balk, they offer to either unload your stuff out into the street right now or to take it to their storage facility, and you'll get it back when you pay up in full. What do you do?

Let's back up a bit and ask a couple of important questions: When you hired your movers, did you go over the price of packing materials? When you got a cost estimate, was it binding? Did you get an estimate at all? And did you make sure that the company was operating legally? If you've answered no to these questions—particularly the last one—then you're quite possibly in a world of shit. Do yourself a favor and avoid this scenario by taking the following steps:

- Before you hire your company, call the Department of Transportation in your state and make sure the mover is licensed. If the company offers a DOT number, double-check it with the department anyway. If the company is not licensed, do not hire them under any circumstances.
- Call the Better Business Bureau and find out if there are complaints lodged against the mover. Keep in mind that a list of complaints will not differentiate between the serious and the frivolous, but if a company has been reported numerous times, you can assume that they've had their share of ugly dealings with customers. Find another company.
- Try to get a binding estimate, in writing, from the moving company. You may be charged for such an estimate or required to put down a deposit. But with a binding estimate, the movers cannot require you to pay another dollar more, regardless of how many hours they take or how many wardrobe boxes they use.
- If you can't get a binding estimate, at least get a nonbinding estimate.This doesn't guarantee the cost of your move, but according to the Interstate Commerce Commission, a mover cannot require you to pay more than the original estimate plus a percentage (25 percent if you're being charged by the hour, 10 percent if by weight) at the time of delivery. You'll then have thirty days to cough up the remaining charges, which you might choose to dispute, but at least you'll have your furniture back.

This is all well and good, but let's say you didn't do any of that, and now they've got your stuff like the Lindbergh baby. What now? Unfortunately, while the law is theoretically on your side, neither the ICC nor your local police can do anything to resolve a dispute between a customer and an illegal moving company. You will have to file a civil action, if it comes to that; in the meantime, file a claim with the movers, then contact both the state DOT and the BBB immediately and submit formal complaints. Then, call a lawyer, beg for mercy, and chalk the whole thing up to experience. You got swindled, baby.

Know Your Rights and Responsibilities

The more you know about your rights, the less likely you are to get fleeced. The Interstate Commerce Commission has prepared two booklets to that end, one for interstate moves, one for intrastate; both are called *Your Rights and Responsibilities When You Move*. Your movers are required to make these booklets available to you. Ask for them.

Did You Forget To . . .

- Change your address with the post office, so your mail will be forwarded?
- Change your address with any magazines you subscribe to?
- Make special arrangements for pets, if necessary?
- Make a thorough inventory of all boxes and what they contain?

if you have homeowner's or renter's insurance, check and see if it extends to transportation.

When the movers arrived, after all the packing was done, I was useless until we arrived at my new apartment and I got to direct them—put this box in here, put the bed over there in the corner, and so forth. Again, four hours later, everything was done, but this time I had to fork over quite a bit of cash: $56 an hour for two men, plus almost $100 for packing materials, plus tip (three dollars per man per hour is reasonable). In the end, hiring movers cost me six times as much as I spent doing the job with my friends.

If you can cram everything you own into the back of a fourteen-foot truck, and you're not one of the blessed whose new employer is funding your relocation, you should try to move yourself. But DIY moving is appealing for more than just budgetary reasons. It's something like the difference between going out for a meal and cooking one yourself; the first way is convenient, but sometimes you get more out of an experience from partaking in the minutia of the process. Even if it's only a profound understanding that moving is a huge pain in the ass and a sobering reminder of how much crap you've accumulated over the years. I, for one, have had my fill. This flower is going to work on her roots for a while

member: Bonquilt

SURVEY: MOVING

Next time we move, I'm selling *everything* we own and starting over from scratch! We hired a moving company (supposedly "the official movers of the NFL") when we moved from Nashville to Seattle. And the usual mistreatment of the stuff wasn't as much of a problem as dealing with the company was. They didn't even leave Nashville until the date they promised delivery. Every day that week I called to check on the status of the truck and was given some kind of story or other how they couldn't reach the driver to see where he was. Well, when I found out that the truck was just leaving, I asked why I hadn't been told that five days ago . . . the response from the manager? "Well, you would have been mad five days earlier, wouldn't you?" Never again!

> Moving Resources Online

Here are some Internet resources that can help you with your move:

- The International Salary Calculator (www2.homefair.com/homefair/cmr/salcalc.html) can help determine the cost of living, typical salary range, and real estate prices for the area to which you're thinking of moving.
- The Moving Guide (www.moving-guide.com) will allow you to access information and prices (for the United States, Canada, and most other countries) from household movers, commercial movers, storage companies, international movers, even auto transport specialists.
- The U-Haul website (www.uhaul.com) has helpful tutorials for planning a DIY move. And if you do find yourself hiring one of those big boxy eyesores, prepare yourself by visiting MapQuest (www.mapquest.com) for free travel instructions and maps. The All Hotels Guide (www.all-hotels.com) can help you find decent, affordable lodging along the way.

Roommate Politics

Friends can be fun but suffocating. Strangers can be less encroaching but boring. Lovers can be intimate but volatile. And then there's living with your parents.

by David Kushner

The only thing that's tougher than living alone is living with someone else. How could you have known that the guy you rented your other bedroom to would brush his teeth six times a night? Or that your dream girl would snore like an asthmatic walrus? When delving into the unpredictable politics of cohabitation, the question isn't whether to live with someone or not, it's how you're going to survive.

Generally, there are three (not necessarily mutually exclusive) reasons for choosing to have a roommate: money, love, or friendship. In urban centers like New York, Los Angeles, Boston, San Francisco, and Washington, D.C., one-bedroom apartments can run over $1,000 per month, making living on one's own fairly implausible. Michael Santomauro, owner of Roommate Finders, a roommate referral service that has operated in Manhattan since 1979, says the majority of his clients have bottom-line objectives. "Most people under thirty-five are looking for a roommate for financial reasons," he says. "Few are looking for companionship only."

What everyone is looking for, of course, is someone with whom he or she can get along. This is no easy task. First impressions are often way off base. Neil, a twenty-seven-year-old law student, finally thought he found the perfect roommate after weeks of searching. The apartment was big and clean. The price was right. Just after he

member: TripodMichelle
CONFERENCE: MOVING IN TOGETHER
I did the living together thing, for a summer. I don't regret it by any means, but it did make me reevaluate whether I would do it again so casually. I did it because we felt like it and we could, and it was just for the summer. But the fact that we knew we were leaving made it easy not to deal with the hard issues that living together raises, even if it's only for a few months. If I were in the position again to make that choice, I would consider it more carefully. I'm for it in principle, but its a big step.

member: LParsons
CONFERENCE: MOVING IN TOGETHER
For some, living together gives a false taste of intimacy. I say false because it often lacks the commitment. Intimacy without commitment is building a house in an earthquake zone.

member: Wholzer
CONFERENCE: MOVING IN TOGETHER
I moved in with my boyfriend two weeks after I graduated from college. At first, I felt like we were closer than ever before—choosing new furniture and decorating our new place really made us feel good about each other and the relationship. Now the pictures are hung and the couch is in the perfect position, but somehow we're not as close. Maybe all those changes spurred the excitement and energy in our relationship, and now that our life is somewhat routine, we're not sure what to do next.

signed on the dotted line, however, his prospective roommate made a confession: "I have to be honest," the roommate said, "I find you very attractive."

The best way to avoid such misunderstandings is to get everything out on the table from the start. Think long and hard about what's important to you in a roommate before you start looking or renting. Here's a test: Let's say there's a prospective roommate named Alex. Do you care whether Alex is a man or a woman? Whether Alex is an accomplished yodeler or a diehard Loverboy fan? Whether Alex sleeps with men or women or both? Also, it's a good idea to make sure the roomie's job is secure, unless you like melancholic leeches. As Santomauro says, "The last thing you want to do is move in and have your roommate lose her job, then she's just hanging at home, depressed."

member: MattyG

CONFERENCE: MOVING IN TOGETHER

Though it seems rather cold and utilitarian to suggest as much, I believe that cohabitating is often used as a way to deal with skyrocketing rents, lack of time to deal with domestic duties, and, in the case of urbanites, as a cheap way to stave off the particular brand of loneliness often engendered by big cities. I'm not saying that the feelings aren't there in abundance; I'm simply stating the fact that cohabitating has dimensions having nothing to do with emotions, which might be a reason fewer cohabitational situations lead to legal marriage than people might expect.

No matter whom you choose as a roommate, though, there are going to be pros and cons to every arrangement. Friends can be fun but too suffocating. Strangers can be less encroaching but boring. Lovers can be intimate but volatile. Then there is the idea of living with members of the opposite sex. And, of course, parents.

Larry, a twenty-seven-year-old financial analyst, spent a year living with his parents after he had an argument with his roommate. "The best thing was that I wasn't paying rent or cooking as much," he says, "the worst thing was that my parents were always in my business. They always wanted to be kept abreast of information I really didn't want them to know: Who I was dating, where I was going, the usual stuff." Eventually, Larry moved out of his parents' place and moved in with a few other guys. Soon enough, he started to see that the new arrangement had drawbacks as well. "Sure these guys might be more fun to hang out with," Larry says, "but then again, at least my parents didn't use up all my toothpaste."

The more roommates someone has, the more potential conflicts. Although someone can save money by living in a *Real World*–style group house, the fights that crop up are usually a lot more tiresome than those on MTV. Karen, a twenty-five-year-old bookkeeper, lived with five roommates: a Danish photographer, a struggling actor, two waitresses, and her boyfriend. "There were constant battles," Karen admits. "Who wasn't cleaning, who wasn't cooking, who wasn't paying—it never ended." Nonetheless, Karen saved a couple hundred bucks a months in rent so in the end, she found it kind of worth it. Plus, Karen says, "We had amazing parties!" Soon enough, Karen and her boyfriend realized it had become "impossible to be intimate with everyone else around," so they got their own place.

Here's one key to survival: separate phone lines. How many roommate conflicts would be resolved if everyone got his or her own messages and didn't have to wait in line to use the phone? "One phone line is not enough for two single professionals who are looking for mates and friends," advises Santomauro. "If you're a woman who's dating and some guy calls for you, how's he going to feel when another guy answers the phone?" After all, who's going to believe you when you tell them, "It's just my roommate"?

According to Dr. Judy Kuriansky, nationally syndicated radio talk show host and author of *Generation Sex*, "having a roommate is like having a lover without the sex." But sexual attraction between roommates sometimes becomes a reality. It's easy to understand: Living together implies a certain intimacy. You immediately start seeing each other in all states of distress and undress. When you're

member: nvolkers

CONFERENCE: MOVING IN TOGETHER

I grew up hearing from my mother that I *should* live with someone before marriage. This was not a widely held view at the time, to be sure. But in her opinion (and now mine), dating someone does not give you the whole picture. To go from movies and dinner to marriage would frankly scare the hell out of me.

> Roommate Survival Kit

LIVE WITH YOUR FRIENDS?

1. Buy as many phones and phone lines as you can afford.
2. Have a "gripe box" in which to file all your complaints, then have a meeting to discuss them.
3. If you must sleep with your roomies, wait until the day before the lease ends.
4. Don't sleep with their friends either.
5. Set an overnight guest policy.
6. Designate a phone message center.
7. Only consume stuff you've paid for, regardless of whether it's shampoo or Doritos.

LIVE WITH YOUR PARENTS?

1. Don't (unless you really, really have to).
2. Keep a fridge in your room.
3. Get your own phone line.
4. Pay for your own groceries.
5. Cook meals for them now and then.
6. Pay rent or do chores or both.
7. Have sex elsewhere (see #8).
8. Buy a car with a large backseat.
9. Go away for a weekend now and then (parents need space, too).

LIVE WITH YOUR LOVER/SPOUSE?

1. Get two phone lines.
2. Have separate spaces for your bathroom stuff.
3. When one person cooks, the other cleans.
4. Have separate closets.
5. Get the other's permission before inviting over houseguests.
6. Designate one person to deal with the landlord.
7. Have sex frequently (force yourself if you must).

single and unattached, the prospect of fooling around with someone who happens to be under the same roof might seem like a perfectly natural (and convenient) thing to do.

But, when the living situation is supposed to be platonic things can get extremely complicated. There are a couple ways to deal: Bite your tongue until the lease is up or broach the topic in a casual way. Just remember, if you choose to say something, you might get what you wish for. Then what's going to happen if you break up?

Maybe, in fact, the sexual politics are too much of a hassle. Or maybe the idea of any roommate at all is just not your style; you don't want to see other people's dishes in the sink, other people's

hair in the bathtub drain. "People look forward to autonomy," says Dr. Peter D. Kramer, clinical profesor of psychiatry at Brown University and author of *Should You Leave?*, a book about the trials and tribulations of living alone. "Then once they have it, they're panicked." Dr. Kramer suggests to people living alone for the first time: "Distract yourself so your worries about loneliness don't promote further loneliness."

But some personality types are just not meant to share living space. "If you really don't like people," says Santomauro, "you shouldn't be living with strangers or even your friends." And if your greatest joy in life is smoking cigars and dancing naked around the living room to Debbie Gibson's first record, it might be worth the extra bucks to get your own apartment.

member: irisheyes

SURVEY: ROOMMATES

It is most important to ask very specific questions of potential roommates. Do you party a lot? Do you tend to have lots of guests? Do you mind pitching in to keep the house clean and the grounds tended? Are you able to pay rent and utilities on time? Are you planning on living here long- or short-term? Do you use drugs? I now provide a written set of crystal-clear ground rules that a potential housemate must agree to before moving in. And requesting references sure doesn't hurt!

member: MOON_LIGHT

SURVEY: ROOMMATES

You think you know your friends? You *don't* until you live with them! Move in with complete strangers. If you like them, great! If you don't you can tell them how you feel . . . and you won't lose any of your best friends!

member: gforman

SURVEY: ROOMMATES

If you are young, in a college situation, your chances of finding the ideal roommate, I think, are nada! Both are going through "growing pains," trying to find themselves. Just hope you don't get a selfish egomaniac who believes everything you own is his!

Fix-it Basics

Some people start to have palpitations at the thought of repairing a leaky faucet or fixing a stuck window. But it doesn't need to be so hard: With the right tools and a little confidence, you too can be self-reliant around the house.

by Suzy Banks

Contrary to circumstantial evidence, aging Anglo males with perpetually exposed butt cracks haven't cornered the market on home repairs. Are you blessed with at least minimal dexterity and a twinkle of curiosity? Are you sick of waiting all day for the plumber to charge you $89.95 an hour (one hour minimum) to pluck the olive oil cap from your jammed garbage disposal? Then strap on a leather tool belt hung with a thirty-two-ounce waffle-head hammer and a neon green twenty-five-foot tape measure and dare something around the old homestead to break.

While the tool belt is indeed a sexy and empowering accessory for do-it-yourselfers, it isn't absolutely necessary. The right tools, however, most definitely are. You shouldn't try to unscrew a P-trap under the sink with pinking shears anymore than you should tighten a screw with the tip of a loved one's Henckels chef's knife. I should know; I tried both before I saw the light of salvation in the tool aisle at the hardware store. There, the indispensable majesty of the pipe wrench and the screwdriver overwhelmed me. And you can't imagine how much easier it is to drive a nail with a hammer than with the heel of an Italian loafer. Next time you're out shopping, forgo the 150-year-old Balsamic vinegar or the cutting-edge, soon-to-be-obsolete software and splurge instead on a basic tool collection. Think of it as a first-aid kit for your home, in ten steps definitely worth taking:

member: TripodJosh

SURVEY: FIX-IT BASICS

I've always preferred to leave electricity to the experts. Why mess around with all that voltage? So I've never fixed or changed a light fixture, rewired a lamp, or any of that good stuff. But one day my mother came over to my house and saw that I had a crappy light fixture hanging from the ceiling and asked "Why don't you replace that with a nice new light fixture?" I told her my bias against high voltage, but she scoffed at me. An hour later, she was up on a ladder installing a lovely new light fixture herself. I guess if you aren't a total idiot, you can fix pretty much anything!

1. A hammer, preferably two—a sixteen-ounce straight claw and a smaller curved claw. (The claw is the handy peace sign at the back of the hammer. With a straight claw you can hack away at things that make you mad, like an ill-placed shelf bracket in the garage. With the dainty curved claw you can slip nails from their hold without gouging the Sheetrock.)
2. A wide tape measure, at least twenty-five feet long. Measure stuff to the nearest 1/32 of an inch and entertain cranky toddlers, too. They'll watch the tape slide out and pop back in *forever*, as if they expect Barney himself to spring forth.
3. An assortment of screwdrivers in various sizes, both slotted (a minus sign) and Phillips (a plus sign). Buy the best you can afford.
4. Pliers. The bigger the variety the better, but you can cut back on your Prozac by springing for long-nose pliers, cutting pliers (sharp, for cutting and stripping wires), and big, old, multi-versatile tongue-and-groove pliers (which also function as a pipe wrench if you hold your tongue right).
5. Wrenches. Two pipe wrenches, which are so heavy they can serve as doorstops or workout weights when your plumbing behaves. A pipe wrench has a serrated square jaw that tightens around objects automatically as you apply pressure. You need two because you hold the pipe with one wrench and turn the fitting with the other. A couple of crescent wrenches—big and small—wouldn't hurt either. These have adjustable jaws and are used for loosening nuts and bolts.
6. A two-foot carpenter's level. Use it to make sure your shelves, towel bars, and automatic dog feeder are hung evenly.
7. A helping hand, in the form of a pair of vise grips, a sturdy clamp or two, or even a few giant rubber bands.
8. A cordless drill—a good one—with a set of drill bits. With a variety of bits, the drill can bore holes, drive or remove screws, sand, buff, mix paint, and so on. This will set you back a bit, but what the hell are charge cards for anyway? I've always said that if I chopped my hand off (accidentally, we hope) with the Salad Shooter, I'd replace it (my hand, not the nefarious Salad Shooter) with a Bosch or Makita cordless drill.

member: Heplock

SURVEY: FIX-IT BASICS

If the job requires an expensive tool that I'll only use that one time, and I can't rent it, then I call in a pro to do the work. Otherwise, it's my house and my work. I prefer doing it myself so that I'm assured of the quality of the job.

9. A ladder. You'll never realize just how short you are until your pilot light goes out in the middle of winter and you can't reach the furnace in the attic even if you stand on tiptoes on top of a New York City yellow pages balanced on top of a rickety bar stool.
10. A snappy tool box. Don't forget to grab a little bottle of carpenter's glue, a tub of spackling, a utility knife, and a single-edge razor blade scraper. You'll need stuff to fill up all those little compartments in your new tool box, so stock up on a variety of standard and finishing nails, Sheetrock screws (sharp black beauties, from half an inch to four inches long, more universally useful than Velcro), and wall anchors for hanging those heavy bowling plaques on hollow walls.

member: harkn

SURVEY: FIX-IT BASICS

"Fixes" regretted: Plumbing jobs that seem simple and end up requiring enough tools, supplies, time, and money to enable a real plumber to happily retire . . . Installing skylights (don't ask) . . . Roofing (don't ask) . . . *All* repairs started late on Friday or Saturday night.

While we're at it, let's stick a variety pack of sandpaper (coarse 80-grit, medium 100-grit, and fine 150-grit) in there somewhere. And don't be caught without a cartridge of Liquid Nails, PL400 or other construction adhesive, and a cartridge of caulk. Both products come in big cardboard tubes that look like they should hold Pop 'n fresh dough. Although it'll never bake into tasty sweet rolls no matter how much icing you drizzle on it, the adhesive will come in handy when you want to reattach a loose ceramic tile to the bathroom wall or tack down a flap of carpet. As for caulk, you can use it to weatherstrip around leaky windows, hide gaping joints in painted baseboards and moldings, seal vermin entrances into your abode, and so much more. You'll need to purchase a caulk gun (no waiting period or background check is necessary), a nifty little metal device that cradles a tube of your goo and lets you direct the sticky gunk precisely where you want it with the flick of a trigger.

A Do-It-Yourselfer's Glossary

AC CONDENSER COILS: The copper tubes and metal waferlike material in an air conditioner.

AERATOR: The device at the end of the faucet that directs the flow of water and catches sediment in its screen.

OVERFLOW TUBE OR OUTLET: This is where the water is supposed to exit when you forget you're filling the bathtub—rather than onto the floor and down into your neighbor's place below.

PACKING NUT: This is the big nut that screws down and holds all the inner workings of the faucet handle in place.

PLUMBER'S SNAKE (or trap-and-drain auger): Although these can take a variety of forms, they all boil down to a springy metal cable with a curly pig tail of steel on the end that you fish through the pipes. I'm partial to the kind where the cable is coiled into what looks sort of like a salad spinner with a handle you can turn to give the cable the necessary twisting action to make it churn down the pipes and through clogs.

SEAT: The little cup down at the bottom of the hole when you remove a faucet handle and the stem assembly. The stem sits in this seat.

SEAT WRENCH: An L-shaped tube of metal with a square tip on one end and an octagonal tip on the other end to fit either of the two most common types of faucet seats so you can grip them, unscrew them, and replace them when they're worn.

WASHER: Generally speaking, it's like a nickel with a hole shot through it. In the wet world of plumbing where it usually acts as a seal or gasket, it's usually made of some resilient material—rubber, cork, plastic, or even graphite-impregnated twine.

WAX TOUCH-UP STICKS: These are crayons for adults with scratched wood surfaces. They come in a variety of wood tones and are available at hardware stores, paint stores, and home centers.

WOOD PUTTY: Finally, another use for sawdust besides hamster bedding. It's mixed with a binder such as glue or lacquer and colored to imitate a variety of wood stains. Don't buy this stuff until you need it because it dries up faster than Jell-O in the Sahara.

member: jakrinda

SURVEY: FIX-IT BASICS

I'm the "fix-all" person for all my neighbors! And they have the nerve to say, "Is that all they teach you in college?"

All tooled up and itching to fix something around the house? If you have plumbing, you won't have long to wait.

To begin with, never use corrosive commercial drain cleaners on a clogged drain; they seldom dissolve the clog and you're usually left with a sink/toilet/tub full of toxic, caustic soup.

To prevent clogged drains the natural way, feed your sinks and tubs a monthly diet of homemade drain cleaner by pouring a cup of baking soda in the drain, followed by one cup of vinegar, then flushing the pipes with very hot water. Should your ungrateful drains plug up anyway, first grab the plumber's helper (a plunger) and churn away like a butter-maker on NoDoz. You'll get better suction if the rubber cap is underwater and if you plug any overflow openings on the fixture. You and everything around you will stay drier if you drape the operation with a towel.

Use either your pipe wrenches or your tongue-and-groove pliers to remove the P-trap, the section of pipe under the sink that looks more like a U than a P. Look inside. Globs of hair, soap, grease, toothpaste, and cherry pits turn into a veritable primordial ooze in the moist valley of the P-trap.

Speaking of thick sludge, if the toilet's clogged, go back to the hardware store and get a plumber's snake (or trap-and-drain auger).

> Do-It-Yourself . . . Not!

Self-reliance is a progressive disease. The more you do yourself, the more you'll want to do yourself. It's a noble addiction, to be sure, but one whose limitations must be acknowledged. There are certain jobs that require a professional's touch.

This is a lesson my husband, Richard, and I, two stalwart do-it-yourselfers, learned a couple of years ago when we sold our house (ourselves), which we had built (ourselves). We moved our mountain of possessions (ourselves) to a barn and cabin we'd built (ourselves) on our new land. We began to build another house, completing the slab, the framing, the electrical work, plumbing, and roofing (ourselves). Toward the end of this frenzied activity, Richard fell off a ladder and broke his ankle. I fell off the roof and broke two ribs. Work progressed very slowly and very unhappily after that.

We decided, persuaded in part by our injuries and by county health regulations, to turn the septic system over to a professional.

But the bids were coming in double what we expected and, because contractors were so busy, we'd have been in Depends by the time the system would have been completed.

"I know," said my independent husband, waving his crutches around, "I'll go to septic school, get certified, and do it myself." I started to laugh, but my ribs hurt too much and, I realized with horror, he wasn't joking.

The moral of the story is that it's okay to admit you need help. I immediately enlisted masons, Sheetrockers, and painters to finish the house. We threw a bundle of money at one septic engineer, who took pity on our Porta-Potty existence and completed the system in a few weeks. I learned that while I *can* do it all myself, there are times when I simply don't want to.

Perhaps you're looking for a list of things you should never try yourself. Refinishing the hardwood floors in your entire house over the weekend, rewiring the whole house if you can't even set the clock on the VCR, or pouring your own perimeter foundation beam if you don't know the difference between concrete and cement are but a few biggies that spring to mind. But the world of home improvement isn't as simple as a list. There are all these darned personalities involved. You may thrill at the mathematical challenge of designing and building your own trusses, yet cringe at the prospect of staring down a toilet drain. One person's Sisyphean chore—say, floating and taping dry wall—is another person's cathartic ritual. Deciding what tasks are beyond your physical, mental, or emotional capacities is the one instance where you *must* do it yourself.

When you start to fish this springy cable down through the inner canals of the toilet, be as gently patient as a bomb-detonator. The deceptively sturdy-looking toilet is made of vitreous china, same as Granny's dainty tea cup.

Use the snake to unclog tub drains as well. You can access the hidden world of tub clogs through the drain or through the overflow tube. To snake your way down the drain, you may have to remove the strainer by prying it up or unscrewing it. Some tubs have an unremovable crosshatch strainer. Believe it or not, the loosely coiled end of your auger can be twisted around and through the crosshatch like some magician's puzzle of metal rings. To feed the auger through the overflow tube—a more direct route—you'll have to remove the metal plate that often sports the stopper lever and a couple of screws. If the tub has a plunger-type drain or a pop-up drain, when you pull the plate off you'll also pull the drain assembly out with it. Be sure to also remove the drain stopper itself on a pop-up assembly as it extends into the overflow tube. If you're lucky, you may even find the culprit tangled around the stopper's spring and hinged parts.

member: StoneyJB

SURVEY: FIX-IT BASICS

One tool you should always have handy is the old brain box. Think a repair or project through before you start and figure that no matter how simple you think it will be, it will be more complicated and time consuming than you thought.

To fish the auger cable down the drain, loosen the set screw on the auger, pull out a length of line, and slide it into the pipe until you feel resistance. Tighten the set screw and crank the auger handle clockwise until the cable shimmies on down the line. Run water down the drain at intervals to flush the lumps of goo down into the big, old main drain. Continue this process until you're certain you've exorcised the fur ball. Reverse the procedure to remove the snake. Hopefully, you'll receive the instant gratification of finding a big gunky wad attached to the snake's tip.

So much for the water leaving your house. Water coming into the house can create its own set of problems, less stinky perhaps, but more intricate.

If the water flowing out of a faucet slows to a dribble, the faucet aerator needs cleaning. Unscrew the aerator. If you're lucky, it'll be on much too tight to loosen with your fingers and you'll get to use your slick tongue-and-groove pliers, introducing you to the wonderful power of torque.

Take the aerator apart, rinse the screen, and clean out the mystery chunks that accumulate in the holes of the perforated disc. If mineral deposits have built up, soak the parts in vinegar before carefully replacing them in the exact order you removed them. They typically stack in the following order from top to bottom: washer, perforated disk, screen, screen holder, and aerator body.

If all went well during this simple procedure, you're ready to graduate to repairing leaky faucets. Maybe. Does your health plan cover mental illness?

Every faucet, it seems, is different. But don't worry. First, plug the sink drain so you don't drop tiny parts down it. Next, if you're working on a stem faucet (it has two handles, as opposed to a single lever faucet), use the tip of your slotted screwdriver to pry off the "decorative buttons" on the top of the handle. You'll find a screw hidden underneath that holds the handle on. Unscrew it and slip the handle straight up and off. You should now be staring down at a packing nut with the gnarled end of the stem sticking out. (On older faucets, the packing nut is accessible without having to remove the

> The Pro Program

So you've decided to hire a pro. The bigger the project you hire an expert to undertake, the more strictly you should adhere to the following rules:

1. Get at least three bids. This may not be appropriate for the delightfully brief augering of your sewer line, but the disparity between bids on projects like kitchen and bathroom remodeling can be enormous. Resist the temptation, however, to go with the lowest bid without question.

2. Get references and check credentials. Disregard shiny pickup trucks, mobile phones, and flashy business cards with a string of association acronyms after the workman's name. (We had one contractor try to convince us that his AARP membership had been awarded him by the American Association of Remodeling Professionals rather than the American Association of Retired Persons.) Instead, ask for the names and numbers of people he's done similar work for and call those people. Quiz them relentlessly. Visit them if possible. Make sure some of them have lived with his finished work for at least a year and are not out gunning for him.

3. Write up a contract with reasonable completion and payment schedules. Sign it and stick with it. Harden your heart to any unexpected requests for advance payments, no matter what sob story the contractor pours out. Not even if his brother-in-law ran over his cousin's foot and now he has to help pay for corrective shoes and new tires or else he can't borrow his brother-in-law's truck to pick up the Sheetrock to complete your job. Remember, money is power.

4. Trust your intuition. If a contractor rubs you the wrong way during the courtship phase of bidding the job, just imagine how you'll loath him after the kitchen sink's been ripped out and your new one has been held hostage in a Swedish shipping strike for two months and the cabinets are stained blood red rather than cherry.

handle from the stem.) If you've lived right for the past few years—given to charities, adopted stray pets, eaten your mom's stuffed bell peppers without complaint—then you will be able to remove the locknut with your crescent wrench. You will then be able to unscrew the stem easily, turning it in the same direction as you do to turn the water on. Now you've exposed the probable culprit behind the drip: the washer. Gunk and calcium particles can grind away at these soft pieces of rubber. The seat in which the washer sits can also get marred. As long as the thing's dissected, take a look. If the seat's pitted and scarred, you will need to replace it.

You'll need a special tool called a seat wrench to remove it. Some older seats cannot be removed and you'll need to grind it smooth using a valve seat dresser. Once you've popped out the washer (and possibly the seat), trot on down to the hardware store with your old one and try to find a match.

At home, plunk your new seat into place and reverse the order of your previous actions.

If you live in a house, you might want to drink your victory beer outside. While you're out there you can do as I do: inspect the roof for straying tree branches, clean the gutters, spy on your neighbors, and put screens over plumbing vents so squirrels don't fall in (no joke—it happened to me).

One of the simplest and most overlooked chores is cleaning or replacing your air conditioner or forced-air filter. If you have a central air unit, use one of your shiny new screwdrivers to open the return air plenum (this is a grill located somewhere inside your house on the wall or ceiling) of your central air-and-heat unit. If you've lived in your house for any time and you've never done this, when you swing open the grill work you'll see what looks like a rectangular swatch of angora. This is your air filter clogged with dust bunnies. Buy a box of replacement filters and change the filter once a month. A half-year supply of filters is cheaper than a six-pack of microbrew.

If you live in a house, you, your electric bill, and your AC condenser coils will breathe easier with an annual cleaning as well. You know that big thing outside your house that whirs constantly in the summertime and looks a little like R2D2? That houses your condenser coils. Before you do anything else, *Turn off the power to the out-*

member:
Uncharted territory
SURVEY: FIX-IT BASICS
Build a computer—no problem. Build a shelf to fit an alcove—no chance. It isn't the building that is the problem but the measuring. I measure the gap, measure and mark the wood, cut the wood and you guessed it, the shelf is always too long or short. I am lucky, my father and grandfather are both carpenters so any wood working and it's a call home:
Me: Daaaaad, can you do this for me?
Father: I guess so.
But then I tend to provide tech support for their PC, so it works out in the end.

side unit. In general, you can best clean the coils by removing the cover, covering the electrical parts with a plastic bag, and, using a garden hose, spraying the coil from the inside of the unit toward the outside.

Even those tiny inefficient window units deserve a yearly cleaning. Remove the front grill, remove the screws that fasten the unit to its exterior housing, and slide the unit into the room onto a table you have placed conveniently underneath the window. Use a toothbrush to loosen the dirt. Then vacuum it up and slide the unit back into place.

You can camouflage scratches in tables with one of those handy wax touch-up sticks available in a wide range of colors. Canyon-sized gouges will have to be filled with wood putty, sanded, and stained—and then hidden beneath a book or ashtray or something since those big repair jobs on tabletops can often look worse than the gouge itself. Next time, cover the table with an old blanket before you slide the beast across it.

Patch that hole in the wall before anyone discovers the depths of your rage. Make like a sculptor: Square up the ragged hole you made by chiseling at it with your utility knife. Dig through your box of party favors to find a nice sturdy balloon. Go to the hardware store and buy the smallest piece of wallboard they'll sell you. Cut a piece of wallboard a little wider and longer than the hole. (Note: If you don't cut a piece wider and longer, you're doomed to fail and will probably become so frustrated you will put another fist hole in the wall.) Size the piece so that you can slip it into the hole and position it as a back brace for the final patching piece.

Dig a little hole in the middle of the scrap you've cut and poke the business end of the balloon through the hole from the back of the scrap. It will look like a wallboard belly button, especially if you use a pink balloon. Now, take that tube of silicon adhesive or Liquid Nails and squirt a little on the parts of the scrap that will overlap the wall around the hole. Slip the scrap into place, using the balloon belly button as a handle.

Are you ready for the fun to begin? Blow the balloon up. Once the balloon's inflated, tie a knot in it. The balloon will hold the back piece in place until the adhesive has dried.

Next, cut another piece of wallboard to fit the hole. It doesn't have to fit tightly; you're not making a piano. Cut off the balloon belly button and glue the patch piece into place with Liquid Nails (no, this is not product placement).

Then go to the store and get some "mud"—the hip term for drywall compound—some drywall tape, a tray, and a four-inch blade. Dip your blade into the mud and make a nice trail, about three or four inches wide, around the patch. Cut some tape strips and stick them onto the mud, over the seams. Drag your blade across the tape to remove the excess mud, holding down one end of the tape to keep it in place.

Once the mud is dry, you still have about ten more coats to put on the patch. Remember: Dents or divots are okay. Those will fill in easily. What you want to avoid is bumps and lumps because they have to be sanded. *Avoid sanding at all costs.* Just keep floating on thin layers of mud, letting each coat dry thoroughly, until the patch is smooth.

By now you should be so self-confident that you're strutting around the house with your chest puffed out like a World Federation wrestler. But be forewarned. The gratification that comes with self-reliance is addictive.

Rather than going shopping, you'll chose instead to rehang a cabinet door that's drooping on its hinges by jamming wooden matches (or toothpicks or wooden golf tees) coated with carpenter's glue into the overwrought screw holes, letting them dry, cutting them off flush, and twisting the screws into their fresh new digs. Instead of a night on the town, you'll discover you'd rather recaulk the tub, unstick windows that are painted shut by *gently* tapping the tip of a slotted screwdriver into the seam, or run a new phone line to your closet for those private calls. Suddenly, there's no time to go mountain biking; you're too busy lubing your door locks by rubbing a soft lead pencil back and forth across your key and then working the graphite-laced key around in the lock. Then there's the belt to replace in the washing machine, shelves to install, floors to refinish . . .

Setting Up Shop

A freshly painted apartment with a shiny hardwood floor and some handcrafted furniture is only a few short lessons—and a few trips to Home Depot—away.

by J. P. Partland

The walls in your new place look terrible. The carpet is disgusting. They say that when we love a person, we also love everyone they've ever loved. When we move into a new house must we, similarly, love the taste of every other tenant who has ever lived there? Fortunately not. You can break away from the stained tile and the grimy walls and make your new place like new. Here's how.

member: rootie
SURVEY: CHEAP CHIC
Repurpose some items and give your apartment a little flair. Lots of people use old footlockers as coffee tables, but if you go to the hardware store and buy a sheet of glass to set on top, suddenly you've given it a little class and your old trunk is now furniture! You can also make your own lamps (make sure you get instruction from the hardware store or a book) just by running an electrical cord through an old bottle or vase. Then you can add the switch and socket and plug, which you buy separately. Pick a shade and voilà, light!

REMOVING WALLPAPER

That peeling, skanky wallpaper most likely has something even nastier under it. The walls far beneath, however, might be prime for painting. The real fun of removing wallpaper is discovering the walls' often colorful histories.

Materials

- Hot water
- Dishwashing liquid
- Dif glue-removing liquid (find at hardware store)
- Big, water-retaining sponges (natural or cellulose sponges work best)
- Wallpaper scrapers

Action

1. Before you do the whole wall, start by scraping off some paper in a corner to see what comes off. One danger is that the wallpaper was put on over unpainted drywall (a.k.a. plasterboard, the stuff covering "hollow" walls), which will rot from soaking. Generally drywall is painted before being papered, but sometimes it isn't. If this is the case, visit the hardware store for suggestions.
2. Dampen the walls with sponges soaked in hot soapy water.
3. Let the water soak through.
4. Start scraping with the edge of the scraper, acting as if it were a razor blade and the wall was skin.
5. After all old paper is off, use clean hot water and a sponge to loosen all the stuck glue. If glue won't come off, apply Dif glue-remover as per instructions.

Painting

If the walls were once covered with wallpaper, the walls underneath might need a few coats of paint. Generally, painting is a fairly managable enterprise. Just make sure cerise is really your favorite color before you cover your living room with it.

Materials

- Covering materials (newspaper, old sheets, drop cloths, tarps, plastic sheeting)
- Masking tape
- Paint, either latex (water-based) or alkyd (oil-based). Latex is much easier to work with, but alkyd often weathers better. Latex's big advantage is that it cleans up easier (water is the only necessary solvent).
- Damp cloth
- Paintbrushes (synthetic bristles are for latex, natural bristles are for alkyd): two inch width for edging jobs, three inch for covering wide surfaces quickly, one inch for detail work.
- An angled brush, sometimes called a sash tool, is used for getting into tight spaces.

- Rollers (ask at hardware or paint store to determine which kind of roller goes with which wall and which paint. Textured walls often need a deeper nap than smooth walls).
- Roller tray—make sure to match the width of the tray to the width of the roller.
- Broomstick—to screw into roller handle for reaching high walls and ceilings.
- Spout—fits on lip of paint can. Makes pouring paint easier and cleaner.
- Mixing stick—any clean, splinter-free wooden stick will do. They usually come free from paint store.
- Hammer

Hints

Determine how much square footage needs to be covered before going to the hardware store. Tell the salesperson how much wall space needs painting and he'll tell you how much paint you should buy. Remember, you'll probably need at least two coats.

member: Emma

SURVEY: CHEAP CHIC

Speaking of making your own lamps, my housemate made a great lamp from a bowling ball! If you go to someplace like Kmart (or a bowling store), they can drill the right size hole in the ball to hold the lamp fixture. Then, all you need is a small rubber ring (look in a car parts store), which acts as a great base for the lamp.

Action

1. Clean ceilings, floors, and walls before painting.
2. If painting exposed wood, make sure it's first been treated with sealant.
3. Paint when there's good light; either do it during the brightest part of the day or bring as many lights as you can into the room. Also, try to paint on days with low humidity because painted surfaces will dry faster. Another reason to paint on rain-free days is that it's more likely you'll be able to open the windows and allow for better ventilation.
4. Move furniture away from surfaces that are to be painted and cover with tarps. Cover the floor. If this is a room where you are sure to throw out the carpet, be careless and use the existing carpet as a drop cloth. Make sure you are going to throw the carpet out immediately after painting, however. If the surface being painted is a single wall, newspaper is all the floor covering needed. When the ceiling is being painted, go for the bigger floor covers.

5. Cover things on the edge of walls, or in the walls that aren't supposed to be painted, with masking tape: floor and ceiling moldings, door frames, window frames, window panes, light switches, electrical outlets, brass hardware.
6. Open the paint can and mix the paint with the stirrer.
7. Snap on the spout.
8. Pour some paint into the roller tray, enough to slightly overfill the bottom.
10. After dipping the roller and rolling off the excess paint on the ribs of the tray, put the roller on the surface. Roll a W. Then go back over the W by rolling an M. Think about filling rectangles, without touching the edges of the space. Continue with the roller until a space (like a wall), minus edges, is filled.
11. Brush in edges before the paint in the middle dries. Never dip the brush more than halfway down the bristles. Except for painting the ceiling and high edges, the brush handle should always be higher than the bristles. These techniques prevent the brush from getting saturated with paint. It is usually best to paint in one direction to prevent lines and bubbles from forming as the paint dries.
12. After the first coat is finished, pour the leftover paint in the tray back into the can and seal the lid by tapping the edge of it with a hammer.
13. Assuming you're using latex paint, clean brushes, rollers, and trays with cold water. The tray should clean out rather easily. The roller should be wrung by hand to squeeze out the paint and water. The brushes should be held as they were when painting, with the handles above the bristles. Here, too, squeeze out the paint.
14. When a brush feels and looks paint-free, form the wet bristles back into the shape the brush came in and let it air-dry by leaving it hanging from the hole in the handle.
15. When the second coat is dry, determine whether a third coat is necessary. If the color is too thin, or old wall markings are showing through, it probably needs a third coat.

Carpet Bagging

So you think that wall-to-wall shag is about to give out, or that the floor beneath might be in excellent condition. You want to get down to the bare wood and take a look.

Materials

- utility knife
- pry bar
- tack lifter
- pliers
- broom
- dust pan
- vacuum cleaner
- garbage can

Action

1. Pull up the carpeting in one corner first; either cut a small bit along the wall and pull up or try to get the pry bar underneath the carpet but above the tack strip.
2. Remove all furniture from the room in question. If the furniture can't be removed, you'll have to shift the stuff around; start by putting all furniture in one-half of the room. Remove the carpeting from the other half. Cut the carpet an inch from the walls, making sure you're getting through the base fabric. Once it is removed from enough of the walls, it can be rolled to the point where all the furniture is. Underneath the carpet is disintegrating padding. If it, too, can be peeled, do so. If not, pick up the large pieces and throw them away.
3. Use the pry bar to remove the tack strips that are along the walls. Stick one end of the bar under the strip and use leverage to lift it off the floor. The strips should go right in the garbage can (a bag won't do because these things are sharp).
4. After the strips, the padding, and padding dust are off the floor, inspect for staples. Pry the staples up with the screwdriver or pry bar. If the pry bar only gets some of a staple up or the staple breaks, use the pliers.

5. Inspect the floor. If it appears to be in good shape, you've got an attractive hardwood floor. Wax it, sweep it often, and enjoy. If not, either cover bad spots with area rugs or go to the library or bookstore and read up on refinishing hardwood floors.

DIY Furniture

Bookcase

Cinder blocks and wood planks are just *so* college. It's time to consider a real bookcase. It's a bit harder than putting up shelves, but you can take it with you if you move.

Materials

- wood (For this project, you might as well buy long boards from the lumber yard as you'll have to do a lot of cutting. The quality of available wood can vary. If the bookcase is going to be on display and the wood is going to show through, buy better wood for the sides than for the shelves. You'll also need some one-by-two-inch wood for cleats that will support the shelves.)
- screws—#8 or #10 wood screws
- wood conditioner (This is meant to be swathed on the wood with a rag and allowed to air dry, preferably as soon as you get the wood home from the yard, in order to prevent bowing.)
- wood glue
- level
- pencil
- tape measure
- drill
- drill bit—1/4-inch wood bit
- screwdriver
- saw (A cross-cut saw, which is designed to cut across the wood grain, is probably the most essential saw.)
- sandpaper
- square
- mitre box (Usually made of wood or plastic, a mitre box is designed to hold wood in place and help administer perfect cuts at 45- and 90-degree angles.)

- c-clamp—a C-shaped device for holding two pieces of wood together.
- sealant (optional)
- stain (optional)
- paint (optional)

Action

1. Plan on building a bookcase no wider than thirty-three inches and no more than six feet high. If only books are going in this case, you probably don't need to build the shelves more than nine or ten inches deep. You'll want to put the largest books on the bottom.
2. Coffee-table books are rarely more than fourteen inches tall, so make the first shelf fourteen inches from the bottom. After that, you can probably get away with ten inches in between shelves, or less if your collection consists mostly of paperbacks.
3. Since you are buying many feet of wood at a time, buy some extra so there's room for error to the tune of two shelves. You need to consider the height of the case (for the sides), the width (for the top), and the depth of the shelves.
4. You'll need enough cleat material so that each shelf is supported by two cleats. Buy extra cleat material as well.
5. Once you have the boards that are the side pieces, lay them next to one another on the ground. Make sure they are the same height. Then lay the tape measure down the length, marking where the shelves should go.
6. Take the square and use it to draw a line across both boards. Below the line is where the cleats will go, above the shelves themselves.
7. Cut the cleats. Don't have the cleats sticking out of either side.
8. Cut the shelves. When marking the boards, remember to include the width of the saw blade in your calculations.
9. Glue and screw the cleats into place. First drill the hole through the cleat and into the board while holding the cleat in place. Put down the drill. Add glue. Screw into place; wipe off excess. Repeat with the second screw.

10. Start by putting on the top piece of wood. It will also be glued and screwed. Mark two drill points in the top piece above where the side will meet it. Drill straight through. Then butt the side against the top. Drill through the top into the side.
11. Take the pieces apart, add glue, butt together again, and screw into place. Wipe off excess glue. Do this to the other side. Next, put on the bottom shelf. Slide the shelf into place. Use the C-clamp to hold the shelf to the cleat. Drill through the sides into the shelf. Remove the shelf and spread the glue in the corners made by the cleat and the side. Put the shelf back in, taking care to match up the holes and sides. Screw into place. Repeat the process until all the shelves are done.
12. If the shelves seem unstable, add a thin sheet of plywood to the back of the case. Make sure the plywood has the same dimensions as the case. For a little extra stability without all the weight, just use plywood to cover the back of the lowest shelf or two.
13. Finish as desired, with sealant and stain or paint.

Secondhand World

It's an exhilarating act of consumer rebellion not to buy this year's model. And if you know where to look, you can get some really cool stuff, too.

by Al Hoff

I've spent my life buying used wares, sometimes due to the state of my checking account. But if I crashed into a trust fund tomorrow, I'd still shop secondhand. Nearly everything you need for easy living is out there already. What might you find today? Who knows?

At least you won't be limited to the same soulless megamall schlock. And, unless you can cough up some serious cash, new merch is often of poor quality and designed to be disposable. I say, Don't fall for that new pressboard desk. Go get a solid old wood or metal one instead.

Advertising sets the agenda for retail shopping, but there are fewer such rules in the secondhand world. Out of a gazillion random-use items, you must use your imagination to furnish your life. I relish the fact that my pad looks like nobody else's, filled with odd and unique items, each with its own mysterious past life, now being reused and reloved by me. Save those functional items from eco-miserable landfills! It's an exhilarating act of consumer rebellion not to buy this year's model.

Where should your treasure hunt commence? Well, that depends. Like to sleep in? Love the rush of competition? Have less than $5? Here's a short guide to help you find your way.

member: PhoenixElaine

SURVEY: FRUGAL FINESSE

I try to reject the impulse to acquire, acquire, acquire. For "social shopping" with friends I go to thrift stores or nice vegetable markets like Reading Terminal here in Philly. And for my software needs, I run Linux, enjoying the benefits of "free software," hoping eventually I'll be able to contribute something back. But when it comes time to buying something significant, quality and technological sophistication are worth paying for.

Sales

Negotiating secondhand sales can be the true test of the proverb, "One man's junk is another man's treasure."

Garage/Tag/Yard/Stoop Sales

Advantage:	Generally low, low prices, goods that ordinary folks are ditching, and little danger of "collectible" prices. Best chance of getting a chair for a dollar.
Disadvantage:	It's appalling what pure junk some people put out for sale! Selection is usually limited to one household's tastes. It can be hard searching for clothes, which are often piled up on the ground.
Haggling Potential:	High
Chance Item Will Be Broken:	60 percent (but you can ask and/or test it on site)
Time Needed:	Garage sales are typically held from 8 A.M. to noon.

Flea Markets and Swap Meets

Advantage:	A good-sized flea often boasts acres of merchandise. Best bargains are found at the amateur tables, especially at day's end. Open Sundays, an otherwise dead secondhand retail day. Good venue for knickknacks, housewares, tools, and small furniture.
Disadvantage:	Some fleas suffer from too many dealers or regulars, rendering them outdoor antique stores.

	Other fleas are bogged down with crappy new merchandise. Clothing is limited or difficult to examine. Summer heat can be brutal. Wear comfortable shoes.
Haggling Potential:	High. When purchasing more than one of the same item, insist on some sort of bulk rate.
Chance Item Will Be Broken:	60 percent
Time Needed:	Fifteen minutes to all day, depending on size.

Stores

Depending on which variety of used-goods store you go to, you may be acquiring glamour or just collecting lint. At a consignment store, for example, you can find some fine, albeit pricey "office drag." On the other hand, at a junk store, you'll be lucky to score a bottle of half-used Charlie perfume and a tube of Chapstick.

Thrift Stores

Advantage:	Thrift stores offer the widest selection of goods (from hundreds of sources), stable pricing (including sales!), and high merchandise turnover. Ever so many clothes! Thrifts are located everywhere and open year-round.
Disadvantage:	Everybody knows this. Thrifts are increasingly crowded and picked over. Perseverance is an art.
Haggling Potential:	Low
Chance Item Will Be Broken:	30–40 percent
Time Needed:	Five minutes to an hour, depending on size.

member: HKoseff

SURVEY: CHEAP CHIC

A former roommate (and current friend) is a master at the art of trash picking. Some of the things he picks up are astounding: 1930s standing brass ashtrays, 1950s kitchenettes, a funky wood dresser, and all at the best price in the world—free. Although it's not for everyone, particularly the timid or anyone without a car or a couple of strong friends to carry the take home, it's a great source of furniture and home accessories. One word of caution: Ask permission if people are around. You don't want to take off with something that someone just bought! If you go at night you can generally avoid people, and it's easier to start under the cover of darkness. And if you ever get a twinge of guilt, consider this: You're doing your part in the recycling effort!

Junk Stores and Used-Goods Stores

Advantage:	Lots of appliances and furniture. The deeper the junk, the more likely there's hidden treasure.
Disadvantage:	Most often located in rundown areas and staffed by kooky, unshaven old men. Mountains of disorganized junk make searching hard. Dust, dirt, and grime galore.
Haggling Potential:	Medium—may be proportional to time spent listening to stories.
Chance Item Will Be Broken:	60 percent
Time Needed:	Five minutes to two hours, depending on density of junk and garrulity of owner.

Locating Secondhand Venues

Your best pal is the Yellow Pages. Look under "thrift store," "secondhand," or "used." Check local bulletin boards and community papers for notices on garage and rummage sales. At thrift stores, ask about other thrifts (they often come in clusters). Estate sales and garage sales are advertised in Friday's newspaper. This is "estate" as in "last will and testament" not as in a "palatial home," and they are held anywhere people die, replete with the uninteresting things a person's heirs no longer want. Sadly enough, estate sales are good sources for odd, personal things like matchbook collections, stacks of old magazines, and family snapshots.

Some General Tips For Shopping Secondhand

Set your own price limits before you go shopping and stick by them. If you are remotely interested in an item, grab it and hold on to it. Make your final decision later. Secondhand goods are rarely guaranteed or returnable. Examine items carefully (and test or try on if possible) before purchase.

Warning

Not all so-called secondhand shopping is kosher or worth the effort. I studiously avoid shopping (browsing is always okay) at antique, retro, and vintage stores. Sure, the goods are shiny, fab, and immediately accessible. That's ideal for those with more money than time, but I enjoy the hunt and dig those low prices! Remember, they got that item from one of the above sources cheaper first.

Steer clear of lame secondhand places like motel and office close-outs. Do you really want to do your pad in last year's Motel 6 cast-offs? And stay away from fake used goods! Some "hip" stores cater to young people by selling slavishly copied new "retro" furnishings and clothing. That knock-off gas station jacket has no more authenticity than a windbreaker over at the Gap. Don't let them charge you for ersatz history, so unique that everybody else is wearing it.

Thrifty Decorating

Don't limit yourself to "traditional" wall decorating—paintings, photographs, things in frames. Toss anything up on the wall and watch it become art! Game boards: Candyland! Life! Snazzy old taffeta and netting cocktail aprons—so impractical on the body, so snappy chic pinned to the kitchen wall. LP covers! The tunes on *Music for Lonely Lovers* suck, but that cover photograph of a '50s blonde bombshell tumbling out of a pink feather boa is something else entirely. Line the staircase with LPs of women cha-cha-cha-ing. Clothing that's too weird or too small to wear, like that psychedelic op-art nylon mini-dress, but too wonderful to pass up can be pinned to walls and doors.

Don't overlook the "art potential" of unwanted mass-market paperbacks. For years I collected silly nurse novels from the '50s, '60s, and '70s. Nobody else wanted them: *Soul Nurse*, *Surf Safari Nurse*, *Television Nurse*, *Nurse on the Run*. They looked fabulous when I put them, covers out, on my bookshelf.

Postcards are groovy little art snaps too quickly thrown away. Save them up and use them for art collage. Any unskilled, nonartistic person can pin or tape up postcards in colorful mosaics. If you have loads of postcards, specialize—beach scenes or just booze ads.

member: xiabelle

SURVEY: CHEAP CHIC

I bought a table from IKEA one day then happened to decide to run by one of the open-air market stores in town. I asked about tables and promptly got shown two lovely oak tables. And the one I bought, while not as big, cost me $150—$25 dollars more than the slightly bigger, flimsier, clear-stained, knotty pine table from IKEA (which was promptly returned, since it wasn't opened yet).

(Don't pass up all those free advertising postcards! Subvert their capitalist meanings by pasting them all over your fridge or cellar stairwell.)

Secondhand shopping lets you cheaply engage in fake-out decorating. Make your Ramen preparation area look more upscale with a colorful shelf of fancy cookbooks. Jumpstart your athletic career with other people's discarded trophies.

Storage Ideas

Storage begets neatness. Open your mind to the storage possibilities of kitchen canisters (nylons, hankies, nails), old colored aluminum ice cube trays (toss the cube divider and the tray holds pens, stamps, cat food), index file drawers (photos), or bread tins (lots of junk). Low on closet space? Dressers cost too much? Store rarely used or out-of-season clothing and linens in secondhand suitcases. Cases slip neatly under the bed, slide behind doors and other nooks, and flat-sided suitcases can stack. (Hey! It's an end table!) Hat and wig boxes and old makeup cases with handles are nifty for stashing smaller items.

Ad Hoc Improvements

Wicker and rattan screens are versatile and inexpensive moveable "walls." If they're too plain, paint them or decorate by sticking things through the holes: plastic flowers, weird sunglasses, little paper drink umbrellas. Use bent paper clips, Christmas tree ornament hooks, or small bits of wire to hang goofy little knickknacks.

Use glass blocks to support book shelves or slab-o-something coffee tables (door, extra heavy mirror, or picture frame). They're more expensive than regular bricks, but they look sensational.

Thrift Party?

Potluck thrift parties have a long tradition. It's a variation on what was once known as a "Harlem Rent Party." That's a term that popped up during the '20s Harlem Renaissance when many folks were pouring into NYC and other northerly urban areas from the

South. They'd arrive with the clothes on their backs and little else. A party would be thrown and the neighborhood would turn out with household donations to get the hosts started on their new life.

A simple and fun way to begin stocking your brand-new pad is to throw a thrift party. Request that your guests bring an easily obtained, cheap (used is just fine) item for admission. Be as specific as you like—knife-fork-spoon sets, drinking glasses, ashtrays, throw pillows, plates, coffee mugs, cookbooks, houseplants, and so on. Announce a prize for the best item received!

member: doncolin

SURVEY: FRUGAL FINESSE

Living frugally just isn't living. Spend it when you have it. Don't when you don't. That works for me.

part 4
food

Kitchen Basics

Setting up a well-stocked and well-appointed kitchen certainly takes a little work. But it's one of the best things you can possibly do to make life a bit more enjoyable for you and yours.

by Sasha Smith

A food memory is the foundation for any cook. I can still taste the scrambled eggs my friends and I devoured in Sparks, Nevada, on our way across the country, and the crayfish and Camembert cheese I consumed with my boyfriend on a terrace in Normandy, France, as we tried to prolong our doomed long-distance relationship.

What does this have to do with cooking? I hold that before you learn to cook, you need to know how to eat. This means slowing down and paying attention to what you put in your mouth. Along with opposable thumbs and sex for nonprocreative purposes, eating for pleasure is one of the distinguishing characteristics separating humans from the rest of the animal kingdom.

Try this experiment. Sit down in a comfortable chair with an apple. Does the apple taste different the closer you get to the core? Is the peel getting stuck between your teeth? Is it better than the apple you ate yesterday or last week? I promise eating good food slowly and deliberately will make you a better chef.

While serious cooking means paying attention to food, it doesn't have to mean slaving over it. In college, my roommates and I had no utensils or appliances, save for a tea kettle. Nontheless, instant oatmeal and soup from a cup never tasted so good. I was so happy to be eating what I wanted when I wanted that those were some of the most satisfying meals I've ever made.

member: Rachel

SURVEY: RECIPES

One of my favorite low-budget meals is curry. You need:

- rice (1/2 cup per person)
- curry powder (or Thai curry paste, if you've got a spare buck; it's pricier, but better)
- one or two cans of coconut milk any vegetables you can find (I usually use potatoes, carrots, onions, and garlic as a base; sometimes add corn, green peppers, whatever)
- cooking oil
- other spices optional (salt, pepper, ginger, hot sesame oil, turmeric)

Make the rice in one pot. In another, or a wok if you've got it, sauté onions and garlic first. Boil the potatoes, diced, for about 15 minutes until they soften; add potatoes to the sautéeing onions. Add whatever other vegetables you've got. Toss in one or two spoonfuls of curry paste or curry powder (powder gives a more Indian flavor; paste is more Thai), pour in a can or two of coconut milk, simmer for a few minutes and serve over rice.

If you want to be fancy, of course, this dish can be augmented with chicken—fresh limes to squeeze over each plate before serving—fresh scallions, cilantro, and mint to sprinkle on top—etc.

Of course, more elaborate cooking can be just as, or more, emotionally rewarding, though it does take some time. But compared to the days you've spent repainting your apartment or putting in overtime at work, spending half an hour mincing garlic isn't such a time suck. And once you do commit to cooking—whether once a day or once a month—you'll begin to find the moments chopping vegetables or stirring the stockpot incredibly soothing.

So go to the market, buy the best quality ingredients you can afford, surround yourself with good company—whether that means twenty friends or your own solitude—and get into the kitchen.

Guide to Knives

One of the first rules of cooking is never skimp on essentials. And when it comes to essentials, nothing is more important than a good knife. With a second-rate knife, cutting, chopping, and slicing are difficult and downright dangerous, as dullness encourages the cook to use greater pressure, increasing the odds of bloodshed.

Metallurgy 101

The quality of any knife depends largely on the blade's composition. Standard stainless steel knives, usually the cheapest kind, are too brittle to be sharpened and, like high school boyfriends, become irreparably dull and outlive their usefulness. A more expensive but, in the long run, more economical solution is the high-carbon stainless steel knife, a durable, evenly weighted blade that can be easily sharpened and starts at about $40. Not cheap, but it beats severed fingers any day.

Cuts Like a Knife

The utility infielder of kitchen cutting tools—the chef's knife—can do it all, from mincing garlic to spearing a potato to carving a chicken. Blade and handle sizes vary, but the most important criteria is what feels good in your hand. Blade lengths range from eight to fourteen inches, but most are in the eight- to ten-inch range. Keep in mind that size and sharpness aren't the same thing. Better to find a blade length that works for you rather than a massive Wes Craven–inspired model. The following blades make good additions to any budding cook's collection:

PARING KNIFE: This smaller version of the chef's knife is perfect for mincing and paring small fruits and vegetables.

SERRATED BREAD KNIFE: This blade's scalloped edge cuts through bread, cakes, and brownies without squishing them or creating messy shards and crumbs. A smaller version, called the tomato knife, prevents juice and seeds from splattering all over your clothes and kitchen. For those obsessive-compulsive sharpeners out there, neither of these blades should ever be sharpened.

CARVING/SLICING KNIFE: The essential holiday dinner tool, the carving knife has a long, narrow blade and usually comes in eight-, ten-, and twelve-inch lengths.

BONING KNIFE: Small, sturdy, and flexible, this blade bones chicken breasts in no time.

Maintaining Your Edgc

When storing knives, keep them out of the all-purpose drawer where they'll collide with other utensils. Wood blocks or wall-mounted magnetic strips are better alternatives.

Make it a habit to use the dull edge of the knife for scraping food off cutting boards, which themselves should be made of a material considerably softer than the knife—don't even think about glass. Frequent use causes the knife edge to chip, curl, and lose its sharpness. When the blade makes a hideous "crunch" instead of a nice sharp slicing sound when cutting through hard vegetables such as onions, it's time for a little sharpening. Home sharpeners range from $30 to $100. Locksmiths and some butchers will also sharpen knives for a small fee.

COOKWARE

Cooks rely not only on ingredients and know-how, but also on good kitchen tools. Good, however, does not necessarily mean a pricey set of gleaming Calphalon cookware from Williams-Sonoma. Raid thrift stores, tag sales, hardware stores, or the kitchen of a friend

member: MSnowman

SURVEY: RECIPES

When the fall harvest is at its most bountiful, the markets are full of wonderful, inexpensive vegetables. Here are a couple of ideas that are too good to resist:

Roasted peppers: Toss some red or green bell peppers (big, sweet peppers—not the hot ones) on the BBQ grill or under the broiler. Roast them, turning often, until the skins are black on all sides. Toss them into a paper grocery bag, fold down the top of the bag, and let them steam until they are cool enough to handle. Peel off the black skin and discard it and the seeds. Rinse the peppers under cold water and cut into wide strips. Drizzle with a little olive oil and a little lemon juice or wine vinegar. Enjoy! Good as an appetizer or side dish or topping a salad or with cheese on bread as a sandwich.

Roasted corn: Pull back the husks on fresh corn and remove the silk. Pull the husk back to cover the corn and tie it together at the end with a bit of string. Soak in water for half an hour. Put the corn on the grill for about 20 minutes while you are barbecuing. Delicious! (You can roast the corn without soaking in water but the husks tend to catch on fire.)

or relative who's about to move. Often the homeliest, cheapest equipment, like a battered, well-seasoned cast-iron skillet, is also the best.

To maximize space for storing tools and equipment, use hooks to hang pot holders, towels, measuring cups and spoons—just make sure they'll be far away from fire and burners. Stick frequently used utensils in empty glass jars or mugs. Clear canisters for flour, rice, and sugar, and watering-can style oil dispensers make measuring cleaner and easier and lend an aura of expertise to even the most primitive kitchen. (See sidebar on page 175 for a full list of recommended cookware and kitchen tools.)

Spices and Pantry

Once upon a time, wars were waged and fortunes founded on the salt and spice trade. Thanks to canning, refrigeration, and the availability of fresh meat, fish, and produce, those days are pretty much over, but herbs and spices should still play a central role in any cook's kitchen.

Herbs derive from leaves, while spices come from the other parts of a plant, such as the flower (saffron), the bark (cinnamon), or the berry (pepper). Dried herbs are usually more concentrated in flavor than fresh herbs, which should be added to a dish at the last minute to preserve their flavor. Buy dried herbs and spices in small quantities, store them in a cool, dry place away from light, and renew them at least once a year.

Get to know which herbs and spices you like in which forms, combinations and quantities. Experiment with the mild licorice taste of star anise, the tang of ground ginger, the pungent sweetness of cardamom, and the subtle elegance of saffron. Try buying spices such as cumin and coriander in whole form, toasting them for a few seconds in a dry skillet over high heat and pulverizing them in a coffee grinder for more intense flavor. Don't be shy—most cooks make a few inedibly hot chilis and other odd combinations before learning how to season properly. If you do OD on the heat, add a little lemon juice to the dish to tame it (or dilute with whatever liquid you're using in the dish) and serve with plenty of bread or potatoes to absorb the heat. A sip of water spreads the spice and will actually intensify the sting.

`member: hardpack`

SURVEY: RECIPES

Tomatoes ala hotdogamissimo: Slice hotdogs diagonally, so they are long and fairly thin. Fry in olive oil over medium heat. Pour a splash of room-temperature spaghetti sauce on a plate. When the hotdogs are done, slap them on top of the sauce. The hotdogs will heat up the sauce a bit and the sauce will compromise the saltiness of the dogs. While they are sitting, use the leftover oil to fry some bread. Eat and enjoy.

`member: Dataphone`

SURVEY: RECIPES

Mock Angel Food Cake

1 cup milk
2 teaspoons baking powder
1 cup flour
2 egg whites

Heat milk to boiling point, sift dry ingredients several times and stir into hot milk. Fold well beaten egg whites into mixture. *Do not* grease or flour pan. Bake about 40 minutes in a moderate oven.

> Terms and Techniques

Don't know your braising from your deglazing? This lexicon explains some of the most frequently used cooking terms and techniques.

ADJUST: to alter seasonings according to the cook's taste

BASTE: to brush or pour liquid over food (usually meat or poultry) as it cooks to keep it moist, flavorful, and brown

BEAT: to combine ingredients at high speed until well-blended

BLANCH: to plunge food briefly into boiling water and then remove

BLEND: to mix ingredients, usually wet and dry, until combined—it requires less speed than beating

BOIL: to heat a liquid until large, regular bubbles break its surface

BONE: to remove all bones from meat, poultry, or fish

BRAISE: to cook food with a small amount of liquid in a covered dish, until done, either in the oven or on the stove

BROIL: to cook food briefly, directly under high heat

BROWN: to cook food in fat over medium-high heat until outside is golden to dark brown in color

CHOP: to cut food into even-sized pieces

CREAM: to beat ingredients until smooth and fluffy

DICE: to chop into pieces approximately 1/8 inch in size

DEGLAZE: to pour liquid (usually wine or broth) into a pan after meat, poultry, or fish has been cooked in it and simmer or boil briefly while scraping at the browned bits in the bottom of the pan

EMULSIFY: to bind together two ingredients that usually separate (e.g., oil and vinegar) by whisking, creating a smooth, homogeneous mixture

FOLD: to incorporate a light ingredient (such as egg whites) gently into a heavier ingredient, being careful not to deflate the mixture

KNEAD: to work dough with hands until it forms a smooth, elastic mass

MARINATE: to soak food (if it's fruit, this technique is often called "macerate") in a liquid usually with an acidic ingredient (citrus juice, wine, etc.) to tenderize and add flavor

MINCE: to chop food very finely, smaller than 1/8 inch

MIX: to blend ingredients until just combined

PARE: to remove skin or outer layer of fruits and vegetables

POACH: to cook food by submerging it in simmering water

PURÉE: to mash solid food until reduced to a soft, smooth, almost liquid state

REDUCE: to boil down a liquid, reducing its volume and concentrating its flavor

ROAST: to cook food in an oven at moderate heat

SAUTÉ: to cook and brown food in a small amount of fat over high heat

SCALD: 1. to heat milk or cream until it almost boils, 2. to blanch

SCORE: to make shallow, regular incisions into food, without cutting entirely through it

SEAR: to brown meat, fish, or poultry quickly over very high heat and with little or no fat

SIFT: to pass dry ingredients through a sieve to remove lumps

SIMMER: to cook food at a very low boil, usually when just a few occasional bubbles break the surface of the liquid

STEAM: to cook food, often fish and vegetables, by placing it over, but not touching, boiling water

STIR-FRY: to cook food in a wok very quickly over high heat with a small amount of oil

TRUSS: to tie poultry or meat together (or secure with pins) to ensure even cooking

WHIP: to beat rapidly with a whisk or electric beater to incorporate air and increase volume

ZEST: to grate the outside colored skin of citrus fruit, making sure not to grate the bitter white skin underneath

SALT: Oversalted food tastes salty; well-salted food tastes like itself, only more so. Regular table salt does the job, but sea salt is more nuanced. It's a little more expensive, but worth it.

BLACK PEPPERCORN: Go for the real McCoy, fresh-ground pepper from a pepper mill, rather than that pre-ground powdery stuff.

WHITE PEPPERCORN: Milder than the black kind and wildly overrated, its main purpose is to appease those anal folks who don't like black flecks in their mashed potatoes.

Herbs

BASIL: Intense and faintly licorice-tasting when fresh, basil loses most of its power when dried.

BAY LEAF: Essential to most everything cooked in a huge pot (stews, soups, beans, red sauces) these dried leaves shouldn't be eaten and are usually removed right before serving.

CILANTRO: You either love it or you hate it—a key ingredient in Latin American, Thai, and Indian cooking.

DILL: This herb marries well with lemon and fish. Use sparingly, however, as too much can be overpowering.

MINT: The fresh kind works well in a variety of sweet and savory dishes. Save the dried kind for dressings or marinades.

OREGANO: The green flecks on a pizza parlor slice, it's one of the few herbs that has its own assertive flavor when dried. Fresh oregano matches well with tomato-based sauces, Mediterranean dishes, and Mexican cuisine, although the Mexican variety is slightly different (and can be found in Latin American specialty food shops).

PARSLEY: Look for the fresh, flat-leafed variety; don't even bother with dried.

ROSEMARY: Piney and aromatic, rosemary is the perfect partner for lamb, but also works well with all meats and poultry. Its flavor usually overpowers all but the most assertive fish and shellfish dishes.

Spices

CAYENNE PEPPER: Ground from the pods and seeds of red chiles (which are also used to make red pepper flakes) cayenne adds heat and should always be added a little bit at a time and the dish

member: hmma

SURVEY: RECIPIES

This is easy to make and has a flavorful & distinct taste. It's not all that expensive, but I wouldn't normally put some of these ingredients in my shopping bag.

Basil Vino Chicken

1 teaspoon olive oil
1 Tb. minced garlic
1/2 cup white wine (sweet)
1/4 cup lemon juice
1/4 cup sun-dried tomatoes
1/4 cup fresh basil
1/2 cup fresh spinich
2 deboned, skinless chicken breasts
2 Tb. grated Parmesan (fresh is best!)

Combine olive oil and garlic in a sauce pan at medium heat until garlic begins to brown. Add wine and cook for another minute or two. Remove the pan from heat and stir in the lemon juice, tomatoes, basil, and spinach. Spray cooking spray in a baking dish. Spread chicken in dish and cover with the wine mixture. Cover the dish. Bake at 350 degrees for about 40 minutes or until chicken is done. About 5 minutes before cooking time is up, sprinkle the cheese on top of each chicken breast. Serve chicken in some of the sauce.

should be tasted after each addition. Remember, it's a lot easier to add a little bit more spice than to take some away.

CUMIN: Smoky and spicy, cumin balances the bright heat of cayenne and matches perfectly with pork.

> The Well-Stocked Kitchen

SOME OTHER SEASONINGS TO ADD TO YOUR PANTRY INCLUDE:

LIKE LICORICE, ONLY BETTER

- anise
- caraway seed
- fennel seed
- star anise

TRÈS FRANÇAIS

- marjoram
- tarragon
- thyme

BAKER'S HALF-DOZEN

- allspice
- cloves
- ground ginger
- mace
- nutmeg
- vanilla

EXOTIC AND EXPENSIVE

- cardamom
- coriander
- saffron

HERB AND SPICE MIXES

- Chinese five-spice powder
- curry powder
- garam masala
- herbes de Provence
- ras al hanout (from Northern Africa)

GENERAL TOOLS

- colander
- sieve
- box grater
- wooden spoons, scrapers
- rolling pin
- slotted spoon
- serving forks, spoons
- rubber spatulas
- metal spatulas
- tongs
- measuring spoons
- microwave-safe measuring cups for liquids
- metal measuring cups for solids
- wire whisk
- mixing bowls
- corkscrew
- vegetable peeler
- can opener
- kitchen scissors
- potholders
- cloth towels
- paper towels
- sponges, scrubbers
- aluminum foil
- plastic baggies
- plastic wrap
- wax paper
- twine

POTS AND PANS

- cast-iron skillet
- stainless steel wok with wok stand
- 8-quart pot with lid
- 3-quart saucepan with lid
- 1-quart saucepan with lid
- 10-inch skillet
- 7-inch skillet
- 9-inch cake pan
- 9-inch pie plate
- 9-inch loaf pan
- 9-inch square baking pan
- 13 x 9 x 2-inch baking pan

BAKING DISHES

- 3- and 4-quart casserole dishes—Pyrex (ovenproof glass) or ceramic, preferably with lids
- enamel cast-iron baking dish (2- or 3-quart)

ELECTRIC APPLIANCES

- blender, standing or handheld
- electric mixer, standing or handheld
- electric coffee grinder
- food processor with simple blade and disks for chopping and shredding

CHILI POWDER: A blend of spices—cayenne, oregano, cumin, coriander, cloves, etc.—chili powder mixes vary, so shop around for one that suits your tastes. It adds complex heat to dips, dressings, marinades and, um . . . chili.

CINNAMON: It's not just for applesauce and toast anymore. Cinnamon adds spicy sweetness to North African and Indian food, in stick and ground form.

Recipes for the Would-Be Gourmand

Before starting in on these or any other recipes, a few tips:

Read the recipe through at least once before starting. Pity the cook who discovers the chocolate mousse he's whipping up twenty minutes before guests arrive was supposed to have chilled for six hours before serving.

Just like in algebra, the order of operations makes a big difference. A cup of flour, sifted, means measuring a cup of flour first, then sifting it, while a cup of sifted flour means measuring the flour after it's been sifted.

Know when to rebel. Adding a splash or a sprinkle of a favorite ingredient to a BBQ sauce recipe can be a great idea; improvising a recipe for puff pastry almost never is. Familiarize yourself with new ingredients before experimenting with them, and respect the rules when baking. Don't underestimate preparation time. Sure, the pasta for capellini with fresh herb sauce only takes eight minutes to cook, but finely mincing several cups of herbs can be an all-evening affair.

member: mark_bradley

SURVEY: RECIPIES

Thai Style Pizza (vegan)

Thai peanut sauce
1 package oyster mushrooms
8 oz. seitan or sautéed, crumbled tofu or similar meat substitute (for you omnivores use chicken)
Pizza crust
1 cup bean sprouts
1/2 cup shredded carrots
2 cups shredded soy cheese (mozzarella style tastes best, make sure it is really soft in the package)

Preheat oven to 450 degrees. Use the peanut sauce as your base. Cut oyster mushrooms into thirds and sauté in canola oil with seitan until lightly brown. The main thing here is to get them heated up. Spread the sprouts and seitan-mushroom mixture on the crust.
Sprinkle with shredded carrots. Cover liberally with your choice of cheese. Bake until the cheese is melted. If you are using soy cheese *do not* let it burn. Takes about 15 minutes.

Romantic Dinner for Two

For the couple who's not always on the same page food-wise, dining together at home can be a tension-filled experience. The following menu, which satisfies two very different appetites, is sure to restore a little romantic culinary harmony. One appetizer is vegetarian and the other is meat-based. The salsas served with the main-course fish appeal to spicy food lovers and tamer palates. For dessert, each person can indulge in his or her own chocolate candy favorite. Beer, wine, or margaritas would all work equally well with this menu.

> The Cook's Bookshelf

The Essentials

These classics offer important reference information as well as tons of recipes—no cook's library is complete without one of them.

The Joy of Cooking, by Irma S. Rombauer and Marion Rombauer Becker (Scribner, 1995) $26.

The Fannie Farmer Cookbook, by Marion Cunningham, (Knopf, 1996) $30.

Better Homes and Gardens, by (Meredith, 1996) $15.95.

Easy

Recipes 1-2-3, by Rozanne Gold (Viking,) $22.95.
No dish in this book features more than three ingredients.

Madhur Jaffrey's Quick and Easy Indian Cooking, by Madhur Jaffrey (Barron's, 1994) $24. The doyenne of Indian cooking serves up simple recipes, defying this cuisine's notoriety for long, complicated preparations.

Just Cook Something, by Mitchell Davis (Macmillan, 1997) $19.95. This book has unintimidating recipes for beginning cooks.

The Surreal Gourmet: Real Food for Pretend Chefs, by Bob Blumer (Chronicle, 1992) $14.95. Dishes in thirty minutes or less.

Intermediate

The Classic Mediterranean Cookbook, by Sarah Woodward (Dorling Kindersley, 1995) $24.95. Clear directions and photographs make even bouillabaise seem easy.

The New Basics, by Sheila Lukins and Julee Rosso (Workman) 1989. $19.95. Overlook the book's cloying cuteness to find some truly great recipes.

Trattoria, by Patricia Wells, (Avon Books, 1993) $12.50. Her personal confessions might get on your nerves (should we care that she eats penne with zucchini when she's in a bad mood?), but her elegant, opinionated recipes and tips will find their way into your repertoire.

http://www.epicurious.com
Recipes from *Gourmet* and *Bon Appetit* magazines, and a thorough food and drink dictionary.

http://www.tvfood.com
Cooking show celebs go online with tips and recipes.

http://www.kitchenlink.com
Overwhelmingly big, but a good source for mail-order goods.

Advanced

The Way to Cook, by Julia Child (Knopf, 1989) $35. A more ambitous alternative to the "essential" guides, from the woman who changed the way Americans eat.

The Essentials of Classic Italian Cooking, by Marcella Hazan (Knopf, 1996) $30. Demanding, but worth it.

Field of Greens, by Annie Somerville (Bantam, 1993) $26.95. Delicious, if at times overly complicated, vegetarian fare.

http://www.starchefs.com For serious foodies only.

Off the Beaten Path

My favorite cookbooks are the eminently impractical kind, for people who have a bit more time and energy to devote to cooking and entertaining.

The Chocolate Bible, by Christian Teubner (Penguin Studio, 1997) $29.95. Tortes, truffles, and more to help you get in touch with your inner pastry chef.

Cooking without Recipes, by Cheryl Sindell (Kensington Books, 1997) $13.00. Hints and tips for when you're ready to go freestyle.

Last Dinner on the Titanic, by Rick Archbold and Dana McCauley (Hyperion, 1997) $24.95. For those who *really* want to know what it was like that fateful night.

Appetizer:

Quesadillas with Roasted Peppers, Jalapeño Jack Cheese, and Sausages or Portobello Mushrooms

You can roast the peppers yourself if you want: Place one red pepper on a baking sheet in a 475-degree oven. Roast for about 15 minutes, or until pepper has collapsed and skin is blistered, but not completely black and charred. Place the pepper in a paper bag until it's cool enough to handle. Peel the skin, remove the stem and inner seeds, and slice into thin strips.

3 ounces (usually the size of one small link) sausage, such as andouille, chorizo, or spicy Italian
1 portobello mushroom
salt and pepper
1/8 teaspoon dried oregano
1 teaspoon olive oil
2 flour tortillas
2 ounces Monterey Jack jalapeño cheese, grated
1 red pepper, roasted, or a jar of roasted red peppers

1. Heat a small saucepan over medium heat. Add the sausage and sauté until cooked through and browned (how long depends on the type of sausage you choose). Remove from the heat. Wipe the skillet clean once it's cool.
2. Trim the tough stem from the mushroom. Sprinkle the other side with salt, pepper, and the oregano. Heat the olive oil in the skillet over medium-high heat until hot. Place the mushroom in the skillet, top side down, and sauté until soft and browned, about three minutes. Flip and sauté on the stem side for another two minutes. Remove from the heat.
3. Finely chop or crumble the sausage and thinly slice the mushroom crosswise.
4. Heat a nonstick or cast-iron skillet over high heat. Place the flour tortilla in the skillet and quickly add the cheese, a few strips of peppers, and either the mushroom or sausage on one half of the tortilla. Fold over the other half and press down with a spatula. Once the tortilla has browned (about 30 seconds), flip carefully onto the other side and brown for another 30 seconds.

Repeat with the second tortilla, cut both quesadillas into wedges, and serve immediately. Once you've got the quesadilla technique down, experiment with different kinds of cheeses, sausages, and vegetables.

Entrée:

Fish with Two Salsas

Fresh salsas are simple to make and taste infinitely better than the store-bought kind. The secret is the interplay of tastes and textures—the acidity of the tomato, the sweetness of the mango and avocado, and the peppery crunch of the red onion. Once you've tried your hand at making these, experiment with whatever looks fresh in your market.

The general rule for cooking fish is 8 to 10 minutes per inch thickness, depending on how well-cooked you like it. Here I suggest broiling the fish steaks, but feel free to slap them on the outdoor grill if you're lucky enough to have one. Serve with white rice or red new potatoes pan-fried with olive oil and a little cumin and cayenne pepper.

1 large tomato, cored and diced
1/2 small red onion, diced
1/4 medium mango
1/2 medium avocado
1 fresh jalapeño
3 tablespoons fresh cilantro
3 tablespoons fresh flat-leaf parsley
1 lime
Two 5-ounce fish steaks (tuna or swordfish work especially well)
salt and pepper
olive oil (optional)

To make the salsas:

1. Divide the tomato and onion evenly between two small bowls.
2. Chop the mango: Slice the fruit lengthwise, being careful to avoid the center pit. Take one of the slices and make regular horizontal and vertical incisions in the flesh (making a crosshatch pattern), being careful not to cut through the skin. Run your knife down the slice to separate the flesh from the skin. If you

member: HWLane

SURVEY: RECIPES

Chicken Marbella

Start 24 hours ahead

2 1/2 lb. of chicken breasts
1/2 cup pitted green olives
1/2 cup pitted prunes
1 1/4 heaping Tb. of minced garlic
2 Tb. dried oregano
salt and pepper
1/4 cup wine vinegar
1/4 cup olive oil
1/2 cup capers
1 Tb. liquid from capers
3 bay leaves

(Add the next day prior to baking)
3/4 cup brown sugar
1/2 cup white wine
1/4 cup finely chopped parsley or cilantro

Put chicken in large Ziploc bags. Finely chop olives and prunes. Mix everything except brown sugar, wine, parsley, or cilantro and pour into bags over chicken to marinate. Seal and refrigerate overnight, turning and mixing several times. Remove chicken and arrange in single layer in shallow baking pan. Spoon marinade over evenly; sprinkle with brown sugar and pour wine around inside edges of pan. Bake uncovered at 350 degrees about 33 minutes, basting occasionally with pan juices. Transfer chicken to serving platter and moisten with pan juices. Sprinkle generously with finely chopped parsley or cilantro.

need to, dice the mango finer so it's the same size as the tomato and the onion. Add to one of the bowls.

3. Chop the avocado: Make a cut all around the fruit lengthwise and then twist to separate the two halves. Whack your knife into the pit, twist, and lift to remove. Cut the flesh as you did the mango. Add the avocado to the other bowl.
4. Finely mince about 1/8 teaspoon of the jalapeño and add to the mango bowl. You might want to wear gloves for this. Be sure to avoid the seeds (the hottest part of the pepper) and wash your hands, knife, and cutting board very carefully when you're done.
5. Mince the cilantro and add it to the mango bowl; mince the parsley and add it to the avocado bowl. Squeeze one half of the lime into each bowl and season with salt and pepper to taste. You can let the salsa sit up to an hour before serving.

To make the fish steaks:

6. Preheat the oven to broil.
7. Place the fish on a baking sheet, season with salt and pepper and rub with a little olive oil if you want.
8. Broil the fish for 8 to 10 minutes per inch of thickness, turning it halfway through the cooking time. Transfer the fish to plates, top with the salsa, and serve immediately.

Dessert:

Candy Ice Cream Sauces

These sauces are unbelievably easy to make. Just make sure to take them off the stove as soon as they're smooth and melted or else you'll end up with a grainy mess. For an even more decadent dessert, you can garnish the ice cream with crumbled candy and a dollop of whipped cream.

member: KatherynJ

SURVEY: RECIPIES

Hungarian Chicken

While in a Budapest hostel, this little old babushka-wearing grandmother cooked up her famous "tennis turkey." After everyone fell in love with it, and being the quick-fix lover that I am, I tried to find something easy that tasted like it once I got home. It may not be the authentic Hungarian grandmother's "tennis turkey," but it does add a little international variety to your menu.

2–4 chicken breasts
1 family-size can of Campbell's Cream of Mushroom Soup
1-4 Tb. dill
wild rice (those little bags of instant rice work well)

Brown the chicken in a sauté pan. Cook the soup (microwave or stove). Stir dill to taste into the soup (this will be your sauce). Cook your rice (microwave or stove). Use the rice to cover the plate. Top with chicken breasts. Use the soup as a sauce over it all.

Peppermint Patty Sauce

Two 1.5-ounce Peppermint Patty candies
1 tablespoon plus 1 teaspoon heavy cream

Break the candy into little pieces and place in the top of a double boiler over medium heat (alternately, place in a heatproof bowl set over a pan of boiling water—just make sure the bottom of the bowl doesn't touch the water). Add the cream. Stir until melted. Pour over the ice cream immediately.

Reeses Peanut Butter Cup Sauce

Two 1.6-ounce packages Reeses peanut butter cups
1 tablespoon heavy cream

Follow the same procedure as for the Peppermint Patty sauce.

Dinner Parties 101

One of the advantages to throwing a dinner party is a refrigerator full of great leftovers. These recipes serve six and will give you at least a weekend's worth of post-party meals. The dip and the dessert are mildly Mediterranean and Middle Eastern in flavor, while the main course is an adaptation of a favorite in the Spanish-speaking Caribbean. Despite these exotic touches, none of the ingredients are particularly expensive or hard to find.

Appetizer:

Poor Man's Caviar (Roasted Eggplant Dip)

Although this dip tastes absolutely nothing like caviar, it's silky texture and smoky flavor are very luxurious. You can make it the day before and keep it in the fridge (just make sure to take it out a few hours before serving) and deal with the garnishes and accompaniments right before your guests arrive.

member: Jenoise
SURVEY: RECIPIES
Frugal can be downright delightfully elegant.

Orange and Yogurt Pankakes with Strawberries
1 cup hulled strawberries
2 teaspoons sugar
1 cup all-purpose flour
pinch kosher salt
3/4 teaspoon double-acting baking powder
1/2 teaspoon baking soda
1 teaspoon grated zest
1/2 cup skim milk
1/2 cup nonfat yogurt

In a bowl, add strawberries and 2 teaspoons of sugar and allow to macerate while you make pancakes. In large bowl, combine flour, salt, baking powder, and baking soda. In another bowl, mix together zest, milk, and yogurt; add to flour mixture. Combine until it just comes together; mixture will be thick. Spray or lightly brush a preheated nonstick skillet with canola oil. Cook pancakes over medium heat. It will take about 3 minutes for the first side and about 1 1/2 minutes for the second. Keep them warm covered with a cloth towel or on plate in an oven set at 150-175 degrees. Top pancakes with strawberry mixture and eat. Serves 2 generously

2 medium-size eggplant
2 small heads of garlic
olive oil
1 cup torn basil leaves
juice of one lemon
salt and pepper
1 tomato
1 red onion
1/4 cup crumbled feta cheese

1. Preheat the oven to 400 degrees. Prick the eggplants several times with a knife and place on a baking sheet, along with the heads of garlic. Drizzle the garlic lightly with some olive oil. Place in the oven and roast until the eggplants are soft and have collapsed somewhat and the outer cloves of garlic are mushy, about 30 to 40 minutes.
2. Remove the eggplants and garlic and set aside to cool.
3. When the eggplants are cool enough to handle, slice the stems off and halve them lengthwise. Scoop out the flesh, discarding as many of the seeds as possible, and put in a food processor or a mixing bowl. Peel the garlic and add it to the eggplant. Add the basil leaves and the lemon juice and turn on the food processor. While it's running, add 1/3 cup plus one tablespoon olive oil in a stream. (If you're doing this by hand, mash the eggplant and garlic together with the back of a spoon until smooth and combined; stir in the basil and lemon juice and whisk in the olive oil.) Season with salt and pepper to taste. Garnish the top with diced tomato, red onion, and/or feta cheese and serve with pita bread, crackers, or slices of good Italian bread toasted and rubbed with a clove of garlic.

   Variations: Use more olive oil for a richer dip or add plain yogurt if you prefer a creamier mixture. You can try this with other herbs—cilantro, oregano (these herbs are strong so start out with 1/4 cup, taste, and add as desired) or parsley with a little thyme—and add pitted black olives or a few anchovies (trust me, no one will know they're in there, but they'll add a delicious saltiness).

   Leftovers: The dip and garnishes make a great omelet or sandwich filling.

Entrée:

Arroz con Pollo

Delicious, hearty, and easy to prepare, chicken is the perfect one-dish entertaining meal. You can use two chickens, each cut into eight pieces. You can buy them packaged this way, get your butcher to do it, or, if you know what you're doing, do it yourself. Alternately, try any combination of white or dark meat you prefer, including skinless, boneless chicken breasts, although this is the blandest way to eat the bird (skin and bones always add flavor). Just make sure to adjust cooking times as noted in the recipe.

As for the wine in the recipe, don't even think about using anything labeled "cooking wine": Never cook with anything you wouldn't drink. If you don't have any wine on hand, substitute with more stock or water.

The *sofrito*, a savory mix of peppers, garlic, onions, and herbs, can be made earlier in the day and refrigerated, and you can brown the chicken right before guests arrive. Once the crowd starts arriving, start the rice and be ready to sit down to dinner in about an hour.

Sofrito
1 red pepper
1 green pepper
1/2 cup onion, chopped fine
3 cloves garlic, minced
3 tablespoons minced parsley
3 tablespoons minced cilantro
salt and pepper

2 chickens, each cut into 8 pieces (or the equivalent)
salt and pepper
1/4 cup olive oil
2 cups regular white rice (not the instant kind)
1 3/4 cups chicken stock (canned or from bouillon cubes is fine)
1/4 cup dry white wine
1 bay leaf

1. Core peppers, halve, and remove seeds and white parts. Chop fine. Combine with the rest of the *sofrito* ingredients and season with salt and pepper to taste. (This can be done in a food processor on "pulse" but be careful not to overprocess; it should still be kind of a chunky mixture, not a purée.)

member: ipswitch

SURVEY: RECIPES

Deli Coleslaw
1/2 cup wine vinegar
1/3 cup vegetable oil
1 teaspoon granulated sugar
1/2 teaspoon salt
1/8 teaspoon pepper
8 cups shredded cabbage
1 cup shredded carrots
1 cup chopped celery
1 small onion, grated

Combine first five ingredients in a jar. Cover and shake vigorously. Chill to blend flavors. In large bowl combine cabbage and remaining ingredients. Shake dressing and pour over cabbage mixture. Toss lightly. Makes 8-10 servings.

member: Andrew_D_G

SURVEY: RECIPES

Cold Sesame Noodles
1/2 lb. thin spaghetti
1/4 cup peanut butter or tahini
1/4 cup warm water
3 Tb. soy sauce
2 Tb. wine vinegar
1 Tb. sesame oil
1 teaspoon chili oil
1 cucumber, cut in 2-inch long slices
1 scallion, chopped

Cook pasta until *al dente*, drain and rinse in cold water. Mix together peanut butter/tahini, water, soy sauce, vinegar, and oils. Toss noodles with cucumber, add and toss the sauce. Top with scallions.

2. Rinse the chicken pieces and trim some of the fat. Season on both sides with salt and pepper.
3. Pour about half the olive oil into a skillet large enough to hold the chicken and rice. (Remember that rice expands a lot during cooking. If you don't have a large enough skillet, you can divide the dish between two smaller ones.) Heat the oil over medium-high heat until hot. Add the chicken, skin side down, and brown for about five minutes. Turn and brown on the other side, about three to five minutes. Whatever you do, don't crowd the pan—only do a few at a time to give them room to cook properly. When browned, but not cooked through (don't worry about salmonella, you'll finish cooking the chicken later), set aside on a plate and cover.
4. Discard the fat from the skillet and wipe clean. Add the rest of the olive oil and heat over medium heat. Add the *sofrito* and sauté until it starts to smell really delicious, about 3 minutes. Add the rice and stir to coat all the grains with the oil. Pour in the stock, wine (and pour a glass for yourself while you're at it), and bay leaf and bring to a gentle boil. Add a few pinches of salt, cover tightly with a lid or aluminum foil so that no steam escapes, and turn the heat way down.
5. After 15 minutes, add the chicken, skin side up. Cover. (If using light and dark meat, add the dark meat first and cover, wait five minutes, then add the light meat and cover.) Let simmer for another 15 minutes or so (less if you're using boneless skinless chicken breasts), until the chicken is cooked through but not dried out.
6. Uncover the chicken, remove from the heat and allow to sit 5 to 10 minutes before serving. At this stage, you can also stir in a 15-ounce can of chick-peas, 1/2 cup of green olives, or a few roasted red peppers cut into strips to warm through. Serve.

   Leftovers: Nothing's better to pick at than cold chicken, but rice doesn't hold up quite as well in the fridge. Try making croquettes: Throw some stale bread (such as any leftover pita from the first course) in a food processor to make bread crumbs. Season with salt, pepper, and paprika and add to some shredded chicken and rice. Stir in an egg or two (just enough to bind the mixture together), form into patties the size of your palm, and sauté in a skillet with a little melted butter and a little olive oil until browned.

Baked Apples

You can prepare the apples up through step 3 in the afternoon and keep them in the refrigerator, well-covered. Take them out right before you sit down to dinner and finish them after you're done eating the main course. While they bake, your guests will have plenty of time to digest and appreciate the smell wafting from the oven. Serve with heavy cream, ice cream, or frozen yogurt.

8 apples (Red Delicious work especially well)
1 cup chopped walnuts
2 Tb. honey
1 teaspoon ground cardamom
8 teaspoons butter
1 1/2 cups water
1/4 cup sugar
4 strips of lemon zest

1. Core the apples to within 1/2 inch of the bottom and cut a strip of peel off the top of each one.
2. Combine the nuts, honey, and cardamom in a bowl.
3. Stuff the apples with the nut mixture, dot with a teaspoon of butter and set in a baking pan.
4. Pour the water into the pan, add the sugar and strips of zest, and bake, covered with foil, until soft but not mushy, 40 minutes to an hour (if you feel like it, baste the apples a few times as they cook). Remove from the oven and serve immediately.

   Leftovers: Left whole or mashed with vanilla yogurt, baked apples make a great morning-after breakfast.

member: shauna_ru
SURVEY: RECIPIES
Pacific Chowder
Cream of potato soup
1 can tuna
dill, to taste
optional:
bacon flavored bits
chopped onion
chopped celery
chopped fresh parsley or cilantro

Warm the soup and tuna, flavor with dill. You can add any of the optional ingredients—or some of your own favorites—and simmer. If you have the time and desire, make homemade potato soup, put all ingredients in a slow cooker and simmer most of the day.

Eating Well

If the "four food groups" are still your idea of good nutrition, you may be eating yourself into an early grave.

by Andrea Coller

Gone are the days when a bacon cheeseburger with lettuce and tomato passed for a balanced meal. Low-fat eating has become a near religion, red meat's gotten rarer (if you'll pardon the pun), and you can get a salad practically anywhere—even at McDonald's. Unless you've been part of a cryogenics experiment for the last thirty years, you've probably got a pretty good idea about what you shouldn't eat.

But short of glib prescriptions like "eat more vegetables" or "drink more milk" it's hard to get any really useful advice on what you *should* eat—that is, what your body needs and how a busy, modern person like yourself can manage to work these things into your diet without turning it into a full-time job. Here's some basic info and some helpful hints to start you on the path from not eating badly to really eating well.

Face Reality

The first thing we can do is stop kidding ourselves. It may be convenient to pretend that coleslaw is a vegetable, or that chicken salad is good for you because it's made from chicken, or that whatever you eat while you're standing up—or off someone else's plate—doesn't count, but this kind of willful ignorance can go a long way toward sabotaging your diet, both nutritionally and calorically. There are no "miracle" foods. If you eat a whole box of fat-free cookies, you've still eaten a whole box of cookies and all their attendant sugar (and calories). Use your common sense. Those softball-sized muffins you buy in the store? These are not the same as the 2.5-inch muffins your granny used to bake for breakfast. They're about five times bigger and, as is the case with much mass-marketed food, have more fat and sugar than your granny ever imagined cramming into one of her brans. They taste like cake because—that's right—they are cake. The worst ones can pack a whopping 1,000 calories. The point being, if you want cake, have cake, but don't confuse it with a healthy breakfast.

Ditto for bagels, which have also grown to elephantine proportions. Don't think that just because they're fat and cholesterol free they don't count—just like any other kind of basic bread, they have about eighty calories per ounce—and some of those super-dense monster bagels can weigh up to six ounces. That's nearly 500 calories—not including the butter or cream cheese. Read labels, compare serving sizes, trust your instincts. Control your own portions, even when eating out. You can ask the deli man for less meat. He may look at you funny, but you can. You can also take meat off a sandwich. The average person's protein needs can be filled with a piece of meat, fish, or poultry that's about the size of a deck of cards. If you've got two or three decks on that roll, you've got too much. Which brings us to a related issue: Size does matter.

The good old four basic food groups from grade school—meats, fruits and veggies, dairy products, and grains—have given way to the USDA's Food Guide Pyramid, which offers general guidelines on how much of what we're supposed to be eating. This lovely graphic element, used to illustrate magazine articles on nutrition or to add a health-conscious note to the back of your cereal box, advises us to eat between six and eleven servings of grains daily, and two to three servings of protein, including lean meats, fish, poultry, and legumes. The widespread use of the Food Guide Pyramid in this manner has, however, left the national collective mind harboring one unanswered question: What the hell is a serving? This question lurks in the heads and hearts of all Americans, yet it goes largely unasked, probably because we understand, on some instinctive level, that what the government considers a healthy serving is not going to turn out to be the standard portion size at Denny's.

"The food pyramid was never designed to stand alone, but it

member: nurse

SURVEY: EATING WELL

It does not have to be expensive or inconvenient to eat better. Most people simply have to evolve into better habits. Some relatively new studies have revealed some very simple ways to enhance longevity and quality of life. Here are several basic steps to start on a more healthy diet:

1. Eat butter or olive oil, throw away any hydrogenated oils in your pantry. Hydrogenated oils contribute to cancer, heart disease, and a host of other ailments.
2. Fish, broiled or baked, two times a week will lower your cholesterol.
3. Try to eat fresh fruit and vegetables, frozen and canned foods lack essential nutrients for good health.
4. If it's processed it lacks nutrients, only whole grains contribute to colon health.

member: WendieS

SURVEY: EATING WELL

Eat organic! The FDA "maximum allowable" for different pesticides does not consider that they are all joining up in our livers and the results are exponential increases in toxicity! Don't believe the big food corps or the government.

took on a life of its own," explains John P. Foreyt, Ph.D., director of the Behavioral Medicine Research Center at Baylor College of Medicine in Houston. "It's supposed to be accompanied by other materials." Like the ones that tell you how big a portion is.

If you wish to remain in the comforting dusk of ignorance, clinging to the hope that a 22-ounce porterhouse is considered one portion, skip the following section. If not, without further ado . . .

member: TieDy
SURVEY: EATING WELL
My husband was recently diagnosed with Type 2 diabetes, so our whole lifestyle had to change. We used to go for convenience every time, even though we both knew it was not good for any of us. Now we eat a lot of skinless, boneless chicken (breasts) and lots of vegetables. Its been the hardest on the kids, who lived their whole lives eating junk. As far as transgressions, yeah, we do allow a little junk food in our lives, if we didn't we'd really binge.

Portion Sizes

OILS AND SWEETS: The pyramid says "use sparingly." They won't even give a serving size. But they're talking teaspoons, not cups. This includes salad dressing and the greasy brown sauce on your Chinese food.

MILK, YOGURT, AND CHEESE: Two to three servings per day. A serving is 1 cup of milk or yogurt, 1.5 ounces "natural" cheese, or 2 ounces processed cheese.

MEAT, FISH, POULTRY, AND LEGUMES: Two to three servings a day. A serving is 2–3 ounces of lean meat, poultry, or fish. Or substitute 1/2 cup cooked beans, 1 egg, or 2 tablespoons peanut butter per ounce of meat.

VEGETABLES: Three to five servings a day. A serving is 1 cup raw leafy vegetables; 1/2 cup all other vegetables cooked, chopped, or raw; or 3/4 cup of vegetable juice.

FRUIT: Two to four servings a day. A serving is 1 medium apple, banana, or orange; 1/2 cup chopped, cooked, or canned fruit; or 3/4 cup of fruit juice.

BREAD AND GRAINS: Six to eleven servings a day. A serving is 1 slice of bread, 1 ounce dry cereal, 1 ounce cooked cereal, rice, or pasta.

Okay? Now you know. A typical meal should look more like what you get on a hospital or cafeteria tray than what they serve you at Red Lobster's Crustacean Fest. Sorry.

Taking It to the Next Level

It's shocking, but it's true: You can fulfill the guidelines of the food pyramid perfectly and still have a lot of room for improvement in your diet. Starting at the top of the pyramid, one oil is not necessarily as good (or as bad) as another. Studies show that monounsaturated oils, like *olive* and *canola*, can help reduce the LDL (bad) cholesterol while maintaining the HDL (good) cholesterol levels. Polyunsaturated oils, like corn or safflower, lower both—which is better than butter or lard, which are saturated fats and raise the LDL. Somewhere toward the bottom of the churn are partially hydrogenated and hydrogenated oils—known as trans fats—like margarine and Crisco, which are found in many packaged foods and turned from liquid oil to a solid through a chemical process. There's evidence that they raise cholesterol (how much is unclear) and some believe your body doesn't really know how to deal with these manmade hybrids. It wouldn't hurt to steer clear of them in favor of some nice olive oil.

Getting enough *fiber* and *calcium* are concerns that are largely ignored, but that are important to good health. Calcium helps maintain bone density and can prevent osteoporosis in later life, and fiber helps clean toxins out of your system, lowering your risk for such nasty ailments as colon and rectal cancer (and, yes, fiber helps prevent occasional irregularity). Calcium is present in some vegetables, like kale and collard greens, and in dairy products. And fiber is found in both fruits and vegetables and in whole grains.

Both *fish* and *soy* are currently being touted by experts as nutritional powerhouses, and both are worth including in a balanced diet. Two servings of fish a week have been associated with lower heart attack risk, among other benefits, and groups who include a lot of soy in their diets have lower rates of heart attack, breast cancer, endometrial cancer, prostate cancer, colon cancer, and osteoporosis than those who don't. Soy can be eaten in many forms, including tofu, soy "nuts" (roasted soybeans), soy milk, soy burgers or franks, and textured soy protein that stands in for meat in vegetarian entrées (like veggie chili).

member: brownfox

SURVEY: EATING WELL

I used to have a horrible diet. I would eat meals at random times and some meals would be junk food while others would be huge dinners. And I thought that since I was skinny, I didn't have to worry about fat and calories and other health concerns. Then I found out that I was anemic and had high cholesterol. Now, I've changed my diet completely. I make sure that I eat salads at least once a day, and if I don't have money for a full meal, I make sure that whatever I do buy is healthy. I still splurge though, but every time I eat a pint of ice cream or a ton of candy bars, I make sure I balance it by drinking water, and eating salads and fruits.

member: Lynnguist

SURVEY: EATING WELL

Occasional "transgressions" are a normal, healthy part of any diet regimen. Eating healthy is a lifelong commitment but if you deny yourself certain foods because you believe they are bad for you, you will only sabotage your commitment to a more healthy diet. Remember, it is what you eat *most* of the time that counts.

These are just some of the places where simple changes within a nutritional category can make for major payoffs. In short, they're ways to help you get more nutritional bang for your calorie.

Eating well is about making smart choices. Once you begin to see the differences between your options in nutritional terms, you can make decisions about what you eat based not just on taste, but also on what you're getting for the calories you consume. Here are some tips for making eating more healthily as painless a process as possible.

Snack Smart

- Keep a fruit bowl in your office. Bring in a variety of fruit at the beginning of each week so you'll have a choice of healthy options on hand.
- Popcorn is a better snack than chips—not super nutritious, but fat free if you air-pop your own and skip the butter. Baked corn chips with salsa, fat-free bean dip, or dip made from nonfat yogurt instead of sour cream is also a good bet. Or try a cereal snack blend (remember Chex Mix?), which is bound to have more fiber and less fat than regular chips—add a sprinkling of nuts, or, even better, soy nuts, for a protein kick.
- Dried fruits are a good sweet snack—a bit high in sugar, but nutritious and fiber rich.

Sneaking in Those Fruits and Veggies

- You can substitute beans for meat in lots of recipes—lasagna, chili, casseroles. Or try sandwich spreads like hummus, which is made of chick-peas, instead of meat or cheese.
- Add raisins, grapes, pineapple, or apple chunks to meat dishes or to stuffing to get a little more fruit into your diet.
- Stick vegetables wherever they'll fit. Get as many veggie toppings as they'll give you on your sandwich (lettuce, tomato, sprouts, onion, whatever). Bulk up soups or chili or add interest to salads with grated carrots or zucchini. Add chopped broccoli or spinach to tomato sauce for use with pasta. Order veggie toppings like broccoli or spinach on your pizza instead of pepperoni.

member: alison22

SURVEY: EATING WELL

I cut out animal products because of my horror at how animals suffer on factory farms, but I was happy to discover all the health benefits that came along with my decision. I hardly ever get sick, I have more energy, my skin and hair are healthier, and I never have trouble maintaining my weight. I'd be vegan even if there weren't a single health benefit, but it's so nice that there are!

member: rgould

SURVEY: EATING WELL

Our entire family has shifted our diet to include nothing with more than 25–30 percent of calories from fat. Even the kids have adapted. I find that I do not have trouble with heartburn and we have all slimmed down some and become more healthy.

- Make your own soda by mixing seltzer and 100 percent fruit juice (not punch or "juice drink"), or dilute fruit juice by half to cut the calories while adding more fruit to your diet.

Fitting in Fiber

- Leave peel on when you mash potatoes.
- Try a high-fiber cereal at breakfast—it will fill you up and go a long way toward helping you fulfill your fiber needs for the day.
- Try oat bran as filler in meatloaf or as a breading on chicken instead of using white bread crumbs.
- Ditch refined white flour from your diet as often as possible. Eat sandwiches on whole wheat, buy whole grain pasta, eat bran muffins instead of blueberry, oatmeal cookies instead of chocolate chip—you get the idea. It's the difference between empty carbs and more nutritious, high-fiber ones. And foods made from whole grains also fill you up better than ones made from refined flour.

Substitute

- You can use low- or nonfat plain yogurt instead of sour cream in almost any situation—for dips, dressings, whatever—and save yourself tons of fat intake.
- Use skim milk instead of whole or 2 percent in everything—including cakes, puddings, and other recipes.
- Two egg whites can stand in for one whole egg in recipes—without the cholesterol.
- Applesauce can often substitute for butter or shortening in cakes, breads, etc. Experiment.
- The array of reduced- and nonfat substitutes for full-fat products is dizzying. Trade in your whole milk cheeses, full-fat mayonnaise, and oil-heavy dressings as often as you can. "Right now you can get anything nonfat," says Kimberly O'Brien, Ph.D., an assistant professor at the Center for Human Nutrition at Johns Hopkins University School of Hygiene and Public Health in Baltimore. "A lot of people are afraid to take dairy because of the calories, but it's an excellent source of nutrition, including calcium. Nonfat dairy is very good for you."

member: CROOKB
SURVEY: EATING WELL
The healthiest diet I've found is the American Diabetes Diet. I'm not a diabetic but the amount of food allowed on even a 1,500 calorie a day diet is a lot.

member: maria99
SURVEY: EATING WELL
I maintain a balance between exercise and healthy eating that allows occasional treats like ice cream. But yes, I do feel guilty if I haven't exercised in days and am eating a candy bar.

member: ThorTrains
SURVEY: EATING WELL
I don't think "vegan" diets are all that healthy—any herbos I know have to take vitamins to supplement their diets. Humankind is an omnivorous species. I think the Quakers said it best: "Eat, and take no shame!"

Make Eating Well Easy on Yourself

- Buy precut carrots and bagged, prewashed salads. It may seem absurdly extravagant, but healthy convenience foods are worth the cost if buying them means you'll actually use them instead of letting that head of lettuce turn mushy and brown in the back of the crisper while you order in Moo Shu pork. And if you toss in some tuna, some capers, and a light dressing, you've got a very healthy lunch for less than a Big Mac meal would cost—and in less time than it takes to say "Supersize it."
- Used canned or frozen veggies. They count, and they require less preplanning than fresh ones, which have to be used in a timely manner.
- Garlic and onions are high in antioxidents—if you hate to chop (or know you'll never get the smell off your hands) buy a bag of chopped frozen onion and toss it into recipes.
- Make your own convenience foods. Freeze small portions of healthy meals—like soups, stews, chili, and pasta sauces—to reheat later. Never cook for one meal—make enough to freeze and eat on a night you don't have the energy to get the pots out.
- Keep some frozen Weight Watchers or Lean Cuisine meals on hand. They're quick dinner in a pinch (which just might save you from a pizza with everything after a terrible day at work) and they're relatively balanced, reasonably low fat, and calorie and portion controlled.
- Have a canned meal if you must. When you're on the run, a low-fat granola bar, or even a Slimfast or Boost is better than nothing. These drinks have some nutrients, and they're a source of energy, so at least you'll keep your body running until you have time for a real meal—and you won't be as tempted to gorge yourself when you do.

member: Ian W Halliday

SURVEY: MOOD FOOD

While I was at college, it was marzipan. About 3 pounds a week. Now that I am older and wiser, I don't go quite so mad. I used to buy 1/2 pound blocks and cut them up into chunks about 1/2 inch square. It was great. Nothing could improve my mood like a couple of mugs of coffee, a slab of marzipan, and the fragrance of a couple of josssticks burning in my room. But that was a *very* long time ago.

Don't Make It Too Easy

A diet of bran cereal at breakfast, an apple and a turkey sandwich on whole wheat for lunch, and a vegetable stew with brown rice for dinner may sound impeccable, but not if you eat it every day. Eating healthy in busy and demanding times isn't easy, and it's very tempting, when you find something you like that fits the bill, to stick with it. Sure, it's a little boring, but at least you know it's good for you, and you can stop worrying about it. Well, actually, it's not as good for you as it sounds. Fish and turkey both fit the protein category, but each contains somewhat different nutrients. Variety is integral to eating well. "Even if you have the same ten recipes you use for dinner, get something different when you eat out," says Belinda Smith, a registered dietician with the Metabolic Research Group at the University of Kentucky at Lexington. "Or rotate side dishes, but somehow get some variety into your diet."

Don't Get Sabotaged

- Don't just ask for turkey when you order a sandwich at the deli counter. You'll probably get "turkey roll," a processed pressboard version made of scraps that's much higher in fat than turkey breast. Ask for turkey breast, or check the display for a brand name you know and ask for it specifically.
- Take the skin off your chicken or turkey. That's where 25 percent of the fat is. And go for the white meat, which has less fat than the dark.
- Read labels. Before you buy what you think is whole wheat bread, check the ingredients—if whole wheat isn't the first ingredient, the bread doesn't contain enough whole grain to make it any better for you than Wonder.
- Normally low-cal, low-fat foods can be turned into monsters in the hands of a deli-counter staffer or the short-order cook. Save your tuna salad sandwiches for home consumption—commercial tuna salad is one of the worst choices behind the glass (chicken salad and egg salad are right up there too). Remember—mayonnaise costs far less than tuna fish, so restaurants and delis add as much mayo as the tuna will take.

member: angelblue

SURVEY: MOOD FOOD

Comfort food depends on the kind of comfort . . . Morning courage: oatmeal, steaming hot, with raisins. Anger at East Coast winter weather is soothed by hot spiced apple cider (none of this warm apple juice business). Refuge from office politics means a bowl of soup and bread. Heartbreak is always a call for chocolate (of course). Nothing too surprising.

A WORD ON WEIGHT-LOSS DIETS

Low-calorie dieters have about as much success losing weight and keeping it off as drunken macho men have at winning those carnival games where you try to knock down the toy cats with a baseball. If you'd like to be slimmer, try to stop thinking about food as recreation or as an indulgence, and think about it as fuel. Instead of counting calories, add some exercise to your routine, including a weight-training program that will increase your muscle mass, which raises your metabolism.

If you want to maintain a healthy weight, don't skip meals—eat early and often. "We tend to overeat or to make bad choices when we're really hungry," explains Rebecca Reeves, assistant professor at Baylor College of Medicine in Houston. And eat three meals a day. "They don't have to be at seven, twelve, and five, but regular meals are important," Reeves says. "Even if you need a couple of snacks, that's fine too. Study after study has shown that the body needs frequent sources of fuel. The meal everybody skips the most is breakfast," she adds. "They say they're not hungry, but ask them how late they eat at night—that's probably why."

Here's a positive way to help curb overeating: Instead of trying not to eat certain foods, or relying on willpower to keep yourself from eating unhealthily, try a more active approach. Most Americans don't even get close to their recommended daily intake of dietary fiber. Try to make getting enough fiber a daily goal, and you may find you're way too full to binge on a full bag of corn chips or to find yourself so hungry you'll settle for whatever's close at hand.

member: sue o'neill

SURVEY: MOOD FOOD

Chocolate. There's nothing like it, and no good low-calorie substitute, either. It has to have the feel, the bulk, and the melt to make it comforting. Mood altering? I should say so! It should be a controlled substance. And I'm a chocolate snob, too; I like the *good* stuff, the pricey Merkens or the Toblerone or, if I'm desperate enough, Newman's Own milk chocolate. In fact, the anxiety of setting down these thoughts for public consumption is stressing me out; I've gotta get a handful of chips out of that five-pound bag I just mail-ordered from the King Arthur catalog.

A Note to Aspiring Vegetarians

Vegetarianism can be a healthy lifestyle *if* you recognize that you still have to follow all the same rules as everyone else—and then some. In addition to eating your quota of fruits, veggies, and grains in order to make up for the lack of meat protein in your diet, you'll have to increase consumption of certain foods, including peas, beans, lentils, nuts, seeds, whole grains, soy protein products like tofu, and, if you're willing to eat any animal-based foods at all, milk, cheese, yogurt, and eggs. So if you're considering becoming a vegetarian for health reasons, understand that you'll have to work a little harder to get all the nutrients your body needs. And if you want to live a meatless life because you can't bring yourself to eat Bambi, don't do it on a diet of peanut butter and jelly sandwiches and moral superiority.

Taking Responsibility

Finally, eating well means accepting the idea that what you eat affects the quality of your life. You can't change your genes, but you can make good choices based on good information when it comes to your diet. This means following the rules, but it also means being skeptical sometimes, and trusting yourself, since different studies sometimes offer conflicting information on the benefits or dangers of different foods. With that said, here are two warnings.

Just because the government says you can eat it, doesn't mean it's good for you.

Olestra, an artificial fat, has been approved by the government despite studies that show it flushes vitamins A and E from your system and can cause gastrointestinal distress, resulting in (you'll excuse the expression) "anal leakage" and "loose stools." Most experts agree that Olestra probably isn't unsafe if used in extreme moderation—and, as Belinda Smith at the University of Kentucky put it, "If you eat enough you'd self-regulate—with the GI problems, and all."

member: VLemley

SURVEY: MOOD FOOD

There's nothing like making bread to sooth one's ire. The very act of beating the living #%*$ out of the dough is soothing. And you get *praised* and *rewarded* for it! The harder and longer you "work" it the better the loaf! And when the sweet smell of baking fills the house all one can think of is hot bread with real butter.

If fat-free french fries still sound too good to pass up, don't say you weren't warned.

Personal discretion is also advised regarding aspartame, a.k.a Equal or NutraSweet—the sugar substitute. "The studies on it look okay," says Smith, "but there may be individual sensitivity, so judge for yourself." There are no concrete answers about the long-term effects of aspartame, but some individuals have reported side effects they attributed to the artificial sweetener that range from headaches to brain tumors. Again, you decide.

Just because the government doesn't say you can't eat it doesn't mean it's not bad for you.

The Food and Drug Administration does not regulate "dietary supplements." They don't ask what's in them, they don't set guidelines for dosage, they don't ban the dangerous ones until enough people die. Just because something is "all natural" doesn't mean it's healthy or safe. Even too much of certain vitamins can be toxic. Most physicians feel it's unnecessary even to take a daily multivitamin—especially if you have a well-balanced diet. If you do choose to venture into the world of dietary supplements and herbal remedies, advise your doctor, buy yourself a good guide by a reputable expert, and proceed with caution.

Homebrewing

If you like to cook and drink beer, there may be a talented homebrewer inside of you. Hey, as a hobby it sure beats stamp collecting.

by Ethan Zuckerman

There are ninety bottles of beer in my bedroom. I'm not throwing a party, and contrary to popular opinion, I'm not an alcoholic. Instead, I've been seduced by the world of homebrewing and I can't escape. Nor would I want to. Homebrewing combines two of my great loves: cooking and beer. And as a hobby, it sure beats stamp collecting.

It's remarkably easy to start brewing at home. To get started, you need less than $100 of equipment and about four hours, split between two weekends. Plus you've got to have access to a decent kitchen, and it helps to have a dishwasher and a bathtub. Oh yeah, you'll also need a few folks to help you drink the brew afterward.

Warning: Don't take up homebrewing to save money. Yes, once you've built a good brewing kitchen, you can brew two cases of fine beer for about $20. But by the time you've built a good brewing kitchen, you'll be hooked and buying all sorts of neat gadgets and spending even more money. This is a great hobby but a lousy money saver.

So how do you make beer anyway? It's pretty simple. When you mix sugars with yeast and leave them alone for a while, you get alcohol. If you're using fruit to provide your sugar, you get wine. If you use malted barley to provide your sugar, you get beer. A beer made solely with malted barley would be pretty vile—very sweet and syrupy. Several hundred years ago, some bright folks figured out a solution to the problem—hops. Hops are aromatic, bitter herbs, which give beer its characteristic bite.

member: Rachel

SURVEY: HOMEBREWING

My favorite homebrew ever was the ginger beer I brewed about two years ago. It was a pretty basic nutbrown ale-type recipe, with four or five inches of fresh gingerroot grated into a cheesecloth bag and steeped in the wort for the last fifteen minutes before it was siphoned into the carboy and the yeast was pitched. The beer turned out great—just gingery enough to have a real kick, but not so gingery that it didn't taste like beer anymore.

People have added thousands of different items to beer over the years, but all beers come down to the same four essential ingredients: water, malt, yeast, and hops. In fact, there's a law in Germany that these four are the *only* ingredients allowed in beer. Of course, if you're not in Germany, you can toss in honey, Irish moss, cherries, coffee, orange peels, or chili peppers. Sounds like fun, huh?

Building a Brew Kitchen

It costs a little money to put together enough equipment to make your first batch of beer. Try not to think of the money as one lump sum, but as an investment that you can amortize over your first few brews. Or, get a bunch of friends interested in brewing to chip in and share the equipment.

Here's what you absolutely, positively need to buy:

- A honking big kettle. Preferably 20 quarts; at least 16 quarts. The cheapest kettles you can get are enamel canning kettles. They run about $10–$15 bucks at your local grocery store. But you'll be a much happier person if you buy a decent stainless steel one. Mine cost $25 at Walmart.
- A long plastic spoon.
- A glass carboy. Basically, this is the same thing as the 5-gallon water containers you find on every watercooler in every office in the United States. Except you need a glass one.
- Stopper and airlock for the carboy. Don't get the three-piece "bubbler" airlock—get an S-lock.
- Big plastic funnel for filling the carboy.
- Bottle capper.
- Racking tube and bottle filler. These are a couple of pieces of Plexiglass tubing that make it a great deal easier to get beer out of the carboy and into your bottles.
- Five additional feet of standard plastic tubing.
- Fine mesh bags for your malt and hops. Look for ones with drawstring and very fine mesh.
- Iodine, to sterilize all your equipment, an investment that will save you a great deal of heartache (not to mention possible heartburn, dysentery, or botulism) in the long run.

- Bottle caps. You'll need fifty for your first batch.
- Bottles. You need bottles made for pry-off caps. Screwtops won't cut it. Some brew stores will sell you clean bottles. Or you could just make the commitment to drink forty-eight bottles of beer. The most valued are those reusable Grolsch bottles with the white flip tops.

Total cost to put all this together—under $60, less if you've already got a suitable kettle.

For a Few Dollars More...

Here are some items that will make your brewing life a good deal happier for just a few extra bucks.

- Hydrometer, which measures the specific gravity of fluids. The specific gravity of your brew is the best indication of the right time to move it from the fermenter into the bottles. Also, you need accurate hydrometer readings to calculate the alcohol content of your beer.
- Thermometer, so you don't have to rely on guesswork to figure out the appropriate time to add yeast to a brew.
- Scale. You want a scale that's big enough to weigh a couple of pounds of malt, but fine enough to measure down to a quarter of an ounce.
- Five-gallon plastic bucket. Make sure it's "food-grade" plastic and not one previously used to hold drywall compound. A clean plastic bucket is a huge help when you're bottling your beer.
- Brushes. One to clean the carboy, another to clean the bottles.

Choosing a Beer Recipe

It's time to pick a recipe for your first beer. For your first brew, try a recipe that uses malt syrup rather than all grains. What's the difference? Professional brewers make a "mash" out of a mixture of different kinds of malted barley. They cook the barley in water at temperatures between 150 and 170 degrees. Once the grains are strained out, there's a sweet, thick liquid called "wort" left.

member: Waldhorn

SURVEY: HOMEBREWING

I had been brewing some decent suds and I was ready for something unique. As I finished off the last of my ale I made a decision. I like beer and I like margaritas, why not combine them? It is a decision that haunts me to this day. It was a simple idea really; to my carboy I added a bottle of tequila and the juice of a dozen limes (did I mention I had been finishing off some ale at the time?). Well, within twelve hours the concoction was bubbling and hissing loudly. The brew seemed sinister, and yes . . . alive. Never had I seen such a powerful fermentation. I would not have been surprised if the carboy had asked to borrow the car keys. As it was I am convinced that the brew was moving around my apartment as I slept. Thankfully, soon the rumbling subsided and the bottling process went normally. Two weeks later, I returned from a camping trip to find glass on the carpet and a greenish stain which had hardened into a gelatinous mass in the kitchen. A bottle had exploded. No problem, one bottle, big deal. I sat down to collect my thoughts before tackling the mess. Suddenly a blast shook me from my reverie. We now fast forward to a man wearing a borrowed catcher's chest plate and a welding mask making twenty-six trips to the dumpster. Friends shouting directions due to my impaired welder's vision, "Right a bit, now left, slower! Now throw!" Yes, we did try to drink the brew, some even kept a small sip down for more than three minutes. But the vast bulk of liquid ended its life explosively with a sickening smell of lime hanging in the air.

You can make wort from grains, but it's an undertaking and probably not something you want to try for your first brew. Instead, you can buy malt extract, which is basically condensed wort in a can. A lot of folks try to combine the convenience of extract brewing with the flavor of grain brewing by making a wort out of a combination of extract and grain.

And that's what I did. I tried to mimic Bass Ale, one of my favorite British beers. Follow this recipe, or choose a recipe of your own (see sidebar on page 208) and follow the same steps:

Wyeast #1028 (London Ale) (If your brew store doesn't sell Wyeast, or if you're hoping to save some money, try one of the better dry yeasts: EDME, M&F, or Whitbread.)
1 pound crystal malt (Lovibond 40)
1 pound dark brown sugar
5 pounds bronze Tru-Malt extract syrup (If you can't find Tru-Malt, you can substitute a golden or pale syrup, preferably a British Pale.)
1 ounce Northern Brewer hops
1 ounce Fuggles hops
1/4 pound corn sugar for bottling

Cost of materials for this brew: $21.50 or thereabouts ($18.50 if you use a dry yeast).

The Brewing Process

1. Preparing the yeast (if you're using dry yeast, skip this step). You'll need to plan your brewing a little bit ahead of time, since Wyeast needs to be started twenty-four hours in advance to give the yeasties a chance to get lively. Wyeast comes in a flat foil package with a bulge in it. Lay the package on a counter or a table, press the package so that the bulge is near the top, and hit the packet hard with your hand until you break the bulge. Knead the package for a little while and then put it in a warm place and leave it alone for 24 hours. The package should puff up as the yeast starts producing CO_2. If it doesn't puff up, you may have gotten dead yeast. Toss it and try another package.

2. Preparing your kitchen

When your yeast is ready, get your kitchen ready for some brewing. Clean off the counters and empty the sink. Fill up your brewing kettle with four gallons of water and put it on to boil. Grab four clean gallon milk jugs. Fill them with tap water and add iodine solution in the proportions described on the bottle. Swish the iodine around and then let the sterilizing solution sit in the jugs for at least ten minutes. That should kill off anything nasty that might have been growing in the jugs, waiting to contaminate your beer.

3. Cleanliness is next to godliness

A brief digression about cleanliness: No matter how big a slob you may be, you've got to make sure that anything that touches your beer is clean. The art of brewing is getting yeast to grow in your beer while preventing anything else from doing so. Some brewers use chlorine bleach to sterilize their equipment, others run stuff through the dishwasher. My brewing partner and I have ruined two batches because of nonsterile equipment, so I'm now a convert to iodine. Don't let anything touch your beer unless it's been boiled for several minutes or soaked in an iodine solution. Period.

Why are you boiling this water? To sterilize and dechlorinate it. (If you don't feel like purifying all this water, you could buy a few gallons of spring water from the grocery store instead.) Once the water is boiled, put a stopper in your sink and dump all the iodine water into the sink. Now you've got a sterilizing bath for all your brewing equipment. Fill the sterilized jugs with the boiled sterilized water and put them in the fridge.

member: jbuss

SURVEY: HOMEBREWING

Coriander seed freshly crushed (but not chopped to bits) is a *great* addition to any beer recipe. The seed will also hide commonly made mistakes, making beers more palatable when they have had too much malt (tastes like alcohol) or too many hops (tastes too bitter) added in the boil.

4. Make a mini-mash

Pour the pound of crystal malt into a large mesh bag and tie it off. Use a rolling pin (or any other blunt object) to crush the grain. You want to crack open the kernels, exposing the inside, not turn the grain into dust.

Put a gallon of cold tap water into your brew pot, add the mesh bag, and heat the water until it boils. When the water boils, remove the mesh bag, letting the water drain into the pot. You'll notice that in the few minutes the grain was in the pot, it turned the water yellowish brown and you've got a pungent smell filling your kitchen. You've got the beginnings of a wort.

Add two more gallons of tap water to the brew pot and let the water temperature increase to a boil again. Pour in the brown sugar, a cup at a time, stirring vigorously. When the sugar dissolves, add the next cupful until you've used the entire pound of sugar. Open the malt extract and let it drain into the pot while you stir (this is probably a two person operation unless you're remarkably strong). You've got to stir like crazy, because there's a lot of sugar in this brew and you don't want anything sticking to the bottom and burning.

Once the wort is boiling again, put the ounce of Northern Brewer hops into your smaller mesh bag, tie it tightly and toss it into the brew. These are your boiling hops, and they'll sit in your brew for the next hour. In fifty-five minutes, you'll add (in their own small mesh bag) an ounce of Fuggles hops—your finishing hops.

5. Prepare for fermentation

Keep stirring the brew every couple of minutes, making sure that nothing's sticking to the bottom of the pot. While the brew boils, you can get your carboy ready. Fill it with 5 gallons of tap water and add an appropriate amount of iodine solution. Put your airlock assembly, carboy stopper, funnel, thermometer, and 5-foot length of tubing into the iodine solution in the sink. When they've soaked for fifteen minutes, drain the water out of the carboy, fill the airlock with boiled water (from one of the jugs in the fridge), and fit the stopper and airlock onto the carboy.

When the finishing hops have been in the brew for five minutes, take out both hopsacks and turn off the heat. Take the airlock and stopper out of the carboy and put your funnel there instead. Pour the hot wort from your boiling pot into the carboy.

It helps to have at least two sets of hands for this step. One person should hold the funnel so that it's not completely seated in the neck of the carboy. If air can't get out of the carboy at the same time that liquid is getting in, the wort will pop and spurt, possibly burning you. Be very careful.

Once you've poured the wort in, add water from one of the jugs to fill the carboy almost to the top. Swish the mixture around to mix the water and the wort.

6. Cool the wort

Your beer should now be pretty hot—if you were to pour yeast into it right now, the yeast would die. You've got to cool the wort down. Unfortunately, you've got to cool the beer in a hurry—if the beer remains hot for too long, the chance that the mixture will get infected increases and certain flavor compounds will break down, making the beer less tasty. Take the airlock off the carboy but leave the stopper in and slowly lower the carboy into a bathtub filled with cold water. Be very careful not to bang the carboy against the tub, and don't place the carboy directly under the faucet—the carboy is quite fragile while undergoing this temperature change.

When the bottom of the carboy feels cool to the touch, stick the thermometer into the carboy. When the temperature has dropped below 80 degrees (but is preferably still higher than 60 degrees) take the carboy out of the bathtub. If you're taking hydrometer readings, pour off a small bit of your beer and record the reading. This reading is the original gravity of the beer. My OG reading for this brew was 1.022, which means that my chilled wort was 1.022 times as heavy as water—pretty light, but not unusual for a beer this pale. If your reading is way off this number, you may well have botched something.

member: Kat_Gurl

SURVEY: HOMEBREWING

I'm new to homebrewing and have made only three batches: two Irish stouts and one pumpkin lager. There's nothing like sitting down to a brew you made yourself, even if the results weren't quite expected; the second batch of stout wouldn't carbonate and the jury's still out on the pumpkin lager. I'd like to see a commercial raspberry stout hit the shelves. I'll make my own someday!

7. Add the yeast

Your packet of Wyeast should be big, puffy, and happy by now. Sterilize it and a pair of scissors in the iodine solution. Take the airlock off the carboy, open the yeast with the scissors, and pour it into the beer. Swish the carboy around vigorously. Fit the stopper back into the carboy but instead of adding the airlock this time, attach the 5-foot tube instead. Move the carboy into a warm dark place.

Fill a jug or pot with water and place the 5-foot tube running from the carboy stopper into the basin. You've just made a sloppy but functional airlock. Carbon dioxide can get out of the brew, so your carboy won't explode, but air can't get in through the water. Why do this instead of using the airlock you paid perfectly good money for? Because in the first few days of brewing, your yeast is going to be very busy, and it's likely to produce a good quantity of foam. This foam can pop a store-bought airlock right out of the carboy. The basin and tube system allows the foam to overflow into the basin.

8. Fermentation

The next part of the brewing process requires very little work and a whole lot of patience. About twelve to twenty-four hours after you've added the yeast to the beer, you should see foam begin to appear toward the top of your carboy. (If you don't get any foam at all for forty-eight hours, you may have what's known as a "stuck" fermentation. Some brew shops sell a chemical solution that may restart stuck fermentations.) For the first few days of foaming, you'll probably see foam creep through your airlock tube and accumulate in the basin. Change the water every day so that your house doesn't smell too raunchy and wait for the fermentation to calm down a bit.

When the beer is still foaming, but no longer pushing foam out through the tube and into the basin, it's time to put on the airlock. Make a quart or so of iodine solution, and boil a little water. Soak the airlock in the iodine; fill it with cooled, boiled water and replace the tube in the stopper with the airlock. Visit your beer every day for the next week or so. You should be able to see bubbles of carbon dioxide float up through the water in the airlock and out into the air. When these bubbles stop appearing, your beer has made it through its primary fermentation. This can take as long as two weeks in a heavy beer with a weak yeast, and as little as three days in a light beer with an aggressive yeast.

If you've got a hydrometer, you can be certain that your beer is ready to bottle by taking a reading of its specific gravity. As fermentation takes place, the sugar in the wort, which makes your beer heavy, is converted into carbon dioxide and alcohol, which are a good deal lighter. Consequently, when the specific gravity of the beer gets very close to that of water—around 1.008 or so—it's time to bottle your beer. If your hydrometer reading reveals that the gravity is around 1.015, the beer needs a few more days to ferment.

9. Bottling

Bottling is a major pain in the butt, but be consoled that it's the last major step before you get to drink your beer! I'd recommend recruiting at least one friend to help you with this step in the process. With three folks, bottling gets even easier.

Start by washing the forty-eight pry-top bottles you've been saving for the last few weeks. Then, fill your bathtub with cold water and a small amount of household bleach. Put the bottles in the tub to sterilize them.

member: Waldhorn
SURVEY: HOMEBREWING
We added 1 ounce of high grade marijuana buds that had been steeped in vodka to twenty-three liters of beer. Man, it was good.

While the chlorine is busy taking out millions of innocent bacteria, get your beer ready for bottling. Take your 5-gallon plastic bucket and wash it out with the iodine solution. Sterilize your long spoon, racking tube, bottle filling tube, and 5-foot length of plastic tube. Take the airlock out of the carboy and put the carboy up on a sturdy table or counter. Put the bucket down on the floor. It's time now for a demonstration of the principle behind the siphon.

10. The siphon

Attach the racking tube to one end of the 5-foot tube. Place your finger over the open end of the racking tube and put the other end of the tubing under the faucet. Fill the tubing and racking tube with cold water. Ask whoever's helping you bottle to put her thumb over the end of the tubing and bring that end down into the plastic bucket. Take your finger off of the end of the racking tube and put the tube into the carboy. Once the tube is in the carboy, your partner should remove her finger. If all goes well, the water in the tube should flow into the bucket, followed by your beer.

11. Racking the beer

The process you've just begun is called "racking" the beer. The idea is to separate the beer from the dead yeast, which has probably settled to the bottom of the carboy. With this in mind, it's a good idea to have one person holding the racking tube in the carboy, keeping it about a half inch above the bottom.

While your partner holds the racking tube, mix 3/4 cup of corn sugar with 1/2 cup of water and put that on the stove to boil. Put a couple of cups of water in another pan, along with 50 bottle caps and put that pan on to boil as well. Are you beginning to understand why you need a friend to help in this phase of brewing?

12. Carbonating your beer

Stop racking the beer when you've hit the sludge level. Put the carboy somewhere safe and, if you're forward-thinking, fill it with water and bleach so that it'll be easier to clean later. Move the bucket up onto your counter or table. Dump the corn sugar solution into your beer and stir it up with your sterilized spoon. Corn sugar is junk food for yeast—it loves it and turns it into alcohol very quickly. More important is the carbon dioxide that this secondary fermentation will create, because that carbon dioxide will carbonate your beer. Without a secondary fermentation, beer would be alcoholic and fairly tasty, but completely flat. While the sugar is diffusing itself throughout the beer, take your bottles out of the bathtub and let them drip dry. While the bottles dry, you need to get another siphon started. This time, attach the racking tube to one end of the tubing and the bottle filler to the other end. Put the racking tube end under the faucet and fill the tubing up with water. Place the racking tube into the bucket of beer. You're ready to bottle.

13. Delegation

If you've got three people involved with the bottling process, here's how to deploy them. Have one person hold the racking tube steady in the bucket of beer. Your second person gets to sit on the floor and actually fill the bottles. The bottle filler is pressure activated. You need to press it against the bottom or side of a beer bottle to make it fill. Fill the bottles up so that there's a half-inch or so of air at the top of each and hand them off to the third person in the assembly line. The third person gets to cap the bottles. Take the bottle caps out of the boiling water, holding them by the edges. Each capper works differently, so follow the instructions that come with the capper.

14. Patience is a virtue

Five gallons of brew should produce about forty-five 12-ounce bottles of beer, or 7 ½ six packs. Resist the temptation to take the cap off a bottle and give it a shot—it won't be all that pleasant an experience. Instead, put the bottles in a dark place and do your best to forget about them for two weeks.

15. Test run

After two weeks have gone by, chill a bottle of your brew and give it a try. If it smells right and doesn't have mold or anything else floating in it, it's probably not going to kill you. Pour it into a nice glass and have a taste. If the gods of zymurgy have smiled, you've just produced the first of your many homebrews.

16. Give it space

If you're not happy with how your brew tastes after two weeks, leave it alone for a few more weeks. Many beers get better with age—more time in the bottle means more time for the flavors to mix together and for the rough edges to smooth out. If you put your beer into green or clear glass, make sure you keep the bottles in a dark room—exposure to light can "skunk" beer, giving it a nasty smell and taste. If the beer isn't better after a few more weeks, you've got a couple of alternatives. If you enjoy cooking or baking, you might want to try beer-batter onion rings, beer bread, or beer-based chili.

> Homebrewing Online

Cat's Meow
http://hbd.org/brewery/cm3/index.html

Recipe Exchange
http://pekkel.uthscsa.edu/Beer/Recipe/recex2.html

Usenet
rec.crafts.brewing

No Longer a Wine Spectator

Despite some of its more highbrow connotations, wine really can be a populist beverage, enjoyable by even those folks on a pretty tight budget.

by Ethan Zuckerman and Rachel Barenblat

You probably associate wine with money—that is, spending a lot of it on a little bottle that will be empty in the blink of an eye. That's understandable; it's commonly understood that wine appreciation is something of an art. There's a culture centered around wine and if your knowledge of that culture is limited, walking into a well-stocked wine store can be intimidating. But don't throw out your corkscrews in despair; good wine—not just the low-end cheapo stuff, but really good wine—comes in all prices, and there are bottles that suit even the most no-frills budget.

member:Villon

SURVEY: WINE

New wine drinkers are safe with a white zinfandel or (if they're more adventurous) a vin gris, most of which can be found in the under $10 price range for a 750 ml bottle. For the conventional, or the "have to have a crowd-pleaser since I'm going to a party" taste, you're always safe with a Kendall-Jackson chardonnay. In general, you can find Fetzer for under $10, and they make a decent chardonnay and a pretty good merlot, unoffensive at worst, and quite drinkable at best. Also try Sterling Vinyards, Chateau Ste. Michelle, and (although this may push the $10 limit) the Paul Jaboulet Cotes du Rhone. Stay clear of cheap Italian, Australian, and Chilean wines as a rule, and Oregon pinot noirs and California chardonnays generally go over well with just about anyone.

Wine Gear and Storage

Wine drinking doesn't require much sophisticated equipment. Wineglasses are the best, but juice glasses or even mugs will do in a pinch. The shape of the glass is more important than what it's made of—wineglasses are designed to send wine to a particular part of your tongue so as to be received by the proper taste receptors. Really good glasses can cost $30 a pop, but grocery stores and homeware shops often have a set of four decent glasses for $5.

When choosing a corkscrew the priorities are ease of use and ability to remove the cork without breaking it (otherwise known as "corking the wine"). The lever-action corkscrew, which is sometimes called the "waiter's corkscrew," is reminiscent of a Swiss Army knife and least likely to shatter a cork. The "screwpull" makes life extremely easy, as it removes the cork from the bottleneck as you twist the handle. There are also unbelievably elaborate corkscrews that look like a combination of a Victorian-era planting urn and one of the gynecological gizmos in *Dead Ringers*. There's something for everybody, so go with the one you prefer.

Wine needs to be stored horizontally so the cork doesn't dry out. Cheap wine racks can be bought at most kitchenware stores, but you can do about as well with some boards and bricks. Keep your wine away from severe cold and heat; storing bottles outside is a bad idea. If you've got a basement, that's an ideal storage area, as it will most likely stay cool in the summer. It also gives you the opportunity to make stupid jokes about your "wine cellar."

Buying Wine

The great thing about wine is that you can try a different vintage each evening and not repeat yourself for years. But the varieties of wine available can make it difficult to know where to begin.

Start by discovering what types of wine you like. Some people are convinced that they don't like wine because it's too sour. They've probably never tried a sweet wine like a white zinfandel or a Riesling. It's true what they say: Wine is an acquired taste and genuine appreciation of wine's subtleties and nuances takes practice. The more different grapes and vintages you sample, the more attuned your tongue will become. Be adventurous and give it some time.

Next, find a wine shop. Really good wine stores tend to have three things to recommend them: a large selection, decent prices, and, most important, a knowledgeable staff. If your chosen store lacks the staff, you can, of course, start by picking bottles randomly and over time your choices will inevitably be informed by past experience. But a novice wine buyer will be better served by a guide who can tell you what's good and what's crappy. There are also a number of resources on the Net (try www.wineenthusiast.com or www.wine-advocate.com) and many useful wine magazines as well. *Wine Spectator* is particularly indispensable; every issue lists dozens of wines and rates them on a scale of 1 to 100. Any wine rated over 85 is bound to be tasty. A wine that gets 95 or better will most likely rock your world, but you'll probably have to shell out a tad more cash per bottle. For those who truly appreciate wine, though, such an investment is well worth the price.

Keep a wine diary where you can take notes on the wines you try. You can get fancy if you like and keep a detailed tasting notebook with labels from wines you've sampled and your observations. But even a simple "loved it/hated it" list will give you something to work with when you go to pick a wine at a restaurant or as a gift.

Now on to the specifics. As far as terminology is concerned: Some wines are named according to the region in which they were made (Bordeaux, Burgundy, Chianti, champagne, Beaujolais) while others are referenced by grape (cabernet, merlot, shiraz, port). "Table wine" means that it's a mutt, a blend of grapes. There are a few good table wines out there, though, so don't be a snob about them.

Good Cheap Reds

Cabernet sauvignon, shiraz, and Chianti are generally heartier wines, best-suited for cold weather, strongly flavored food, and people who like wine with a little bite. These wines tend to be described as "peppery" and as having overtones of raisin or plum. The more pretentious wine books and magazines will use adjectives like "piquant," "powerful," and "chewy." Chewy? Whatever.

Merlot, Bordeaux, and red zinfandel are kinder, gentler, more delicately flavored reds. People who live in warm climes tend to favor these wines, as will those who prefer milder foods. These wines would be overpowered by wasabi or strong curry; they lend themselves well to meals featuring fish, mildly spicy chicken, pastas of various sorts, and pretty much anything that doesn't aim to make diners dab at their streaming eyes with their napkins.

Almost all red wines should be kept at room temperature and are generally served in large-bowled wineglasses. (Some very young Beaujolais wines are served slightly chilled.) If you want to impress fellow dinner party guests with your finesse and all-around suavity, cup the bowl of the glass in your palm so that the wine is slightly warmed by your hand.

name: DearAbbey

SURVEY: WINE

Personal satisfaction for money spent is the only criteria for wine. If you are looking for a wine to "lay down" for a few years, buy a good, current vintage and let it age. Many a cheap, average wine has become a sought-after classic years later. Basically, if you like it, buy it, to hell with what anyone else thinks.

Under $5

Avia is made in Slovenia and bottles generally retail for around three bucks—it's almost cheaper than soda. Avia has a rich, almost creamy flavor; it's decent table wine and as long as you pull the price tag off, you can probably fool people into thinking it set you back ten or twelve bucks.

Concha Y Toro makes a cabernet, a merlot, and a blend of the two. The price is roughly comparable to Avia; Concha Y Toro is a little smokier and spicier.

Cavit Wineries, Trentino Merlot is full-bodied wine with a gently spicy flavor and it goes well with anything, especially good hearty soups and crusty loaves of bread.

Under $10

Straccali Chianti is robust, full-bodied, and a wonderful general table wine to keep around to drink with Italian food, meats, and anything cooked with garlic or rosemary.

MC Vallejo Cabernet Sauvignon has strong overtones of black cherry. It's a pretty glorious wine, especially for the price. And we don't think the vintner is a rapper, but it would sure be cool if he were.

Rosemont Estate Shiraz/Cabernet is a really nice blend, slightly mellower than many full cabernets and likely to appeal both to cabernet fans and to those who prefer something milder. It has notes of plum and spice, which are fairly common to shiraz grapes.

Merlot de Jacques et Francois Lurton: Bordeaux is actually a merlot/Bordeaux blend and surprisingly full-bodied. Notes of currant and cassis, beautiful clear garnet color—definitely the kind of wine you could drink a few bottles of and not mind the repetition.

Georges Duboeuf Merlot (Vin de Pays Doc) is a mild wine and it's a great match for less spicy Indian dishes or anything containing fennel. The label calls this "red table wine," but we think it's nicer than that. At least, if it is a table wine, it's for a very fine table.

Under $15

Heron Merlot is worth searching your wine store for. Made by a female French vintner, this wine goes great with stew, cheese, country bread, or any honest, hearty food. Better suited for cabernet fans than merlot lovers.

White Wines

Sauvignon, fume blanc, and pinot blanc are good white wines for those who like reds; they're dry and brisk, fairly crisp in flavor, sometimes lightly spicy or fruity, but they're definitely not sweet. White wines should be kept chilled and are usually served in smaller-bowled glasses (held at the stem so the warmth of your hand doesn't heat up the wine). Never serve a white wine at room temperature; it's considered gauche and the wine will taste awful. White wines tend to go well with "white" meats (chicken, fish, veal, and pork), and they're particularly nice with stir-fry or sushi as a substitute for the more traditional Asian plum wines. White Bordeaux and white Burgundy are also dry whites worth considering. Don't be

confused by the name "white Burgundy"—Burgundy refers to the name of the French province where these grapes originated, not the color of the wine.

Chardonnay is generally considered a "fruity" wine—not as sharp as a red, but not sweet either. It's usually redolent of apples and white grapes.

Riesling, gewurtztraminer, and white zinfandel (which is actually pink) are all sweet whites and are often referred to as dessert wines. Those who prefer wine coolers to actual wine would probably enjoy giving these a whirl.

Under $5

Kronendal Sauvignon Blanc is extremely fruity and surprisingly dry for an inexpensive sauv blanc. It starts off sweet but turns lemony and it's very cool and refreshing. This is a good wine for warm weather, particularly picnics.

Under $10

Chateau St. Jean Fume Blanc, like a lot of fine scotch, is aged in oak barrels, which lends it a slightly smoky flavor. There are strong notes of citrus and melon, but the wine itself is still very dry. Fish and citrusy foods—anything with wedges of lemon—or Thai soups that rely on lemongrass and fresh lime bring out the wine's citrus notes nicely.

> Cooking with Wine

Red wines are great for cooking meats, fungi, and hearty stews. Pour red wine over chicken breasts, add some whole canned tomatoes and chick-peas and a lot of spices, and stew it for an hour or so. (Be forewarned: If you cook chicken in red wine, your chicken will turn out purple.) You can also add red wine to chili, spaghetti sauce, or anything tomato-based.

White wines are also good for cooking fungi, as well as vegetables, chicken, and fish. If you've cooked chicken in a skillet, once you remove the chicken pour a little wine over the scorch marks and residue the chicken leaves behind, add some butter and spices, simmer, and presto: you've just made sauce. Or try this: Cook mushrooms, onions, and garlic in white wine at low heat, then ladle it over boxed couscous or wild-rice pilaf. This is an impressive-looking (and tasty) meal for in-laws, guests, or friends.

Erath Vineyards Pinot Blanc is crisp, with a hint of citrus and lemon and something like fresh-cut grass.

Rosemont Estates Semillon-Chardonnay is dry and full-flavored, with notes of butter and citrus.

Luna di Luna Chardonnay-Pinot Grigio is unassuming and gentle, which makes it the perfect companion for mild foods. Besides, it comes in a splendid—if unorthodox—blue glass bottle.

Say *Fetzer Gewurtztraminer*, and the response might be, "Gesundheit!" This is a spiced German wine (*gewurtz* means "spicy"). It's almost like a sweetened cider. Gewurtztraminer goes well with apple pie, especially if you're a Northerner and eat your pie with a wedge of sharp cheddar. If you want to drink it with dinner instead, something autumnal, like butternut squash, would be most appropriate.

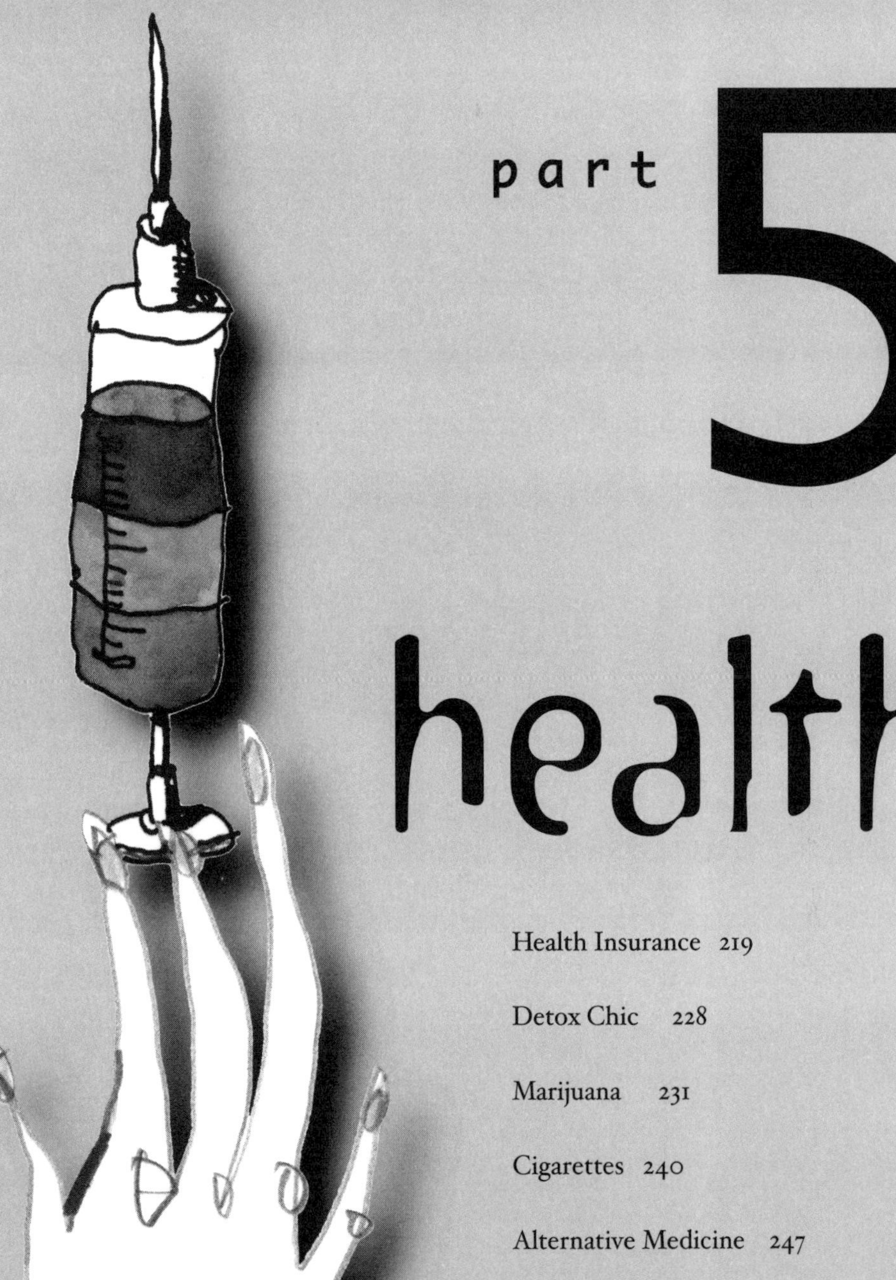

part 5

health

Health Insurance

When you're living on rice and beans for the last week of every month, having good insurance can seem like a luxury. But bite the bullet and keep reading—a little information could wind up saving you your money and your life.

by Andrea Coller

Not sure whether you really need health insurance? Here's a short quiz to help you decide.

Question: Your money or your life?

That's really what the decision boils down to, yet every day an amazing number of people go for the dough without really considering what might happen in the unlikely event that they aren't, as it turns out, invincible. And according to a study released by the Census Bureau in 1996, eighteen- to twenty-four-year-olds were among the worst offenders: They're one of the groups most likely to be uninsured. More and more of them are even saying "no thanks" to health plans offered by their employers.

Skimping on health insurance is almost as common as skipping it altogether: Young adults who *do* have coverage most often join HMOs—the cheapest option—but rarely bother to find out exactly what it is they're buying, which can be as bad as or even worse than having no insurance at all.

When you're living on rice and beans for the last week of every month, having good insurance can seem like a luxury—and even if

member: xprof

SURVEY: APPLE A DAY KEEPS THE DOCTOR AWAY

I practice what I call "Defensive Medicine." Recognize that M.D.s more closely resemble priests (i.e., proponents of an orthodoxy) than they do physicists (objective scientists), and take the responsibility upon yourself for learning about your body and the latest relevant research. If you must see an M.D., establish clear objectives for treatment and seek outside opinions when they are not met in a timely fashion.

member: jdfrost

SURVEY: HEALTH INSURANCE

I worked in health insurance for years, and here's my three cents: 1. Don't trust managed care any more than you have to—they barely manage and they don't really care; 2. If you're fairly healthy, you can probably get a high-deductible policy for under $80 per month that will protect you from homelessness; 3. If you're uninsured and not healthy, about all you can do is go broke and go on Medicaid, then fight like hell for your right to survive.

you're living large, doing your homework on the topic is no damn fun. But bite the bullet and keep reading—a little information could wind up saving you your money and your life.

Some Common Arguments Against Buying the Best Available Health Insurance, and Why They're Lame

I'm too poor to afford health insurance.

You and the government probably have different ideas about what poor is. If you're a single person making minimum wage you may feel poor, but the feds expect parents to support families on that same paycheck. So if you're poor—but not Uncle Sam poor—you won't be eligible for Medicaid, and if you don't purchase coverage, you're simply not covered. Many folks think, Hey, this is America, if I need medical care for something serious, I'll get it. Well, actually, no. Unless you're an adorable five-year-old from a war-torn country who needs an organ, don't expect hospitals to do you any favors. They won't deny you emergency care, but that doesn't mean they'll give you a free pass. You'll still wind up with what could be a whopper of a bill—and if you couldn't scrape together enough to buy health coverage, how will you begin to pay that? As one hospital spokesman put it: "If something really serious happens, that twenty dollars a week is going to look like chump change. If you thought paying off that student loan was bad, this will be *much* worse." In short, without insurance, a serious illness or accident could leave you with chronically ill credit (or leave your parents with a second mortgage on their house).

member: KAMBILL

SURVEY: HEALTH INSURANCE

I am a twenty-two-year old college student working part-time. I still live with my mother, and if I did not have her to help with my doctor bills, I don't know what I would do. I have recurring sinus infections and am always going to the doctor for prescriptions. Last year, I was having bad headaches and my doctor sent me for CAT scans. The bills came to at least $1,500. I had to apply for Medicaid and after waiting for an answer from them for five months, they thankfully paid for my bills. I don't know what I would do if they did not pay for them.

member: sawtooth

SURVEY: HEALTH INSURANCE

My employer offered three different plans from which to choose. I chose a popular HMO and have been very satisfied. There is very little out of pocket required. I am in the insurance business, so I carefully read and understand the policy and ask questions when needed. Most policies have similar coverage and similar exclusions, so price is a deciding factor.

The indemnity deductible is so high I'll never hit it. Why have insurance when I'll end up paying all my expenses out of my own pocket anyway? If I choose the HMO, I can see a doctor for only five bucks, no deductible.

Newsflash: Generally healthy folks in their twenties and thirties with limited incomes should not be buying health insurance to cover their basic annual medical bills. If you're seventy-two-year-old Ida and you see eleven different doctors twice a month, you're going to want a plan that helps you meet those expenses. But if you're income is limited and you "never get sick," you should let your good health buy you the greatest freedom in the event of a catastrophic illness or accident—which is really what you're insuring against. Don't be angry that you'll never meet your deductible—rejoice. It means you're not sick.

All the plans suck, so what difference does it make which one I choose?

You're right. All the plans do suck. But they suck in a glorious, prismatic spectrum of different ways. You may know the plan your workplace offers is an HMO, but is it a "network" HMO (meaning it has its own staff) or a "non-network" HMO (which means it contracts with other institutions and individuals who provide services to its members)? Not sure? It could take you six weeks to get an appointment with a specialist at the first kind; you could wind up getting physical therapy from the worst hospital in town from the second. The point is, it does make a difference and even though no one knows for sure what kind of care they'll need in the future, you can certainly do some homework and make an educated guess.

member: Rebecca

SURVEY: HEALTH INSURANCE

I'm a full-time college student and have two part-time jobs, neither of which offers any benefits. How do I get by? Well, orange juice, aspirin, and sleep cure most ailments. Failing that I'm lucky in that the Planned Parenthood office takes care of all my "female" problems and my college campus has a health center. Worst that's happened so far was minor surgery that cost three grand. Used my Visa gold. Still paying. It's not easy, but I'm making it.

YOUR CHOICES AND HOW TO MAKE ONE

Old Faithful: The Indemnity Plan

Traditional health insurance, also known as "fee-for-service" insurance means you pay 20 percent, they pay 80 percent. They don't cover your yoga classes or your checkups. They cost the most and often have heinous deductibles that can mean hundreds, even thousands, in out-of-pocket expenses—but they let you go to any doctor or doctors you choose.

member: sonny321

SURVEY: HEALTH INSURANCE

I am stuck in an income bracket where I have very few options as far as health insurance is concerned. The insurance offered at my husband's job is just *too* expensive for us to afford and we make just enough not to qualify for Medicaid. It scares me to death what would happen if something major were to happen. We have two small children and though they are very healthy, they still do have to go to the doctor, and paying cash for the visits hurts our budget big time. But what do you do? One of the boys will probably need braces and I shudder to think of what that will cost! My husband and I have both gone without medical care for years and as a direct result of this I ended up in the emergency room with a ruptured cyst that could have been detected with a regular exam at a doctor's office. This country *needs* to do something about this problem.

In and Out: PPO and POS Plans

In this model, you are the one who makes the cost-benefit calculation. For that reason alone, it can be the best choice for the young and the cash-strapped. A PPO (preferred provider organization) can be used like an indemnity plan, but it also has a network of providers who have agreed to provide services for reduced fees. If you chose one of them, you pay very little (and so does the insurance company). The main drawbacks here are that if you have a serious problem and choose to go "out of network" to consult a specialist or for hospitalization, your payments can be even higher than with an indemnity plan—for example, many PPOs pay only 70 percent of costs incurred at "out-of-network" hospitals, whereas indemnity plans usually pay 80 percent wherever you go. And if you do go to an out-of-network doctor, you'll have to meet a deductible, just like you would with an indemnity plan. You may also have to pay the difference between what the service costs and what the plan is willing to pay (see sidebar on page 225 for a discussion of "reasonable and customary" charges). A POS (point of service) plan also allows you to go "out of network," but it comes with all the bureaucracy of an HMO. Your primary care physician is still the "gatekeeper" who approves (or not) many services—and he or she must be chosen from within the network.

You Get What You Pay For: The HMO

That stands for Health Maintenance Organization, and it's the cheapest health care option, in every sense. You pay the least to join the plan, you pay the least to see a doctor (usually a copayment of $5 or $10), and in return, they try to provide you with the fewest services possible. The only exception to that assessment is in preventative care—HMOs are best at covering screenings, checkups, and other services that, by keeping you healthy, are apt to save them money. You choose your primary care physician (your regular doctor) from within the HMO's network. That doctor then decides when, whether, and to whom all referrals are made—and HMO doctors often receive financial incentives not to refer patients. If you convince your doctor to send you to a specialist, he or she will choose one from within the network. If you don't like a specialist, can't get an appointment with the one you've been referred to, or want a second opinion, you're almost guaranteed a fight. And if you wind up having to go "out of network" to see a doctor you trust or to get the kind of care you need, you can end up owing as much as you would have if you had no insurance at all. (And if HMOs can seem wonderfully caring before you get sick, be warned: They take no similar interest in helping you recover once you fall ill. Benefits like rehabilitative therapy—which can help determine how much you'll recover if you've been in an accident—can be brutally limited.)

member: Dickj

SURVEY: HEALTH INSURANCE

Living without insurance coverage is equivalent to working a week and gambling your paycheck at the track on the weekend. Whether you live by principal or lack of access it is a crapshoot that many suffer. Many like myself choose to forego out-of-this-world rates for private insurance coverage but fail to provide an emergency net for accidents or illness. Single individuals, like children, believe they are invincible until something happens to educate them. I use this method. Find out what it costs to pay for insurance coverage. Figure the percentage of your income; cut the percentage by half and put that amount in savings. That type of "trust fund" will always be there in an interest-bearing account until needed. And the beauty is—it's your money. The best-selling tool for insurance is catastrophic illness. Paying insurance does not guarantee good health. It's still a crap shoot.

member: deborahstone

SURVEY: HEALTH INSURANCE

The medical field is a self-creating business, if insured I might be induced to access such care and would then be unhealthy. I have basic prevention tests as needed but would not approve most treatments if I were diagnosed (at least not on this bod!). Most of these prevention tests I wish I could perform more independently . . . teeth cleaning and pap smears could be made to be more accessible to persons wishing to monitor their own health. Living without health insurance is living healthy.

How to Get It

The simplest way to get health insurance is through work. This is cheaper than buying insurance as an individual, but it means you're limited to the options your employer offers. It's fairly common for an employer to offer a choice of plans at varying prices, but not every company does. If an HMO is the only choice at your workplace, consider lobbying for another, either through your union if you belong to one or by banding together with like-minded coworkers to pitch the idea. Even a POS would give you more freedom, and a PPO or indemnity plan would eliminate the primary care physician as "gatekeeper." (If lobbying for a better health care option sounds weird, remember that your benefits package is part of your deal with your employer. If you wouldn't hesitate to ask for a raise when you deserve one or to cut a deal for more vacation time, remember that your health plan is just another part of your benefits package, which can be upgraded in much the same way.)

If you're unemployed, self-employed, or employed by a company that doesn't offer health insurance (and you don't meet the "Uncle Sam poor" test) you still have a few choices.

If you get fired or laid off from your job, you can pay to extend that coverage for eighteen months under a federal law known as COBRA (for the Consolidated Omnibus Budget Reconciliation Act of 1995). The same law lets you extend your coverage if you are insured under your parents' plan when you graduate from school.

If you're not eligible for a COBRA extension (or if you use it up) you can often obtain insurance through unions, trade guilds, and other organizations. If you can't attach yourself to any group, contact an insurance broker who will be able to present you with options for individual coverage—which is apt to be expensive but is still better than being uninsured.

member: p040700b
SURVEY: HEALTH INSURANCE
I am an insulin-dependent diabetic without health insurance, and since 1992, when I returned to Florida from New Jersey, my unpaid medical debts are well over $5,000.

member: spiritual1
SURVEY: HEALTH INSURANCE
I don't have health insurance at the present time, and I personally like it that way. I take preventive measures and am a strong believer in vitamins, herbs, and good nutrition. I save thousands a year by not going to doctors and hospitals. I spend far less money than I would normally spend on health insurance and doctor visits and put it toward the health food products and herbal teas at the health store and I feel better too!

member: lazydaze
SURVEY: HEALTH INSURANCE
It's a shame that the wealthiest country in the world does not have socialized medicine! Our political system supports "something for nothing" only for those who are wealthy.

Three Simple Ways to Keep Yourself Out of Trouble

1. Read the literature with your needs in mind before you choose a plan

Reading the insurance info before you pick an insurer is an excellent way to ferret out a lot of potential problems. Only you know what's most important to you, but some examples of what to check for when you're comparing plans include caps on mental health costs, limits on the number of rehab sessions they'll cover, limits on medical tests or surgery, and limits on what the plan will pay over a year or over a lifetime. If you have any kind of chronic problem or history of illness, you'll want to find out in detail how the different plans you're considering stack up in your particular area of concern and how each plan handles ongoing conditions in general. If you're considering having a baby in the foreseeable future, check out ob-gyn and family-planning services. If you're on medication of any kind (and even if you're not) find out if prescription drugs are covered, what kind of copayments you'll be responsible for, and how to obtain refills. If you're thinking of joining an HMO, you should also find out what kind of coverage you'll have if you have a medical problem when you're away from home.

2. Get a copy of the contract—and read it

It's no accident that many insurers don't include a copy of your contract with their "welcome" package. That shiny advertising brochure that explains your health care plan's benefits tends to . . . er . . . gloss over some important details. If you break both your legs, it won't do you much good to scream at a customer service rep because "doesn't cover crutches" wasn't in the brochure. They'll just refer you to the "durable medical equipment" clause of your contract. So it's wise to know what that document says before you test out that black-diamond trail. Look at it this way: If the thought of reading your health insurance contract makes you want to barf now, just imagine trying to slog through it once you're already sick.

member: Johnny_Poppyseed

SURVEY: HEALTH INSURANCE

Upon leaving my employer, I suddenly became ill with acute pancreatitis. Had I *not* opted for continued coverage, I would have had 1.25 *million* dollars in health costs! *Plus*, external physicians that billed a total of $10,000.

member: dolphenix

SURVEY: HEALTH INSURANCE

I live without health insurance and its a nightmare! I'm so scared that I will get sick and die because there is no way I could afford to go to the doctor. It's not easy to live like this. There have been many times I would have liked to have seen a doctor and couldn't. I have two large moles now that according to some are cancerous. What can I do about it? Nothing because I have a minimum wage job and I'm trying to support two kids. I'll probably die of cancer—that is what living without health insurance is like.

member: JackForge

SURVEY: HEALTH INSURANCE

If not for the VA I would be at a loss about what to do for health care. That is one reason I am glad to have been in the army. Unfortunately dental care is not included for nonservice connected veterans. So, I recently decided to buy dental insurance simply out of necessity. The out-of-pocket costs are far too high. As for socialized medicine, I think it is long overdue in the United States. In that area we have a long way to go to catch up to the other leading countries of the world. After all, if society is not formed for the benefit of all members, it is not functioning at full purpose.

3. Choose your primary care physician carefully

This is for all of you out there (you know who you are) who choose a primary care physician by locating the address closest to you on the list of network providers. Cut it out. Just because doctors are in the same plan doesn't mean they're of the same quality. Convenience is nice and it may make you more likely to visit your physician for a checkup, but let's face it: Most of you wouldn't buy a pound of coffee from a store just because it was close to your house—why on earth would you choose your doctor that way? Get a reference from your last physician, or ask friends, kin, or coworkers for a recommendation.

member: MaryBeast
SURVEY: HEALTH INSURANCE
Why is the president always giving to other nations when we need so much right here? Wouldn't the government taking care of our health be in the country's best interest?

> Health Insurance Lingo

Two of the most insidious epithets you'll find in the insurance language are "reasonable and customary" and "medically necessary." These seemingly empty bits of blather are actually massive loopholes that limit what insurance companies are obligated to pay and block your access to services.

Reasonable and Customary

These days most insurance contracts, including indemnity plans, include a "reasonable and customary" clause; even if you don't need to get prior approval for a procedure or appointment, the company may refuse to pay part of your costs on the grounds that your physician charges more than is "reasonable and customary": i.e., more than other doctors in the same area charge for the same thing. If, for example, you're planning to have surgery, ask for a list of charges up front (the hospital, surgeon, and anesthesiologist usually charge separate fees, although no one will tell you this) and then run them past your insurance company. If you don't, and your surgeon charges $6,000 for the same procedure many doctors in the same area perform for $3,500, the insurer will pay you 80 percent of the "reasonable and customary charges"—say, 80 percent of $3,500—and you'll be responsible for 20 percent of the $3,500.

Plus $2,500.

If you don't ask, its very possible that no one will mention any of this until a bill for your share comes in the mail. If you do ask, and you discover that your surgeon charges more than your insurer will pay, you can do one of three things:

1. Tell your surgeon that your insurance company won't pay that much, and try to renegotiate the fee (yes, you can negotiate with your doctor).

2. Shop around for another doctor whose estimate is more "reasonable."

3. Suck it up and pay the difference.

Medically Necessary

This phrase means exactly what it says, even when it makes no sense. Insurers will claim to cover a service, like speech therapy, as long as it is "medically necessary"—which, if you think about it, it never is. Although it can certainly have an enormous impact on the quality of your life, not being able to speak clearly, or at all, is not life threatening. With that disclaimer, insurers can provide or withold certain benefits as arbitrarily as they choose. One speech therapist cited an insurer who only considered speech therapy medically necessary for children born with cleft palates, which is a pretty narrow definition of eligibility for a supposedly covered service. Unfortunately, there's not a lot to do if this phrase crops up, except to take note of where it appears and to fight like a dog when your insurer tries to use it to deny you what you need.

Three Hints to Help You Get Out of Trouble Once You're in It

1. Keep a log

Write down dates of conversations and the names of people you speak to; keep a list of failed attempts to contact providers and administrators. Tape record conversations if you can and if it's legal in your state. Keep copies of all correspondence, bills, invoices, and so on. This way, should you need to do battle, you'll be armed.

2. Yell

Pick the most obnoxious person you have regular dealings with and, the next time you're 100 percent in the right, let them have it. Health care is one of those arenas in which the squeaky wheel really does get the oil. But remember, especially if you're in an HMO, your access to care is in their hands. You don't want to make them *too* mad unless you're willing to . . .

member: selfsame

Survey: Health Insurance

I had what I thought was great workplace insurance when I became pregnant with my first child at age forty. It was a terrible crash and burn birth mostly because of the way the insurance company manipulated the doctor and hospital to comply with their cost-cutting policies. The best interests of my baby and me were not considered. The final cost for her birth and subsequent three-month hospitalization came to a quarter of a million dollars, of which my share of cost was about 20 percent. Fortunately I live in California, so a social worker at Children's Hosptial took steps to have California Children's Services pick up the remainder of her bill. I remember being shocked at being assigned a social worker. My husband and I both worked and both had insurance through our jobs.

> If You Don't Have It

Okay, so you've read all our good advice, but for some obscure reason, you choose to ignore it. To heck with health insurance, you're flyin' solo—you're a rebel. Well, should you find yourself in need of health care, here are a few options. They all come with paperwork and hours-long waits, but they're relatively cheap ways to access reliable care without coverage.

- Many people without insurance skip the primary care stage entirely and seek medical help only when the problem is pressing enough to send them to the emergency room. Instead of waiting for your health problems to get bad enough to put you in the ER, see if there are any community clinics in your area. They offer good quality care to low-income patients on a sliding scale—meaning they'll expect you to pay something, but they won't charge you more than you can reasonably afford.
- If your problem isn't an emergency and clinic hours are over, many hospitals now have "after hours" health care centers that are cheaper than emergency rooms and are better equipped to tackle not-quite-urgent health problems.
- Many nonprofit hospitals are built with federal Hill-Burton funds, on the condition that they provide designated amounts of free and reduced-cost care. The income threshold for free care for a one-person "family" is $7,890; the lowest qualifying income for reduced care is $15,780. For referrals to hospitals that provide such care, call the Hill-Burton toll-free hotline at 800-638-0742.
- If you've received care but can't afford to pay a hospital or doctor's bill, don' t just ignore it—talk to the billing department. Most will be happy to set up a payment schedule you can afford. That way they won't have to hound you for the dough, and you can keep the bill out of the clutches of a collection agency.

3. Go over their heads

If you've got a serious beef and you're not getting anywhere with the lower downs, take your troubles to whomever handles grievances. If you get nowhere doing that—make some more noise. Contact a local politician or newspaper. There's nothing insurance companies hate worse than bad PR—except maybe lawsuits.

One last word, however: If you're fighting to get them to cover treatment for something that could be serious, *do not wait* for the issue to be resolved. Even if you're in an HMO, go out of network if you have to, but see a doctor. You can fight for for the money later, but if you put off getting the care you need, you'll be gambling with your health.

Detox Chic

Once perceived as a true scourge on one's character, detox is now worn by many as something as a badge of distinction. Strange? You don't know the half of it.

by Jessica Willis

Thirty years ago, if a cranky, bedraggled, and sick coworker vanished without a trace, only to return to his desk three weeks later with rosy cheeks and under-eye circles gone, what would the whisperings around the watercooler sound like? "Gee, that grouch who usually stank of whiskey and cigarettes at 9 A.M. must have fallen in love and raced off to Madrid."

Barely fifteen years ago, at the tail end of the Me Decade and at the dawn of Greed is Good, perhaps the rumors would have taken on a slightly more vicious bent. "Thank God he was sent off to the Farm to dry out. That loser was shuffling off to snort coke every ten minutes," the office coterie might be heard muttering.

In the upwardly mobile late '90s, however, if a twenty-five-year-old worker bee calls for an informal meeting around the watercooler and announces to his boss and his subordiantes that he's getting on a plane tonight for Minnesota for some serious detox, everyone nods compassionately and pats his back.

Purity in the wake of pollution is something to crow about, but the visions of modern detoxification read like a tabloid feature, if not an Oscar-winning script. Celebrities brag publicly about having to do a detox "tour" at the height of their fame. In films, scenes of

member: TJanes

SURVEY: VIRTUES OF VICE

Do vices have virtues? You bet! Why would we continue to engage in an activity if it didn't serve us in one form or another. People smoke because on some level it calms them down, drinking can help numb us to things we aren't ready to deal with, etc. I think a truly nasty vice is trying to fix other people. Fucking with other people's vices is the nastiest vice of all.

member: boetticher

SURVEY: DRUGS

I take exception to the whole war on drugs party line about all drugs being 100 percent bad and deadly 100 percent of the time. There's quite a big difference and quite a long road between occasional use and full-on, hardcore, Sid Vicious-style abuse. Drug use is occasional recreational use. Drug abuse is needing it to get out of bed in the morning.

young heroin addicts barricading themselves in their bedrooms to kick the habit provide comic relief. Cheerleaders are dragged into the hospital by their fathers, ex-boyfriend's initals carved into their forearms and their stomachs full of diet pills. Lithe women expose their nicotine patches with pride at cocktail parties.

Quitting—whether it be cigarettes or amphetamines—used to be for weaklings and terminal cases, a miserable plan Z. But now everyone seems to be doing it, even if some of the old stigmas apply. Judges usually send convicted drunk drivers to detox out of state, and many addicts who voluntarily seek inpatient treatment avoid the local hospital. Maybe the detox process is more successful if the patient feels like they're going on vacation.

What is detox? Is it a noun or a verb? Is it a warm bed and an IV drip after a massive coke binge? Is it a gentle at-home ritual used to expel the harmful effects of smog from the body?

Several generations ago, the average detox patient was a fifty-year-old family burden with a swollen liver and jaundiced eyes; now it's the barely thirty-year-old wunderkind, suffering from clinical depression, multiple piercings, and a gym-built body. "Detox" used to mean shakes and sweats in a hospital, now it can mean trying to beat a nagging case of the blues by going to the health food store and buying a jar of herbal pills with labels that claim to "promote well-being," like extract of St. John's Wort. What it all boils down to is this: Detoxification, an act that once was a secret kept in the immediate family now has more cachet than a suntan from the Côte d'Azur. Past sufferings, excesses, intensities, and surrenders are good. Admitting to them is even better.

Not surprisingly, today's on-the-move detoxers want their discomfort to be relieved at an accelerated rate. Drive-thru detox, once a cynical joke for anyone with typical health insurance—one that supports the minimalization of money spent on addicted clients and is opposed to inpatient treatment—is now becoming a reality with the advent of Ultra-Rapid Opiate Detoxification (UROD), an extreme form of detox detailed in both a prime-time TV hospital drama and a late 1997 edition of the *Journal of Addictive Diseases*.

With UROD, the opiate-addicted patient's short-term memory is impaired with sedatives or general anesthesia before repeated

member: anniesparkle

SURVEY: DRUGS

More time should be spent educating about drugs and less time and money on the scare campaigns. People want relief from everyday problems, pressures, and pains and one way or another will find it. If they do so with an understanding that it's a temporary reprieve, not a solution or an actual escape, so much the better!

member: societyisahole

SURVEY: DRUGS

I smoked marijuana for years and didn't have a bit of trouble quitting. On the other hand I've been smoking cigarettes for years and I've tried one too many times to quit with no such luck.

doses of naloxone (a drug tyically used in the emergency room to revive heroin ODs) are administered, putting the patient in a state of accelerated physiological withdrawal. Approximately five hours later, the patient is opiate-free. UROD is currently an intensive (and expensive) inpatient treatment, but it's not so far-fetched to imagine that within a few years, a white-collar professional whose job is in jeopardy (it's pretty hard to shoot junk and make it to work by 8 A.M.) will be able to have a UROD as an outpatient treatment. And those nicotine patch–wearing ladies are already passé; the FDA recently approved a fast-acting nicotine nasal spray to curb tobacco cravings. Perhaps we'll see silver spray holders worn as pendants in the years to come.

> The Many Faces of Detox

Perspiration is the body's natural detoxification mechanism. The ancient practice of "sweating it out" via saunas, sweat lodges, or exercise remains a viable method of bodily cleansing. The following is a list of new or nontraditional treatments for drug addiction:

ST. JOHN'S WORT: "It stopped the angry voices in my head," says Matthew V., a new user of St. John's Wort, who has been clean of dangerous drugs for over four years. St. John's Wort has its share of skeptics. As one doctor who has been running a detox center in Western Massachusetts for fifteen years says, "I see many people come through the door saying 'I tried it, but . . .' "

SELECTIVE SERATONIN REUPTAKE INHIBITORS (SSRIS): Prozac and Zoloft are prescribed for depression. They also break the cycle of abstinence and relapse. SSRIs, however, have their own side effects—nervousness, weight-fluctuation, lethargy, and lowered sexual response.

MOVEMENT THERAPY: Clinics are now experimenting with movement therapy for easing the physical and existential discomfort of severe or mild detoxification. Fluid movement, coupled with steady breathing, elevates the patient's seratonin levels. One example of movement therapy is yoga. With recovering addicts, yoga teachers like Rhana Harris use breathing techniques that consciously direct oxygen into specific parts of the body. "The patients seem to really like the yoga program," Harris says, who along with doctors and nurses, makes regular rounds on the ward at Stuyvesant Square Drug and Alcohol Rehabilitation Clinic in New York. "We can show the patients simple postures that they can do in street clothes," says Harris. "Spinal twists and side bends are good for people who are detoxing, because exercising the spinal column makes the connection between the nerves stronger and the energy flow becomes more direct."

MASSAGE THERAPY: A Chinese form of touch based on redirecting the energy flow of the twelve meridians—defined areas of the body that correspond to specific bodily functions and organs—is considered a good complement to emotional and physical detox. "If someone were detoxing off of cigarettes, I'd work with the lung and immune system meridian, which runs down the inside of the shoulder joint to the thumb," says Ester Fischer, a Shiatsu therapist who has a busy practice near Manhattan's Union Square. She massages with a deep, sweeping stroke away from the extremities and toward the heart—the best way to purify the blood and remove toxins.

Marijuana

The most commonly used illegal drug is also one of the most misunderstood. Clearing the air, so to speak, is a hard job but someone's gotta do it.

by Adam Heimlich

"It won't make me go schizo, will it?"

In the movie *Animal House*, a young fraternity pledge wants to know if trying marijuana just once will drive him stark-raving mad. The answer is easy: No way. It's indisputable—a single experiment is completely safe. Of course, if everyone tried marijuana once and never smoked it again, pot wouldn't be much of an issue and you wouldn't be reading about it right now.

Perhaps you weren't quite satisfied with the lab conditions or investigative procedures of that first trial run, necessitating that your experiment with marijuana be performed again and again over a period of several years. Such are the ways of science. As one question is settled, others are inevitably raised.

But to ask what's likely to result, health wise, from sporadic, habitual, or (God forbid) constant pot smoking is to swing a mighty uppercut at a particularly sticky tar baby. You'll probably remember why, if you cast your mind back to a college lesson on research methods (not that after-hours one conducted in the dorm). It's that insidious problem of bias.

Lab experiments are funded, designed, conducted, and interpreted by human beings. And the biological and psychological effects of marijuana are simply too controversial to be approached

member: prickly

SURVEY: DRUGS

When I was smoking every day or every other day, I was able to function when I was in school, and I suffered no negative physical effects. On the other hand, I have an acquaintance who is addicted to codeine and gets physically sick when she isn't able to get a hold of some Tylenol 3 or 4. As Frank Zappa once said: "A drug is not bad. A drug is a chemical compound. The problem comes in when people who take drugs treat them like an opportunity to behave like an asshole."

evenhandedly at every stage. The maze of conflicting data emanating from media, government, medical, and counterculture sources incontrovertibly proves one thing—our culture is flatly unable to reach a bottom-line verdict on pot.

Summarizing the results of recent marijuana research is like condensing a plot synopsis from a cyclical, epic melodrama. Typically, research funded by your tax dollars discovers some possible harm caused by marijuana. For example, a 1985 study found that THC, the "active ingredient" of the cannabis plant, weakened the immune system of laboratory mice, thus increasing their risk of herpes infection. Then, the media inevitably goes hog wild with the story, in the case of the '85 study, suggesting that smoking pot will directly cause you to develop nasty sores on your private parts. Eventually, critics of marijuana laws weigh in with any number of troubling observations that call the scare-story into question. In our mice-with-herpes example, some of the unlucky lab animals were primed with up to 1,000 times the effective dose of THC. Yowsa.

member: sexychicken gangbang

SURVEY: DRUGS

I used marijuana four to seven times daily for several months, and I did not become physically addicted. However, I became mentally addicted—I forgot what it was like to be sober.

In other research, massive doses of synthetic THC (more than you could ever sit down and smoke, tough guy) have been found to cause not only impairment of the immune system, but also brain-cell damage, physical addiction, and temporary dysfunction of sex hormones. But the brain-cell findings were decisively repudiated in the early '90s, under far better lab conditions than had been used in the early experiments. Neither physical addiction nor sex trouble has stood up to repeated experiments on lab animals. (And that's not for lack of trying. The National Institute for Drug Abuse's 1990 budget for marijuana research was $26 million. In the end, considering the vast number of humans happy to volunteer as guinea pigs in marijuana research, it makes sense to question whether or not such mouse-abusing reefer madness has anything to do with you.)

Studies involving human beings would indeed be more relevant. But the U.S. government hasn't funded many of these lately; marijuana's undue "Schedule 1" status—a designation indicating that it is a dangerous substance with no medicinal value—makes it nearly impossible for American clinicians to conduct experiments involving human subjects inhaling real pot. In 1970, however, the United States did pay for an extremely comprehensive one—a $1 million project called the National Commission on Marijuana and Drug Abuse (better known as the Shafer Commission). That commission's report, issued in 1972, showed that potheads were as healthy and horny as their abstaining peers and asserted that the plant did

> The Drugs Index

Hours after smoking pot skills related to attention, memory, and learning are impaired: 24

Percentage of heroin in the U.S. that comes through South America: 96

Factor by which juvenile arrests for marijuana possession or sale increased from 1991 to 1994: 3

Factor by which heroin-related hospital visits increased from 1991 to 1994: 3

Percentage of drug-related hospital visits involving heroin: 14

Percentage by which these visits increased from 1988 to 1994: 64

Millions of pounds of pot seized by U.S. law enforcement in 1995: 1

Rank of cigarette smoking among leading causes of death in U.S.: 3

Millions of pounds of tobacco seized by U.S. law enforcement in 1995: 0

Factor by which stressed-out rats self-administered cocaine compared to rats not exposed to stress: 2

Billions of dollars spent by Americans on illegal drugs in 1995: 57.3

Billions spent on alcohol: 103.9

Percentage of all retail sales of alcoholic beverages that were spirits in 1970: 49

In 1995: 28

Millions of dollars spent on advertising by the liquor industry in the U.S. in 1996: 100

Rank of Sam Perkins among most stoned-looking NBA players: 1

Rank of Kurt Loder among most pro-drug TV news anchors: 1

Number of court-supervised treatment programs to which drug offenders may be sentenced instead of prison in 1989: 2

Number in 1997: 289

Number of Rohypnol (the "date-rape drug") pills seized by U.S. customs in 1990: 207

Number seized in 1995: 139,414

Number of known species of psychoactive mushrooms: 17

Number available at the Burning Man festival: 17

Years it took the National Institute on Drug Abuse to figure out that injecting heroin and smoking it caused "similar effects": 20

Percentage of college students admitting to use of any illicit drug in the past year, in 1980: 56.2

Percentage in 1995: 33.5

Percentage of brain cells using dopamine destroyed by a single high dose or prolonged low doses of methamphetamine: 50

Rank of the "Will you be my Mommy?" scene in *Boogie Nights* among most accurate filmic portrayals of how stupid cocaine will make you: 1

Maximum length of a federal prison term for sale of a Schedule I drug, in years: 15

Estimated number of infants born annually who are affected by the mother's drug use: 375,000

Degree to which the preparer and editors of this fact sheet will deny its derivation from the Harper's Index™: Completely

Number of Americans who try marijuana for the first time each day: 3,792

Number who try cigarettes: 5,064

Price of a single dose of Ketamine, in dollars: 5

Years the coca leaf and opium poppy have been used for their psychoactive properties: 3,400

Number of psychoactive drugs ever tried by the preparer of this fact sheet: 9

—Paul Tullis

"not constitute a major threat to public health." Twenty-three years later, the British medical journal *Lancet* assessed the extensive paper trail left by a generation of stoner scrutiny and expressed absolutely no doubt that "the smoking of cannabis, even long-term, is not harmful to health."

Confused yet? Well, keep in mind that you can often cut through the Gordian knot of marijuana lab research with some simple common sense. Take, for example, our original case study—the one with the socially diseased rodents. Unless all your news comes from *Sports Illustrated* or *Allure* (and maybe even then), you've heard that some AIDS patients suffering acute weight loss smoke marijuana for its ever-reliable effect on appetite. Maybe you even heard that in 1992, the FDA approved the drug Marinol (oral THC) for this very purpose. AIDS is, of course, an Immune Deficiency Syndrome. If THC wreaked havoc with the immune system, you'd have to be completely twisted to give it to AIDS patients.

member: SpittingLlama

SURVEY: DRUGS

The war on drugs is Politics as Usual. It's a way for politicians to make us think they care. Think about the effects of the legal drug alcohol—drunk driving, violent mood shifts, violent crimes, liver problems. Think about the effects of the illegal drug marijuana—dulled perception, loss of reflexes, calmed personality, deadened brain cells. Alcohol is obviously more dangerous than marijuana! Yet which is legal?

At the far end of the spectrum of dismissability is the mythical "gateway" theory: the notion, popular among Just Say No drug educators, that pot smoking inevitably leads to experimentation with "harder" drugs like heroin and cocaine. If you follow this logic, you'll end up concluding that riding a bicycle leads to riding a motorcycle. Another sitting duck is the myth of marijuana-induced "amotivational syndrome," which has been demolished by studies showing that pot actually increases worker productivity (at least in regard to boring or repetitive tasks).

Followers of the marijuana debate must learn to distinguish between words commonly used to refer to the results of a single study and statements of scientific fact. "Concerns" about possible "links" between marijuana and medical or social ills cannot be equated with confirmed certainties like "Cigarette smoking causes emphysema," or "Alcohol impairs your ability to operate a motor vehicle." There is an arena in which habitual marijuana users can't compete with the nonsmoking population: respiratory functioning. Like heavy tobacco smokers, dedicated pot smokers report more wheezing, chronic coughs, and bronchitis than nonsmokers. However, it's unlikely, according to a Canadian study, that inhaling burning cannabis can lead to emphysema. Other permanent respiratory damage and the risk of cancer haven't been ruled out. The only certainty is that, as with tobacco, pot's respiratory risk increases with the amount of smoke inhaled over the long term; if pot is slightly easier on the lungs than tobacco, it may just be because one

> Charting Illegal Drugs

Drug: Marijuana (THC)

Immediate Effects: perceptual distortion, increased heart rate, increased appetite, social ease, relaxation or anxiety (depending)

Long-Term Effects: extreme lethargy, short-term memory loss

Okay, but can it kill me? No one has ever OD'd on marijuana

Scribe: Jack Kerouac: "This madness would lead nowhere. I didn't know what was happening to me and suddenly I realized it was only the tea that we were smoking."

Myths: Dangerous "gateway" drug; totally harmless (holding smoke in your lungs just can't be good for you)

Betcha didn't know: 10 million Americans use pot monthly

Drug: Cocaine

Immediate Effects: alertness, confidence, paranoia

Long-Term Effects: psychosis, hallucinations, emaciation, antisocial behavior

Okay, but can it kill me? Oh, yeah. Even if you're a young, healthy, super-athlete, like, say, 1985 #3 NBA draft pick Len Bias.

Scribe: Sigmund Freud: "I hastily wound up my investigation of cocaine and contented myself . . . with prophesying that further uses for it would soon be found."

Myths: That it's an aphrodiasic; that it's having a big comeback—it never went away.

Betcha didn't know: Men are more sensitive to the effects of cocaine than women.

Drug: Speed (amphetamines, methamphematime)

Immediate Effects: alertness, feeling of well-being, increased physical stamina

Long-Term Effects: psychosis, paranoia, emaciation, respiratory problems

Okay, but can it kill me? Yup

Scribe: Ted Berrigan: "I wonder if I'm fooling myself . . . about pills?"

Myths: Better than caffeine

Betcha didn't know: On the West Coast, cocaine use has been eclipsed by methamphetamine.

Drug: Heroin

Immediate Effects: sweating, nausea, expansion of ego, overwhelming sense of well-being, reduction of fear and pain perception

Long-Term Effects: clouded consciousness, narcosis, respiratory and heart failure

Okay, but can it kill me? Start with Charlie Parker and follow the trail of corpses to the guy from Sublime. Yes, heroin can kill you, both sooner and later

Scribe: William S. Burroughs: "*KICK THAT HABIT MAN/KICK THAT HABIT/ MAN KICK THAT/HABIT MAN KICK/THAT HABIT MAN*"

Myths: Needle-exchange programs don't increase heroin use in a community; studies have produced contradictory findings and are inconclusive.

Betcha didn't know: To really get off on heroin, you have to vomit. Sexy, huh?

Drug: LSD (Lysergic Acid Diethylamide)

Immediate Effects: hallucinations and perceptual distortion, heightened sensory perception, altered sense of self, makes the Grateful Dead and rave music sound good

Long-Term Effects: People with psychological problems or a history of multi-drug abuse are likely to suffer long-term psychological problems from exposure to LSD. Otherwise, probably none, though there are occassional reports of extended and drastic reactions. Prediction is basically impossible.

Okay, but can it kill me? Only if, in your tripped-out state, you

continued on page 237

doesn't tend to smoke as much of it. (Committed bong-hitters should note that bongs don't mitigate pot smoke's harm to the body and that holding smoke in the lungs for a longer time not only fails to produce a better high, but has been shown to cause more damage.)

The only other evidence of marijuana-related health problems in humans comes from a 1996 study, published in the *Journal of the American Medical Association*, in which heavy pot smokers didn't do quite as well on memory tests as light pot smokers.

Thus, the most relevant question for cautious experimenters becomes, "How do I avoid becoming a long-term, heavy marijuana smoker?" Which invites exploration of what may be the thorniest of pot-related issues: psychological addiction. One problem is that it's difficult to argue that addiction per se is a serious crisis—caffeine, for instance, can be difficult to quit, but many coffee junkies enjoy the habit and report no negative health effects. Another problem is that addiction of any kind is extremely difficult to define usefully.

member: ez2bkind
SURVEY: DRUGS
Prohibition began because the Secretary of the Treasury (Andrew Mellon) had a ne'er-do-well nephew-in-law (Harry Anslinger) who needed a job. Hearst wanted hemp paper out of the picture to further his wood pulp paper business, DuPont was about to introduce nylon, which they were billing as synthetic hemp (Mellon Bank was one of the chief financiers of DuPont), the drug companies had all these "modern" synthetic drugs they had patented and wanted to create a market for. Congress was bought and paid for and the marijuana tax act passed despite the objections of the AMA. It doesn't take a rocket scientist to understand—they weren't outlawing *dope*, they were outlawing *rope*.

Any kid who passed her government-sponsored drug education class will tell you that you have an addiction when you keep doing something, even though it messes up your life. But people with more experience know that just because something screws you up in some ways doesn't mean it's not worth doing. Maybe the benefits outweigh the costs. And heroin is certainly addictive, but it doesn't hurt you until it's absent. "Okay," counters our Just Say No kid, "addiction is when something makes your whole life revolve around it, and you can't give it up because that would hurt very bad." Congratulations, kid—you just defined love.

Trouble is, while it can be pretty easy to recognize when a friend or loved one's use of a substance is destructive or unhealthy, it's usually impossible to pinpoint what it is about the person or the drug that has created that situation. In fact, addiction may have less to do with "bad" substances or "bad" people than with bad relationships between people and certain drugs. Science and statistics may help guide you through the convoluted maze of marijuana decision making. But in determining what kind of relationship you're likely to have with the stuff, it might be best to consider the most biased sources of information around—people with a lot of marijuana experience and a genuine concern for their own health and well-

decide to do something that will kill you. The fatal dose is several thousand times the normal dose.

Scribe: Tom Wolfe: "The whole thing was . . . the *experience* . . . this certain indescribable feeling . . . The *experience* of the barrier between the subjective and the objective, the personal and the impersonal, the I and the *not*-I disappearing . . . But these are *words*, man! *And you couldn't put it into words*."

Myths: A certain number of doses makes one legally insane; LSD crystals accumulate in the body, causing flashbacks.

Betcha didn't know: Hoping it would work as a truth serum or psychological weapon, the CIA tested LSD on hundreds of Harvard and Stanford volunteers in the late '50s and early '60s.

Drug: Mushrooms (Psilocybin)

Immediate Effects: tendency to think the not-funny is funny, tremendous physical rush, heightened sensory perception.

Long-Term Effects: See LSD. Also, anecdotal evidence suggests paranoia, dim-wittedness, and depression may result from heavy ingestion over time.

Okay, but can it kill me? See LSD.

Scribe: Terrence McKenna: "If the expansion of consciousness does not loom large in the human future, what kind of future is it going to be?"

Myths: They're easy to grow.

Betcha didn't know: There are at least seventeen different species of psychoactive mushrooms.

Drug: Ecstasy (MDMA)

Immediate Effects: empathy, euphoria, enhances interpersonal communication and emotional awareness (uncontrollable urge to hug strangers and tell them your most private thoughts)

Long-Term Effects: MDMA has been shown to cause partial (although not necessarily irreparable) damage to serotonin-receiving neurons in lab animals (serotonin is a brain chemical that that affects sleep, mood, sexual function, appetite regulation, and pain perceptions). The *Journal of the American Medical Association* reports that "humans presently using MDMA may be incurring damage" to their brains. Some psychiatrists who favor the study of MDMA as a psychotherapeutic agent doubt the outcomes and conclusions of these experiments.

Okay, but can it kill me? Death appears to be rare, but it does occur; a healthy eighteen-year-old died after taking 1½ hits of MDMA in 1985. May be more common in individuals with underlying cardiac disease.

Scribes: Thomas Pynchon: "The circuits of the brain which mediate alarm, fear, fright, fight, lust, and territorial paranoia are temporarily disconnected. You see everthing with total clarity, undistorted by animalistic urges. You have reached a state which the ancients have called nirvana, all-seeing bliss."

Myths: accumulates in your spinal cortex; is harmless; is the love drug.

Betcha didn't know: Thomas Pynchon was such a wild man!

Drug: Special K (Ketamine, an animal anesthetic taken orally and nasally; not to be confused with Vitamin K)

Immediate Effects: nausea (compounded by movement), extenuated sense of touch, loss of smell and taste; overall, "disassociates" mind from body

Long-Term Effects: comalike state or "k-hole"; belief that you have been plugged into a realm of the "hyperreal." Anecdotal evidence suggests that the more people do K, the crazier they sound.

Okay, but can it kill me? On its own, probably, and when mixed with alcohol or other depressants, or with hallucinogens, K becomes extremely dangerous.

Scribe: John Lilly, the model for the anthropologist character in the film *Altered States*, claims to have communicated with aliens while on K.

Myths: That it's a hot new drug.

Betcha didn't know: At least one person has compared the K experience to the film *Tron*. That good, eh?

—*Paul Tullis*

being. Consider the following examples, from interviews with people who started puffing in their teens.

Gary, age twenty-six and employed as a Web site administrator, reports that he doesn't enjoy pot smoking as much as he used to, but he's having great difficulty quitting. For him, what was once an adventure has become a routine. "My entire lifestyle has changed since college, when I started getting high," he says. "It used to be a tool for seeing the world through new eyes. Now I have a family and [I'm] far more likely to smoke alone, in secret, and then experience difficulty dealing out in public. I have much less fun being confused and disoriented now that people rely on me. But still—if I'm at a movie and I'm not high by the time the lights dim, I feel disappointed and wish I'd had a couple of hits." More often, Gary says, he'll smoke but end up fighting the effects. "It's absurd," he says, "but I still do it."

Another veteran smoker narrative, at least as common as Gary's, involves even more unpleasant effects, including paranoia and panic attacks. "My heart would pound so hard the sound would fill my ears—I couldn't even hear people asking me if I was okay," recounts Erin, a twenty-nine-year-old assistant chef. "Sometimes it would happen right after smoking pot, but on occasion I also found myself overcome with fear upon waking and on the bus after work." Erin saw a doctor about her attacks. "He said to stop smoking marijuana, and I didn't believe it would help. I thought he was just reciting the medical establishment's party line. But the panic attacks stopped as soon as I quit." Once Erin associated pot with unpleasant feelings, she experienced no difficulty abstaining.

Stories like these are no less common than tales of incorrigible ganja lovers who experience no ill health effects after decades of steady use. Brian, age thirty-two, a photographer and a regular pot smoker for over ten years, claims that he's never found the effects of marijuana anything but agreeable. "If I didn't smoke pot," he says, "I'd be less creative, less successful, and less happy. I don't see how that could be healthier."

If you're interested in marijuana—whether as a drug, medicine, or cultural phenomenon—reading up on it is a good idea. *Marijuana Myths, Marijuana Facts: A Review of the Scientific Evidence*, by Lynn

member: Johnny_Victory

SURVEY: DRUGS

I've seen husbands trying to trade their wives' sexual favors for $40 worth of crack, fifteen-year-old girls with abcess-covered arms trying to shoot up into their elbow, and people trying to cash their mother's forged checks. I've also seen a lot of good come out of the drug scene—junkies who find "God" in the end of their needle and start doing good for those less fortunate than themselves (believe it or not, lots of people are worse off than drug addicts). I've seen the camaraderie that the short, sharp relationships of the underground inspires—people pulling together and helping each other to get high. And even though that may seem like a ludicrous target to reach for, I have seldom seen that kind of caring and cooperation in the "real" world. I hold down a $40,000 a year job, have a thirteen-year-long relationship with a non–drug using girl, and own my own home—and I'm a drug addict.

Zimmer, Ph.D., and John P. Morgan, M.D., is (though published by the unabashedly pro-legalization Lindesmith Center) an excellent place to start. So is Dr. Andrew Weil's first book, *The Natural Mind*, which fundamentally challenges our culture's prevailing understanding of how drugs and medicine work. Weil argues against the notion that drug "highs" are contained in the drugs themselves, and shows how the "effects" of many drugs, including marijuana, are better understood as conditioned responses. A Harvard-trained medical doctor, Dr. Weil guides readers, step-by-step from the atomizing mind-set of hard science to a holistic view in which drugs, users, medical philosophy, political culture, and human nature all play a part in the drug problem.

Incidentally, though Weil's recent best-selling books on natural healing have brought him international guruhood, his early work on drugs has yet to achieve the same level of mainstream acclaim. It seems most people aren't ready for a practical approach to drugs. If you are, it's out there. But watch out—trying to keep your head clear while following our national conversation on marijuana is like trying to think sober when everyone else at the party is stoned.

> Not Your Average Resource Guide

FACTS AND STATISTICS ON DRUGS AND DRUG USE

http://www.hyperreal.org/drugs
http://www.lycaeum.org
http://www.deoxy.org
http://www.nida.nih.gov/
http://www.health.org

NONPOLEMICAL BOOKS ABOUT DRUGS AND DRUG USE/ABUSE

Alcoholism and Substance Abuse, Thomas E. Bratter & Gary G. Forrest, eds. (Free Press).

A Primer of Drug Action, 7th edition, by Robert M. Julien, M.D., Ph.D. (W.H. Freeman & Co., 1995).

ARTISTIC INTERPRETATIONS OF DRUG ABUSE

The Electric Kool-Aid Acid Test, by Tom Wolfe (Bantam, 1983).

Junky, by William S. Burroughs (Bucaneer Books, 1994).

Trainspotting, by Irvine Welsh (W.W. Norton & Co., 1996).

Play the Piano Drunk, by Charles Bukowski (Black Sparrow, 1997).

Leaving Las Vegas, Mike Figgis (Columbia Pictures)

Sticky Fingers, The Rolling Stones (Columbia Records)

—*Paul Tullis*

Cigarettes

What most folks find so hard to figure out is how they got so hooked to begin with. Here's one explanation.

by Matt Goldberg

> It is my conviction that nicotine is a very remarkable beneficient drug. You are all very aware of the very great increase in the use of artificial controls, stimulants, tranquillisers, sleeping pills, and it is a fact that under modern conditions of life people find that . . . they must have drugs available to take when they feel the need.
>
> —*Speech given by a tobacco industry executive at a 1962 research conference in England*

Spontaneous sobbing. Powdered laxatives. I had a hard time deciding which of these two unexpected results of having quit smoking cigarettes was more pathetic. Adding orange-flavored Metamucil to my diet seemed to be the shoe-in for that distinction. After all, spooning the same facilitative dried and ground wheat husks I'd grown up watching my father administer each morning before work into my own Tropicana shed too bright a light on some of the less than desirable changes being wrought on my body. Needing assistance with that function, a kind of aid I'd never before required, was a clarion call that I really could no longer rely on my smokes.

But as it went (colon-clenching, blood-vessel-on-the-forehead-ballooning sessions on the porcelain notwithstanding), these excretory difficulties proved, I decided, less deserving of pity than the inescapable reality that I had twice already imploded into tears since Quit Day, which had passed not three weeks previous. Immediately following the second of these mini-breakdowns came the conclusion that crying was clearly a more deplorable cigarette withdrawal symptom than losing the ability to defecate with ease. Sure, constipation does no wonders for one's self-image, not to mention how poorly a sludgy helping of medicated juice substitutes for one's morning puff. But at least this dilemma has a direct physiological cause, I told myself. You can't really will yourself into taking a dump. The bawling on the other hand belied a flawed character and declared (to all the folks hanging around and tossing bread crumbs into the terribly quaint little duckpond where I flipped the switch on my tear ducts) my inability to ride it out, to suck it up, and as they say, take it like a man.

That I was totally misguided in the above self-disgust didn't become apparent until I delved further into the literature on smoking, a vaguely quixotic academic quest I set upon further along the quitting path as part of the continuing experiment that is keeping me off the Evil Weed. The one that still, twenty years after we first heard it in health class, kills more people each year in the United States than all other forms of substance abuse combined—a number that's often quoted as being around 400,000 but that the World Health Organization claims is closer to 530,000.

member:
bluegrassrainbow

SURVEY: DRUGS

I have smoked cigarettes for some thirty odd years, drunk myself into oblivion upon numerous occasions, smoked marjuana off and on over a period of years, and sniffed cocaine *once*. By far, I've found nicotine the most addictive.

One of the first facts I unearthed was that cigarettes function as a sort of ad hoc antidepressant, not only increasing the release of the neurotransmitter dopamine, which is related to feelings of pleasure, but decreasing *at the same time* the rate at which dopamine dissipates in the brain, according to research on cigarette smoke by scientists at the Brookhaven National Laboratory in New York. So lighting up butt after butt contributes to a precisely managed ebb and flow in the brain of the chemicals responsible for making us feel contented. "Over-the-counter therapy" is how author Alan Brody describes this attribute of smoking in his book *Cigarette Seduction*. Such a pharmacological and therapeutic perspective on smoking, one that envisions smokers using cigarettes to micromanage their moods, helps begin to explain why so many hundreds of millions of people around the world continue to smoke—even though overall cigarette consumption, at least in the United States, has decreased over 30 percent since 1970 because of ever-increasing alarm over the health-related damage wreaked by smoking on its practitioners and the people who share the planet with them.

As with much research and revelation having to do with smoking, the discoveries getting play in the media and the public sphere now are extremely old news to the tobacco companies. In 1996, University of California professor Dr. Stanton Glantz penned *The Cigarette Papers*, a damning assault on the tobacco industry fostered by the anonymous shipping of several thousand pages of confidential internal documents to the author two years earlier. Therein, a tobacco company research report dating from 1963 posits "the 'pleasure of smoking' must be found partly in the relief of anxiety that cigarette smoking brings so constantly, and in such a very short time." Then and now, smokers, in essence, medicated themselves with cigarettes, continuously warding off depression and anxiety in a fashion whose insidious gradualism eventually creates the illusion that the cigarette-induced shifting biochemical tide is the norm. Cessation of smoking results in a sort of El Niño of one's neurotransmitters, the often disastrous effects of which are no less physiological (nor less inevitable) than constipation, say, or weight gain, another of the recognized ways that quitting impacts the body.

All of this helps explain the biggest development in the realm of kicking the habit since the advent of the patch. In the spring of 1997, the Food and Drug Administration approved a drug called Zyban for use by people seeking to cease smoking. Not only is Zyban the first FDA-approved nicotine-free cessation aid, it's also the first stop-smoking system to come in tablet form. The one thing not new and revolutionary about Zyban is its actual composition. For Zyban is not a new drug at all, but a new name for the well-known antidepressant Wellbutrin.

In a pair of clinical trials, the drug's manufacturer, Glaxo Wellcome, set out to experimentally corroborate mounting anecdotal evidence suggesting that depressed smokers being treated with Wellbutrin *wanted* to smoke less and hence consumed fewer cigarettes or even stopped smoking entirely. The results of this research, which garnered the FDA's stamp of approval, demonstrated that after four weeks of taking the drug 49 percent of the participants were smoke-free, as compared to 36 percent for the patch. When the two methods were combined—the Wellbutrin (or Zyban) to fill the antidepressant void left by the absent cigarette smoke and the nicotine patch to alleviate the pangs of withdrawing from this elemental compound of inhaled tobacco smoke—a whopping 58 percent remained off cigarettes. A late 1997 article published by the *New England Journal of Medicine* indicated that the longer-term chances of quitting with Zyban were slightly less spectacular though, in all honesty, still pretty encouraging: The *NEJM*'s figures showed 23 percent of people attempting to quit with the aid of Zyban were smoke-free one year later. This compared to the 10 percent success rate among the 17 million Americans who try to quit each year, a stat reported as part of testimony heard by the House Subcommittee on Health and the Environment in 1994.

The odds seemed good enough for me.

I made an appointment with a faceless Dr. Martin at the clinic nearest my office agreeable to accepting my insurance. Doc Martin glanced at the story about Zyban's approval I'd printed from CNN's Web site, cocked his head as prelude to a mental tour through the office's pharmacological inventory, and slid out of the exam room . . . only to return a moment later with a case of Wellbutrin. The original. Without the new agency-concocted name but with all 150 milligrams in each and every smooth-edged, purple tablet of sure-to-keep-you-awake-for-a-fortnight psychoactive bupropion hydrochloride.

Before getting too involved with the specifics of my experience customizing the biochemistry of my brain, it's worthwhile to investigate the mechanism by which one gets so direfully dependent on cigarettes that quitting requires measures as drastic as a regimen of prescription antidepressants (especially a brand with a one in a thousand incidence of seizures), not to mention any number of fairly expensive nicotine replacement devices like transdermal patches, gums, and nasal sprays (this last also recently approved by an apparenty ultra-smoking-conscious FDA).

And it's with the just-mentioned alkaloid, nicotine, that that story starts. Nicotine, a substance found nowhere else in nature but the tobacco plant, is the primary agent responsible for the antidepressantlike, anxiety-soothing effects of inhaled cigarette smoke. But as Cornell comp lit and French prof Richard Klein states in his 1993 *Cigarettes Are Sublime*, a wonderfully hyberbolic exploration of smoking's literary, philosophical, aesthetic, and cultural dimensions, "it is not enough to merely assert that though bad for the health, cigarettes provide remedies for ills of the spirit. Cigarettes are more than therapy."

Researchers at Brown and Williamson (the tobacco giant whose pilfered files comprise the bedrock of Stantz's book) concluded the same thing, thirty years earlier. Their report noted "increasing evidence that nicotine is the key factor in controlling, through the central nervous system, a number of beneficial effects of tobacco smoke." Smokers intuitively understand what these people are talking about. You're sleepily behind the wheel late some night somewhere . . . what invariably winds up lightly clenched in your fingers, jiggling a bit with each bump in the road? Or you're writing something . . . a magazine story, say, or a paper for a grad school course . . . and you keep hitting the wall. What without fail helps you break through? You get the point.

But what's happening here? Why does nicotine make you more alert and nimble minded? By racheting up your brain functions, plain and simple. The September 22, 1997, issue of the journal *Science* reported findings that support this assertion: "The researchers believe that nicotine's ability to strengthen signals between neurons may account for the complex behavioral effects [of smoking] such as alertness and improved short-term memory." By enhancing the connections between the nerve cells in your brain, cigarettes become a tool with which smokers can, at will, perform (indeed, exist) at a higher level. So it should come as no surprise just how attached people get to them. For, as Klein writes, "a smoker lives through his cigarettes . . . making systematic use of [them] to perform tasks and procure pleasures, in a wide variety of situations, accompanying all his moods and movements . . . any smoker will tell you what Sartre says is true: 'Life without cigarettes is a little less worth living.' "

This was clearly my feeling as well, as the Wellbutrin reached optimal levels in my brain and I affixed my first patch to one of the few mostly hair-free places on my body. I didn't really feel as bad (or depressed) as I'd anticipated—isolated bouts of teary-eyed gloom notwithstanding—but it did seem like life was somehow paler and less interesting. I was on a pretty even keel, which I guess is better than swinging wildly between the extremes but might not be quite as satisfying as minor yet regular modulations in consciousness—precisely the experience afforded to one who smokes butts.

That life's edge seemed to have dulled, that I was just less enthusiastic about . . . stuff in general, could not be attributed simply to the now absent pharmocological mechanations of cigarettes upon my pyscho-physiology. The antidepressantlike action of cigarette smoke was replaced by the Zyban and the essentially irremediable withdrawal one faces when kicking nicotine (the 1988 Surgeon General's report concluded that "the processes determining tobacco addiction are similar to those that determine addiction to . . . heroin and cocaine") was being combatted by my extra-large 21-mg nic patch (which, I should divulge, stirred up in my subconscious such vividly surreal dreamscapes that I had to cease wearing said patch twenty-four hours a day as I'd been doing). And though I was additionally deprived of the performance-enhancing attributes of smoking, life appeared lackluster not because I couldn't stay awake late at night while driving or think of a clever way to end an argument in some essay or what have you. No, the ultimate reason why I felt so blasé about everything around me and all that I did once I'd stopped smoking isn't specifically physiological or biochemical in nature. It's less tangible than noting increased levels of dopamine or examining the signals traveling to and fro between neurons in the brain and is more aligned with the previously referenced Sartre quote. Because this French philosopher, who smoked fat, robust cigarettes, knew the secret to smoking's unrelenting grip on its practitioners. As Klein tells it, Sartre conceived of the cigarette as "an instrument for symbolically appropriating the world . . . its smoke bathes the light and shadows, mitigates the press of hard reality."

Sartre further maintained that the only way to quit was to find other methods for "taking possession of the significant events in daily life: the savor of a dinner, the pleasure of a performance, the act of early morning writing." But this is so much easier said than done. I mean, Sartre couldn't—and didn't—quit for any sustained period of time. Moreover, it damn well isn't a coincidence that the same philosopher responsible for delineating the angst of a millennium's last century and giving it a name had a life-long (and fatal) love affair with the cigarette. Smoking allows smokers a measure of control over lives that are increasingly out of control and out of sync. This has been true since tobacco's introduction to the Western world in the sixteenth century (the dawn of what Klein terms the "Age of Anxiety") but it is only more pronounced now, at a time when people have more evidence than has ever been available as to why they shouldn't smoke and yet pay no heed. Quitting smoking, for some time if not forever, carries with it a curse of sorts; one may live longer, but that longer life may just feel a bit less like a set of deliberate actions and more like a series of events that just sort of happen and wash over one.

I know how melodramatic much of this may seem, especially to someone (un)lucky enough to have never indulged in a cigarette in some truly made-for-smoking moment like the ones spoken of by Sartre. And I feel more than a little embarrassed at how much truth I ascribe to these ideas about why cigarettes still exert such an absurdly strong influence over the not quite 1 billion people who insist on smoking them. (Others focus more on how cigarettes represent the biggest dupery of the world's population by the capitalist industrialist complex in the history of our species—which is true but outside the scope of this piece.)

But in the end, I'm haunted by something Richard Klein posits in his book, the writing of which, incidentally, was the author's personalized method of quitting. "One thinks of the many great men and women who have died prematurely from having smoked too much," Klein writes. "It does them an injustice to suppose that their greatness did not depend in some degree on the wisdom and pleasure and spiritual benefit they took in a habit they could not abandon."

The more you ponder that notion, the scarier it becomes.

Alternative Medicine

One out of every three Americans uses some form of "unconventional" medicine. From the age-old to the New Age, here's a look inside the alt.med universe.

by Alissa Quart

In the last decade, more Americans have had their shoulders realigned, their energies recalibrated, and their nerves massaged than ever before. They have swallowed flowers to help them sleep, chewed roots to improve their memory, and received flavored enemas for whatever ails them. Curatives from the age-old to the purely New Age have—in news media parlance—"mainstreamed."

This increased attention is being encouraged and institutionalized on all sides. According to a study by the *New England Journal of Medicine*, 34 percent of Americans use "unconventional" medicine. The National Institute of Health has underwritten ten investigations into various herbs and plants to determine whether or not they are helpful in treating cancer. And in 1992, Congress even mandated the creation of the Office of Alternative Medicine (OAM), to serve as an information clearinghouse and produce and cofund research on everything from manual healing methods to "mind/body interventions." In 1997, it had a budget of $12 million.

Why are people so interested in what are now called "complementary" treatments and tonics? At a time when huge pharmaceutical concerns control the cost and quality of America's health, herbal remedies can appear at the very least an assertion of individual will. And as America's managed medical care grows ever more business-like, with higher deductibles and more impersonal attention, the appeal of natural remedies grows as well.

member: Applecheeks

SURVEY: ALTERNATIVE MEDICINE

As an R.N. who worked twenty-five years (mostly in hospitals), I can say without hesitation that most M.D.s are only interested in how much money they can make! Disease starts in the mind and then shows up in the body as illness. The homeopath knows this and treats the entire individual. Unfortunately, since the AMA does not recognize them as "legitimate" doctors, it is quite difficult to find a homeopathic doctor outside of California.

member: Apel

SURVEY: ALTERNATIVE MEDICINE

Look at it this way: homeopathy, herbal remedies, witch doctors, and religious healing were all very popular in the 1600s, and the life span was thirty years. Now, people go to medical doctors with high-tech equipment and powerful, FDA-approved, scientifically tested drugs—and the life span is over seventy years, and increasing. The improvements in technology and medicine in just the last twenty years have drastically increased the quality and length of the average life. Homeopathy had hundreds of years to do the same thing—and it just plain hasn't.

Melissa Cooperman, a twenty-eight-year-old New York–based photographer and a skeptic of traditional health care had her suspicions confirmed once and for all after what she calls her "Gen-X injury"—an infected eyebrow piercing. She incurred a bill of $350, which took her a year to pay off. "I don't trust doctors," says Cooperman, reciting one of alternative medicine's mantras.

Adds Paul Rush, director of publications for the Open Center, the largest holistic learning center in the United States, "My personal opinion is that young people's increased interest in acupuncture, nutrition, yoga, and tai chi stems from a distrust of conventional medicine's impersonality. America's HMOs are primarily interested in satisfying Wall Street."

Nonetheless, even bureaucratic behemoths have opened up some of their insurance coverage to alternative medicines. Microsoft employees now may have unlimited access to a number of "in-network" chiropractors, naturopaths, and Christian Science healers. Blue Shield of California offers an HMO policy option that allows employers to cover a fixed number of acupuncture visits. Even the stodgy Oxford Health Plans, after finding that 33 percent of its members had used an alternative provider in the previous two years, now covers alternative medicine through a credentialed network of providers.

member: KerrinWhite

SURVEY: ALTERNATIVE MEDICINE

Many years ago, as a faculty member in a psychiatric residency training program, I was asked to mentor a young lady on a fellowship who had been trained in Israel to believe in homeopathy. Actually, they wanted me to check out whether she was crazy or not. I didn't believe in homeopathy then and I don't now. Specifically, I don't believe in their contention that drugs that have been diluted so much that not a single molecule remains in solution can have biological (versus psychological) effects. In any case, this "fellow" and I set out to review the literature on homeopathic treatments for psychiatric disorders. Eventually we published two articles on the subject. What surprised me was that, where I half expected to see a lot of incredible claims of "miracle cures" that would reveal the practitioners as charlatans, instead I found a lot of modest, seriously presented series of cases, and even a controlled study or two. What became apparent was that, considering the kind of patients the homeopaths reported treating, such as acutely depressed people, you would expect them to get better in a reasonably short time anyway, without any treatment or with a placebo. The authors of these reports mostly didn't seem to realize that; instead they seemed to feel that anybody who got better on a treatment represented evidence that the treatment worked, quite a naïve point of view.

Snake Oils and Media Hype?

The media, always eager for breakthroughs of any sort, has been quick to jump on stories of miracle cures. But in the ephemeral media spotlight, today's wonder herb may be tomorrow's poison. Dabblers in alternative cures are right to ask, How much of the new interest is simply media-generated hype? Jan Lynch, the manager of herbal medicines at the New York City health food store Commodities, attributes the rise in sales at her store over the last year to "a media blitz," the power behind consumer interest in her top-selling remedies: St. John's Wort for depression, echinacea for colds, and Alpha Lipoic Acid, an antioxidant, to slow aging. "People come rushing in, a lot of them young," says Lynch. "Lots of students use gingko, especially around exam time. These are regular people who read about it in the newspaper."

Retired psychiatrist Stephen Barrett spends much of his time disparaging the consumption of alternative medicine. "There's no research that shows a fear of doctors is making people turn to alternative medicine," says Barrett, coauthor of forty-three books and an editor of *Quackwatch*, a Web magazine that seeks to undermine the

> Alt.med Dictionary

ACUPUNCTURE: Needles are inserted into the skin at specific points and manipulated. The points are on purported energy channels—or meridians—thought to be connected to internal organs. Pain is supposedly relieved by rebalancing energy flow, which prompts the nerve cells to produce endorphins.

ALEXANDER TECHNIQUE: One-on-one lessons that improve posture. An Alexander instructor pushes and prods her pupil's body into perfect alignment, adjusting the limbs, shoulders, and jaw. F. M. Alexander recommended at least thirty individual lessons. Benefits are said to include easier and more efficient movement, improved posture, the development of poise, freer breathing, and increased energy.

CHIROPRACTICS: Chiropractors manipulate the musculo-skeletal system of the body, usually by hand. They specialize in helping people with spinal problems, such as low back pain and neck pain. State-licensed practitioners, chiropractors adjust the tissues of the human body, particularly along the spinal column, factoring in neurology and nutrition, as well.

HERBAL MEDICINE: This combines a holistic philosophy with the exclusive use of plant material. Herbalists claim to treat the patient as an individual, not just a collection of symptoms. Although remedies from gingko to goldenseal are broadcast and debated on television the world over and achieve sales in the billions of dollars, users should still approach these natural substances with caution. They are not to be used without sufficient knowledge and may have negative effects. Speak with a doctor, herbalist, or naturopath before you take herbal remedies or supplements.

HOMEOPATHY: Samuel Hahnemann founded homeopathy in 1789 on the principle that a little bit of the disease can be the cure. An infinitesimal amount of an organic substance, like bark, in a pill that is almost entirely composed of sugar supposedly cures or eases malaria, asthma, and a host of other conditions. One example of this is syrup of ipecac, derived from a plant that causes vomiting—ipecac is supposed to counteract the effects of having ingested certain poisons.

REFLEXOLOGY: Reflexologists apply pressure to the feet or the hands to affect changes in other parts of the body. Reflexologists believe that the feet are a mirror of the body, with different parts of the sole corresponding to internal organs. As with acupressure and acupuncture, reflexologists press on pressure points to decrease stresses on the body. According to Jery Whitworth of Columbia Presbyterian's Complementary Care unit, when dogs had their foot pads pressed, there was an increase in lymphatic drainage back to the heart. According to Whitworth, edema, or swelling in the tissues common to heart failure patients, responds similarly after reflexological techniques.

PILATES: A technique of lengthening and strengthening the body using pulleys and other machines that provide resistance. These exercises concentrate on building abdominal strength. Its adherents say this fitness regime is the most holistic and effective exercise model there is.

SHIATSU, ACUPRESSURE: Shiatsu uses the same principles as acupuncture; pressure is applied to specific parts of the body by the hands and fingers, working on acupuncture points.

validity of the healing movement. "It's logical for alternative medicine proponents to say that an aversion to conventional doctors is behind the alternative medicine phenomenon," he says. "Much of what is called alternative medicine is promotion of products: The vast majority of herbs are aggressively marketed. The remedies are sold over the counter, without a doctor in the equation."

For all of his extremism, he has a point. In the fall of 1997, "nature's Prozac," St. John's Wort, surfaced in the *New York Times* and on morning talk shows. The evidence that this Teutonic herbal antidepressant was effective and safe was suggestive but not conclusive. And yet the natural supplement was snapped up.

Even some herbalists are ready to admit to the variablity and the "quackery" to be found among some herbal medicine practitioners. Betsy Levy of the American Botanical Council says that while some herbal medicines are wonders others are indeed placebos. "Herbs work," she says. "A lot of traditional drugs are based on herbs. But like any other product, some work and others don't work nearly as well."

Homeopathic remedies, even more than herbal ones, have been highly disputed and are frequently dismissed as ineffective. Samuel Hahnemann founded homeopathy in 1789 on the principle that a little bit of the disease can be the cure. Interest in the field apexed with a number of American homeopathic colleges in the nineteenth century and then waned, but the discipline has received new attention in the 1990s. In 1996, the homeopathic brand leader, Boiron's flu remedy, generated sales of $20 million. Though homeopathic remedies are often accused of exploiting the placebo effect, the estimable British medical journal, the *Lancet*, stated in the fall of 1997 that they could not prove homeopathy's effects to be solely "due to a placebo [effect]."

In the last few years, there has been a smattering of lawsuits in response to the snake-oil claims of some complementary health care providers and manufacturers. In 1996, a Virginia judge awarded more than $200,000 to the family of a man who died of cancer while receiving homeopathic therapy. The two-week trial revolved around the role of the doctor, Vincent Speckhart, in his patient's decision to reject chemotherapy, a standard treatment for cancer.

member: Mur

SURVEY: ALTERNATIVE MEDICINE

People were taking herbal remedies long before any modern medicine was invented. People in the 1500s didn't run to the apothecaries for Tylenol, believe it or not. Modern medicine is wonderful, but if people decide they want a natural remedy, the remedy can be found out there, and it's not a hoax. It never was.

member: Mixed

SURVEY: ALTERNATIVE MEDICINE

I think that holistic methods aid and remove stress from our bodies, allowing them to work better. However, when something is to the point of needing fixing, Western health care is where to start.

member: OlindaM

SURVEY: ALTERNATIVE MEDICINE

I have used various herbal remedies and acupressure regularly ever since I was prescribed antibiotics that gave rise to a very dramatic allergy. At the very least, homeopathic remedies don't have nasty side effects.

Herb: Echinacea (ek-a-NAY-sha)
A.K.A.: purple coneflower

Where found: North American plains, prairies, and open woodlands. Note: Due to its growing popularity, overcollection is threatening wild *Echinacea angustifolia*.

Most used part: The root

Indications: Echinacea is one of America's most popular herbal products, traditionally used to treat and prevent the common cold and flu, coughs, sore throats, infections, and even toothaches. Echinacea helps the body rid itself of microbial infections and is often effective against both viral and bacterial attacks.

Scientific stuff: More than 400 scientific studies have been conducted on echinacea. Research suggests that the echinacosides in *E. angustifolia* (not *E. purpurea*) are the main antimicrobial constituents. The polysaccharides in echinacea help stimulate the immune system and are antiviral.

Try this: Put 1 to 2 teaspoons of the root (available in bulk at natural foods stores) in 1 cup water and bring it slowly to a boil. Simmer 10 to 20 minutes. Drink three times daily. Tinctures and capsules are also available and should be taken as directed.

Don't do this: Don't take echinacea every day. It doesn't work that way. A regime of five days on, five days off echinacea is recommended because echinacea may lose its effectiveness if taken more regularly. If you're generally healthy, only use echinacea to help fight the common cold. It's not dangerous if you take it more often, but you're probably just wasting your money.

Herb: Goldenseal
A.K.A.: *Hydrastis canadensis*

Where found: North American woodlands, damp meadows, and forested highlands. Note: Goldenseal is also threatened by overcollection. Suitable herbal substitutes include barberry, Oregon grape, and goldthread (which contain goldenseal's active constituent, berberine).

Most used part: The root

Indications: Goldenseal soothes the mucous membranes of the respiratory tract during the congestion and inflammation of colds and flus. Combined with echinacea, it helps enhance the immune system and reduce congestion.

Scientific stuff: Goldenseal's major alkaloids are hydrastine and berberine. Hydrastine has been reported to lower blood pressure and relieve coughing. Berberine has many antibiotic and immunity-stimulating properties and is effective against amoebae, fungi, bacteria, and yeasts.

Try this: Use goldenseal with echinacea to support your immune system during colds and the flu. Goldenseal may be taken every two hours for acute cold symptoms. If taken with echinacea, use two parts echinacea to one part goldenseal in tablet, capsule, extract, or tea form.

Don't do this: As with echinacea, don't use goldenseal every day but rather only when necessary to help clear a cold or flu.

There are other ways to treat a cold naturally: Eat garlic until you stink —three cloves a day minimum for Americans—also available in nonodorous capsules. Take vitamin C (200 mg every two hours during acute conditions). Bioflavonoids (found in the peel of citrus fruits and in rose hips and hawthorn berries) reportedly increase the effectiveness of vitamin C when taken together.

Herb: Ginseng
A.K.A.: *Panax*

Where found: *Panax quinquefolius* (American ginseng) is native to North America, while *Panax ginseng* is found in China and cultivated throughout China, Russia, and Korea. *Eleutherococcus senticosus*, or Siberian ginseng, grows in mountain forests of Japan, Korea, Russia, and northeast China.

Most used part: The root

Indications: Therapeutically, ginseng works best with the weak or elderly. The Chinese value its ability to improve overall health, strengthen resistance to disease, and increase strength and performance. It has also been used as an aphrodesiac. Research confirms ginseng may help improve physical and mental performance and stimulate the immune system, according to Rob McCaleb, president of the Herb Research Foundation.

continued on page 253

Longs Drug Stores and PayLess Drug Stores have settled a number of lawsuits that charged them with deceptive advertising of homeopathic products. The manufacturer of Cold-Eeze zinc tablets, Quigley, got into a hot sitz bath when the company allegedly paid for the research that announced that zinc pills were cold cure-alls.

Energy Healing for Heart Patients

While advocates of traditional medicine may accuse complementary medicine practitioners of irrational faith and deceptive marketing, they also tend to ignore credible data supporting practices like chiropractics. According to a study conducted at the University of North Carolina at Chapel Hill, for instance, patients with acute lower back pain preferred the care they received from chiropractors to that given by primary care physicians.

Jery Whitworth, cofounder of the Complementary Care unit of Columbia Presbyterian Medical Center in New York, says the unit started off by providing services to Columbia patients who had undergone open heart surgery or heart transplants. These cardiac patients were treated using "mind therapies like guided imagery and visualization, and manual therapies like acupressure and reflexology," says Whitworth.

"Three-and-a-half years ago I had one attending physician. Now I have one hundred thirty-seven physicians in eleven different departments, including cardiac, pediatric, oncology. Cancer patients using our therapies need one-tenth the postoperative pain medication," Whitworth boasts.

Dr. Mehmet Oz, who cofounded the unit with Whitworth, is a heart surgeon at Columbia Presbyterian. Oz's cardiac patients can elect to have energy healers and therapeutic touch attendants along with traditional medical attention for heart problems. Similarly, oncologist Dr. Mitchell Gaynor of Manhattan's Strang Cancer Prevention Center combines allopathic and herbal treatments in his practice, prescribing Theragreens, a nutrient supplement, to reduce cancer risk.

But how much faith do these alternative therapies ultimately deserve? "Any healing fad is worth exploring," says Nancy Allison, editor of *The Illustrated Encyclopedia of Body Mind Discipline* and a

member: Louise_C

SURVEY: ALTERNATIVE MEDICINE

My oldest daughter has four boys and at least once a week one of them used to be in an emergency room getting stitches. But now she just grabs the cayenne pepper and sprinkles some on the cut, slaps on a butterfly bandage, and the whole thing usually heals in about two days. A lot of people ask if this doesn't burn like fire . . . only a teeny bit; even the five-year-old doesn't seem to mind it much.

member: Sartori

SURVEY: ALTERNATIVE MEDICINE

Current standard medical practices attack the symptoms. Homeopathy treats the root of the problem.

Scientific stuff: Ginseng is classified as an adaptogen, meaning it helps the body adapt to environmental and psychological stressors.

Try this: Place 1/2 teaspoon of powdered root (available at natural foods stores) in a cup of water, bring to a boil, and simmer gently 10 to 20 minutes. You can also buy whole roots, which are steamed to soften and then sliced and dried. "Simply suck on a piece the size of a corn kernel till it dissolves," writes herbalist Brigitte Mars. Limit use to once a day.

Don't do this: Don't expect ginseng to turn you into a superhero. Too much ginseng may make you feel like you're on a caffeine high, so you should use it wisely to help your body deal with physical and mental stress or fatigue.

Contraindications: Chinese herbalism warns against using ginseng during bronchitis and acute inflammatory disease.

Herb: Valerian
A.K.A.: *Valeriana officinalis*
Where found: Throughout temperate North America and Europe, displaying pink or white flowers.

Most used part: Roots and stems

Indications: Used worldwide to aid sleep, valerian's main indications are anxiety, nervous sleeplessness, and symptoms of tension such as indigestion or muscle cramping. Valerian is safe for long-term use and doesn't lose effectiveness.

Scientific stuff: The sedative action of valerian is partially due to its valepotriates, found in the root. The volatile oil found in valerian root has carminative (makes you pass gas) and relaxing properties.

Try this: Try taking valerian before a stressful situation, such as addressing an audience or meeting new mutant in-laws. The tincture or capsules are the most widely used preparations, but you can prepare an infusion by using 2 teaspoons of the dried herb in boiling water.

Don't do this: Don't combine valerian with other sleep-inducing drugs.

Contraindications: Valerian is considered GRAS (Generally Regarded as Safe) as a food additive by the FDA. It may stimulate rather than sedate some people. Large doses over an extended period of time may cause headaches, lethargy, or depression.

Herb: Chamomile
A.K.A.: *Matricaria recutita*

Where found: Roman chamomile (*Chamaemelum nobile*) is mostly cultivated in England. German chamomile (*Matricaria recutita*) is more widely used, however, and is less expensive.

Most used part: Flower tops

Indications: Chamomile has been traditionally used to aid conditions such as insomnia, stress, anxiety, and nervousness; as a soothing ointment for burns to the skin; and for stomach upset and menstrual cramps.

Scientific stuff: Scientists believe some of chamomile's healing properties come from its essential oil azulene, which is anti-inflammatory and hypoallergenic. Chamomile also contains levomenol, which is soothing to the skin. Coumarins and flavonoids also found in chamomile help against muscle spasms.

Try this: Put fresh chamomile tops or teabags in your bath. The fragrance will help calm you while the flowers soothe and soften your skin. If taken orally, the tincture preparation is popular, or you could steep chamomile tea: 2 to 3 teaspoonfuls of the flowers infused for 10 to 20 minutes.

Don't do this: Chamomile is a member of the ragweed family, so avoid it if you have hayfever.

Contraindications: According to herbalist Brigitte Mars, "Chamomile is considered safe, effective, and nonaddictive, although people with sensitivities should use caution. Some herbalists consider it too relaxing to the uterus to consume often during pregnancy."

Herb: Passionflower
A.K.A.: *Passiflora incarnata*

Most used part: Whole plant

Where found: Native to southeast North America, passionflower can also be grown in most any garden.

Indications: Similar to chamomile, passionflower is indicated for cases of insomnia, especially "intransigent insomnia."

continued on page 255

teacher of movement theory at New York University. As a teacher of Pilates, a fitness technique incorporating yogalike movements, Allison herself advocates practicing yoga and other ritual movements as health palliatives that help the body's many systems ward off disease.

According to the World Health Organization, there are, worldwide, 100 million suffererers of "chronic illness." For people in their twenties who wish to avoid being one of the malady-ridden, Jery Whitworth recommends preventative strategies like visualization. "Alternative medicine is not a religious experience or a war," he says. "Chronic illness can be mitigated by changing nutrition, getting exercise, reducing stress, and group therapy."

The media stories about taking vitamin E to stave off cancer and heart disease, folic acid to prevent certain birth defects, and melatonin to induce sleep will continue. But a certain amount of personal research may be the only satisfactory answer to discovering

member: Doc_ZueS

SURVEY: ALTERNATIVE MEDICINE

I was in a grease fire and suffered second degree burns to both hands and one arm. I went to my doctor and he said I would require at least two skin grafts and three to four months of healing and one month of physical therapy. I then went to a plastic surgeon who said that he had good results using aloe vera on burns, something he'd tried about two years previously. I used raw aloe vera plant on my burns for five weeks and all the skin grew back on its own. Two weeks after that I was back to work with only a bright redness remaining, which should disappear in about another month.

Scientific stuff: Passionflower is reported to have a depressant effect on central nervous system activity. One of its flavonoids, apigenin, is well known for its pharmacological actions, especially as an antispasmodic and anti-inflammatory.

Try this: Try passionflower first if you're having trouble falling asleep from mental worry or excitement. Pour 1 cup of hot water onto 1 teaspoonful of the dried herb and let it sit for 15 minutes. Drink a cup before going to bed.

Don't do this: Despite its sedative properties, passionflower is reputed to be an aphrodesiac.

Other tricks to put you out for the night:
Melatonin: This one's a bit controversial. You naturally produce melatonin in the pineal gland in your brain. As a "dietary supplement," melatonin is made from either a natural hormone extracted from bovine pineal glands or from synthetic sources.
Researchers believe that melatonin synchronizes daily and seasonal rhythms and a deficiency may in part be responsible for sleep disorders. Scientific studies on the long-term effects of melatonin supplements are still being conducted. Thus, it's safest to say that until more concrete data is collected about the effects of melatonin and the "supplemental" use of hormones, it's best to use herbal methods to aid sleep.

Herb: Ginkgo
a.k.a.: *Ginkgo biloba*

Where found: If you live in New York City, look around you for the trees with the bilobed, fan-shaped leaves. They're all over. Native to China, ginkgo trees are common in urban settings worldwide because of their ability to survive insect damage, viral and bacterial infection, and chemical pollution.

Most used part: The leaves

Scientific Stuff: Clinical research shows ginkgo extract increases blood flow to extremities, thus helping provide additional oxygen and nutrients to the brain, eyes, ears, and heart muscle.

Indications: "[Ginkgo extract] helps improve memory and cognitive function, prevents senile dementia, speeds recovery from head injury, improves vision and hearing in the elderly, and prevents oxygen deprivation of the heart muscle," according to Rob McCaleb, president of the Herb Research Foundation.

Try this: Try convincing your dad, whose memory is slowly fading, to start taking ginkgo daily. Explain that ginkgo extract is one of the most commonly prescribed medicines in all of Europe.

Don't do this: Don't expect to take a ginkgo pill and suddenly become Einstein.

Contraindications: Studies have shown that ginko may cause diarrhea and irritability, although McCaleb's review of clinical research on ginkgo shows that "no serious side effects have been noted," and "there are no known drug interactions," according to the medical journal the *Lancet*.

Herb: Gotu kola
a.k.a.: *Centella asiatica*

Most used part: The root

Where found: Located primarily in India, China, Australia, Indonesia, parts of Africa, and the South Pacific, gotu kola is considered an Ayurvedic herb, meaning it's part of the 5,000-year-old healing tradition from India known as Ayurveda.

Indications: Gotu kola has gained recent attention in the West as a mental stimulant and may be beneficial for skin conditions.

Scientific stuff: Triterpenes are an active compound in gotu kola that demonstrate both tranquilizing and antianxiety effects.

Don't do this: Don't take a lot of gotu kola. It's a powerful stimulant whose effects can be irritating if you don't like the jitters.

Contraindications: Gotu kola has been shown to cause central nervous system stimulation in high doses, which can cause a "racing mind," insomnia, and headaches.
— *Steve Taormina and Marni Davis*

what truly works. Brian Daly, a Wisconson-based musician and recording engineer, abused alcohol and drugs as a teenager and for years he was "sick with depression, allergies, fatigue, problems with digestion—things that if I went to the doctor and got a physical they would find nothing wrong." Though he still has his doubts about some of the therapies he undergoes, Daly says his frequent meetings with acupuncturists, homeopaths, spiritual counselors, bodywork counselors, and massage therapists, as well as his involvement with edu-kinesthetics and Chinese herbal medicine, have been the most effective regime he has been able to create to date.

And while there's little robust data on the effectiveness of so many natural remedies, from shark's fin to energy healers, these salves have worked for Daly, who is now off antidepressants. "I wanted to take charge of my own life. I realized nobody was going to fix me simply," he says of his involvement with alternative healing. "So I have been trying to fix myself."

member: nathanb_2

SURVEY: ALTERNATIVE MEDICINE

Not everyone knows that conventional medicine is based on natural things that have been tested, where their effects on illnesses, and, even more important, their side effects, have been established. "Conventional" medicine extracted from a plant, for example, contains only those ingredients of the plant that may help overcome the illness and will exclude those that are harmful. By using only "natural" things one consumes both the good and bad parts of it.

Antidepressants

By the late '80s, of nearly 16 million people who visited doctors for depression, 70 percent ended up in drug therapy. Now, on the verge of a new century, Prozac and its ilk are so ubiquitous that they stand to change our very definition of mental health.

by Tom Vanderbilt

Few consumer products ever define the age in which they are introduced, and Prozac might be the first for which one needs a prescription. It has landed on the covers of national news magazines; inspired countless books that came to praise, bury, or channel into memoir-grist its popularity (e.g., Peter Kramer's *Listening to Prozac*, Peter Breggin's *Talking Back to Prozac*, and Elizabeth Wurtzel's *Prozac Nation*); spawned fervent adepts and a concerted backlash; been blamed for the suicide of singer Del (Runaway) Shannon and prompted 28,000 adverse-reaction reports; been used as a legal defense in the trial of a New York City subway bomber; and earned the kind of zeitgeist-check in a Woody Allen film once reserved for the analyst's couch. A decade after the green-and-white capsule known formally as fluoxetine hydrochloride landed on U.S. shores after a successful Belgian launch in 1986, Prozac has become the best-selling mental health drug in history—some $2.6 billion in sales globally in 1997. When the world is depressed, the world reaches for Prozac.

Someone mistaking that for an ad slogan would not be far off

member: KerrinWhite

SURVEY: DEPRESSION

I've had many years of chronic, low-grade depression, punctuated by more severe episodes that incapacitated me. I've tried virtually all antidepressant medications over those years. The majority proved intolerable for their side effects: The worst was feeling groggy or dazed. Prozac I could take, but it did only a little good. I had a remarkably better response to the monoamine oxidase inhibitors (MAOIs), which are hardly ever used nowadays, almost considered "obsolete," but can help about half those depressed people who don't respond to more conventional medications. Nardil in particular did wonders for me, but it took several weeks and a substantial dosage (75 mg per day). Alas, many psychiatrists never use MAOIs so their patients never have the chance to try them. I know. I'm a psychiatrist myself.

member: SILVERLOCK

SURVEY: DEPRESSION

I've suffered from severe depression for years. I was drugged (Thorazine), locked up, tied down, and shocked. I heard voices and imagined plots against me. I couldn't sleep or eat. I was so scared and in such pain that I wanted to die and did try once or twice. Until five or six years ago I could not understand what was wrong with me. I finally found a good therapist and an antidepressant that works—Serzone. There were and will always be people better off and worse off than I am. Life is not fair. I truly understand that now, which frees me to be grateful for the many good parts of my life. I have no time for bitterness.

the mark as America enters the mass-consumer phase of what has been preciously dubbed cosmetic psychopharmacology. Prozac already has its slogan (a two-page spread that contrasted rainy skies—"Depression can hurt"—with sunny skies—"Prozac can help"), but the need for strong brand positioning campaigns will only intensify as the Food and Drug Administration rolls out vast new numbers of prescription drugs, including antidepressants. The FDA's approval rate for 1996 increased by 63 percent over 1995, noted *Medical Marketing & Media*, setting an all-time record for new product introductions (meanwhile, from 1992 to 1995 the agency's review time for new drugs dropped from thirty-three months to nineteen months). Suddenly, behind-the-counter drugs are being marketed the same way as over-the-counter drugs—whatever distinction remained was tossed out in August 1997, as the FDA allowed the makers of Prozac and Effexor to run ads largely devoid of lengthy explanatory text.

So what's the problem if ads start appearing with taglines like "It's the right drug now"? Isn't advertising just getting the word out, helping to inform those who may not have known they were afflicted with a particular malady? There is of course a grand problem putting supposedly therapeutic or medicinal drugs into the realm of consumer culture: Advertising conflates wants and needs into one big metaphysical stew. It creates and identifies problems where none may have existed before; it posits material goods as the solution to immaterial crises; it depicts visions of idealized selfhood, offers instant gratification, and demands little save monetary investment. For some users, Prozac and other antidepressants with a serious biochemical kick are treated as just another consumer product intended to help them get through the day: popping Prozac before going out to get a bigger buzz from fewer cocktails or front-loading pills during finals week.

Anyone feeling sanguine about the drug companies' good intentions in promoting their pills would do well to read the trade press or a Wall Street industry analyst's report. There the vague categories of human discontent and psychic affliction are cast in the most harshly naked lights of market share, brand identity, and revenue growth. Even more unsettling is the oft-stated fillip in the drug

member: jayen
SURVEY: DEPRESSION
I've suffered from chronic depression for as long as I can remember. I tried to medicate myself with narcotics for fifteen years. When I finally decided to seek help for my drug addiction, I also sought help for my depression. Whether or not one caused the other, they are now two separate issues. I was put on Prozac, which has done wonders for me. I describe it like this: Before I was on antidepressants, everything seemed to fall down into this black hole. Antidepressants have laid down a foundation for me and covered up the black hole. I still have to do the work and build on that foundation.

member: lilypad2
SURVEY: DEPRESSION
I have been on one antidepressant or another for the last twenty-five years. I thought at first it was all in my head and it was my fault that I let things get the best of me. Finally I found a doctor who explained to me that the medication was necessary because my depression was caused by a chemical imbalance in my brain. I caused myself a lot of grief trying to get off my medication and control my depression myself. Now that I know what the situation is, I accept it and live a relatively normal life.

member: shysmile
SURVEY: DEPRESSION
I suffered from depression during my formative years. I did attend therapy but it wasn't helpful for me at all. My doctor wanted to put me on medication, but I strongly refused. It seemed hopeless to me if my problems would simply disappear with a brain-chemical-altering pill. I wondered what would happen when I "returned" to reality if I took medication.

industry that the makers of antidepressants aren't competing against one another, they're increasingly competing against other forms of health care. So, beginning in the late 1980s, as Reagan-era deregulation brought new competitive pressures into the drug industry, companies began targeting HMOs, which now provide the majority of the nation's health care and are infamous for their cost-cutting efforts. As *Harper's* observed, for HMOs, Prozac was a panacea. Almost immediately, the average number of insurer-paid visits to talk therapists fell dramatically while drug-therapy numbers soared. By the late '80s, of nearly 16 million patients who visited doctors for depression, 70 percent ended up in drug therapy.

And since the National Depressive and Manic-Depressive Association has reported that most clinically depressed people are either misdiagnosed or undiagnosed, the future looks rosy. Yet the search for higher market shares takes on many faces. Companies now tout their pills as miracle drugs that work wonders, with Prozac being indicated to cure bulimia and the old diehard Wellbutrin trying to do so as an antismoking palliative; another growing if unaccepted practice pairs drugs into crossbranded cocktails like phen-pro, a diet drug that combines the legal part of the outlawed fen-phen with Prozac. The beleaguered FDA has tried to combat the promotion of offline uses (in 1996, for example, Zoloft manufacturer Pfizer got a slap on the wrist for pushing the drug as a treatment for a PMS-related form of depression that afflicts a small percentage of women). And in 1996, Eli Lilly drew criticism when it submitted to the FDA a version of Prozac designed for children—an important market that already receives an estimated half-million adult Prozac prescriptions but could expand enormously were the writing of kiddie Prozac Rxs to be officially sanctioned.

Drugs have long been a fixture of consumer culture, from outlandish ninteenth-century patent medicines to the early, cocaine-fueled Coca-Cola, but their meaning has changed over time. The first popular antidepressant, Iproniazid, emerged in the early 1950s and was prescribed to 400,000 U.S. patients in its inaugural year. Then came Valium, the mother's little helper of the 1960s and 1970s. These earlier drugs, rather reluctantly prescribed by drug-wary U.S. psychotherapists, seemed to approximate Aldous Huxley's

member: HillaryF

SURVEY: DEPRESSION

I have suffered from over a dozen major depressive episodes since I was a preteen (I'm now twenty-five). I have treated my depression with various forms of talk therapy and several medications. I know that if you've had one major depressive episode, you're likely to have another, and once you've had two, the likelihood of your having another goes up again, and so on, and that each episode gets harder to treat. I've had enough episodes that it's virtually guaranteed I'll have another, and they are getting much more difficult to treat. My most recent episode this summer required outpatient hospitalization and a major medication change. My doctors are now talking in terms of long-term disease management, and it looks like I'll be on medications for a long, long time . . . maybe always. This is frustrating (and depressing) for me. I told someone recently that "it's like having diabetes, only you can't tell anybody and everyone thinks it's all your fault" (something I often believe when I'm depressed). Meanwhile, life goes on, and with any luck will for some time, but how will I live with this for the rest of my life? It's becoming more and more real that I am living with a chronic disease. Recently I tried to apply for life insurance (I just got married and we just bought a house), and it's virtually guaranteed I'll be turned down because of my depression. Often I wonder what will happen in a few years years when my husband and I decide to have children. I also wonder what will happen with the next episode. What if they can't find a medication that works?

mythical drug Soma in *Brave New World*: a coping mechanism for or even an escape from the drudgeries of modern industrialized society. Prozac, on the other hand, and the more than half a dozen other antidepressants that followed on its heels, emerged in the go-go '80s as the legal version of coke: It enhanced performance, made its users better than well (in Peter Kramer's words), and was said to come without the weight-gain and other immediate side effects of previous antidepressants. A writer in *Salon* even compared the college experience of taking Prozac to an appropriately contemporized version of the 1960s fascination with LSD: "But we didn't want to come within screaming distance of madness—it would limit our possibilities, screw up our portfolios. Sure, we wanted to be creative, but above all we needed to produce."

Prozac and its ilk also debuted in an America that was largely more willing to talk about mental illness, in which therapeutical rituals and belief systems were well inscribed. Kramer, in *Listening to Prozac*, could offhandedly remark: "For instance, I treated a case of homesickness with Prozac. Prozac wasn't a mind-altering drug, it was a window to the soul, one that could tell a patient how he was constituted and could give social confidence to the habitually timid, to make the sensitive brash, to lend the introvert the social skills of a salesman." This raises hard phenomenological questions. "I got my Mommy back," goes an ad for Effexor, but where in fact did she go? Who was she before? As medical historian David Rothman asks: How can our individual biological selves be identified as distinct from our social selves? Does the drug simply raise one's spirits without ever revealing—as therapy might—why they were down? When is a spell of mourning or a bout of melancholy normal and when does it cry out for medication? (One is reminded of a mental health PSA that asks: What if Picasso had never had a blue period?)

The invention of relatively safe antidepressants has undoubtedly helped a great number of people who may have once been beyond help. Yet in light of the pharmaceutical companies' recent push to boost sales of antidepressants and other drugs and wed their products to the great cornucopia of American capitalism—and for managed care systems' imperative to control costs—it is worth speculating on the long-term social outcomes. With depression we have

member: sexymuffin

SURVEY: DEPRESSION

I have been chemically depressed since I was four. Recently I began treatment with a psychiatrist and Wellbutrin, a new antidepressant, which also helps my ADD. I have been in therapy for a year now with another psychotherapist. These things have helped clear my head and given me room to relearn how to cope with and project the future. These drugs are only "addictive" to people who have a need for a crutch and refuse to help themselves when given the means. It is true, however, that some people (like myself) *may* have to stay on some form of antidepressant for the rest of their lives. This is not because we are weak or because we won't "cheer up." Often it is because of a situation similar to mine; I have been depressed, somewhat severely, for twenty years without any help or treatment. The best thing to do for depression, in my opinion, is to look out for it and acknowledge its presence; the second best thing is to have understanding for those who have no choice but to deal with it (including yourself).

member: Tericot

SURVEY: DEPRESSION

I was depressed about a year ago. So I went to a psychiatrist and he prescribed Paxil. I was on it for a few months but got off because I didn't like the side effects. After all of this, I figured out that the depression was a result of being on four different types of birth control pills within five months. My hormones were way out of whack. My medical doctor also told me to stop drinking coffee. I quit the Paxil, the birth control pills, and coffee all at once. Within a couple of months, I was myself again. So don't be so fast to allow doctors to prescribe these medications for you. They are a big moneymaker for drug manufacturers and doctors.

> Depression Resources

It is estimated that anywhere from 5 to 8 percent of the population is affected by some form of depression. While depression cuts across class, race, and age, people between the ages of twenty-five and forty-four are particularly susceptible. Women are also twice as likely to suffer from depression as men. It has been argued that the incidence of depression is rising in America, but it is yet unclear whether this can be traced to societal causes or simply to better reporting.

Antidepressants have proven to be a viable tool in combating depression (the Mayo Clinic reports that antidepressants seem to help 60 to 80 percent of those who take them), but there is some dispute whether psychotherapy can be equally effective. The price pressures of HMOs have tilted the balance in favor of drug therapy. In any case, no pharmacological regimen should be embarked upon without the consent of a reputable doctor, and antidepressants should not be used as a substitute for therapy. And just as one should only go on an antidepressant on the basis of sound medical judgment, one should only go off of one under the equally rigorous watch of a doctor.

The sheer number of antidepressants and their myriad side effects are far too vast to list here. While it is true that the so-called SSRIs (Selective Serotonin Reputake Inhibitors), which include Prozac, Paxil, and Zoloft and the Seratonin/Nonrepinephrine Reuptake Inhibitors (SNRIs), most famously, Effexor, have been generally shown to have far fewer side effects than the older antidepressants or the more powerful tricyclic antidepressants (such as Anafranil and Imavate), both classes have been found to have significant side effects in some people. Prozac, for example, which has been used (without FDA approval) to treat everything from alcoholism to Alzheimer's to sleep apnea, has been found to diminish sexual drive in some people; Effexor, meanwhile, counts anorexia and weight loss among its known side effects.

Stories abound in the mainstream press about new drug developments and sizable literature already exists on antidepressants. Peter Kramer's *Listening to Prozac* and Peter Breggin's *Talking Back to Prozac* are the two main pro- and anti-Prozac volumes, but there are scores of others, ranging from the satirical to the serious. There's *Barking at Prozac: My Diary*, a spoof that examines time spent on Prozac from a canine point of view, or even *Cooking with Prozac from Nuts to Soup*. On the serious side there is Carol Ann Turkington and Eliot F. Kaplan's *Making the Prozac Decision: A Guide to Antidepressants* or William S. Appleton's *Prozac and the New Antidepressants: What You Need to Know About Prozac, Zoloft, Paxil, Luvox, Wellbutrin, Effexor, Serzone, and More*. For alternatives to chemical antidepressants, check out Michael J. Norden's *Beyond Prozac: Brain-Toxic Lifestyles, Natural Antidotes & New Generation Antidepressants, Nature's Prozac* by Judith Sachs, or Joel C. Robinson's *Natural Prozac: Learning to Release Your Body's Own Antidepressants*. Edward Shorter's *A History of Psychiatry: From the Era of the Asylum to the Age of Prozac* is an interesting cultural study.

In addition, there are dozens of Web sites dealing with depression and antidepressant drugs. Breggin's Center for the Study of Psychiatry and Psychology is generally critical of psychopharmacology and features articles on the negative side effects of antidepressants. Dr. Ivan Goldberg's Depression Central Web site (www.psycom.net/depression.central.html) also contains a wealth of information and links to specific drug-related articles in the medical press. The Mayo Clinic's Health Oasis, MedScape (www.medscape), Online Psych (www.onlinepsych.com), and InfoSeek's Health Channel (www.infoseek.com/health) also contain much useful information. It should also be noted that the drug manufacturers also have their own Web sites, where they dispense the kind of information that is no longer legally required in television and print campaigns. In addition, groups such as the National Mental Health Association (800-969-6642) can be a good place to start when gathering information.

seen a normalization of what was once considered abnormal, yet will we also see the abnormalization of what is normal—the rush to medically fix what isn't broken? Is there a point where someone who would have once been a candidate for a happy life now becomes a carrier of physical or mental dysfunction? As science historian Roy Porter has written, neuropharmacological advances, breakthroughs in diagnostic technology, the economics of medi-business, the new consumerism, and capitalism's instant hedonism are bound to make the next century the age of the drug. Proposals floating around D.C. about the future of health care posit ATMs for pharmaceutical disbursement and drug company/patient interfacing. In the end, the ubiquity of medication may prove as socially beneficial as the polio vaccine, or an irrevocably bitter pill to swallow.

member: Keath

SURVEY: DEPRESSION

I was clinically depressed for years and didn't realize it. It has a lot to do with hostility, not just being moody. The death of my mother pushed me to the brink and led me to get help from a doctor. I was placed on antidepressants and the difference in my life was like the scene when Dorothy leaves the drab black-and-white farm and opens up the door to colorful Oz. There was a dead witch under my house, too, at the time but it was the witch of depression and her ruby red slippers are the equivalent of the pills I take to remain serene.

member: nonobaddog

SURVEY: DEPRESSION

A couple of years ago my life seemed to fall apart as everything became negative. I was sure no one liked me. I drank too much and chain-smoked pot. I saw a psychiatrist who put me on Zoloft. At first it worked, then I overdosed on it. I went into recovery for alcohol and drugs and remained on Zoloft and added trazodone. The combination worked but I became impotent, which was more frustrating than the depression. The whole experience with the drugs has taught me a lot about patience, tolerance, and basically retrained my way of thinking. I don't want the drugs anymore. They made me feel indifferent, like a zombie. But I don't think I need to modify my personality in order to survive. I'm me and unless I'm a danger to myself or others, which I'm not at the moment, I'm just saying no to medication.

member: sharons_forest

SURVEY: DEPRESSION

The problem I had with Prozac was that I wasn't getting a good night's sleep. And the longer that went on, the worse I began to feel. Currently I'm not taking anything and I'm finding that I'm just fine as long as I get the sleep I need every night.

Therapy

In these days of short-term managed care, the talking cure is not quite as pervasive as it once was. Which is not necessarily a good thing. One much touted study shows that almost every form of therapy helped two-thirds of the people who used it. Who wouldn't want a piece of those odds?

by Emily Nussbaum

As Morissey once sang, shyness is nice, but shyness can stop you from doing all the things in life you want to—as can depression, panic attacks, generalized anxiety, eating disorders, phobias, and plain old dissatisfaction. Is counseling the answer? Most likely, you already speak the language—therapy-talk has become a bona fide American dialect, turning love affairs into "relationships" and creeps into "abusers." Counselors on talk shows blithely analyze complete strangers; "low self-esteem" explains away everything from shoplifting to genocide.

But in what an analyst might term a "reaction-formation," there's also a current backlash against the talking cure. The bottom-line values of the managed care/pharmaceutical complex have shifted the treatment du jour to short-term, symptom-focused modalities, heavy on the antidepressants. (One look at those creepy Prozac ads—turn your rain clouds to smiley faces!—should be enough to alert you to the economic forces encouraging drug treatment for even mild unhappiness.)

member: search2

SURVEY: DEPRESSION

A combination of meds and talk therapy is best for the treatment of clinical depression. On a personal level keeping active and socially involved is also extremely important whether you are clinically depressed or just have a case of the blues.

member: Polymath

SURVEY: DEPRESSION

Some years ago I was seriously depressed and almost suicidal. I then studied the Bible with members of the International Churches of Christ and so I learned to give up the selfish habits that were making me depressed. I started focusing on God and on the needs of others, whilst learning to be more responsible in my own life too. I became happy, peaceful, and patient. Occasionally I get PMS, and sometimes I'm sad about things like animals who suffer, but I have never felt anywhere near as depressed as I did before I became a disciple.

member: IcecreamC

SURVEY: DEPRESSION

One thing I've learned to keep me going: Whatever you're going through, if it hasn't killed you, you can get through it.

member: stephid

SURVEY: THERAPY

Therapy can help remove the "blinders" placed on us by our environment to see who we really are or can be. You have to use caution in selecting a therapist. Good psychotherapists will not bring religion into the session, but they will offer ethical advice that most likely will not go against your own principles.

member: Twyla

SURVEY: DEPRESSION

What helps: sun, tea, time, writing it out of your system. What doesn't: People trying to "jolly" you out of it.

This messy zeitgeist has fueled a lively debate over the nature of depression. If debilitating sorrow is simply a biochemical glitch, what does that imply about our emotional lives? Are we just bags of boiling chemicals, deluding ourselves about our own free will? (After all, schizophrenia and manic-depression—once blamed on "refrigerator mothers"—are now universally treated with drugs.) Other critics question the value of pathologizing misery: Depression, they argue, is just a fancy word for the human condition. Why are we entitled to happiness, anyway? Call it the grumpy old man critique: "In my day, we were miserable—and we loved it!" Finally, there are those singing the generational blues, à la *Reality Bites*: Hell, of course we're bummed out—we're the disgruntled, atomized, Nintendo-playing, disenfranchised spawn of those damned divorced, self-indulgent boomers.

But what do these abstractions have to do with men and women in their twenties who simply want to understand their problems, feel better, and get past date three? There's copious evidence that meeting with a therapist *does* work for most people dealing with nonpsychotic types of adjustment problems—the kind almost everyone experiences to one degree or another after adolescence. One much-touted study in the mid '70s found that almost *every* form of therapy helped two-thirds of the patients who used it—whether the therapist was a psychiatrist or a social worker, a drive-theory Freudian, an object-relations empath, or a cognitive-behavioral Adlerian with a secret yen for Jung. "There are factors that cross therapies," points out Michael J. Lambert, Ph.D., a member of the clinical psychology program at Brigham Young University. "You're in an office with walls, in a safe place, with a person who is understanding, respectful, nonjudgmental. Since they feel safe, patients can open up to aspects of themselves they usually defend against and take risks," says Lambert. "And therapists are typically optimistic, so the patient gets 'remoralized.' Effective therapists, whatever the theory, operate in similar ways."

member: ScaMingLee
SURVEY: DEPRESSION
Had I actually died once in the hundreds of times I tried to kill myself, I wouldn't be able to be here now, enjoying this really cool computer, and creating awesome homepages at Tripod!

member: realife_records
SURVEY: THERAPY
It is not wise to blindly accept anything anyone tells you. A fair amount of skepticism should be displayed and a true therapist expects it. All a therapist can do is help reveal your options, your choices, your situations. It's up to you to internalize the information and make it your own.

member: czfz
SURVEY: THERAPY
Eventually biochemical technology will be developed that will enable people to order their personalities from a therapist.

member: txhern
SURVEY: DEPRESSION
I have always suffered from chronic depression. It was only when I was in the military that things got really bad. I had gotten to the point that if there were more than three people in the room I would leave, I just couldn't handle a "crowd" larger then that. I then realized that there was a problem and asked for help. First I was in therapy. It was the first time that I really started to deal with the fact that I am gay. The only way that I had to deal with it was to paint. Some of my best work was done when in the midst of a major depression. That was about twelve years ago. Now, I still have some bouts with the depression, but I have found that the only thing that helps is to just decide to move on, and that whatever it is really isn't that important.

What Kind of Therapy Should You Get?

Of course, this doesn't mean all therapists are alike. There are chilly, eye-blinking types who say "hmm" in response to hysterical sobbing; there are emotional gesticulating chest heavers who will enthusiastically join you in your tears. For a postmodern test-drive of the profession, take a look at media portrayals: You've got your cuddly ethnic model (Judd Hirsch's character in *Ordinary People*; Dr. Katz); your bright repressed WASP (the Brothers Crane on *Frasier*; Bob Newhart); and your oddly well-coiffed big city narcissist with red talons, impressive pipes, and questionable professional ethics (Barbra Streisand's role in *The Prince of Tides*.)

To simplify things a bit, the two major schools are psychodynamic therapy and cognitive-behavioral therapy. (A slew of other approaches, such as Gestalt, Jungian, relational, and more systems-oriented theories, are often blended into these two like crumbled Heath Bar into soft-serve frozen yogurt.) Broadly, in psychodynamic therapy, you'll hash out unsettling past experiences. In cognitive-behavioral therapy, you focus on the here and now. In practice, though, whatever they *say* they do, many therapists are privately eclectic—cycling through practical, emotional, confrontational, and supportive approaches depending on the patient.

member: aunt_tonto

SURVEY: DEPRESSION

Journaling is a wonderful tool for dealing with depression. If you keep a journal daily, it can help you track issues that can trigger a depressive episode. When you ascertain a pattern, then you can devise a plan of action to help cope with your depression. Another option is to "lean" into your depression, experience it, contemplate it, find out what purpose it serves, and then look for alternative ways to deal with the issues.

member: Lorcalon

SURVEY: DEPRESSION

I seem to get depressed on Sundays because I have nothing to do, so what works for me a lot is to *do* something. My "Sunday depression" is definitely caused by boredom, so kicking back and relaxing just doesn't work for me. I've played basketball, soccer, started a model car, and other things to keep me busy. Once I took two or three showers just to take up time.

> How to Find a Therapist

WHAT TO LOOK FOR

- Good listening skills.
- Honesty and straightforwardness.
- Nondefensiveness: If you question their approach, do they take your concerns seriously?
- "Chemistry": Could you spend a significant time talking with them?
- A feeling of safety.
- Mutual respect: Do you feel like they're intelligent, do they understand what you're saying, or are they trying to fit you into a theory?
- Clarity in terms of what you can expect in therapy with them.
- Someone in sync with your values about medication.

WHAT TO LOOK OUT FOR

- Arrogance, ignoring what you say.
- Sexually suggestive intimacy, such as touching or compliments.
- A controlling approach, advising you to isolate yourself from friends or family.
- Talking an excessive amount about him- or herself.
- Insisting you take his or her advice and getting angry if you don't.
- Irresponsibility, such as being late or cancelling appointments.
- Handing you pills without discussing how you feel about this approach.
- Boringness, a flat affect, a distant manner.

Psychodynamic Therapy

Freud has certainly taken his lumps over the years. To some, he's a misogynistic, sexual-abuse-denying fiend; to others, simply a provincial quack, mistaking local Viennese conditions for universal truths. And Woody Allen's progress after all his years of psychoanalysis isn't exactly inspiring. Nonetheless, most current therapy—and much of Western culture, for that matter—owes a heavy debt to Freud's notion that we are driven by sexual and aggressive impulses even in childhood, and that taboo desires are "repressed" into the dark, unknowable unconscious from whence they bubble up to wreak mischievous havoc on our everyday lives. One big appeal of psychodynamic approaches is that they are aimed at providing genuine self-understanding, allowing you to delve into the complex path that has led you to this couch (or chair, more likely—these days, few shrinks actually haul in a green-leather, curl-backed divan with claw feet).

Almost nobody does classical psychoanalysis anymore. The five-days-a-week, free-associative, ten-year approach is out of vogue, if only because it requires a massive time commitment and a trust fund. Nonetheless, a huge proportion of therapists use Freud-derived approaches; they will talk through past experiences with you, looking for patterns and interpreting dreams. Psychodynamic therapists also use "transference"—the strong feelings of love and hate patients feel for their therapist—as a tool to illuminate your . . . um . . . "issues" with other people.

There's a caveat: Psychodynamic therapy can go on for a real long time. But that might be okay. Some people view therapy as akin to going to the gym: It's good for you and you should do it over the course of your life as a way of "shaping up" your psyche. Ask your therapist how long he or she expects your treatment to go on: Till death do you part? Till you feel like an adult? Till you stop obsessing about Jodie Foster?

member: Aiyana

SURVEY: DEPRESSION

I have suffered from depression most of my life. Some days are good and some days are bad. Mine is caused by a chemical imbalance, which means I have to watch what I eat and so forth. I have learned to listen to my body and know when I have a bad episode coming.

member: Dunahein

SURVEY: THERAPY

I do recommend the use of medications to help one focus and center, to bring one to a point where other methods of healing can be effectual. For myself, I preferred to use medications briefly, to abandon them for less toxic therapies as quickly as possible.

member name: RrakkaDog

SURVEY: THERAPY

Therapy is just a way for you to pay someone to listen to you. All the therapist has to do is look interested. Just get some friends. It is cheaper.

member: zipper_and_teddy

SURVEY: THERAPY

When I was eleven, I was diagnosed as anorexic, simply because I was underweight, and all the talk shows were telling the nation that "one out of every <insert random number> girls in America have an eating disorder!" I've never been worried about my weight, certainly never have thought of myself as fat. When I told the therapists this though, they told me I was in denial, and committed me to an institution.

Cognitive-Behavioral Therapy

Cognitive-behavioral therapy tends to be shorter term and more symptom focused, and your HMO will love you for choosing it. Which doesn't mean it doesn't work (there's tons of evidence that

CBT is especially good for phobias and anxiety disorders), just that it happens to have the bottom-line, trackable appeal that insurance companies go for. Unlike a Freud-loving shrink, a cognitive-behavioral therapist isn't really all that interested in the Day Your Mom Forgot Your Birthday. Stop living in the past, he says—you're unhappy because you're thinking wrong. Learn how irrational you're being, fix your mental mistakes, and you'll feel better. This in-your-face approach is good for pragmatists and for those who relish a direct therapeutic challenge. And anyone who has experienced the self-destructive mental leaps that CBT discourages—"all or nothing" thinking, "mind-reading" negative judgments in others, and a form of mental self-abuse the puckish founder of the field, Albert Ellis, called "musterbation"—can relate to its underlying insights.

Expect to do a lot of writing with a cognitive behaviorist, in addition to exercises intended to make you aware of your "illogical" thoughts and replace them with "logical" ones. Critics see CBT as somehow shallower than psychodynamic therapy, but proponents sneer in return at the touchy-feely wallowing in memories inherent in a psychodynamic approach. "For most people, all they want to do is to reduce their symptoms," points out Benjamin S. Fialkoff, Ph.D., a cognitive-behavioral therapist. "Why isn't that enough?"

How to Find a Therapist

Your best source for a referral is someone you trust. If you're in college, you're in luck: Most university health centers have a built-in mental health system that will steer you to a shrink who has at least some experience with people your age. If you're out of school, you can get a list from your HMO or by contacting your local chapter of the national organizations, such as the American Psychological Association. What you pay is going to depend on how well certified your therapist is and whether the modality you're seeking is covered. An M.D.-wielding, medication-prescribing psychiatrist will cost more than someone with a master's in social work, but she won't necessarily be better. There's no evidence that more years in graduate school equals better results.

If at all possible, check out a couple of therapists before you pick one. Some will let you have a freebie session before you decide,

member: Rachel

SURVEY: THERAPY

Therapy can work. It's not a cure-all, but it works for a lot of things. Therapy can help a person understand herself better, and understanding oneself can lead to unraveling (and fixing) the problems in one's psyche and one's life. There are disorders that require medication—OCD, ADD, serious depression—and therapy can help in those cases, too. In almost any instance, from mild distress to acute anxiety attacks, therapy (when properly done) can help one come to the root of what's going on in one's mind.

member: New_Mexican

SURVEY: THERAPY

The last person most people can be totally honest with is themselves, and therapy is the safe place someone can explore that possibility. Of course, you have to define "work." Some people expect therapy, like religion, to save them from all their troubles. It can't and won't. But, if "work" allows you to be honest with yourself and those you love in a positive way, and allows you to achieve something approaching your potential, then, yes, it works.

member: Artaed

SURVEY: THERAPY

I have been in psychotherapy and from my experience it is very hard work for the depressed person. I don't think that psychotherapy is for everyone. Sometimes when you finish a session, you feel worse than you did before you went. The therapist helps you to recall childhood events that may not be pleasant and might be very painful to recall. Many people think that the therapist tells the patient what to do, but that's not true. What he or she does is help you to look at a situation in a different way. Don't be afraid to let someone see you cry, because that's the start of the healing process.

others will make you pay. The first session is not like the first day of class, all syllabus and no content. Instead, you'll usually model what a session with them would be like. It may sound clichéd, but you should trust your instincts: Does the person seem like someone to whom you'd feel comfortable spilling your guts? Are they empathic, distant, smothering?

You might also consider how much it matters to you whether your therapist is a man or a woman, what race they are, what their sexual orientation is. These decisions can be complicated. If you're a woman who feels untrusting with men, you might want to see a woman, since you'll be able to open up to her—or you might want to

member: moebluesman

SURVEY: THERAPY

I have watched many friends who denied therapy go by the wayside. It took me all of those therapy years to only recently acknowledge an underlying problem that has confused me forever. That was my fault for not telling the doctor "where it hurt." My attitude was, your mechanic (doctor) should find what's broken. Professional therapy may not be for everyone but I don't know of anyone it hurt.

see a man, since he'll model a healthier relationship with men. It's easy to say that as long as the therapist is qualified and well-intentioned things will work out, but the truth is, client-therapist relationships thrive on that indefinable quality—good chemistry. If you have special requirements, don't be shy about asking. For special concerns—eating disorders, for example, or sexual abuse—make sure you get someone who has experience with patients with similar issues. Be straightforward during the first sessions about your goals ("I want to figure out if I should stay with my girlfriend, and I'd like to get rid of my insomnia") and then listen to the response.

Therapy is more of an art than a science. To critics of the messy field of clinical psychology that truism merely proves their critique—that there's no way to measure what goes on inside the privacy of the shrink's office (let alone inside someone else's mind). With the current prevalance of psychoactive medications on the science axis of therapy, the art of conversation with a deep structure can seem like a badge of honor.

member: blackheron

SURVEY: THERAPY

My one experience with psychotherapy was very disappointing. The therapist's solution to my depression was to tell me to "get a social life" and pass me off to someone who could put me on Prozac. I figured I could do better on my own and I never went back. I'm sure there are some excellent therapists out there, but I haven't run into one.

member: art_birds_prayer

SURVEY: THERAPY

Therapy cannot replace the need for family, friends, etc. Those of us who are left with no family (or a very limited one) because of someone else's violence have to rebuild the best we can. A good therapist will help you do that.

member: enso

SURVEY: THERAPY

I spent years periodically trying psychotherapy with no real results until I found my current therapist. He was the first to diagnose me as a probable bipolar and recommend pharmaceuticals. The rest just piddled around with cognitive therapy, Freudian therapy, or whatever they were into.

Safe Sex and STDs

When it comes to safe sex in general, and AIDS in particular, there are no guarantees. Which is exactly how you should approach your sex life.

by Chip Rowe

I write the advice column for *Playboy* magazine. Most of the 500 or so letters I receive each month are about sex and some of those are from people who want to know how to avoid sexually transmitted diseases, including AIDS. When people ask me whether they will get AIDS from this or that sexual scenario, I can't provide a yes or no answer. Instead, I discuss risk assessment. Most people are familiar with the concept. For example, the fact that you might be involved in an accident doesn't keep you from getting into a car. Instead, you assess the chances you'll be involved in a crash and accept them as a necessary price of getting where you need to go. In some cases—maybe a drunk driver is at the wheel or the roads are slippery with ice—you might decide the risks are too great.

Risk assessment is also necessary in sexual situations, although some people would prefer that sex educators do it for them. A twenty-two-year-old wants to ease her mind about giving her boyfriend a blow job. A twenty-five-year-old doesn't want to use a dental dam during one-night stands. A twenty-eight-year-old would like to have anal sex without a condom. These people ask me to calculate their odds of survival. I'm at a loss for two reasons: (1) I can't dictate the circumstances of their sexual encounters, and (2) I can't say what unbridled sex is worth to anyone. Even if I could provide a figure, what odds would they find acceptable? Odds are meaningless

member: CurlySue22

SURVEY: SEX

Sometimes I feel old-fashioned in my way of thinking, but I think it's vital for a sexual relationship to involve feelings. I personally have tried it with and without, and I have to say I prefer "making love" to just feeling sexually gratified. After simple sexual gratification, I personally feel like I don't even want to see the person the next day, or maybe even the next minute. It sometimes feels when you are in love that the person can just touch you and get you off, maybe even a look can set things off between you.

member: hip_fan

SURVEY: SEX

I understand that some women prefer to have sex (make love) with people that they have some sort of past or future with. In some cases, I think this is because they trust themselves (and their partner), can relax with this other person, and in turn, achieve orgasm more easily.

member: Mixed

SURVEY: SEX

Sex comes in three basic modes: adventure, relief, and passion. Adventure comes often with first time partners or situations, it is full of will he, should we, and what the hell! Relief sex is when our world is tied up in knots or just needs a boost, or you just haven't had any for a while. This is usually mediocre sex, but you usually feel better after. Finally passionate sex is usually with someone you care about and consumes you in the act. This is the type where your knees are weak after.

if you end up with an STD, particularly if you end up dead. One online resource, the sci.med.aids FAQ (Frequently Asked Questions), puts it this way: "The risk of HIV infection is unlike the risk of losing at the races. Because you cannot recoup the loss represented by infection, you ought not to think of the odds in the same way."

That's why AIDS educators don't put out betting lines. They prefer to categorize activities as "high risk" and "lower risk." Back in the early 1980s when AIDS was picking up speed, my high school sex ed teacher managed to sum up the numbing parade of safe sex warnings in one line: "If mucus membranes are touching, you can get a sexually transmitted disease," she said. "You're not a shmoo. You have these openings." If your partner has HIV and you don't know it, you're in an extremely high-risk situation.

In North America, the two groups who most often get HIV have always been men who have unprotected anal sex with infected partners and people who share needles with infected IV drug users. People who have other sexually transmitted diseases such as herpes or gonorrhea also carry increased risk. STDs break the skin and weaken the immune system, opening a door for the virus. Anal sex without a condom is one of the highest risks because it increases the chances that you will tear the rectum and create an opening where semen can reach the bloodstream. Anal sex with a condom and plenty of lubrication eliminates some risk but not all.

Because my readers are mostly straight men, I am often asked about HIV and unprotected vaginal intercourse. When AIDS first made headlines, the disease was spreading rapidly among gay men. At the time, many scientists felt it would only be a matter of time before it jumped to the straight population, either through bisexual men or intravenous drug users. While many heterosexuals have died of AIDS, an epidemic of the predicted proportions never happened. If you eliminate the HIV-positive men who lie to researchers when they say they've never had anal sex or shared needles, relatively few infections can be conclusively attributed to unprotected vaginal sex. That isn't to say it can't happen, particularly if there is not enough lubrication or an infected man comes inside the woman. After a ten-year study, researchers at the University of California at San

member: SpittingLlama

SURVEY: SEX

I think that having the feelings is as important as having the fun, but they don't have to always be equalized. Why not have one night where you are communicating your deepest devotion and trust, and another afternoon where you dress up in silly costumes and face paint? Ultimately, however, disease puts a damper on everything. Disease makes it imperative to have as few partners as possible, regardless of your morals or standards.

member: wpublishing

SURVEY: SEX

The one person you truly love will preclude *any* desire for other women. They just aren't attractive. Monogamy is a natural effect of True Love.

member: freegirl1

SURVEY: SEX

This is your one and only life, why waste it on one person your whole entire life? Go out, have fun, see what all kind of different sexual experiences you can have.

member: CarolDiego

SURVEY: SEX

I came of age in the late sixties, when knowing your partner's name was not considered relevant to a good time. In many ways, STDs have been a blessing. They gave us a balance, in physical terms, between pleasure and regret, a chance to take a time-out and really think about what we were doing.

member: slan

SURVEY: SEX

After our marriage, sex took a holiday for a while. So when my wife told me of her fantasy about having two men make love to her at the same time I listened. Over the years our threesome has changed and he is now a friend of hers more than a lover. I see them as the typical old couple that fights and carries on about stuff. I'm still married and after all these years things are still good and fresh in the bedroom.

Francisco projected that if you were to track 10,000 unprotected sexual encounters between infected men and uninfected women, nine of the women would acquire the virus. The female-to-male tranmission rate was even lower. These numbers shouldn't make you feel safe—just safer. For if you acquire HIV through irresponsible

> AIDS Testing at Home

I had never taken an HIV test before I bought the $45 Home Access Express HIV-1 Test System, so I knew a maddening wait for results would follow suit.

After a nervous point-of-purchase experience at my local pharmacy, I hid the box in my backpack and mentally prepared to draw my own blood. I wouldn't have had a chance to do so before 1996 when the FDA ended a decade-long debate on home specimen collection by approving two over-the-counter HIV kits, Johnson & Johnson's Confide and Home Access Health's Home Access Express. Confide didn't last very long, however. Corporate behemoth Johnson & Johnson recently discontinued the kits, which proved to be unprofitable in light of the enormous costs of operating a mail-in testing center. Home Access Health, a smaller, specialized company, offers a $35 kit that promises results in a week, and a $45 version that's ready within three days.

Testing for the virus can now be as easy as a walk to the drug store and a stab in the pinky. It takes about an hour and is reasonably painful. The kit comes equipped with a detailed instruction booklet, two "safety lancets," a specimen card, information on HIV, and a prepaid Federal Express envelope in which to send your blood sample. I followed the directions attentively and soon found myself massaging my arm to ensure good circulation so I could produce the blood necessary to fill the specimen card's designated circle. I laid my hand on the coffee table, palm up, and chose my middle finger as the victim. I pressed the cocked lancet against my digit and with a grimace, forced the syringelike plunger through my skin. But in spite of the formidable pain the stab caused, it failed to draw enough blood to fill the circle. I repeated the process with lancet #2, and an excruciatingly deep thrust finally got the blood flowing properly. After soaking the card with my blood, I overnighted it to the lab. I would know my results in three business days.

Most public health groups, such as GMHC (Gay Man's Health Crisis), seem to favor clinical testing over home kits, citing the benefits of face-to-face human notification. The home test model omits some vital procedures—like partner notification or a support system of counselors for those who test positive. At an HIV testing center, blood tests are performed on a person-to-person basis by either a nurse or doctor, both of whom are qualified to offer support if patients test positive. A notification of HIV status is potentially devastating news and home HIV tests don't address this. Clinics also compile the names of HIV-positive patients' ex-partners and notify them of their risk—a major factor in the stabilization of infection rates. Home Access Express offers nothing of the sort, leaving potentially infected customers with the responsibility of contacting their own ex-mates. And there are those who test positive then shirk any responsibility.

In my case, a self-administered HIV test conducted in the comfort of my own home helped me to avoid the anxiety and potential publicity of a visit to the clinic. Moreover, the dried blood sample I FedExed to the laboratory was completely anonymous and only identifiable by a secret eleven-digit code. Nonetheless, no matter how or where you get your test, little can dissipate the fear that is entwined with this undertaking. When I entered that code on my phone, I grappled with memories of last summer, all too aware that a soothing-voiced live counselor would only pick up the line in the event of bad news (negative test results are delivered via a prerecorded message).

Thankfully, after entering my code, the prerecorded voice came on the line to tell me that my sample had tested negative. I had never been happier to hear the sterile tones of a computer-generated voice in my entire life. *—Ben Klipstein*

sex, your chances of getting AIDS are 1 in 1. Comprendé? I don't want that on my conscience.

But what about oral sex? Theoretically, you can get AIDS from an infected woman through cunnilingus, though if you did you'd be the talk of the scientific community. You increase your chances tremendously if there are cuts or sores in your mouth. The same applies to sucking an infected man, particularly if you take his semen into your mouth. Flossing before oral sex may increase the danger of infection because it can create small cuts on your gums. Saliva itself does not contain enough of the virus to be infectious, and scientists know of only one extreme case where anyone acquired the virus through French kissing. Both partners had advanced gum disease, and the infected man had just flossed, which made his mouth bleed.

The high-risk/lower-risk model assumes that one partner has HIV. If your partner doesn't have HIV, you're safe. But how can you be certain? I've gotten letters from people who ask, "I've been in a relationship for five years—do I still have to practice safe sex?" That's a tough call. But I've heard from too many people who were shocked to discover that their partner was sleeping around or shooting up. (One expert says, "If you're going to cheat, at least care enough to do so safely.")

The discussion is more clear-cut when you're talking about short-term romances. It's amazing to me that people will trust someone who tells them he or she doesn't have HIV or an STD but wouldn't trust that same person with their PIN number. Your frat-party partner or summertime fling may not know he or she has HIV—the virus usually does not show up in tests for six months or more after infection. Your afternoon delight may have shared needles while shooting drugs, a common method of acquiring HIV. Your new lover could also be in a high-risk group even if you would never guess that he's bisexual and having unprotected anal sex on the side or that last week he hired a prostitute on a dare or that a year ago she had a nagging doubt after a sloshed quickie but has never felt sick and never been tested. We all have our secrets, including those we keep from ourselves.

Let's say you absorb the message that vaginal intercourse and

member: MelSkunk

SURVEY: SEX

Many people would consider me a very sexed up person, but to my consideration, I'm merely participating in the most initmate form of trust between friends. I enjoy sex in its simple pleasures of exploration and adventure but hope to one day settle down into a firm and loving relationship.

member: elixirmedia

SURVEY: SEX

Sexual intimacy is the higher aspect of sex, and with exploration, affection, playfulness, and mutual pleasure, it's what reconnects us to our humanity. Any pair of morons can insert Tab A into Slot B, but it takes two real humans to make love.

member: rokey

SURVEY: SEX

With someone you trust, sex can be everything and anything you both want it to be, and it can change with your mood and situation. A one-night stand or some other casual relationship just cannot offer you that. Of course, those more temporary relationships have their own positives.The most obvious one is the lack of commitment, which offers you the mental freedom to do what you want without caring about the consequences.

member: Perimus

SURVEY: SEX

It seems that in today's society a lot of people want to protect you from sex. I don't see how that contributes to a "safer" sexual environment. It seems to me that that works to make people more uncomfortable with the subject, and for me it made it harder to come to terms with being gay.

oral sex carry a lower risk of transmitting HIV than anal sex, and you decide that you're going to skip the latex and take your chances. Many people feel so strongly that condoms and other safe-sex methods destroy the pleasure of sex, they are willing to accept that risk. Better to live a short full life than a long dull one, right? If you're prudent and lucky, you may avoid AIDS. But you'll likely pick up another nasty visitor that will make your long life much less pleasant. Despite the death sentence attached to AIDS, you never want to find yourself saying, "Whew! It's only herpes." This is especially true now that, as mentioned earlier, the presence of other STDs can make it easier for HIV to be passed on.

Last year there were 12 million new cases of STDs in the United States (an estimated 40,000 people acquired HIV). Safer sex can prevent herpes, gonorrhea, genital warts, syphilis, hepatitus B, chlamydia, and other diseases that sound like they should be the next villian in a *Batman* movie. STDs spread easily. Herpes, for example, can be passed even if the infected person doesn't have lesions. It sometimes won't matter if you're wearing a condom since it can be present anywhere on the genitals and even on the butt or thighs. Herpes can also be present in and around your mouth. Cold sores, which are a strain of herpes, have been identified as the root of 20 to 30 percent of genital cases. If you have a cold sore, hold off on the licking and sucking until it heals.

member: LauraEllen727
SURVEY: SEX
I strongly believe in monogamy. People who cannot stay with one single partner and are careless about their sexual practices almost deserve to get some kind of STD, as long as they keep it away from those of us who are smart and careful about sex.

member: crux_criticorum
SURVEY: SEX
If everyone had practiced monogamy we would have *zero* sexually transmittable diseases. Think of how many billions of dollars could go instead to education and natural resource preservation, not to mention the hundreds of thousands of lives that would have been saved if HIV had never been introduced into the human race. Now sit back with a smug expression on your face and tell me that your instinctual sexual drives are far more powerful than your ability to control.

> Safe Sex Resources

HOT LINES

AIDS Hotline 800-342-2437
Herpes Hotline 919-361-8488
STD Hotline 800-227-8922
Sex Information 415-989-7374

GREAT SEX BOOKS

The Good Vibrations Guide to Sex, by Cathy Winks and Anne Semans (Cleis Press, 1994) 800-780-2279, http://www.goodvibes.com

The Guide to Getting It On! A New and Mostly Wonderful Book About Sex, by the editors of the Goofy Foot Press (Goofy Foot Press, 1996) 800-310-7529

WEB SITES

American Social Health Association
http://sunsite.unc.edu/ASHA

Center for Positive Sexuality
http://www.webcom.com/-cps

Condomania
http://www.condomania.com

Common STDs & the Organisms that Cause Them
http://www.cdcnac.org/stdpics.html

The Safer Sex Page
http://safersex.org

Who gets STDs? They spread most rapidly among teenagers and young adults. Two-thirds of the victims are under the age of twenty-five and the largest jump since the late 1970s in genital herpes infections has been among white teenagers and twenty-somethings. During the last few years I've been receiving more and more letters asking about the care and treatment of the "nondeadly" STDs. New combinations of drugs have offered some hope that AIDS can be defeated—or at least delayed long enough that something else can kill you first—and people are feeling more carefree. I've even read that more gay men are looking for partners with whom to have anal sex without condoms, a practice known as "barebacking." They prefer risking death than missing out on skin-to-skin. I understand completely. How can a man go through life without ever feeling a lover around his penis? How can a woman live without her clitoris ever being teased by a tongue that's not wrapped in plastic? I hope that every person has that chance, but I can't say if or when it should happen in your life. You have to ascertain what the sex is worth and separate the reasonable and unreasonable risks. You have to decide whether to get in the car.

member: joetruck

SURVEY: SEX

Whoever said "God gave men two heads and only enough blood supply to run one at a time" evidently didn't have the benefit of spending time with a more mature and thoughtful lover.

member: emraldangel

SURVEY: SEX

"I'll show you mine if you'll show me yours" has a whole new meaning! Now it is a piece of paper showing that one has been tested negative for AIDS.

member: samizdata

SURVEY: SEX

Although I've conducted my share of sexual experiments, I have to admit that the rise of AIDS awareness during my college years curtailed my activities, made starting new relationships more complex, and made long-term commitments more attractive. The discomfort of negotiating health precautions with a stranger combined with the medocrity of one-night-stand orgasms dissuades me.

member: Trefor

SURVEY: SEX

If it were just physical, you would not need a partner. Were it just mental, you would not need a body.

member: LatcoEnt

SURVEY: SEX

Having someone know you, who truly cares about you, who goes to great lengths to make sure that *you* have a good time, has been incredible!! I had never associated sex with laughter until I fell in love.

member: AmazonFox

SURVEY: SEX

Despite what many people think, not all women are looking for a relationship before sex. We have normal drives, too, and I see nothing wrong with fulfilling them with someone who I am attracted to, regardless of the depth of our relationship.

Contraception

We may very well be entering the golden age of birth control. But to really reap the rewards, you've got to know what to do with the available technology.

by Sarah Blustain

One of the earliest records of birth control appears in an Egyptian papyrus from nearly 4,000 years ago: Mix crocodile dung, honey, and saltpeter and insert into the vagina. A faint trail of herbal antifertility solutions leads through ancient Egypt, India, and China, where herbal preparations were chewed, brewed, or used topically to prevent or abort pregnancy. Some historians of birth control suggest that even with the great knowledge midwives brought to birth control, the greatest form of population control in ancient Greece was infanticide.

We are, indeed, in the golden age of contraception. It's true that in the last two decades new methods have often failed to catch on in a big way, unable to meet the standards of the FDA (woe for the sponge), fight legal challenges, or intrigue a stubborn market (the female condom). While scientific and legal hurdles have slowed down the availability of new birth controls, we're still comparatively rolling in contraception.

Of course, it's little comfort to the fertile adult that half of all pregnancies in America are unintended, and a solid half of those the result of faulty or improperly used contraception. With perfect use, a condom plus spermicide is nearly 100 percent effective; the birth control pill, 99 percent; the rhythm method, 98 percent. Knowing what to do with the available technology is the key. Below we offer information that should help bring you up-to-date on what's out there and help you decide which methods can work for you.

Sterilization

A woman goes into the hospital to deliver what she hopes will be her last child. She emerges with the baby—and with her tubes tied. Sound like a dramatic move? Perhaps, but millions of American women each year request a tubal ligation at the time of delivery.

In fact, sterilization, which is almost always irreversible, is the most common form of birth control in the United States—used by 42 percent of the people who use any form of contraception, primarily those who have already had their children. (This figure is three times higher than in Western Europe.) About two-thirds of those sterilized are women whose fallopian tubes are blocked by a tubal ligation; one-third of those sterilized are men through the vasectomy, which prevents the sperm from traveling from testicle to penis. The process, in each case, takes about half an hour and costs $1,000–$2,500 for a tubal ligation and $240–$520 for a vasectomy.

member: dawnchristine

Survey: RU-486

Besides giving women a safe alternative to a surgical abortion, the other studied health benefits of RU-486 outweigh the reasons not to approve. It has been shown that it may help women with breast cancer. I think that's reason enough. The federal government needs to approve more research that will help women, not hurt them.

Barrier Methods

Diaphragm/Cervical Cap

The diaphragm and the cervical cap work in a similar manner, though they differ a bit in shape. Available by prescription, the diaphragm is a shallow cup shaped like a dome that is inserted into the vagina, where it blocks the cervix from invasion by sperm. The cap is smaller and recommended for use by women whose pelvic muscles aren't strong enough to hold a diaphragm in place.

The diaphragm has suffered a popularity lag in the last decade as more effective methods, including the pill, have been refined. Used by fewer than 3 percent of American women, and effective only around 80 percent of the time in average use, both the diaphragm and cervical cap should be used in conjuction with spermicidal products. The diaphragm can be left in for up to twenty-four hours. Beyond that, the user runs the risk, though unlikely, of getting toxic shock syndrome, characterized by sudden fever, stomach upset, rash, and low blood pressure. The cervical cap can be left in for forty-eight hours.

Sponge

The Today sponge may be the only birth control innovation in this decade to win the applause of a wide American audience. As effective as the diaphragm, it benefited from being available without a prescription. But when the FDA challenged Whitehall-Robins Healthcare to meet higher standards in its manufacturing of the sponge, the company opted instead to pull the product from the shelves. Even Elaine, from TV's *Seinfeld*, deplored the action and went so far as to stockpile all the sponges in New York City.

Made of polyurethane foam and soaked in three spermicidal gels, the sponge is intended to block semen from entering the uterus. Used perfectly without additional spermicides, it was 92 percent effective.

Despite the public's enthusiasm, the sponge has not returned to the shelves. It is available in Canada and remains on the FDA's list of approved contraception, but no new manufacturer has taken up the challenge in the United States.

Condom

Condoms have inspired a cottage industry of stores with names like Condomania and Condomnation selling all varieties of textured, flavored, and colored prophylactics. You can get them in corner delis, gas stations, and, in France, from sidewalk vending machines; college health advisers hand them out to students by the handful, pushing them hard on all nonmonogamous folk as the only safe way of preventing the transmission of STDs.

Despite this high public profile, condoms are used only by 18 percent of those who use birth control. Men complain it's uncomfortable; it's easy to use wrong; and female-centered techniques have been developed to much more sophisticated and less intrusive levels.

All of the varieties of condoms fall into one of three basic categories: garden variety latex, up-and-coming polyurethane, and lamb-skin. Polyurethane condoms have been welcomed by those allergic to latex, but they also have a leg up for other reasons: They emit no rubbery smell, they are more durable, and they will not break down in the presence of oil-based lubricants the way latex condoms will. Some men even report greater sensitivity when using the polyurethane condom.

Like latex condoms, the new polyurethane condoms are not porous and therefore can prevent the transmission of STDs. They are also, in a perfect world, 98 percent effective at preventing pregnancy. However, condoms in average use are only around 84 percent effective. For all condoms, their effectiveness jumps when used in conjunction with a spermicidal product.

The lamb-skin condom is really misnamed, made not out of skin but out of the lamb's intenstines. More natural looking (and some say more aesthetically pleasing) than synthetic varieties, the lamb-skin condom is porous and offers no protection against AIDS or other sexually transmitted diseases.

member Whitewave

SURVEY: RU-486

I am not a prolifer, or a prochoicer, however, I do think that abortion should not be used as a form of birth control. This method makes abortion way to easy and accessible. I think allowing this pill in the USA will only heighten the number of abortions.

Vaginal Pouch

The Reality Female Condom was approved for use in 1993, but its awkward mechanism has discouraged widespread use. Reality is shaped like a condom with a ring at either end; the closed end is placed over the cervix while the open end dangles out, covering the labia and the base of the penis during intercourse. This "dangling" effect coupled with a slight sqeaking noise have been among the female condom's most off-putting features (see sidebar on page 286).

Nonetheless, Reality has drawn high praise as the first contraceptive device that a woman can use on her own body to prevent HIV and STDs. At three times the cost of a regular male condom, the disposable female condom is made of polyurethane, emits no smell, and is said to conduct heat better than latex male condoms. Though it is stronger than the male condom and theoretically more effective, Reality has been found to be difficult to insert, testing as less effective because of improper use.

Chemical/Hormonal

Oral Contraceptive Pill

In 1959, when the oral contraceptive pill—soon to be known simply as The Pill—was first approved by the FDA, it was greeted as a scientific miracle. And as it marked the first time in history that a woman could control both her reproductive ability and her menstrual cycle with a daily pill, it nearly qualified as such.

The pill has been developed significantly since its appearance. Today's pill contains much lower doses of estrogen than the earlier pills did, reducing greatly the risk posed by the first pills of aneurysm, stroke, and heart attack. Two kinds are available, one with progestin only, called the mini-pill, which works by thickening cervical mucous and preventing sperm from reaching the egg; and the more common combination pill, in which the more active ingredient is estrogen, a hormone that prevents the development of the egg in the ovaries. When taken properly (every day, around the same time), the pill is 99 percent effective at preventing pregnancy, makes menstrual periods more regular, and reduces cramps. The pill has also been reported to reduce the chances of ovarian cancer by as much as 75 percent if taken for ten years.

Though the FDA reports that taking the pill is safer for most women than having a baby, there are some side effects. In the first few months, many may experience nausea, headache, breast tenderness, weight gain, irregular bleeding, and depression. In addition, it may harbor more serious dangers such as stroke, heart disease, and high blood pressure in certain women, particularly those who smoke or are older than thirty-five. In addition, taking the pill for longer than ten years is discouraged as some studies have found that such long-term use may lead to a slightly increased chance of breast cancer.

So, should you take the pill knowing it will reduce the chances of ovarian cancer or avoid it because of the fear of breast cancer? Since the pill has been proven to have overwhelming impact on reducing the chances of ovarian cancer while the breast cancer studies have shown only a slight (and unproven) impact over many years, we can probably feel safe in taking it for a decade or less.

Norplant

Norplant was introduced in 1991, and there were soon more than 1 million American women walking around with the six matchstick-sized capsules in their arms. Containing only progestin, Norplant avoided some of the problems of estrogen-carrying birth control pills and was expected to be easy to use—once inserted, a woman could forget about birth control for five years. Side effects were no greater than those of the pill and the method was completely reversible—depending on her cycle, a woman could be fertile two or three days after removal of the sticks.

The hassle-free reputation of Norplant was marred, however, when doctors came to remove the device about five years after implantation. Most medical schools, even today, do not train ob-gyns to remove the device and reports flooded the press in the mid '90s that the device was difficult and painful to remove. Some users experienced swelling in the arm as well as infection. A class-action suit filed by 50,000 women also claimed that they had not been adequately informed of what they claimed were Norplant's side effects: bleading, tumors, and diminished fertility. Although that suit was denied by the courts, demand for Norplant has dropped dramatically.

Many health care researchers still encourage the use of Norplant, focusing on its convenience, safety, and effectiveness. Norplant costs about \$500–\$750 to put in and \$100–\$200 to remove, making it less expensive than the birth control pill.

member: bill54494

SURVEY: RU-486

Until someone can demonstrate to me that the products of human conception are not genetically human, not genetically distinct from the parents, and not alive, I will be unable to accept that abortion in any form is morally acceptable. I realize that there are many others who agonize over this complex issue, and I respect those who do so.

Depo-Provera

It's eerie to realize that Depo-Provera, which was approved by the FDA in 1992 as a form of birth control, is the same drug generally used by California and other states to chemically castrate sex offenders convicted of child molestation. But the drug, which in men reduces testosterone and sex drive, in women has only those side effects and potential dangers experienced with Norplant and the pill.

Injections into the buttocks or arm every three months might discourage some women from using this method, though it is 98 percent effective, carries similar, mild side effects and benefits as Norplant and the pill, and costs about the same. As with Norplant, the greatest boost to Depo-Provera's effectiveness comes because the woman does not have to do anything—use is always perfect. Since 1969, it has been used by 30 million women worldwide.

Vaginal Spermicides

Used alone, spermicides such as nonoxinal-9 have been found to be the least effective form of birth control—less successful, in fact, than withdrawal. In part this more than 20 percent failure of all forms—foams, creams, jellies, suppositories, tablets, and films—is due to the complexities of using spermicides, which are easily available over the counter but need to be inserted at least ten minutes before intercourse and left in for six to eight hours afterward. Spermicides, however, are nearly 100 percent effective when used in conjunction with a condom or other barrier method.

In recent years, researchers had hoped that new forms of spermicides would prevent the transmission of HIV along with other STDs. In fact, they were able to kill the HIV virus with spermicides in a test tube. This research is still in development, however, since spermicides were not found to block the HIV virus nor protect from gonorrhea or chlamydia in regular human use.

IUD

The notorious intrauterine device is one of the most popular forms of birth control in the world, used by more than 90 million women and by 15 percent of women on birth control in Western Europe. In the Unites States, however, it has never recovered from the Dalkon Shield disaster of the mid 1970s, which was associated with a high incidence of pelvic infections and infertility and some deaths. More than 2 million American women had the device implanted in the 1970s; tens of thousands contracted pelvic infections, had miscarriages, and became infertile; eighteen died. Only about 1 percent use it today and although the current IUDs have been shown to be safe, many doctors refuse to put them in.

The IUD has one of the lowest failure rates of any of birth control method (1 percent) although, according to a surprising description from the FDA, "it's not entirely clear how IUDs prevent pregnancy." (Sounds as informed as those ancient camel drivers, who are rumored to have put stones into their animals' uteri to prevent pregnancy!) It seems to work either by immobilizing the sperm on their way to the fallopian tubes or by changing the uterine lining so the fertilized egg cannot be implanted.

There are two kinds of IUDs—one in which the active ingredient is copper, which causes the intended uterine inflammation; the other, which is used for women allergic to copper and which releases the hormone progesterone. The IUD takes about fifteen minutes to implant and costs $250–$1,000. The copper IUD can be left in for up to a decade; the hormonal IUD for only about a year.

The IUD presents serious danger only to those prone to sexually related infections: Women who have an STD and use the IUD have an 8.3 percent chance of a potentially life-threatening pelvic inflammatory disease and a 7 percent chance of infertility.

"Natural"

The world is full of coitus interruptus babies. This method is only 80 percent effective and depends on the rather dubious talents of a man to withdraw just before ejaculation. Even then, however, the damage may be done: Sperm are abundantly present in pre-cum, liquid droplets that escape the penis before orgasm.

The rhythm method, by contrast, has been found to be 98 percent effective by dedicated users who like it because it is completely natural and without side effects. But it is not for everyone, is easy to do wrong, and is also only 80 percent effective in average use. Also called "natural planning," "periodic abstinence," "fertility awareness," or the "ovulation method," this technique is only for the highly motivated, detail-oriented woman. It requires that a woman be aware of changes in her menstrual cycle, her cervical mucus, and her body temperature. Understand that without a significant amount of research or training, your chances of using this method effectively are low.

member: Emma

CONFERENCE: CONTRACEPTION

Much as the idea of the Reality condom turned me off originally, I think it's important to examine the other options out there. I think of the female condom as being a work in progress—just a sign of better things to come. And much as I enjoy pondering the idea of a male pill, this (female condom, etc.) is probably the direction we should be looking for advancement. I can't imagine that good things will ever come from screwing around with our hormones so much.

Emergency Contraception

In Western Europe, emergency contraception in a number of different forms is readily available, by prescription or even over the counter. It is labeled for use within seventy-two hours of unprotected sex and is packaged in one or two pills.

By contrast, there are no products specifically marketed in the United States as the "morning after pill." In 1997, the FDA concluded that "off-label" use of the copper IUD and birth control pills in high doses was safe to prevent pregnancy. If used within seventy-two hours after unprotected intercourse—under the prescription and care of a doctor—a certain number of birth control pills or an IUD can stop pregnancy.

By the time emergency contraception is used, the egg is already fertilized and traveling toward the uterus. But because doctors define pregnancy not by fertilizaiton but by implantation in the uterine wall, this technique falls under the category of contraception, not abortion.

The Future

Birth control may have been revolutionized in the 1960s with the introduction of the pill and the IUD. But in the years since birth control research reached its zenith, activists have been deploring the failure of the pharmaceutical and research communities to successfully develop and market more effective methods of preventing pregnancy and sexually transmitted diseases.

Nonetheless, a number of new birth control methods are currently under development, mostly in the first and second stages of trials on humans:

- The Vaginal Ring—this flexible, doughnut-shaped device is inserted into the vagina to deliver hormones that, like the pill, prevent ovulation.
- Transdermal Methods—delivered through gels or patches on the woman's abdomen, a highly concentrated dose of the hormone nestorone is absorbed into the blood to prevent ovulation.
- Microbicides—under development to prevent the transmission of HIV and other STDs, these drugs, worked into current spermicidal methods, would offer an alternative to the condom. Researchers hope to prevent microorganisms from adhering to the outer layer of the reproductive tract. To date, the drugs work in a test tube, but much more research on effectiveness and side effects has yet to be done.

The list of methods of birth control for men to use is short compared with what's available for women: condoms, withdrawal, abstinence, and vasectomy. Researchers are looking into new methods that would be easy to use, effective, reversible, and would not cause serious side effects or have any impact on sexual activity.

Developing hormonal methods of male birth control—the current direction of research—is a more complex problem than it is for females. For starters, in men, sperm production and the sexual drive are spurred by the same hormones, so a drug that reduced the former would also reduce the latter—which you might say would defeat the purpose. Second, sperm are produced daily (as compared with a woman's monthly egg), so suppression of sperm must be continuous.

Researchers are now working on a combination of hormones that would suppress testosterone and the resultant creation of sperm without having an impact on the man's sex drive, which also depends on testosterone. These studies are only in their initial stages and are not expected to offer a viable product for at least five years.

member: genius17

CONFERENCE: CONTRACEPTION

I myself use the pill, and it has had a number of positive effects for me. Not only does it allow for spontaneity with my partner and me, but it has regulated my cycle as well. I'm much happier. With the pill, mistakes are somewhat predictable. If you miss a pill, you know you may have a chance of getting pregnant. You never know if your condom will break. Even if you miss a pill, there is only a 3 percent chance that you will get pregnant, compared to 12 percent with a condom. The pill may not be the answer for someone who is worried about disease, but as far as pregnancy is concerned, I think the pill is the way to go!

MIFEPRISTONE

Known commercially as RU-486, Mifepristone is not a method of contraception but a drug that causes an abortion to occur in the early stages of pregnancy. It has been hailed as a more convenient method of abortion and cursed by antiabortion activists who fear this nonsurgical method would lead millions more American women to abortions.

A "medical abortion," as Mifepristone abortions are called, is conducted over three sessions in a doctor's office. At the first session, a woman takes Mifepristone and usually experiences the same side effects as a normal pregnancy—nausea, headaches, and fatigue. In the second session, she is given a dose of a second drug, commonly the ulcer medicine misoprostol, which in combination with Mifepristone increases the chances of a successful abortion. Usually within twenty-four hours of this second visit, she experiences cramps and abdominal pain as if she were menstruating or having a miscarriage. If both drugs fail to induce abortion—which happens 5 percent of the time, a tradi-

> Reality Check—The Female Condom

Over the last few years, the Female Health Company has been trying to reach Jane Q. Public through advertising, to convince her that one of the newest forms of contraception, the Reality Female Condom, is the most desirable form yet. If you read any glossy women's magazine whose targeted audience includes women between eighteen and forty, you've probably seen the ad.

"Exactly how *fantastic* was it?" inquires the type laid over the heads of a postcoital opposite-sex couple who only have goo-goo eyes for each other.

"Fantastic enough *once* wasn't enough." Do tell. It's the woman who sells the ad. She looks so . . . sated, mildly amazed, and grateful all at the same time. Curiosity about the female condom made me consider using it. It was that *look* that made me dial the 800 number for my free sample. I wanted it to "Feel so *good*, you won't believe it's *safer sex*."

Before my Reality Female Condom arrived in the mail, I succumbed to the urge to buy one from the mecca four blocks from my home: Condom Kingdom.

It seemed easy enough to use. "To insert Reality, squeeze the inner ring and push into the vagina as far as possible. This ring helps to hold the female condom in place inside, while the outer rim stays outside the body and helps to protect. When both partners are ready, the penis is simply guided into the female condom. Extra lubricant is added for extra pleasure and ease of movement." They'd thoughtfully included a small tube of lubricant with my purchase.

Keeping one for myself, I gave my friend Amadee a pack and told her to call me with a Reality check in the next few days. She called me the next day. "Well, I can see right away that it's going to turn off a certain kind of woman," she told me.

"What?"

"I mean, I know a lot of grown women who can barely deal with having to use a tampon for a few days a month. You've really got to be comfortable touching yourself if you're going to insert it and use it correctly. Now let me tell you about the sound effects, girl . . . "

Amadee told me, but I found out for myself a few days later. Reality in action produced such hilarious sound effects it rendered intercourse nearly impossible. We were laughing too hard. Imagine the squishiest, squeakiest Baggie on earth and you're close. My beau now refers to it as "the whoopee condom." (The mood-deflating sound effects do go away with . . . um . . . practice and a bit of lubricant.)

There's an extra benefit not mentioned in the advertisements: The Reality Female Condom's outer base ring is a girl's best friend. It gives a surprising amount of clitoral stimulation because it hangs externally. I now call it "the whoopee condom" too, but for entirely different reasons.

But the absolute most important reason to give Reality a try is that men *love* it! At least mine did. They can't complain about constriction and the polyurethane conducts heat better than latex. And he doesn't have to be cajoled into wearing the condom because it's on you, girlfriend!

Sound too good to be true? Well, the label on the Reality box emphasizes that "the male latex condom remains the best protection against HIV and other sexually transmitted diseases." I went back and did some research. In Food and Drug Administration tests, subjects had a 26 percent failure rate while using the female condom, compared to the male condom's 15 percent failure rate.

But further FDA research reveals that with perfect use, the female condom has a failure rate of 5 percent, compared with 3 percent for the male condom. So it's 11 percent easier to get pregnant when using the Reality Female Condom improperly than it is when using the male condom improperly.

"We can't really ignore a relatively safe method that prevents pregnancy and sexually transmitted diseases and is under the control of the woman," Amadee, who is a sex-ed counselor, told me. "With a male condom, a man has to agree to wear it and sometimes that just doesn't happen. Also, I notice that the FDA isn't circulating the fact that the rip and tear number for male condoms is as high as 14 percent and Reality's is only 0.2 percent."

I must say, when I first heard about the "femidom" a few years ago, I was underwhelmed. Just what the women of the world were waiting for—another contraceptive prevention method they'd bear all the responsibility for. Now I'm high on Reality. I value a contraceptive/ STD preventative that allows me to protect myself without being dependent on a partner, no matter how nice.

—*Yvonne Jones*

tional "surgical abortion" must be done to remove the embryo.

Women have preferred the medical abortion over the surgical kind for a number of reasons: It can be done earlier in pregnancy, it requires no anesthesia, it is less invasive, and there is no risk to the uterus or cervix. On the other hand, a medical abortion forces a woman to see the "products of contraception," as the bleeding induced may last from one to three weeks; it may also result, in rare cases, in the loss of enough blood to require a transfusion.

Medical abortions have been used by 300,000 women worldwide since 1981. In France, more than half of all abortions are done through this method. In Sweden, where it has been used since 1991, 16 percent of abortions are medical. After much political haggling, the FDA issued an "approvable" letter regarding Mifepristone in 1997. Once the nonprofit Population Council—which owns the U.S. rights to distribute RU-486—shows that it can safely manufacture the method on a factory level, it is expected to be approved.

member: LHoward

CONFERENCE: CONTRACEPTION

I was on Depo-Provera for over a year, and just recently went off it. Although it was very convenient my sex drive became nonexistent. My problem with all of these contraceptives is that they all take away some of your sex drive. What's the use of being on birth control if you never want to have sex? I also recently heard that California is thinking about chemical castration for pedophiles, they plan on using Depo-Provera! Proves to me that this is a man's world. If they ever come up with male birth control you can bet that their sex drive won't be decreased. I am back to using condoms with my husband. I'd rather be inconvenienced than not want to have sex at all.

part 6

money

Credit Cards

The American Bankruptcy Institute reported a hair-raising 1,178,555 personal filings in 1996. A big part of avoiding such a fate is learning to keep your credit record squeaky clean.

by Wendy Cholbi

"I feel I'm very responsible financially. I try not to get into too much debt," says Molly, a twenty-six-year-old writer. "I hardly ever used my card until last year, when I had trouble finding a job. I just wasn't making enough income, so I had to get money from somewhere." Molly quickly racked up a "huge" balance, using the card to pay for basic necessities like food and rent.

David and his wife Julia, both artists in their mid-twenties, have had even worse luck. "We have about seven or eight cards," says David. "I'm not even sure anymore—some of them have been frozen because of late payments."

The couple's total credit card debt is around $25,000. "I've never calculated how long it will take us to pay off the full amount of our debt—it's too depressing," groans David.

Gina and her husband Dan, both professionals in their late twenties, recently faced a similarly scary situation. Says Gina, "We had over $15,000 on four or five credit cards and we both had student loans and car payments."

If you see yourself in any of these stories, you are not alone. Many people who have every intention of being financially respon-

member: Intempo

SURVEY: CREDIT CARD DEBT

I have been trying to be credit card free since I got married. But my husband thinks cards are a great help, and credit helps us cover most of our expenses. But I see it as a big monster eating up our last penny and leaving us with nothing, since half of what we make we pay to credit cards. I don't think it's a wise thing to use all the time, but maybe for an emergency or travel and only using what you can comfortably pay later.

member: dichiara

SURVEY: CREDIT CARD DEBT

Credit cards are a way to gain instant gratification for things you *think* you deserve. We feel like we owe ourselves something so we go out and purchase stuff with money we do *not* have just so we can feel like we have gained some social status in life. Actually what we have done is to lie to ourselves and our friends by getting stuff we really can't afford, then we end up owing everything we earn just to pay the interest on the credit card debt.

sible end up carrying more debt than they know how to handle.

"Consumers are feeling stretched in terms of credit. They've had a long time to [rack up high balances]," observes Michael Durante, a credit-card analyst with Salomon Brothers, Inc., in New York. The economy has "had a long expansionary period and that's given consumers the time and motivation to buy, and buy on credit."

And how.

The American Bankruptcy Institute reported a hair-raising 1,178,555 personal bankruptcy filings in 1996, compared to 926,601 in 1995—that's a 27 percent increase. A whopping 95 percent of those filings were by individuals, and according to the ABI's report, credit was a major factor.

Don't panic. Being a smart credit consumer isn't that difficult. All you need is a healthy dose of common sense and the take-no-prisoners attitude of a bargain basement shopper. Here are a few simple principles:

1. Credit is a loan—not just an easy way to buy things. A credit card is tremendously convenient, but it can also lull you into a false sense of security, making it too psychologically easy to spend money you don't have.

   If you find yourself using cash advances from your credit card to cover routine expenses like groceries or gas because you're waiting for payday or don't have enough cash in the bank, you are treating your credit cards like currency, not like the high-interest loans most of them are.

   David and Julia learned this the hard way. "We've dug ourselves in so deep that our goal now is not using credit much at all," says David.

   But you can recover from a period of credit card overdependence. Now that Molly has a full-time job, she pays about $300 per month, and her balance is down to about $1,500. She plans to be debt-free within six months.

2. Understand how credit card companies make money and use that knowledge to your advantage.

   The first thing to think about is fees. Apply for a credit card that promises no annual fee. "Fees are back," says Durante. "Companies are instituting new late fees, over-

member: vlague
SURVEY: CREDIT CARD DEBT
I teach at a community college in Florida. I really hate it when credit card companies come to campus to solicit business. It never fails that later in the semester or year I have students who are not attending class regularly, and when we talk they tell me that they have to work to pay their credit card bills. These companies are taking advantage of young people who don't understand how credit cards work or how fast they can get in over their heads in debt.

member: c_steiny
SURVEY: CREDIT CARD DEBT
It interests me that so many people seem to think that the issuers of credit are to blame for the irresponsible use of same. Someone here wrote "Don't think that if you have $20,000 available, you won't use it. The credit companies know this too." To which I say, "Not necessarily!" I can see how some folks have gotten into trouble with credit, though. What each of us really needs is someone to educate us at the very start that credit is not for frivolous, gotta-have-it-now purchases.

limit fees, and the like," which you want to avoid at all costs.

Another area, the mother lode for card companies, is the interest on your balance. They can easily afford to give you the card "free," that is, with no annual fee, if you'll use their card and carry a nominal balance. Which brings us directly to the third rule.

3. Always read the fine print. By law, credit card issuers must disclose interest rates and fees when they make an offer of credit. Read the terms carefully and make sure you understand them completely before you accept any offer.

When you carry a balance from one month to the next, you are assessed a finance charge, which is calculated as a percentage of your balance. This charge is expressed as the APR (annual percentage rate). If you have a balance of $100 that you carry for one year, and your APR is 16.5 percent, at

member: promerk

SURVEY: CREDIT CARD DEBT

When I applied for a loan, my banker said that I didn't have enough credit history. I said that I usually paid cash, and I had a service card (AmEx) so I pay my bills within thirty days. Well, I got my Visa, and then my MasterCard, and after one year of "credit history" I got my loan. Now, I have so much debt that about half of my income goes to pay those "monthly minimums."

> Beating the Minimum

If you make your minimum payment reliably each month, and never charge beyond your limit, you will never default on a loan, and you will, therefore, never be seen as a bad credit risk. You'd be a model customer—from the companies' point of view. But you still might saddle yourself with debt that takes a surprisingly long time to pay off. Consider chart 1, which shows how long it would take to pay off a $2,000 balance, assuming that you stop making new charges on your card.

Your monthly payments are first applied to the interest you've accrued before they start gnawing away at the principal. Of course, if you continue to use the card (which is exactly what they hope you'll do), you will probably never pay the balance in full.

Paying more than the monthly minimum, whenever you can, is a good idea. Be realistic—don't plan on making $400 monthly payments that will keep you from paying your rent. But if you're expecting a tax refund or are selling your car, for example, plan on making a few large payments that will really chomp away at that balance.

APR Balance	*Monthly (%)*	*Monthly payment*	*Months to Pay in Full*
$2,000	16.0	$40	83
$2,000	16.0	$80	31
$2,000	7.9	$40	61

CHART 1:
"How Long Till I'm Free?"
(assuming I don't make any new charges)

the end of the year you will owe $116.50 (see sidebar on page 293 for more information about APRs).

4. Finally and most important, keep your head. Though these companies may seem intimidating, ultimately you've got the power because they need your business.

But to make that power work for you, you have to be savvy. Gary Gordon, a credit card analyst with PaineWebber Group, Inc., says that banks and other issuers have been confusing consumers by marketing their cards too aggressively, mailing out solicitations for preapproved credit cards.

"I get those things all the time," says Molly. So far she has resisted these promos, but she admits they can be seductive: "One card is enough for me. Still, last month I got an application for a gold card with a $50,000 credit limit." That's nearly twice her annual income. As sales tactics get sneakier, it becomes more important than ever to educate yourself about credit (see sidebar on page 295 for a comparison of some current card offers, including what to watch out for).

When you apply for credit, you start a credit record on yourself. This file will be used by banks, finance companies, realtors, and other total strangers to pass judgment on you for your entire life (see sidebar on page 297 for information on obtaining your credit report and fixing errors).

Yikes. What a creepy concept. Don't let it overwhelm you, though. If you can keep the electric company from shutting off your power, you should be able to keep your credit record clean. This way, when you need large amounts of credit (for a car loan, a mortgage, or a home equity loan), your chances of getting it will be that much better. One of the slippery things about credit is that you might think you should stay away from it altogether to avoid the hell of overwhelming debt, but in fact you will probably end up needing a credit record sooner or later.

"I've been told when I've applied for loans in the past not that I have bad credit, just that I don't have much credit," says Molly. "I

member: kimmer

SURVEY: CREDIT CARD DEBT

When my little brother recently started college I sent him an envelope full of cut up credit cards and copies of my bills with a stringent warning *not* to get sucked in. When he saw how much I send to the bank every month I think he got the picture loud and clear.

member: Amaranth

SURVEY: CREDIT CARD DEBT

I put all my credit cards in the freezer in a bowl of water that turned to ice. I look at them longingly every once in a while when I'm grabbing the peas and pearl onions or mint chip ice cream, but deep in my heart I know they're where they're supposed to be and shall remain forever more.

member: MFTuchman

SURVEY: CREDIT CARD DEBT

I prefer to use AmEx because their strictness makes sure I can't carry a balance.

member: wildbird

SURVEY: CREDIT CARD DEBT

It isn't the plastic's fault but mine . . . try $10,000 plus in credit card debt with no job, and mortgages and vehicle payments to boot. I did it all by myself. Now I've just got to dig out of this hole but the dirt keeps falling back in on my head . . . trying not to go down for the count.

member: anniesparkle

SURVEY: CREDIT CARD DEBT

I am currently in deep debt. After the divorce and assuming responsibility for my three sons, I see the debt as an investment in my children's future. Debt may be expensive, but I'm providing my kids with a better living situation. I think they deserve it!

> Special Deals

If you're sifting through piles of solicitations for "preapproved" credit cards or searching credit card databases like those maintained by Ram Research (http://www.ramresearch.com/cardlocator/cardlocator.html) or Get Smart (http://www.getsmart.com/), you're probably wondering if the offers you're seeing are really as great as they seem. Here's a look at a few of the slicker offers floating around.

1. Reward cards. These give you points or bonuses for each dollar that you charge. These may look enticing, but most of the cards that offer them have high interest rates or annual fees, and unless you charge large amounts, the rewards don't amount to much. So if you regularly charge large amounts and you can afford to pay off the balance each month, these cards might work for you. Otherwise, pass.

   The GM card, offered by Household Bank, gives you 5 percent of your purchases toward the purchase or lease of a new GM car or truck. Although there is no annual fee, the APR can be as high as 20.9 percent, and you can earn a maximum of $500 per year for seven years (that means charging $10,000 per year). Who knows how much car prices will have gone up in seven years? Bringing a bargain-savvy friend to the car dealership will save you more money than using this card ever could.

   The Discover card offers users a cash rebate equivalent to 1 percent of the amount charged each year. If your local grocery store proclaimed, "1 percent discount on all items!" would you rush out to stock up? Probably not. So why would you pay some 15 percent in interest each year to get 1 percent of your purchases back in cash?

   Frequent flyer miles, free hotel stays, and savings on meals at restaurants are other popular rewards. A typical airline card will give you one mile per dollar charged. Most airline rewards start at 20,000 to 25,000 miles, so you'll end up paying $25,000 for a "free" ticket. It might be more cost-effective to buy the ticket outright.
2. Gold and Platinum cards. Originally, these signified higher charging credit lines, but they have been aggressively marketed to ordinary folks. They play on your desire to feel pampered by offering special perks in customer service, warranty plans on purchased items, and extras like travel insurance. Most ordinary card users won't use half of the "special services" these cards offer. Choose a card for a feature other than color. If a platinum card happens to have the lowest APR or offers warranties for products you buy often, go for it. But if you just want the feeling of importance that you think a platinum card will give you, you're probably applying for the wrong reason.
3. Low interest-rate cards. Here is a feature that—believe it or not—can actually save you some cash. Getting a lower interest rate is often easy to do, thanks to card companies' eagerness to transfer balances for people with good credit.

   "There's no reason [consumers] shouldn't take advantage of low interest-rate offers," says PaineWebber's Gary Gordon. "It's all about the balance of power between the borrowers and the lenders, and right now it's a borrower's market, because competition [for customers] is fierce among lenders."

   Most low-rate cards will only give new account holders the low rate for a specified period of time, usually three to six months, and after that they'll jack it up significantly. If you plan to pay off or pay down the balance within the first six months rather than sticking to the minimum, these "teaser" rates may work for you.

   Chart 2 shows how much you can save on interest if you transfer your balance to a lower APR card.

APR Balance	*Monthly (%)*	*Monthly payment*	*Interest paid in one year*
$2,000	21.9	$50	$420.71
$2,000	16.8	$50	$314.69
$2,000	12.9	$50	$237.04
$2,000	7.9	$50	$141.6
$2,000	5.9	$50	$104.75

Chart 2:
"How Much Will I Save?" (assuming I don't make any new charges)

hate that game! You have to go into more debt in order to establish credit. It makes no sense to me. It seems they would look upon you more favorably if you didn't have a bunch of outstanding loans."

"What do I do," you may be saying, "if my credit record is already trashed? What if my cards are all maxed out?"

Take heart. Even a "subprime" borrower, which is what you are if you've had credit problems, can be rehabilitated back to respectable status.

You'll need to do some basic accounting. How many loans do you have? Besides credit cards, do you have student loans? car loans? What are the balances? What are the minimum payments? Are you in default on any of these loans?

Identify the trouble spots: loans for which you are late making payments, in default, or over your credit limit. Set goals. Your first goal is to make a payment—of any amount each month, to each card, on time. Your second goal is to make the minimum payment each month—on time. But starting a regular payment schedule, even if you can't make the minimum amount, goes a long way toward establishing that you're a paying customer and not a total deadbeat.

member: Shinteetah

SURVEY: CREDIT CARD DEBT

My method of managing the plastic is simple—I have one card, and I do not spend more than what I have in the bank. I pay my card off in full each month. I have never paid a penny of interest on my card, and I have a sterling credit record because I've never been late. Yes, if I want to buy something big, it'll be a pain to wait until I've saved enough to pay for it all at once—but it would be a bigger pain to find myself in debt.

If you find it hard to keep your various credit cards and their balances, due dates, and fees straight, simplify.

"Lack of money was a problem when it came to paying off the cards, but a more serious problem was a lack of organization," admits David. He and his wife, Julia, thought a popular personal-finance computer program might help, but it only muddled and discouraged them further. "It was kind of a pain in the ass," David says. "I didn't need a program to tell me how broke I was, I needed a program that would pay the bills for me." Finally, the couple signed up for an account with a bank that offers online account access. Now they pay more than the minimum payment on every card, every month, and their bank account is set up to automatically deduct the payments.

Transferring your balance to a card with a lower APR may help. But you may not have that option. In which case, especially if you are having a lot of trouble meeting your monthly payments for each card, consider a consolidation loan—a bank loan that will be sufficient to pay off all your current debts.

Consider this example. You have the following debts:
Credit Card 1: $7,500 at an APR of 16.9 percent, minimum monthly payment of $120.

> Your Credit Report

You are entitled to a free copy of your credit report if you have been denied credit within the past sixty days; otherwise, expect to pay up to $8 (depending on where you live).

You can also request that your credit report not be made available to companies that want to "prescreen" you for credit offers. This will cut down on the "preapproved" mail and phone solicitations you receive, although it may take a while to take effect.

Here are three credit bureaus:

Equifax Information Service Center
P.O. Box 740241
Atlanta, GA 30374-0241
800-685-1111
FAX: 404-612-2668
http://www.equifax.com/consumer/consumer.html

Trans Union Corp.
Consumer Disclosure Center
P. O. Box 390
Springfield, PA 19064-0390
800-851-2674
http://www.transunion.com/

Experian
P.O. Box 2104
Allen, TX 75013-2104
888-397-3742
http://www.experian.com/index.html

If you make your request in writing, you'll probably be asked to include the following information. It may seem like a pain, but remember, this prevents thieves and scam artists from getting your credit report, so bear with it.

- your full name and signature
- birthdate
- addresses you've held in the past five years
- phone number
- photocopy of driver's license showing current address
- photocopy of your social security card

Once you receive your report, read it carefully. Going back seven years, it will list all the loans you've taken out and all the credit cards you've held. If you have ever been late on a payment or defaulted on a loan, the report will give the full name of the issuer and a notation. It will also give you the names of any companies that have requested a copy of your credit report in the past year. You have the right to request the addresses and phone numbers of those companies.

If you see a mistake, notify the credit bureau immediately in writing. Enclose any documentation you have that will help refute the error. Under the terms of the Consumer Credit Reporting Reform Act of 1996, the bureau must investigate your complaint within thirty days.

Within five days of finishing its investigation, if the credit bureau finds that there has been a mistake, it must provide you with a corrected copy of your credit report. Whatever the finding, you should also receive a written explanation of your rights under current credit laws, and a written report on the results of the investigation. It is the investigating credit bureau's responsibility—not yours—to report mistakes to the other credit bureaus. Even if the bureau's decision is not in your favor, you have the right to add a statement to your credit file that explains your side of the story. That means that anyone looking at your credit record will see that you believe some of the information on it to be incorrect.

If you need help or are overwhelmed by your credit report, there are agencies that can help you. Start with the non-profit National Foundation for Consumer Credit. For the office nearest you, call 800-388-2227.

Credit Card 2: $9,000 at an APR of 18.9 percent, minimum monthly payment of $155.

Student loan: $5,000 at an APR of 9 percent. Fixed monthly payment of $125 (you have four more years of fixed payments on this loan).

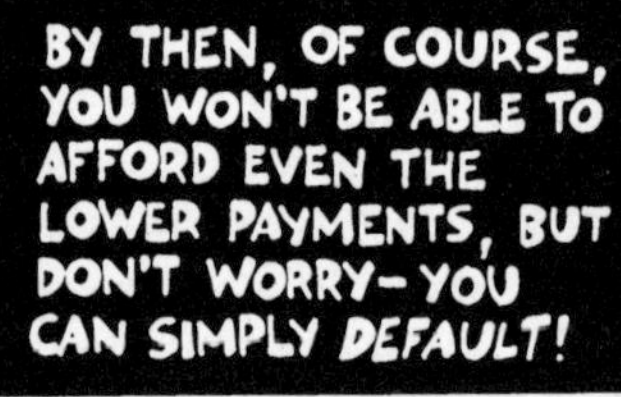

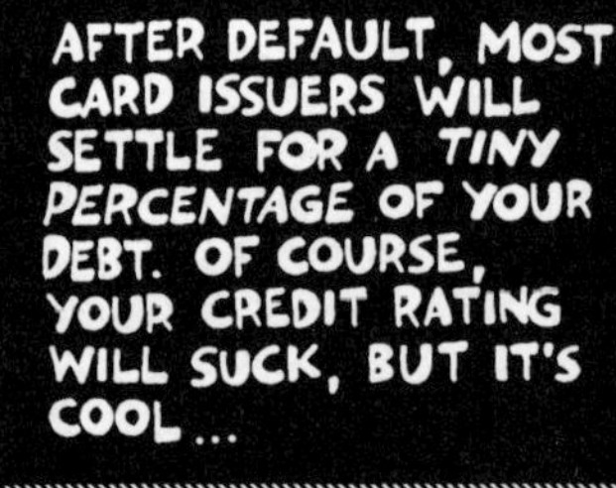

Car loan: $3,500 at an APR of 12 percent. Fixed monthly payment of $170 (you have twenty-three months of fixed payments on this loan).

So your total debt is $25,000, with monthly payments totaling $570. If you get a bank consolidation loan for $25,000, at an APR of 11 percent with a repayment term of fifteen years, you'll have a monthly payment of around $300.

That's exactly what Gina and her husband did: Since they had recently purchased a new home, they were able to get a home equity loan to consolidate their debt. Gina knows that it's risky to trade unsecured debt, like credit cards and student loans, for secured debt; the couple would have to forfeit their home if they defaulted on the home equity loan. "But there was no way we could keep making the monthly payments on everything we were paying," Gina explains. "Now we have a few simple payments and some breathing room, and our credit hasn't been damaged."

Clearly, there is no quick and easy way to pay off bills that you've spent years accumulating. The best strategy, of course, is not to get into debt in the first place, as David readily admits. "Being financially responsible to others means meeting your obligations. Being financially responsible to yourself means not stupidly getting into debt, but it's too late for us—we've already done that."

member: Keath

SURVEY: CREDIT CARD DEBT

I had to file for bankruptcy after amassing $15,000 in debt and felt pretty bad about it until my lawyer "cheered me up." I don't know if he was telling me the truth or not, but he said he files every seven years after amassing huge personal debts. I said, "But isn't that unethical?" He said, "Who cares? It's legal!" He later told me his motto: "You can't blame the water for finding the hole in the boat." He said major companies work like this all the time. The only ones who really suffer are the little people with consciences struggling to meet the payments on their credit cards refusing to file bankruptcy on matters of principle. I can't say I like what I heard from my lawyer but I no longer feel so rotten about filing after having heard his side of things.

Freelance Finance

The best way to ensure that you remain your own boss is to create systems for handling your finances. After all, if you like making money, you should do what you can to maintain its continued flow.

by Michael Kaplan

You've made the big break from corporate shackles. A shingle hangs outside your door and the work pours in like confetti. Clients think you're a genius—at writing software or illustrating book covers or designing clothing—and a degree of certainty has been added to your life. Clearly, the work you generate for yourself is where it needs to be.

Now all you have to do is keep the finances in motion to keep the whole thing from collapsing. It is a three-stage cycle—getting your money, saving your money, paying taxes on your money—that can make or break a self-employed person. And no matter how much passion you pour into your profession, without the right kind of cash flow you will be back on the nine-to-five chain gang quicker than you can say, "Man in the gray flannel suit."

The best way to ensure that you remain your own boss is to create systems for handling finances. After all, if you enjoy earning your money, you ought to do what you can to maintain its continued flow. This series of strategies will assist you in keeping the floodgates open.

Getting Your Money

The work is done and it's time to get paid. As a freelance writer who has been doing this for the last ten years, I can tell you that billing, bookkeeping, badgering of pokey accounting departments, preparing for the inevitable slow periods, and tracking of expenses are among the least interesting—but, alas, the most critical—aspects of my job. Here's how I deal with what seems like a cross between being my own CEO and doing some serious grunt work.

Keeping Track

Chronicling the flow of assignments is imperative to running any kind of business with even a modicum of organization. And considering the computerized bookkeeping programs that are available—Intuit's Quicken and Microsoft's Money being among the best—it's easy to log your jobs as they come in (include the due date and the amount of money you'll be paid) and go out (note the day that the work was submitted, billed, and, ultimately, paid for). This will serve as a guide for the work you're doing and where your finances might stand thirty or sixty or ninety days in the future. It will also give you a fair bit of confidence in dealing with a client who claims to have promised $1,500 when you noted $2,000. To avoid such debates, however, the terms of your work should be confirmed in a written contract or letter of agreement from the client outlining the payment, the due date, the expectations, and the precise nature of what is being purchased from you.

member: thersites

SURVEY: FREELANCE FINANCE

Of course I do my very own taxes. The math is simply ***not*** that involved or difficult. It doesn't cost me more than sixty minutes of my time.

Creating Invoices

Most clients will ask you to bill them for the work you do. The more information you include on the invoice, the less likely the odds of your having to deal with delayed payments. Always include your name, address, phone number, social security number, the job you're billing for, and the amount due. If you're creating invoices individually on your computer, remember to give each one a unique number. This will make it easier for you to keep track of them and for the client's accounting department to locate them as well.

Maintaining the Flow

Among the peculiarities of freelancing are the ebbs and flows that come with the territory. While it is tempting to monitor your cash flow on a weekly basis, tracking it quarterly is a bit wiser. That will allow you to account for slower periods, which a lot of businesses experience in August and December when people take vacations and work cycles slow down. One way to avoid a shortfall is to bulk up with long-term assignments during the busy times in order to see you through the slow periods when clients may be less receptive to your proposals. If this is not possible, then you need to remain aware of your work cycles and prepare accordingly, squirreling away money during the fat months in order to survive the lean—an ideal time for a well-deserved vacation—without freaking out.

Expense It

Most clients reimburse reasonable expenses to independent contractors as a matter of course. But the only way to get reimbursed quickly is to keep receipts and maintain a log for anything that does not come with an actual receipt (say, riding a city bus, racking up wear-and-tear on your automobile, or purchasing publications from a small newsstand). It's a good idea to confirm beforehand that your client's idea of "reasonable" jibes with your own and remember that presentation counts. It's best to tape your receipts to sheets of paper, make photocopies, and submit the copies. In terms of filing your

> Freelance Survival Kit

Once you have your fiscal life in order, here are a few things that can help you to keep it that way.

The Official IRS Site
(http://www.irs.ustreas.gov/)
Unsettlingly upbeat, this site is a place for keeping up on changes in tax laws, receiving some fairly self-serving advice from the IRS, and downloading tax forms that your post office might be out of.

Quicken
(http://www.quicken.com)
Arguably the best bookkeeping/cash-flow/investment-tracking software on the market for a freelancer. It allow you to quickly track money coming and going out, plus the program makes the itemizing of expenses for your tax return a breeze.

Successful Freelancing by Marion Faux (St. Martin's Griffin). While the book is a pretty good general resource on the ins and outs of freelancing, its chapters on taxes and finances will be particularly helpful.

Tax Savvy for Small Businesses by Frederick W. Daily (Nolo Press). Written by a tax attorney, this encyclopedic tome is a great resource on maintaining a beneficial financial relationship with Uncle Sam.

American Express Gold Card
(http://www.americanexpress.com)
It's not the cheapest credit card around, but for a freelancer it can be as good as gold. The card has no preset spending limit, travel services are available twenty-four-hours-a-day at a toll-free number (very helpful when you are working abroad and lack the support system of a home office), and at the end of the year you receive an itemized summary of all your charges for the twelve-month period.

receipts as they come in, keep it simple: Designate a file folder for each job and fill it with your receipts. Just remember to mark the reason for the expense on your receipt, which will make things easier when you need to justify the expenditures. Organizing phone expenses can be a tedious undertaking, though some long distance carriers make the task easier by allowing you to itemize calls through a code number that you key in for each client.

Fighting for Your Money

Every once in a while you encounter a client who can't pay you, who doesn't want to pay you, or who is disorganized and slow in paying you. After five weeks (thirty or so days plus a one week grace period) of waiting for your money, assume the latter and proceed in a gentle, professional manner. First, check with your contact to see what is going on with the payment. Give it another week. If you get nothing in the way of a reasonable response, find the name of the person who writes or at least expedites the checks. What you don't want to do is turn all of your client conversations into discussions about your money. Deal directly with the finance people. Try to get a firm date on when you can expect a check. Sometimes a letter to your client—explaining that you are surprised it's taken so long to get your money, that the slow payment is causing a cash-flow problem for you, that it's unfair and divisive to a good working relationship—will do more than a phone call.

Finally if the money or a reasonable explanation are not forthcoming, your final recourse is small claims court—where disputes for $3,000 and less can be resolved for a nominal filing charge (it is done through arbitration and lawyers are not necessary) over the course of a single evening. This might mean the end of your relationship with the client, but who wants to work for somebody who doesn't pay? Remember to have all your paperwork (particularly contracts or assignment letters) in order.

member: ericmr

SURVEY: FREELANCE FINANCE

I am one of several people I know who do their own taxes to save the cost of having an accountant do them. The first thing I do is find a real quiet spot to work. I then read the instruction booklet that comes with my tax forms from cover to cover. Then I get out the tax forms and my calculator. I then proceed to fill in all the lines on my state and federal forms that I will be using as a worksheet. After I do that I then recheck what I have put down and look in the instruction booklet and see if there are any amounts that I can take and see if I put them down as deductions so my taxes are lower. Then when I'm sure the worksheet is right I put down everything on the form I am sending in making sure all numbers are clear and easy to read. Last but not least, I send it all in.

Organizing Your Money

Making money is only half of the equation. The other half is managing it. Organizing your income is the difference between scrambling to pay your bills each month and having a good idea of what your income will be for the next six months. According to Philip Taxman, a financial adviser in Merrill Lynch's St. Louis office, "The secret to any efficient handling of your financial affairs is this: Be extremely well organized and in one split second know how much money you've got and exactly what it is doing for you in terms of your investments." Here is Taxman's approach to maintaining fiscal sanity despite the unpredictability of the freelance business.

> How to Hire a Tax Pro

You're savvy and smart about your money, but you've found yourself in over your head with the IRS. There's no need to be embarrassed about admitting that you need help sorting out your finances; the real shame is in not getting the right hired gun to tame the taxman for you. Getting the right advice can be the difference between being successful and going broke.

So, how do you know they know their stuff? Simple: Ask questions. One day a woman called and said she wanted to interview me to decide if she would hire me. Naturally, I felt a bit defensive. She then reeled off a comprehensive list of questions and problems she wanted addressed. Her questions told me that she understood her own business and cared enough to be well informed. Definitely my favorite kind of client. She was organized, direct, and to the point. She wasn't antagonistic. She just wanted someone who would do a good job. I can live with that. Should you need to interview a tax pro, here are some questions you may want to ask.

1. Does the tax pro have the expertise you specifically need? Don't waste time asking about experience she may have in fields or areas that aren't related to your problem: e.g., if you are a building contractor, what do you care if the tax pro knows the entertainment industry?

2. Make a list of questions specific to your lifestyle: e.g., you are a trucker, does this person know highway-use taxes or the IRS allowed per diem rates for transportation workers?

3. Does the candidate have a degree? He also should have some understanding of fundamental bookkeeping functions like the difference between loans and expenses. You'd be amazed at how many tax preparers don't know how to do a balance sheet or income statement.

4. How much tax audit experience does she have? This is a trick question. If the tax pro brags about how many audits he has handled or how good his results are, ask an additional question: How many of the audits were on returns he prepared? If a tax pro's clients get audited frequently, there is either something wrong with their work *or* their clients are in industries targeted by the IRS. Personally, I'd be more comfortable with a tax pro who knows how to prepare returns that don't attract IRS attention. On the other hand, you do want someone who can represent you effectively if you are audited.

5. Are they open year round? Five days a week? If they close frequently, who's available to cover for them when they're gone?

6. If they make mistakes, do they fix the return for free? Do they pay any penalties generated by those mistakes? Do they even know how to amend returns? File corrections?

7. How long has their average client (nonfamily member) been with them? Can they provide references you can call or visit?

8. In addition to tax preparation, can you call them during the year to get planning advice? For retirement planning? Tax reduction ideas? Savings and budgeting assistance? Buying a home?

9. Can they advise you or help you with the business aspects of your work or your job? Do they have contacts in your industry? Can they help you network? Are any of their clients successful at least partly because the tax pro has helped them succeed?

continued on page 306

Paying Yourself

Rather than getting checks, cashing them, and living from check to check, hoping that you'll get paid something close to your rent when the rent is due and enough to cover your Visa bill before the interest cycle closes in on you, Taxman suggests creating a pie chart and slicing up the income you expect to earn for a given year. "Break out your salary as a cost center," he advises. "If you're self-employed and you need $40,000 a year to pay your bills and live your life, pay yourself the equivalent in a monthly salary. Arrive at the amount by figuring out what the business is making over the course of a year and what it can pay out to you after all of its expenses."

Dealing with the Excess

You live within your budget, and your earnings exceed your projected needs. This, obviously, is a good thing. But what you need to figure out first is what to do with the excess capital. "Maybe it goes into the business for expanded facilities or prospecting trips or new equipment," says Taxman. "Or else you can take a higher salary for yourself and improve your standard of living. If you're thinking about the future, maybe what you'll eventually want to do is grow the business in a way that you are not equipped to do right now. In that case you can start investing the excess revenue. Five years from now, or whenever you project that the expansion will happen, you'll have the resources for getting bigger."

Staying Organized

Taxman suggests breaking your money out into different accounts or investments that serve various purposes. One might be for the cash you need to operate your business, another for tax payments, a third for long-term savings, but all originate from a single banking or investment source. "Having everything consolidated and receiving a summary statement each month is important," he says. "What we set up for a seedling on the way to becoming a redwood is a cash management account." That account, he says, branches off to include investments, checking services, and perhaps a no-load money market fund in which quarterly tax payments can be accrued.

Make the Money Work for You

Whatever your investing style—risky, conservative, or somewhere in between—you should work with a predetermined strategy and pursue concrete financial goals: e.g., buying a car, having a baby. Freelancers should first stockpile enough money to cover six months of living expenses before thinking about tying up money in other investments. Considering how unpredictable freelancing can be, long-term investments, where there are often substantial penalties for early withdrawals, should be made only with money that you will absolutely not need in a pinch. Because you will not have a pension fund created for you by your employer, it is important to create one for yourself. Specifically designed for freelancers are investment funds such as SEP-IRAs (Simplified Employee Pension Individual Retirement Accounts) and Keoghs, which allow self-employed people to invest anywhere from 15 to 25 percent of their net incomes

> How to Hire a Tax Pro, cont.

What if I hire a pro and he's not much help?

This is a common complaint, but before you cut your tax pro loose, ask yourself if you are partly at fault. Do you call and schedule appointments for consultation on specific issues or do you just show up for your routine tax preparation appointment and expect that, like magic, all your questions will be answered and all your problems solved?

Tax season is an insane, hectic, nonstop grind. During that time, most tax pros only schedule enough time for each appointment to get the tax returns done. Don't expect your tax pro to solve your personal or professional problems between January 2 and April 15. That's what the other eight and a half months of the year are for. Be fair. Schedule a planning appointment with your tax pro and discuss your issues before seeking a new professional.

Where should I look for a tax pro?

Calling on your parents' tax pro is often a good place to start. You should also try asking around among your friends. You may be surprised how many folks have tax pros they just adore! If you can't find someone through your usual networks, get in touch with one of these professional organizations:

Enrolled Agents—EAs and Tax Specialists (licensed by the U.S. Treasury to practice in all fifty states)
http://www.naea.org/

Accounting Associations—CPAs (licensed to practice only in specific states)
http://www.accountingnet.com/prod/prodfr.html

American Bar Association—Attorneys (licensed to practice only in specific states)
http://www. abanet.org/

If you're in business for yourself, you need more than just tax planning: You need to hear about other people's successes, failures, problems, and solutions.

Small Office/Home Office
http://www.soho.org/

Self-Employment Digest
(a free forum on the Internet)
http://aimc.com/aimc/self-employment-digest.html

—*Eva Rosenberg*

annually (resulting in a maximum yearly contribution of $30,000). You don't have to pay taxes on this money (or on any income this money generates) until you take it out. But if you withdraw these funds before the age of fifty-nine and a half, you'll end up paying a penalty. Also worth noting is the new Roth IRA: Money invested in a Roth is not tax deductible, but at the same time you won't ever have to pay taxes upon withdrawal—probably one of the only times in your life that you'll manage to skirt the Tax Man.

Paying Your Taxes

Among the financial transactions that you make as an independent contractor, taxes are among the most important—and the likeliest to get you in trouble if you aren't careful. According to Ronald Andrews, a Manhattan-based certified public account, Schedule C forms (which are filed by all self-employed people) are among the most heavily audited.

Also, as far as Social Security payments go, freelancers carry a heavier burden than salaried employees (whose employers match their contributions): Self-employed people pay double the social security tax (compared to a normal employee) from their adjusted gross incomes, though they can deduct 50 percent of that.

In spite of this, though, there are still a number of tax advantages that specifically apply to freelancers. The trick, says Andrews, is knowing what to deduct and how to do it. In order to deduct, you have to be able to prove that something is crucial to your business only, rather than partly for your business and partly for your enjoyment of life. He suggests beginning by tracking all of your expenses for the year—whether they are business related or not. "From there," he says, "you can weed out whatever is not critical to your business." People in the movie business, he explains, deduct every movie they attend and cable TV. In the eyes of the IRS, that would be an arguable area. However, if you're a movie critic, subscribing to every movie channel would be deductible—but basic cable would not be.

A little bit of organization can go a long way in allowing you to be more aggressive in the tax return that you file. It is more important, Andrews says, to focus on the basics than to devise all kinds of off-beat deductions: "Keep good out-of-pocket, automobile, and travel records. The IRS allows expense amounts less than $75 to be documented in a diary as opposed to requiring actual receipts for expenditures. But you have to be careful that you can justify spending this money through bank records that show that you had the cash on hand in the first place."

Here are a few tips that Andrews offers for making the most of your independent status without raising the ire of the IRS.

Auditors Are Not Idiots

Beware of accountants who promise to bring your net earnings down to zero or anything close to it. An auditor will look at that and instantly realize you are fudging figures. "You have to be able to justify that you can live on the money you have left after expenses," says Andrews. "Otherwise an auditor will simply ask how you live day-to-day if you show virtually no net out of, say, $100,000 in revenues. Getting a 'how do you live?' audit is a nightmare for a self-employed person who files a very aggressive tax return."

Pay Your Taxes on a Quarterly Basis

If you're working freelance, then you are being paid with checks that have no taxes taken out. It's up to you to pay taxes, and—unless you want to get hit with a modest late fee and a potentially staggering tax bill—they are due on the fifteenth of April, June, September, and January. "Generally a rule of thumb—which allows you to avoid underpayment-of-estimated-tax penalties—is to pay 100 percent of your prior year's tax in four quarterly installments or 110 percent of last year's tax if you earned in excess of $150,000," says Andrews, explaining that any overpayments will be applied to the coming year's taxes. "If you are filing your first return, you have to pay as you go. If you're making under $100,000 I would suggest putting aside anywhere from 30 percent to 45 percent of your net income for taxes."

Work Within Walls

In order to deduct a home office, it needs to be literally that, in the strictest sense of the word. "The IRS requires that a home office be a separate room within your dwelling that is used exclusively for your business," says Andrews. "If you use your living room for business during the day and watching TV at night, that deduction would most likely be disallowed. But you can build a wall, dividing the room, and that would make it acceptable." What about a portable or temporary wall? "That is a gray area."

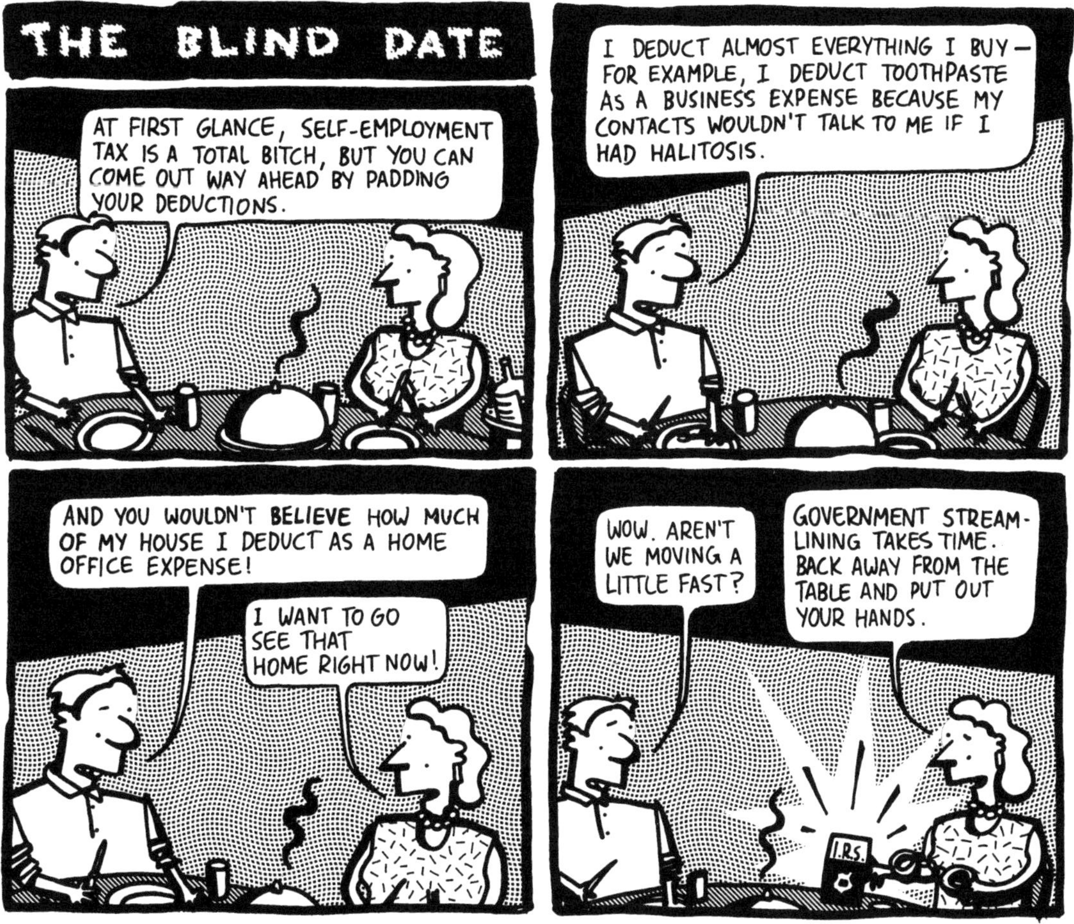

Entertain Often and Lavishly

One of the great perks of being self-employed is the high life you can enjoy while wining and dining clients—hey, it's a business expense that allows you to eat in your town's best restaurants before attending the hottest concerts or sporting events. "Travel and entertainment get broken up into two areas," explains Andrews. "Entertainment is any kind of expenditure in which you are taking out a client to, say, a basketball game or a dinner. Only 50 percent of that amount spent can be deducted, but it includes your expenses as well as his. Since this is basically on the honor system, it's a good thing to document who you took out and the purpose of the meeting. The other type of expense is travel. It's 100 percent deductible as long as it's attributable to your business. However, if you take a spouse or frat buddy with you, then their expenses are not deductible. And, as with everything on your tax return, you want all of this to be seriously documented."

Investing

You like money. You'd like to have more of it. You have two (legal) options: Either work harder or make your money work harder. Kind of a no-brainer, huh?

by Ken Kurson with Dan Reines

Whether you're a doctor or a dancer, a broker or a baker, payday means pay dirt. Maybe you write a check to your landlady and breathe a sigh of relief—you don't have to worry about paying the rent for another month. Maybe you pick up a swanky new shoe tree for your closet, or a brand-new pine tree for your rearview mirror. Or after a beer or two with your friends, maybe—just maybe—you stash a little something away in your savings, at a whopping 3 percent growth rate. So you're not J. P. Morgan, what's the big deal? You're getting by just fine, right?

The thing is, down the road, "getting by just fine" isn't going to cut it. With more and more companies farming out the workload to independent contractors without benefits, your job security may be sketchier than it's ever been, and Social Security is, well, badly named at best. And suppose, in five or ten years, when you've got a spouse and a couple of kids, you want to buy a modest, three bedroom bit of suburbia to house them all? Think about your parents' life for a minute. Do they take vacations and own a couple of cars? Did they pay your way through college or part of it? Do they find some cash to loan you when you really need it? If your parents do have that kind of financial leeway, it didn't just "appear" from nowhere. They got it by practicing smart money management—which essentially means socking away a little now so that you'll have a lot more later.

member: KMorrison

SURVEY: RETIREMENT

Take $5,000 (I know, first you have to come up with that!) and put $1,000 in a one-year CD, $1,000 in a two-year CD, $1,000 in a three-year CD, $1,000 in a four-year CD, and $1,000 in a five-year CD. The five-year CD earns much better interest, but it's hard to commit money for five years, when you might need it. Anyway, now when your one-year CD matures, you open another five-year CD. Next year, your two-year CD matures, and you open another five-year CD, and so on. By the time you've rolled all your CDs, they are all five-year CDs, earning the better rate, but you have one maturing every year so that it's more available time-wise in event of an emergency.

There are all sorts of reasons not to invest your hard-earned cash. You may be thinking you're too young to be investing or that it's boring or that you don't have that kind of money.

Let's start with "I'm too young." Actually, the younger you are, the better—the more time you'll have, over the course of your life, to accumulate money. It's known as a "time horizon," and if you're somewhere in your twenties or early thirties, yours is enormous.

How about, "It's boring"? Sure it is, right now. But the business section is like a day at the dog track: It gets a lot more interesting when you've got some money riding on it.

"I can't afford it"? Again, you couldn't be more wrong. Granted, it's sometimes tough enough to scrape together money for groceries, much less a hundred bucks a month to appease some guy at Fidelity. But imagine how much tougher it gets with a family, two cars, and a mortgage. "People make the mistake of thinking that the more money you make, the more you invest," says James Lowell, author of *Investing from Scratch* and *How to Survive in the Real World*. "In fact, the older you get, the more you acquire, and the harder it gets to support what you've acquired. It's not more money, but more discipline you need to be able to invest." You can't afford not to.

member:
toby not the dog

SURVEY: INVESTING

Never underestimate the power of compounding. A little bit earlier is a lot later.

Here's the essential argument for investing: You like money. You'd like to have more of it. So you have two main (legal) options: Either you can work harder (if that's possible), or you can make your money work harder. Not much of a choice, is it?

The following cautionary tale illustrates the value of getting an early start on your financial portfolio.

Two women, Alice and Trixie, begin working for Acme Products on the first day of 1960. Alice, her conservative father's words still burning in her ears, diligently put about $100 a month in a solid growth-oriented mutual fund. Trixie, on the other hand, blew her discretionary dollars on mambo lessons.

Exactly ten years later, Alice decides not to put a penny more in her mutual fund. Trixie, however, has met the vest-wearing sewer repairman of her dreams and has decided to mend her derelict ways. Starting that year, she puts $100 a month into the same fund Alice invested in.

Fast forward to 1990. The fund has performed well, but not marvelously, earning 10 percent over the past thirty years (about the average that stocks have earned since 1926). Trixie now has $75,937, tripling her original contribution of $24,000. But Alice, who contributed a total of only $12,000, is now sitting on over $150,000—more than twelve times her investment.

> Specialty Mutual Funds

There are plenty of funds that cater to particular social or political sensitivities. Let's say, for instance, you don't want your dollars going into R. J. Reynolds's coffers. No problem—put your money into a tobacco-free fund like Domini Social Equity. Remember, though: This is your future, not a T-shirt, and you should be careful not to base your investments solely on your politics. That said, the following is a list of some of the more exotic fund flavors that offer security without sacrificing integrity.

Domini Social Equity (800-762-6814) and Citizens Index Portfolio (800-223-7010)

Funds that invest only in do-good companies: No gambling, smoking, labor-hostile environmental criminals are welcome. Socially conscious funds take a lot of heat in the financial press, which has been skeptical about their returns, sometimes for good reason. But Domini's fund (ranked in the top half of all large-blend funds), Citizens Trust (formerly Working Assets), and a company called Calvert (the Calvert Social Investment Fund Managed Growth Portfolio is what's called a balanced fund—in short, pretty safe but won't dazzle you with high returns) are working to change the perception that good deeds involve financial sacrifice (contact Calvert at 800-368-2748).

Meyers Sheppard Pride (800-410-3337)

This fund seeks to invest in companies that have gay-friendly workplaces and employee benefit policies. Started in June 1996, the fund produced a return of 26.8 percent in its twelve months of existence. And it's easy to get into, too: The Pride fund has no load and features low minimums to start accounts—$1,000, or $250 for IRAs and those who opt for automatic direct deposit.

Beacon Cruelty-Free Value Fund (800-892-9626)

This fund invests only in companies that don't use animals in their product testing, don't support the "inappropriate" use of animals as entertainment, and whose corporate policies don't cause pain and suffering in animals. Still brand-new, the fund is off to a quick start, returning 11.84 percent in its first six months.

Here are some other specialized funds that are just plain fun:

Stein Roe Young Investor's Fund (800-338-2550)

This fund provides an entry point for younger investors, capturing their interest by snaring the stocks of youth-oriented companies. Ironically, its investment in eco-bad boys McDonald's and Procter & Gamble makes this youth-friendly fund almost diametrically opposite to the pious folks listed above. Rated five stars by Morningstar.

Sportsfund (888-82-SPORT)

This fund looks to tap into America's obsession with professional sports, investing in companies such as Nike, Disney (which owns the Anaheim Mighty Ducks hockey team and a piece of baseball's California Angels), and publicly traded teams in "the big four" sports, like the Florida Panthers and the Boston Celtics.

Morgan Funshares (800-446-2987)

The antithesis of the Socially Responsible Investment, this fund invests only in a limited spectrum of companies tied to liquor, sex, tobacco, cosmetics, and gambling (along with other habit-forming products like toilet paper). Its octagenarian founder and manager, Burt Morgan, doesn't smoke or drink, but he does know that some habits are recession-proof. And while the fund's lack of ownership of high-flying cyclical and technology stocks has punished its performance during Wall Street's record-breaking bull run, it's worth noting that FunShares (originally called SinShares) is designed to perform best when the chips are down.

Amazing, huh? What's more, Trixie will never catch Alice, even if she continues to contribute another $100 every month. (In case you're interested, the numbers after another ten years are $226,049 for Trixie and $406,349 for Alice—and remember, Trix had to pour in an additional twelve grand for that while Alice sat back and raked in the dough.)

So get started—the mambo lessons can wait. But how? You're not exactly a financial whiz. The business pages make your head spin. And no wonder; they're not written for normal folks like yourself. Lowell says, "[The business press] has a private form of speech for the people who are inside it. I think a lot of reporters forget that their real job is to translate stuff, and not just to toss around a bunch of jargon."

member: mazdamanzz

SURVEY: INVESTING

Invest in things you know, and in companies whose products you use yourself.

So what chance do you have of succeeding in the fast-paced world of high finance where slick-haired, Armani-clad MBAs roam the landscape like so many T-rexes? Actually, plenty. You may not be Warren Buffett, but if all you're looking to do is make a little dough, you don't have to be. The more time you spend worrying that you don't know enough about the market, the less time you spend learning about it—by diving in and rolling around. Remember the cost of Trixie's hesitation: about 180 grand so far—and counting.

Everyone tells you to read every last line of fine print before you slap down your first red cent. But much of that print is just there to protect the fund company from litigation and to assure you that the fund managers have all the details worked out so you can relax and let them do the work. All those prospectuses, bless their pointed little words, are intimidating. But don't be overwhelmed; you're a lot smarter than you think. Keep in mind that you're already equipped with an investor's most powerful tool: common sense.

Don't buy a stock because the logo reminds you of your high school mascot; investigate before you invest. Put your money in companies (and industries) you understand. Don't get cocky, and remember, that "can't miss" stock tip is usually no better than that "can't miss" horse tip. Ask yourself: If your Uncle Jimmy knows so much about playing the market, why's he still tooling around town in a Dodge Dart?

But enough preaching. Let's get specific.

"Where should I put my hard-earned cash?"

Okay, we can't get that specific. This isn't a late-night infomercial—we don't pretend to hold some mystical, foolproof key to untold riches. But while we can't tell you what stocks to buy, we can give you some sound advice on how to choose a stock for yourself, as well as on some of your other investment options.

The first thing you have to do is to set goals for your investing.

> Investing Resources

Web Sites

Morningstar
(http://www.morningstar.net/)
From the Chicago-based publisher that puts out *Sourcebook*, this excellent site provides instant reports on any fund's performance. Claims its mission is "the democratization of investment information."

Kiplinger's Online
(http://kiplinger.com/)
The online home of the ubiquitous personal finance journal, this site also offers reports on top funds, as well as personal finance advice and information culled from the print magazine.

CNNfn
(http://cnnfn.com/)
One of the most complete sources for business and financial news online from CNN's little-seen sister network. Connected to CNN's own interactive site, CNNfn provides stock quotes along with news from Wall Street and other markets around the world.

The Street.com
(http://www.thestreet.com/)
Financial reporting and commentary on markets, companies, and mutual funds. Note: Citing the maxim "you get what you pay for," The Street charges a membership fee for access to many areas of the site.

Good Money
(http://www.goodmoney.com/)
Devoted to socially responsible investing (SRI), consuming, and business practices. Includes stock averages, company profiles, and information on funds screened for social and environmental responsibility.

The Social Investment Forum
(http://www.socialinvest.org/)
Also devoted to promoting socially responsible investing, this nonprofit group's site focuses on news pertaining to SRI, as well as networking opportunities and an on-line guide to investing.

Other sites offering personal finance information:
Stein Roe Mutual Funds
(http://www.steinroe.com/)
Fidelity Investments
(http://www.fidelity.com/)
The Vanguard Group
(http://www.vanguard.com/)
Mutual Funds Interactive
(http://www.brill.com/)
Stock Smart
(http://www.stocksmart.com/)

Books

The Only Investment Guide You'll Ever Need, by Andrew Tobias (Harcourt Brace, 1996). This update of the 1978 classic incorporates Tobias's sequel guide, *The Only Other Investment Guide You'll Ever Need*, into its commonsense approach to basic investing.

A Random Walk Down Wall Street: Including a Life-Cycle Guide to Personal Finance, by Burton G. Malkiel. (W.W. Norton & Co., 1996) Shows why a broad portfolio of stocks selected by chance will perform as well as ones carefully chosen by the experts.

Investing from Scratch, by James Lowell (Penguin USA, 1997). Aimed at readers in their late twenties and early thirties, this book tackles current economic issues and offers advice about reducing the risks of investing while achieving a decent financial return.

Periodicals

Wall Street Journal, Money, Worth, Smart Money

"You don't try to go somewhere without knowing where you're going," says Bill Rice, director of corporate marketing for Liberty Financial Companies. "If you want to go from point A to point B, you have to know where point B is." Are you looking to pack away a little money each month in something without much risk but with a decent payout? Then you'll probably want to consider something like a mutual fund. If you've got the basics covered, and what you really want is to send your bank account on an upward spiral, you'll probably want to put your money directly into the market, which can be a bit riskier, but has the potential for much higher returns. But let's start off easy, with one of the most popular moneymakers of the past few years.

Mutual funds: We've established that you don't know all that much about the market; no problem—you're not alone. But with a good mutual fund, you can get your feet wet in the shallow end of the financial pool, where you're pretty unlikely to drown. Your task is simple: Pick out a good fund—we'll get to the criteria in a minute—and leave the wheeling and dealing to some blurry-eyed sap who spends his or her every waking hour in front of the stock ticker. These fund managers spread your money out among stocks, bonds, options, money markets, commodities, and more, but for you, it's as simple as making a deposit into a savings account. Difference is, instead of giving you a lousy 3 percent back on your investment, a decent mutual fund can bring you returns in the double digits. Here's how it works.

Mutual funds allow you to fulfill the mantra of investment strategy—diversity, diversity, diversity—while spreading your risk over lots of companies, all for a very low cost per company. Let's say you had a million bucks. Obviously, it wouldn't be smart to put it all in Coca-Cola, because even a well-run blue chip like Coke can have a bad year or a bad several years. Instead, you'd divide it among, say, twenty companies. If fifteen of these did well, you'd more than make up for the five that didn't.

Unfortunately, you don't have a million bucks. You have just the five grand you managed to squirrel away last year. But to divide five grand among twenty companies is a bad strategy because each transaction you make costs you a commission. Investing $250 in twenty companies doesn't make much sense because even if three-quarters of the companies do well, your commissions will eat up a much greater percentage of your profits than if you were investing $50,000 in each as in the example in the previous paragraph.

Basically, all a mutual fund does is take, say, 200 people with $5,000 each and invest the total as though it belonged to one millionaire with a well-diversified portfolio. A mutual fund pools small investors' money to get the diversity and buying power that one small investor couldn't get alone.

So there you go—mutual funds are a beginner's dream. But how do you decide which fund is your best bet? Their popularity keeps growing and there are more than 8,000 out there to choose from—that's more funds than there are publicly traded companies. You'll want to do a bit of research; start with Morningstar, the Chicago-based publisher that puts out *Sourcebook*, an invaluable reference for both new and experienced fund pickers (you can find it at your local library). Or check out www.morningstar.net, where you can get instant reports on any fund's performance. Although Morningstar makes a big production out of downplaying its one-to-five-star rating system, it is smart to stick with a four- or five-star fund. Also, be sure to avoid large loads (fees to get in or out of a fund) when there's a "no-load" equivalent that's as highly rated.

Look for aggressive growth stock funds. Use your age and time horizon to your advantage by riding out inevitable market dips and keeping your eyes on the historically sound returns. There are also, of course, overseas funds, precious metal funds, and specific sector funds that focus on technology or utility stocks. In fact, there are all sorts of specialized funds available, including some that promise to invest your money according to specific guidelines that don't necessarily follow just the bottom line (see sidebar on page 313).

It's also important to note the difference between "open-end" and "closed-end" funds. Most funds are "open-end" funds. That means that when you put your money in, you essentially own a fraction of all the securities that the fund owns. In other words, if you put $1 million into a fund that previously had $9 million, you'd then own one-tenth of everything the fund owns. As the companies held by the fund rise and fall, so do your share values.

But "closed-end" funds resemble stock in that they contain a fixed number of shares and a fixed amount of money. Unlike an open-end fund, its share value depends on public perception. So if a magazine calls the fund's manager "one of the year's hottest" the public might suddenly find that fund more desirable—and its shares would then be more valuable. Since you're buying shares not from the company but from other investors, closed-end funds don't need the 800-numbers that open-end funds always have; you invest in them through a broker.

If you're not yet ready to go it alone, mutual funds are your best option, but they aren't your only option—many beginners like investment clubs. An investment club acts as a sort of miniature mutual fund: A group of investors, often centered around a collection of friends or business associates, pools its money and begins investing.

Usually, each member puts up a certain stake, like $1,000, and is expected to add to that at regular intervals. If there are ten members, the group starts a portfolio with the initial $10,000. The buying power of the group lowers the percentage spent on trading costs in much the same way a mutual fund does.

Investment clubs can be a good way to learn the market; they provide much more hands-on experience than mutual funds do, and they allow each investor to benefit from the knowledge and resources of his or her clubmates. But investment clubs are far from perfect—troubles inevitably arise when one or more of the members withdraw. Unlike mutual funds, which keep a small percentage of their assets on hand to cover redemptions, clubs are typically fully invested. So when someone bails, the club has to buy the party pooper out. That means selling shares, which market conditions may not favor. If you do decide to start an investment club, get in touch with the National Association of Investors Corp. (810-583-6242). For an inexpensive fee, they can set you up with a kit to help you get off the ground, as well as give you access to discounted software, free research reports, and their own magazine, *Better Investing*.

But enough, you say. Enough with the mutual funds. Enough with the investment clubs. You're not looking to drop your money off at day care and let someone else take care of it. It's your money, you're a player, and you're ready to play the market. So what's your first move? Take a quick step backward, accompanied by a slow deep breath. Yes, we did say you could handle the market and you can. But there are a few things you ought to consider before you plunge in. And they bring us right back to—you guessed it—common sense.

When buying stocks, stick to companies and industries that interest you and that you can keep track of in the news. How else would you know when to cut bait or when to up your investment if it's doing well? And you should also know not to plunk down your life savings on a stock tip that seems just too good to be true—as with most things, if it seems that way, it probably is. Besides, if your information's so good that it'll make you money, you're likely to end up sharing a cell with another chastened arbitrageur. But beginning investors more frequently drive into another pair of potholes: trying to time the market and thinking they're somehow smarter than everyone else.

We'll start with the timing issue. Everyone wants to buy low, sell high, and get out with a wad of cash and a private jet to Barbados. It all sounds fabulous, but guess what? It's a sucker's game. Yes, any given stock will go up and down in value over the course of time, but figuring out when it'll be up and when it'll be down requires that you be a psychic, which you're probably not. One thing you can be sure of, though, is that over time the market as a whole moves upward. So sit tight and be patient. Figure out where you want your money to be in the long run and put it there now. Sure, it'll hurt if you dump your funds there today and the market tanks tomorrow. But in the long term, total catastrophe is unlikely.

Here is a particularly instructive investment fable, courtesy of the legendary Peter Lynch, former chief of the Fidelity Magellan Fund, the country's largest mutual fund. Three siblings, call them Robert, Jane, and Kenny, each put $1,000 into the stock market every year from 1965 through 1995. Robert is incredibly unlucky and buys his stocks on the day each year when the market is highest. Jane is incredibly lucky, plunking her dough down on the cheapest day of the year: i.e., when the market's at its lowest point. Kenny eschews any system and buys his stock on the first trading day of the year, no matter how the market is performing.

So Jane, Miss Perfect Timing, ends up with way more money than Robert, who has impossibly crummy timing, right? Nope. Robert comes out with an annualized return of 10.6 percent, Jane gets 11.7 percent, while Kenny does 11 percent. So even unrealistic extremes only separate performance by 1.1 percent.

Besides timing the market, the other trap to avoid is thinking that somehow you know something that nobody else has figured out yet. It's virtually impossible to outguess the market consistently. Each time you buy a stock because you think it's headed uphill, someone else is selling that stock, ostensibly because they believe the opposite. Let's take a look at an example from the experience of an investor we'll call Steve.

In spring 1995, the hype that became Windows 95 had just begun. "Wow," thought Steve, "with all this talk about Microsoft, I bet Apple is a pretty good value right about now." Bestowing upon himself that most overused of investor pet names—contrarian—he boldly assumes one of two things will happen: (1) Windows 95 will be a fiasco—slow or buggy, it'll so frustrate PC users that they'll all buy Macs; or (2) Windows 95 will be a sensation, causing Apple to realize that it can no longer go it alone, sparking a bidding war that'll send Apple shares skyward. In July, Steve plunks down for some Apple at $46 a share, convinced he's looking at a win-win.

Cut to early 1996. Windows 95 was a sensation, but Apple, undersupplied through the end of 1995, made the mistake of being drastically oversupplied for a disastrous Christmas season. Steve bails in early February, thankful for the twenty-eight bucks someone else thinks each of his shares is worth.

Now that you've reviewed the most dangerous—and common—rookie mistakes, it's pretty much time to dive into the stock market. Sure, the risks are higher than with mutual funds, but so are the rewards—and we don't just mean the immediate financial returns. There's much to be learned about investing from stocks that can't be gleaned from funds. Most important, you can only track the relationships between news events, earnings estimates, earnings results, and specific stock prices by paying close attention to specific companies and the industries they inhabit. Learning to do that is key to the understanding that will guide your future picks as you become a better and richer investor. Besides, when you're relatively young, you still have plenty of time to recover from the mistakes you're bound to make.

The last bit of advice we can give is, perhaps, the most important: Have fun. Sounds frivolous, doesn't it? It's not. Managing your money's not all that different from any other disciplined, intense activity. Ever played a musical instrument? Investing's just the same: a drag to get started, but if you stick with it, it gets a lot more fun, and you keep getting better. Hey—even Liberace had to start with "Chopsticks."

Retirement Planning

Hope you die before you get old? Just a little planning (and a little money) is all you need to ensure that you won't be the oldest fry cook at the local Burger King.

by John Fried

Retirement planning isn't a luxury, it's a necessity. And ignoring it will only postpone the inevitable (assuming you don't die an early death) and make your Golden Years a hell of lot less golden. Our parents and grandparents collected monthly pension checks for a lifetime's commitment to a company. Unfortunately, deregulation during the '80s allowed many companies to dip into the pension repository. The result: Many pension plans were wiped out. By the time we retire, pension-planning will be extinct.

But what about Social Security, you ask, and the portion of your paycheck that goes to it every time you are paid? Today, 63 percent of Americans age sixty-five and up count on Social Security as their primary source of income. Unfortunately, banking on Social Security these days is like playing lotto: There's a chance you may score but don't count on it.

The reality is that Social Security, under the current plan, will no longer be able to pay out full benefits after the year 2029. For Social Security, that spells an early retirement. How'd we end up in this mess?

President Roosevelt inaugurated the Social Security program in the 1930s. After a brutal stock market crash in 1929 and the depression that followed, many elderly people were living below the poverty line. The Social Security trust ensured that the swell of old-age poor would have some source of income on a monthly basis.

Take a look at your paycheck. Look for the item that sounds like a plant: FICA. It stands for Federal Insurance Contributions Act. The amount that follows is 7.65 percent of your wages or salary, which the federal government deducts for Social Security and Medicare. (We won't get into Medicare here, except to say that it is nearly as fraught with problems as Social Security.) Of this amount, 6.2 percent goes for Social Security and your company matches an equal portion. (If you are self-employed, you know this fact all too well: Self-employed people pay twice as much in Social Security because they don't have the benefit of a company covering half of the Social Security bill.)

Contrary to what you might believe, the money that you pay toward Social Security isn't stuffed in a shoe box with your name on it somewhere down in Washington, D.C. A lot of your money goes to pay out Social Security to current retirees. The government manages to stay ahead of itself, paying and collecting, because there is a surplus of money. In the early years of Social Security there were about forty people working for every person retired. As recently as 1950, that number had dropped to sixteen workers for every retired person. That means that for every one person being paid their portion of Social Security, sixteen people were putting money in.

The ratio is no longer nearly so generous. In 1996, there were three workers for every retired person. In 2030—the date that the current Social Security fund will stop being able to pay out full benefits—there will be two workers for every retiree. Consider all the baby boomers who can technically start retiring in the year 2008. When they start dipping into the till, the Social Security benefits are going to dry up quickly.

For people in their twenties and thirties, this spells possible disaster. Think about it: If you are twenty-five today, you can start collecting Social Security in the year 2035—nine years after the current system will have cut back on its monthly payments. If you are thirty-five, you can start to collect in 2025. That'll give you five solid years. While a lot of proposals have been tossed out to save Social Security—everything from privatization to raising taxes to a subtle combination of both—nothing has changed, yet. And if nothing does change, the refrain "hope I die before I get old" will start to make a lot more sense.

member: Scoobie_2

SURVEY: RETIREMENT

My company is a quasipublic corporation. I was eligible three months ago to become part of the pension plan. I contribute 6.2 percent to Social Security which, yes, I have no faith I will ever see in forty years when it is time to collect. Another 7 percent is going into a 401(k) pension plan. I picked mostly aggressive stocks but also mixed in some moderate stocks. (This was based on the understanding that I would have the time to ride the market's ups and downs.) I am nervous about two things. First, the stock market is not controllable. Second, I am probably going to switch jobs ten times in my life and each time I will have a new plan— this can get complicated. I also hate thinking about retirement when I have only been working two years full-time. At twenty-four, worrying about my old age should not be an issue.

Curious about where you stand with Social Security? The Social Security Administration can give you a breakdown of your history with the ill-fated system, plus an estimate of where you'll stand come your "golden years." Call 800-772-1213 or go to their Web site (www.ssa.org) to request this information. They will send you a "Personal Earnings and Benefits Estimate Statement." The statement will list what you've contributed, the current-dollar estimate of the benefits you'll receive, plus a worst-case scenario—what your children or spouse will receive if you were gravely or fatally injured. And no, they don't include the money you'll be getting if Social Security itself is fatally injured. Still living in denial, I guess.

The Basics

Let's assume the government manages to fix the system and people continue to pay in at the current rate. Do you know how much the average person collects on Social Security? About $700 a month. Now if you have trouble living on $20,000 a year today, how hard will it be to live on less than $10,000 when you're pushing seventy? Remember: When you retire, everything you do still costs money. You go to the store, you spend money. You meet friends, you spend money. You fall down, you spend lots of money.

The Two Maxims of Retirement Planning

1. Take matters into your own hands. If you are looking for the government to take care of you when you grow old, you clearly are living in the wrong country. Try Sweden. Even in its prime, the Social Security system was never supposed to cover all of one's financial needs. (This despite the fact that about half of the people currently on Social Security would be below the poverty line without those monthly checks.) Social security is not an insurance policy.
2. Start early. Time is the key ingredient to an expansive retirement account. The magic of compound interest can make all the difference over the course of a multidecade investment period.

Planning for Retirement Planning

How do you work investing for retirement into your budget? Dropping $1,000 or $2,000 a year into a retirement account sounds like a great idea, but not all of us have a big pile of cash to draw on at year's end. But don't fret; it can be done.

The first step in retirement planning is the often thorny task of figuring out how much you'll need. This involves calculating and comparing how long you have until you retire, what your income is likely to be until then, and the somewhat morbid business of figuring out how long you will live once retired. Keep in mind that medical advances are extending our life expectancy. While the current life expectancy is seventy-two for men and seventy-eight for women, it may be a lot longer when it comes time for today's twenty-five-year-olds to retire. Unless you have a trust fund somewhere, the bottom line is that you will probably need a lot of money if you don't want to end up running the *frites* stand on the boardwalk at the tender age of eighty.

Once you get a rough sense of what you'll need, the next step is finding the right place to put your hard-earned money. Keeping your dollars and cents in a savings account at the local bank earning 3 percent may sound like a safe move, but don't expect to finally "see the world" on the money you'll earn. Inflation alone will chip that money down to pocket change by the time you're gray around the temples. To know the best place for your money, you have to determine which investment tool suits your particular time horizon and risk profile, the two mantras of retirement planning.

A time horizon is simple: It's basically an expression of the amount of time between the beginning of your retirement investing and when you actually retire. If yours is over twenty years, that's considered long-term. Simple enough.

A risk profile, however, is a little more complicated and involves answering the murky question of how much volatility you can stomach. Profiles run from swaggering risk gluttons to nail-biting, risk-averse types. Depending on your profile, there's an investment instrument to match your needs.

Here is what financial planners call the "sleep at night" test: Ask yourself if you're willing to take a chance that between now and

member: mrbrown2

SURVEY: RETIREMENT

Not only do I have myself to worry about, but my father's retirement picture is rather bleak. I feel obligated to supplement his income to some extent, leaving me with the added burden of saving for my retirement fund, while supplementing someone else's.

member: novelty123

SURVEY: RETIREMENT

I always thought I would have enough time, and assumed real estate investments would do the rest . . . until now. After two divorces, my concern is greater than it ever was. Just now started putting the maximum into a 401(k), but I will still have to work much longer than I ever expected . . . I wish I would have started it earlier. Divorces destroy estates and plans for retirement!

retirement your money might lose more than half its value at any given time. The market is bound to take a downturn sometime between now and when you retire. Can you handle that? If you say no or are uncertain, you are probably best adding a certain bit of security to your portfolio.

Long term the stock market has the highest returns of any investing option, providing the greatest opportunity to make money on your money. Take a look. According to Ibbotson Associates, a dollar invested in 1925 in large company stocks grew to $3,822.40 by 1995. A dollar invested in long-term government bonds grew to only $34.04.

Most of us want to grow our money as best we can but would rather not spend the years between now and retirement having heart palpitations every time the stock market swoons. One point bears repeating: Time is the great equalizer. Even if you are not a risk-taking person, the daily fluctuations of the market shouldn't concern you a great deal if you have a time horizon greater than ten or fifteen years.

Where to Put Your Money

Believe it or not, when our government wasn't busy managing a soon-to-be doomed Social Security program, they actually created some effective retirement savings plans. The greatest benefits of these plans is that they lower your tax burden now *and* grow money tax-free for the future. Of course, you'll have to pay the piper when you start to collect your money come retirement, but by then your tax bracket will probably be back around what it was when you were fifteen, anyway.

Which retirement savings plan you choose depends on what options your employer offers and if you happen to be a full-time worker. Some employers grant employees stock options or sponsor plans that allow employees to invest in the company's own stock. While these may be worthwhile, they are less secure than some of the more traditional options. We're going to focus on the most popular types of retirement savings plans: 401(k) and 403(b) plans, Individual Retirement Accounts (IRAs), Simplified Employee Pensions (SEPs), and Keoghs.

401 (k) Plans

Invented only thirty years ago, 401(k)s are known as defined contribution plans and are becoming the standard form of employer-sponsored retirement program. As of the close of 1996, there was $334 billion held by 401(k) plans.

Here's how they work: 401(k) plans allow employees to contribute a percentage of their salary to a retirement plan. That contribution is pre-tax money, so you lower your tax base and therefore pay less in taxes. Best of all, many employers match a certain percentage of your contribution. As of 1997, an employee can contribute a maximum of $9,500 to a 401(k). The combined contribution of employer and employee cannot be more than 25 percent of the employee's salary.

Let's say you work for a company and earn $40,000 a year. Your company allows you to contribute up to 6 percent of your salary and they match up to 3 percent. That first year you would contribute $2,400. Plus, your company would kick in an additional $1,200 for just being there. It's free money—a benefit you don't often find.

Not only have you started saving for retirement, you also managed to lessen your tax burden. That $2,400 you contributed lowered your adjustable gross income to $37,600. If you are in the 28 percent tax bracket, you'll now pay $10,528 in taxes. Without the 401(k) plan, you would pay $11,200. By signing up for the plan, you've saved $672. Take this in slowly: With a 401(k) you can save for retirement, potentially get free money from your employer, and lower your tax bill. It doesn't get any better than that.

Once you've started your 401(k), the word *vested* will inevitably be bandied about around the watercooler. This refers to the rights you have to the portion of money your employer contributes to your 401(k). Being fully vested implies you are entitled to 100 percent of what your employer put in. Typically, it takes five years to be fully vested, with each year adding an incremental amount to what's considered yours. If you leave before being fully vested, you'll receive all your contributions to the plan plus a percentage of your employer's contributions.

WARNING: Many companies allow you to borrow money against your 401(k) plan. This is a dangerous road to head down

member: BernieLucas

SURVEY: RETIREMENT

My financial future freaks me out! And I'm closer to it than most Tripodians . . . because I'm over forty (gasp!) I saved nothing in my twenties, saved a little at thirty and lived off of it after losing a job at thirty-four, repeated that scenario at thirty-eight and again at forty-one. I do what I love for a living, but my jobs seem to run a three- or four-year cycle. Now I save, invest in a 401(k), I'm frantically paying down high-interest credit card debt, plan to keep my car at least two years after it's paid off, etc. I regret not committing to this at twenty-five. A forty-eight-year-old friend did this, and now she is retired and living in Hawaii.

unless you really need the money for something essential like a medical emergency or a home purchase. First of all, you will have to pay that money back with interest. While paying yourself interest may sound like a good deal, it's another expense you do not need. If you leave your company having borrowed against your plan, you may be asked to pay the whole amount back immediately or suffer even more fees.

403 (b) Plans

The 403(b) plan functions pretty much like 401(k) plans except that it is offered by charitable, educational, or other nonprofit organizations. At the end of 1996, there was over $137 billion held by 403(b) plans.

Individual Retirement Accounts (IRAs)

An IRA is a retirement account that allows employed people to sock away up to $2,000 a year, or $4,000 for a couple if they both work. (If one person works and the other doesn't, you can con-

> Money-Saving Tips

- Have your employer withhold more Federal or state income tax than they would normally. Specify this on the W-4 form you fill out when you get a job, or request a new one to amend your previous withholdings. If you have as little as $10 or $20 extra withheld from each paycheck, you'll get back much more money when your tax refund comes, which you can then sock into an IRA all at once. Of course, you won't be earning interest on the money until it's in your hands, and you have to deal with the temptation to spend your tax refund instead of saving it. But this is a good way to amass the money needed to make the initial investment in a mutual fund or IRA.

- Open a savings account and transfer some money to it every payday. You can do this yourself, or you can set up an automatic transfer from checking to savings on a weekly, biweekly, or monthly basis with almost any bank. If your employer has direct deposit, you don't have to think about saving at all.

- While many mutual funds have an initial investment minimum (often around $500 to $1,000 for an IRA), many forgo this if you are willing to contribute a minimum amount on a monthly basis from your bank account. At some companies, the amount can be as little $25 to $50 a month. This is a great way to get started because it allows you to start investing for retirement without taking a big bite out of your monthly budget.

tribute $2,250 as long as the nonworker doesn't earn more than $250 a year.) You can't touch that money until you're fifty-nine and a half or you'll have to pay federal income tax plus a 10 percent penalty. (With the Roth IRA, there are certain exceptions to these penalties if the money you're withdrawing is being used to purchase a first home.) Another caveat: You must start to draw on that money by age seventy and a half or face penalties.

Any bank, brokerage, or mutual fund can help you start an IRA. While the maximum you can contribute is $2,000 a year, don't let that number scare you. Since the financial institutions know that you are giving them money for the long haul, the initial investment can be as low as $500 a year. Even if you can only contribute the minimum, do it. Every cent counts.

One of the big benefits of IRAs is that you may be able to deduct the amount of your IRA contribution from your taxes, just like with a 401(k). Of course, since an IRA is established on your own, you or your accountant have to do the paperwork to take advantage of the tax break. There also are certain rules governing how much people with 401(k) or defined contribution plans can contribute to an IRA. These limits change from year to year so consult a tax expert to be certain. Currently, these are the rules:

- Even if you are in a plan already through work, you can still make a tax-deductible contribution if your income is below $25,000. For married couples who file jointly, your combined income must be less than $40,000.
- If your income is between $25,000 and $35,000 (or $40,000 and $50,000 for married couples) you can deduct a portion of your IRA contribution. This portion is prorated based on tax tables so consult a tax expert.

member: matthewd
SURVEY: RETIREMENT
I have started saving for my retirement; I have invested in a daily interest savings account with a preauthorized payment—I am twenty-three—I started saving in September 1996. I also have some money invested in mutual funds. I invest $60 per month but I'm thinking of increasing it to more by doing a weekly preauthorized payment and putting more into my account to help build it up.

member: nostrand
SURVEY: RETIREMENT
I started purchasing stocks when I was twenty and had very disappointing results. But when you are young, you can make a lot of mistakes and still come out ahead (so don't be afraid to take a risk). All it takes is discipline and time.

Simplified Employee Pensions (SEP) and Keoghs

SEP plans, also called SEP-IRAs, and Keoghs are ideal for self-employed people and small businesses. While these plans work essentially like a regular IRA, the difference is the amount you can contribute on an annual basis. Both SEPs and Keoughs allow for investment of up to a quarter of annual income up to a maximum of $30,000. If you have a company retirement plan but earn money as a freelancer, you can contribute a portion of your freelance income to a SEP. While SEPs are easy to organize and administer, Keoghs are fairly complicated and require a little more paperwork than other plans.

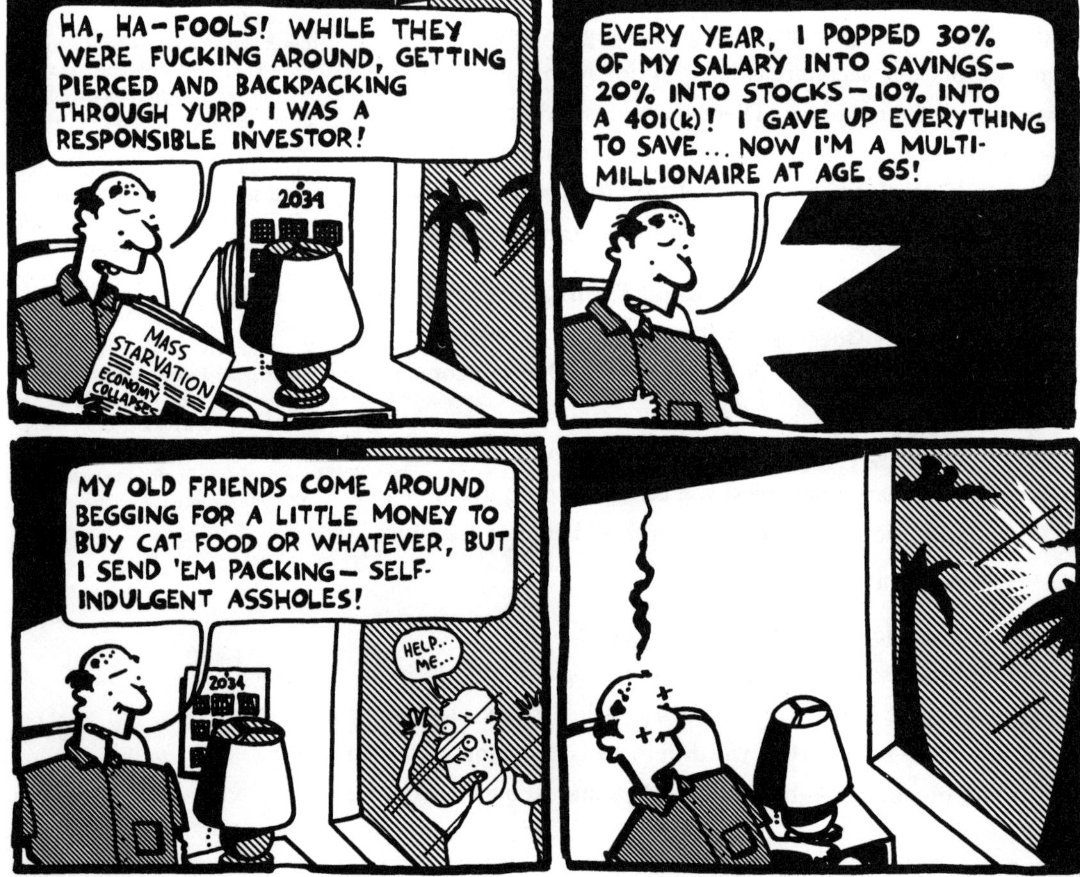

List of Web Sites

The following is a list of Web sites culled from the pages of this book. For good measure, we've thrown in some extra sites that aren't listed in the stories themselves. To have instant access to these sites, point your browser to www.tripod.com/book, where you'll find these resources collected in an easy-to-use format.

The Net

Search Engines

http://www.metacrawler.com
http://www.dogpile.com
http://www.searchengine.com
http://www.humansearch.com
http://www.directoryguide.com
http://www.four11.com
http://www.wsj.com
http://www.dejanews.com

Shopping

http://www.excite.com
http://www.bbbonline.org
http://www.firefly.com
http://www.bignote.com
http://www.yahoo.com
http://www.amazon.com
http://www.compare.net
http://www.jango.com
http://www.onsale.com
http://www.bid4it.com
http://www.zauction.com
http://www.bb.com
http://www.billskhakis.com
http://www.autobytel.com
http://www.lucidcafe.com
http://www.outpost.com
http://www.stocksmart.com
http://www.1800flowers.com
http://www.moviecritic.com
http://www.peapod.com
http://www.cornells.com
http://www.cdnow.com
http://www.cyberrentals.com
http://www.ticketmaster.com
http://www.expedia.com
http://www.virtualvin.com

Shareware

http://www.shareware.com
http://www.happypuppy.com
http://www.freewarenow.com
http://www.netscape.com
http://www.microsoft.com
http://www.galttech.com/ssheaven.shtml
http://www.idsoftware.com

Radio

http://m2.monsterbit.com/brainwash/
http://www.real.com
http://www.timecast.com
http://www.liveconcerts.com
http://www.audionet.com
http://www.pseudo.com
http://espn.sportszone.com/editors/liveaudio/index.html
http://www.grit.com
http://www.news.com/radio
http://events.yahoo.com/
http://www.lalive.com
http://www.real.com/contentp/npr

Privacy on the Web

http://www.cyberpatrol.com/cybernot/
http://www.anonymizer.com
http://www.lpwa.com
http://www.verisign.com

Online Community

http://www.mirabilis.com/
http://www.tribal.com/powwow/
http://www.activeworlds.com/
http://www.thepalace.com/
http://www.talkcity.com/
http://chat.yahoo.com
http://www.tripod.com/planet/chat/
http://www.liszt.com
http://www.communityware.com
http://www.geocities.com
http://www.miningco.com
http://freenet.msp.mn.us/-drwool/webcon2.html
http://www.ForumOne.com
http://www.salonmagazine.com
http://www.utne.com
http://www.well.com
http://www.echonyc.com
http://www.concretemedia.com
http://www.GirlsOnFilm.com

Build Your own Homepage

http://www.justin.org/webpub/whyweb.html
http://www.slate.com
http://www.flotsam.com/PLOTZ
http://www.lysator.liu.se/mit-guide/mit-guide.html
http://thetransom.com/chip/zines/index.html
http://www.links.net/webpub/index.html
http://www.adobe.com/prodindex/main.html
http://screenlife.tripod.com/lifesupport/toolbox/design/webgraphics.html
http://www.yahoo.com/computers_and_internet/software/internet/ftp/index.html

http://www.ispin.k12.il.us/fetch.html
http://www.fray.com
http://www.lpage.com/
http://www.thefinger.com
http://www.typo.com/wcd/wcd.html
http://www.entropy8.com

E-Zines

http://www.benedict.com
http://www.clari.net/brad/copymyths.html
http://www.georgejr.com
http://www.well.com/user/futrelle
http://www.15minutes.com
http://www.primenet.com/~obscure
http://www.ionet.net/~twilken/HITCH
http://www.soundbitten.com
http://www.birdhouse.org/words/pagan
http://members.tripod.com/~boing_boing/index.html
http://www.bust.com
http://www.media.mit.edu/people/dryer
http://www.fatso.com
http://www.inquisitor.com
http://www.teleport.com/~dkossy
http://www.diysearch.com
http://www.zinebook.com
http://www.factsheet5.com
http://thetransom.com/chip/zines/
http://www.meer.net/~johnl/e-zine-list
http://propagandist.com/tkemzl

Work

Career Survival Guide

http://www.abastaff.com/handbook/resume.htm
http://www.careers.net.au/
http://www.tompetersgroup.com/

Internships

http://www.nsee.org
http://www.tripod.com/work/goodworks/
http://www.rsinternships.com
http://interns.org
http://www.studentcenter.com/where/intern/intern.htm
http://www.wetfeet.com
http://www.tripod.com/work/résumé
http://www.dol.gov
http://thomas.loc.gov

The Net and Your Job Search

http://www.hoovers.com
http://www.well.com
http://www.echonyc.com
http://www.dejanews.com
http://www.synapse.net/~radio/finding.htm
http://www.neosoft.com/internet/paml
http://www.lycos.com
http://www.moving-guide.com
http://www.uhaul.com
http://www.mapquest.com
http://www.all-hotels.com

http://www.monster.com
http://www.HeadHunter.net
http://www.careerpath.com
http://www.worldpages.com
http://www.switchboard.com

Temping

http://www.worknow.com
http://www.slip.net/-junodr/twu/index.html
http://www.as-we-are.com/awa/issue3/temp_union.html

Telecommuting

http://www.homeworkers.org/iha.htm
http://www.telecommute.org
http://www.hoaa.com
http://www.att.com/Telecommute_America/
http://www.gohome.com/
http://smartone.svi.org/PROJECTS/TCOMMUTE/TCGUIDE/
http://www.pacbell.com/products/business/general/telecommuting/tcguide/index.html
http://www.officeplus.com/Services/

Start Your Own Business

http://www.idye.com
http://www.sbaonline.sba.gov/
http://www.venturepreneurs.com/
http://www.edgeonline.com

Career Contrarians

http://fdncenter.org
http://home.gnofn.org/-nopl/info/bsinfo/foundres.htm

Home

Apartment Hunting

http://rent.net/
http://www.sidewalk.com/
http://www.tsci.com/
http://www.equifax.com/

Renting vs. Buying

http://www.fanniemae.com
http://www.tenant.net

Moving

http://www.usps.gov/moversnet/
http://www.avatar-moving.com/doc_valuation
http://www.mapquest.com/cgi-bin/mqtrip?screen=tq_main

Fix-it Basics

http://homerepair.miningco.com/
http://www.octane.com/dtjimtim.html
http://www.livinghome.com/livinghome/toolchest

Thrifting

http://www.123sortit.com/RO/garage.html
http://www.retroactive.com/itinerant.html

Food

Kitchen Basics

http://www.slow-food.com/
http://www.homearts.com
http://www.epicurious.com
http://www.tvfood.com
http://www.kitchenlink.com
http://www.starchefs.com

Eating Well

http://sln.fi.edu/biosci/healthy/diet.html
http://www.genius.net/indolink/Health/dietTips.html
http://www.2020tech.com/health/health02.html
http://magazines.enews.com/magazines/ucbwl

Homebrewing

http://hbd.org/brewery/cm3/index.html
http://pekkel.uthscsa.edu/Beer/Recipe/recex2.html

Wine

http://www.2way.com:80/food/wine/
http://www.wine-lovers-page.com/learn.htm
http://www.wineeducation.com/
http://www.winebrats.org/grapejuice/blindtasting/index.html

Health

Health Insurance

http://www.mahmo.org/
http://www.ncqa.org/

Drug charts

http://www.hyperreal.org/drugs
http://www.lycaeum.org
http://www.deoxy.org
http://www.nida.nih.gov/
http://www.health.org

Marijuana

http://www.natlnorml.org/home.html
http://pressenter.pressenter.com/~davewest/hemp.html
http://www.lindesmith.org/
http://www.marijuana-anonymous.org/

Cigarettes

http://ash.org
http://www.cs.brown.edu/people/lsh/docs/whysmoke.html
http://www/gl.umbc.edu/~rfreem1/cigs/cigarettes.html
http://www.library.ucsf.edu/kr/bin/showByTopic.pl?Tobacco/Nicotine/Smoking
http://www.library.ucsf.edu/tobacco/cigpapers

Detox Chic

http://www.hazelden.org/index.dbm
http://www.uniqual.com/medicine.html
http://www.yahoo.com/Arts/Humanities/Philosophy/Eastern/Yoga/Traditions/
http://recovery.netwiz.net/index.html

Alternative Medicine

http://www.healthy.net/pan/pa/homeopathic/natcenhom/index.html
http://cgi.pathfinder.com/drweil/
http://www.HerbNET.com/
http://members.aol.com/permianbry/best.htm
http://www.gardenmag.com/

Therapy

http://www.shef.ac.uk/~psysc/psychotherapy/
http://www.healthguide.com/therapy/
http://www.bath.ac.uk/~hssrilc/psychsn.htm
http://plaza.interport.net/nypsan/

Antidepressants

http://avocado.pc.helsinki.fi/~janne/asdfaq/
http://www.psycom.net/depression.central.html
http://www.medscape.com
http://www.onlinepsych.com
http://www.infoseek.com/health

Safe Sex

http://www.goodvibes.com
http://sunsite.unc.edu/ASHA
http://www.webcom.com/~cps
http://www.condomania.com
http://www.cdcnac.org/stdpics.html
http://safersex.org
http://www.aegis.com/topics/oralsex/oralsex.html

Contraception

http://www.plannedparenthood.org/
http://users.deltanet.com/users/agkid/
http://www.femalehealth.com/
http://gynpages.com/ultimate/

Money

Credit Cards

http://www.ramresearch.com/cardlocator/cardlocator.html
http://www.getsmart.com/
http://www.equifax.com/consumer/consumer.html
http://www.transunion.com/
http://www.experian.com/index.html

Freelance Finance

http://www.irs.ustreas.gov/
http://www.quicken.com
http://www.americanexpress.com
http://www.naea.org/
http://www.accountingnet.com/prod/prodfr.html
http://www.abanet.org/
http://www.soho.org/
http://aimc.com/aimc/self-employment-digest.html

Investing

http://www.morningstar.net
http://kiplinger.com/
http://cnnfn.com/
http://www.thestreet.com/
http://www.goodmoney.com/
http://www.socialinvest.org/
http://www.steinroe.com/
http://www.fidelity.com/
http://www.vanguard.com/
http://www.brill.com/
http://www.stocksmart.com/

Retirement

http://www.retireweb.com/death.html
http://www.northwesternmutual.com/noframes/business/owners/needs/retirement/
http://www.cas.muohio.edu/-security/
http://www.clark.net/pub/x-pac/

Contributor Bios

Jim Adams lives in a small apartment in New York City. He collects cruiser bicycles. Send him one. Really.

Michael Agger is an aspiring book editor. He lives in Brooklyn.

Suzy Banks has been twirling tools and fixing up houses for more years than she cares to admit—and she's got the scars to prove it.

Rachel Barenblat is an MFA student at the Bennington Writing Seminars. Her first book of poetry, *the skies here*, was published by Pecan Grove Press (San Antonio) in 1995. Her poems, stories, and essays have appeared in various places, online and off, and she enjoys singing madrigals and baking bread.

Sarah Blustain lives in Manhattan and is a contributing editor for the *Forward* and an Associate Editor at *Lilith* magazine.

Michelle Chihara is a staff writer and Web editor at the *New Haven Advocate*, a Connecticut alternative weekly newspaper (the free kind you pick up on the corner). Her homepage is "in progress" much like her life, her apartment, and her collection of French rap.

Wendy Cholbi is a financial writer and editor who lives in Boston with her husband, a philosopher. She has written extensively on personal finance (many of her articles can be found on the Tripod Web site) and is a producer of *The Blue Moon Review*, an online literary magazine (http://www.thebluemoon.com)

Andrea Coller is a writer and editor living and working in New York City.

Marni Davis is a graduate student at the New School for Social Research in New York City. She has contributed to the *New York Press*, *BUST*, and Tripod's Women's Zone.

Liza Featherstone is a freelance writer and editor. She has contributed to numerous on-line and print magazines, including *Nerve*, *Salon*, *Ms.*, *Columbia Journalism Review*, and the *Nation*. She lives in Brooklyn.

Adam Fifield is a writer living in New York City. He is currently working on a memoir about his relationship with his Cambodian foster brother, to be published by Avon Books in 1999.

Thomas Frank is editor-in-chief of *The Baffler* magazine, and author of *The Conquest of Cool* (University of Chicago Press, 1997).

John Fried is a freelance writer in New York City. He's written articles for a number of magazines, including *Worth*, *Time*, and *Cineaste*. When he's not writing about retirement, he's denying that he'll ever grow old.

Josh Glenn is the former editorial director of Tripod's Web site, a contributing editor to Great Britain's fabulous *Idler* magazine, and the publisher of his own zine *Hermenaut: The Digest of Heady Philosophy*.

Matt Goldberg tries to squeeze in as much writing as possible in between everything else. He lives in Brooklyn and actually has a backyard.

Harry Goldstein is a writer living in Brooklyn. He divides his time between writing fiction and anything else to make money. He wrote a column for Tripod focusing on workplace politics, and is currently a science journalist writing about everything from genetics research to microelectronics engineering.

Adam Heimlich is a New York–based freelance writer who contributes to *New York Press*, *Miami New Times*, and *The Stranger*.

Al Hoff is the author of *ThriftScore*, a book celebrating the joys of too much thrifting. She lives in Pittsburgh, with lots of junk.

David Hudson is the author of *Rewired*, a "brief and opinionated" history of the Internet and its culture, as well as editor of the ongoing *Rewired* webzine. He has written for *Salon*, Spiegel Online, Netly News, *LA Weekly*, and the *San Francisco Bay Guardian*, and has hosted conferences for Electric Minds and Netscape's Professional Community.

Yvonne Jones is a writer and filmmaker based in Philadelphia. The ongoing battle between her curious mind and a need to pay the bills on a regular basis has led her down many an intriguing road.

Michael Kaplan is a journalist based in New York City. He's written on a wide range of topics for magazines that include *Smart Money*, *Los Angeles*, *Movieline*, and *New York*.

Ben Klipstein is a Tripod contributor who has written for *Time Out New York*, *Blender* and nynow.com. He's also in a band called The Team. Ben is a resident of Brooklyn.

David Kushner is a contributing editor for *Spin*. He has written for publications including the *New York Times*, the *Village Voice*, *Entertainment Weekly*, and *Details*.

Ken Kurson is the founder and editor of *Green* magazine, a personal finance zine for those nauseated by the phrase "personal finance." He is a columnist for *Esquire* and his first book, *The Green Magazine Guide to Personal Finance,* was published earlier this year.

Kathleen McGowan is a New York–based writer.

Emily Nussbaum is a writer living in New York City. She is a contributing editor at *Lingua Franca* magazine.

Our carpenter, *J. P. Partland*, is also an ordained minister and a doctor of divinity. When he's neither damning his errors nor blessing his creations, he writing about cycling, culture, and objects, and trying to prove that comedy is pretty.

Alissa Quart is a freelance writer based in New York City.

J Betty Ray is a Minneapolis writer who revels in the incestuous relationship between media and itself. She is also the editor/producer of Fucker Dot Com (http://www.fucker.com), an online monument to the archetypal Fucker Within.

Ted Rall is a syndicated cartoonist and columnist for Universal Press Syndicate. Winner of the Robert F. Kennedy Journalism Award and a finalist for the Pulitzer Prize, his most recent books include *Revenge of the Latchkey Kids* (Workman) and *My War with Brian* (NBM), both released this year. Rall lives in New York City.

Dan Reines is an editor for Tripod and a freelance writer. His writing has appeared in the *Los Angeles Times*, the San Diego's *North County Times*, the *Orange County Register*, and *ChinMusic*, the nation's premiere digest of baseball and bigrockaction.

Eva Rosenberg, MBA, EA, writes a national tax column, is a frequent talk show guest as the Original GiftSurfer (http://www.mywishlist.com/giftsurfer/) and the Tax Bytes columnist at http://www.tripod.com, in addition to her tax practice in Encino, California.

Chip Rowe is the *Playboy* Advisor. A self-diagnosed anal-inventive personality, he once compiled a subject index to the *Weekly World News* and a 660-entry guide to *This is Spinal Tap*. Last year he compiled an anthology of great zine writing, *The Book of Zines: Readings from the Fringe* (Owl Books). His E-zine of pop culture and fun, *The Chip Electric*, is located at http://thetransom.com/chip.

Formerly Tripod's "Chatmaster General" and Poderator of the Critters Pod, *Christina Simmons* has returned to civilian life as a freelance writer and a teacher of sixth grade Language Arts in Connecticut. Her publishing credits include features in *Catholic Teen Magazine* and the Berkshire–based *Animal Life* newspaper.

Sasha Smith lives and eats well in New York City.

Candi Strecker is a freelance writer living in San Francisco. In her spare time she publishes the zines *It's a Wonderful Lifestyle* and *Sidney Suppey's Quarterly & Confused Pet Monthly*.

Steve Taormina lives and works the organic life in Boulder, Colorado.

Emma Taylor is the editor of Tripod's Women's Zone (www.tripod.com/women). She learned the art of interning at a political consulting company in Oxford, where she made coffee, fixed the photocopier, and used the office fax machine to maintain a long distance love affair.

Bruce Tulgan is a sought-after speaker and consultant. He is the author of *Work This Way* (Hyperion, 1998) as well as *Managing Generation X* (Merritt, 1995), and is the founder of RainmakerThinking, Inc. in New Haven, which is dedicated to studying the working lives of Americans born after 1963.

Paul Tullis is a freelance journalist in San Francisco. From 1994–1997 he was an editor at *Might* magazine. He has written for *The New Yorker*, *New York*, *Columbia Journalism Review*, *Vibe*, NPR, and the *LA Weekly*.

Tom Vanderbilt is contributing editor of *The Baffler* and a columnist for *Mother Jones*, and has contributed to many publications, including the *Nation*, the *London Review of Books*, and *Spin*. He is the author of *The Sneaker Book: Anatomy of an Industry and an Icon* (the New Press, 1998).

Randy Williams is an editor and writer who has supervised the Media, Web/Tech, and Work/Money Zones for Tripod's Web site. Williams's essays, stories, and poems have appeared in numerous publications, and he is the author of two plays. Despite rumors to the contrary, he is not related to crooner Andy Williams; he has, however, been known to belt out a spirited rendition of "Moon River" after downing a few Black & Tans.

Jessica Willis handles money and people. She breathes in New York City.

Ethan Zuckerman lives and works in the Berkshire mountains of Massachusetts with his wife. He works as Tripod's VP of Research and Development, and writes about the impact of technology on society.

Tripod Member Bios

Tripod member Trefor is a published writer of fiction and poetry living in Seattle.

Tripod member mark_bradley is Mark Bradley, a surfer and programmer living in San Francisco.

Tripod member YCantIBU is Tod Beardsley, a Pittsburgh-area screenwriter, NT administrator, and goth.

Tripod member Spinnuendo is Jason Nadeau, a technical evangelist and musical hobbyist living in Victoria, B.C., Canada.

Tripod member MaxGoof is a fifteen-year-old, redheaded boy who loves Weird Al and a goofy movie.

Tripod member rgould is Ron Gould, a software developer, writer, and musician living in Richmond, Texas.

Tripod member Rachel is Rachel Barenblat, a writer who lives in a barn in Williamstown, Massachusetts.

Tripod member Lyn_Nelson is a career development specialist from Boston.

Tripod member VixenOne is Jacqueline Bower, a vocational counselor and online cyber romance columnist in Palm Springs, California.

Tripod member BDScodak is Bruce S. Zoldak, owner of BDScodak personalized children's books, and Personal Protection Products.

Tripod member maxthecat is Dan Reines, a writer and editor who works out of General Cable in Williamstown, Massachusetts.

Tripod member Dataphone is Howard Rice, who loves helping people make money.

Tripod member crux_criticorum is really named Crux Criticorum, a tortured soul, poet, and writer living in San Francisco.

Tripod Member j_rowles is John Rowles, the supreme dictator for life of his Web marketing firm, X-Presso Internet Group, LLC.

Tripod Member elixirmedia is Owl Berg, a one-man-band and web developer living in Seattle.

Tripod member StoneyJB, a former merchant seaman and probation officer, is currently a networking professional living in Springfield, Ohio.

Tripod member JHM42 is John H. Matthews, a web developer in Cupertino, California.

Tripod member hmma is Heather M. Magaw, a graduate student of psychology in Connecticut.

Tripod member rwilde is a practicing attorney with American and European legal degrees who spends every free minute he can find in the state of Maine.

Tripod member Sawmill is Ann Boyles Gerstein, a professional artist who paints on saws instead of canvas in her northern California studio.

Tripod member marnster is a writer and graduate student living in New York City.

Tripod member mec9 lives on California's central coast and is beginning a new catalog business selling Mexican miniatures.

Tripod member SFShan is Shan Schwartz, a freelance writer and marketing research analyst in San Francisco.

Tripod Member MsThing is Lori Tuckett, an editor at Tripod who lives in bucolic Williamstown, Massachusetts.

Tripod member SolutionsEBS is Timi Rosenbaum, owner and operator of a medical billing service in west Texas.

Tripod member HWLane is Helen Lane, who's semiretired, combs Ventura, California beaches and stares at blank pages.

Tripod member MFTuchman is Michael Tuchman, a software developer and amateur mathematician living in Durham, North Carolina.

Tripod member Cybird is Rohit Kamat, a software consultant living in Buffalo, New York.

Tripod member Artaed is Deatra Mitchell, a certified nursing assistant living in Norristown, Pennsylvania.

Tripod member brownfox is a native New Yorker studying counseling psychology at a university in Illinois.

Tripod member mrusk is Mike Rusk, a computer professional by day and writer wannabe by night, living in Howard County, Maryland.

Tripod member Xprof is Leo Toribio, a computer systems consultant and published poet who currently haunts Pittsburgh.

Tripod member shauna_ru is Shauna Russ, a freelance programmer and author's assistant living in the California desert.

Tripod member jemstone, a.k.a. Jessica Millstone, lives in Manhattan and is a technology and media literacy consultant for educators in New York City.

Tripod member Gingerly is S. Boswell, a psychology student from Louisiana.

Tripod member Geenius is Keith Ammann, a writer and editor in Albany, New York.

Tripod member joetruck is actually Joe Chasse, a part-time antiques dealer and bartender living on the beach in Washington state.

Tripod member Doc_ZueS is John Michaud, a systems analyst from Barrie, Ontario.

Tripod member jakrinda is a graduate student of Middle European history and an avid *Star Trek* fan, living in San Diego, California.

Tripod member anniesparkle is actually Julie Jefferies of Garland, Texas, who spends her days constructing prairie houses and her nights writing fascinating comments about world events and events important to her world.

Tripod member Jeni..just jeni is a swimmer, cheerleader, and music lover from Flint, Michigan.

Tripod member Thersites is a political activist, public witch, poet, nursing aide, and essayist from Agawam, Massachusetts.

Tripod member Samizdata is a freelance Web writer who bounces between D.C., Florida, and Illinois.

Tripod member RobertCooper is a Web systems engineer in Atlanta, Georgia.

Tripod member Kimmysue is Kim Johnson, a manufacturing specialist of over the counter drugs living in Allegan, Michigan.

Tripod member seeword is Martha Gifford, an internet librarian in California.

Tripod member Patricia_F is Patricia Frazier, a preschool teacher in Altus, Oklahoma.

Tripod member Irisheyes is a website designer & internet entrepreneur living in Fort Myers, Florida.

Tripod member ThorTrains is Thor Sheil, a publisher, author, and hobby software maker from New York State.

Tripod member sexymuffin is Terri Croop, who lives near the Berkshires and likes to write and argue.

Tripod member XaguamalaX is Dan Lindsey, a student at Oneida High School who is planning on going to college for hotel/resturant management.

Tripod member Barbara_Robertson removes her underscore by day to become 'Barbara Robertson,' social & political psychologist, disability studies researcher, and activist.

Tripod member Kiran Akbar lives in Malaysia and is planning to write books about herbal beauty and Indian cooking.

Tripod member Dunahein is a Career Development Practitioner who lives in a century log cabin on 97 acres in rural Ontario, Canada.

Tripod member KMorrison is Kitty Morrison, ISP Tech Support Team Member and instructor from Port Charlotte, Florida.

Tripod member Waldhorn is Michael E. Loescher, a struggling brewer and psychology intern who really needs to get a life.

Tripod member Richard_Bulger is a retired pornographer, living and breathing in the Sierra foothills. He is the founding publisher of *BEAR* magazine and videographer of other naked, hairy, homo smut.

Tripod member Lorcalon, also known as Amanda Demeter, is a poet, musician, and Net freak living in California.

Tripod member ipswitch is commonly known as David Godfrey, tuba soloist and Ultimate Frisbee player at Scarsdale High School.

Tripod member SleepyCP is Carl Paulson, a physicist living in New Jersey.

Tripod member mbrown2, real name Randy Brown, is old enough to buy liquor for minors, but doesn't.

Tripod member Perimus is Mitch Jackson, a student at Oklahoma State University.

Tripod member Boetticher is Christopher Boetticher, who plays good music, drinks good beer, and lives in Philadelphia.

Tripod member Shazya is Janene Hayes, a software engineer living in Omaha.

Tripod member HillaryF is Hillary Frazey, a help desk analyst in Minneapolis.

Tripod member JackForge is an English teacher and writer living and striving in California.

Tripod Member Johnny_Victory is Johnny Victory, a Seattle media whore who has chronicled the popular underground since 1983.

Tripod member Villon is Rebekah Villon, who currently resides in Portland, Oregon and has more tricks up her sleeve than a circus sideshow.

Tripod member WendieS is Wendie Schneider, who is learning to live on less while enjoying the beach life on Topsail Island, North Carolina.

Tripod member tericot is a twenty-nine-year-old speech therapist and special education teacher living in Califoria.

Tripod member CarolDiego is Carol Mackintosh, an actress and writer living in San Diego.

Tripod member matthewd is Matthew Dunbar.

Tripod member Jenoise is Jennifer A. Kirkgaard of Pasadena, who wishes to one day publish her own cookbook.

Tripod member Twyla is Janice MacDonald, a mystery novelist living in Edmonton, Alberta, Canada.

Tripod member KerrinWhite is Kerrin Leon White, M.D., a psychiatrist living in Providence, Rhode Island.

Tripod member Queenmeow is Debbie Clark, who resides in Sequim, Washington, and is head housekeeper at the Red Ranch Motel.

Tripod member Mixed is Larry (Lawrence) Miller, a student and multimedia artist living in the Minneapolis area.

Tripod member hip_fan is H. Murphy, a full-time mother, wife, office manager, and part-time writer, living in Victoria, British Columbia, Canada.

Tripod Member MoeBluesMan is alive and well in Salisbury, Maryland.

Tripod member nathanb_2 is Nathan Baruch, an industrial psychologist working as a marketing consultant, who lives in Kfar-Saba, Israel.

Tripod member Keath is Keath Graham, age thirty-nine, single, and a Louisiana nudist.

Tripod member BrianOG is Brian O'Grady, a software engineer and documentation manager living in Stockholm, Sweden.

Tripod member kenny_a_j is really Kenny J, twenty-two, male, Scottish and paranoid; he has a Web site devoted to endlessly scanning for hidden agendas and ulterior motives.

Tripod member Silverlock is Karen Ballentine, a medical transcriptionist and writer living in San Antonio.

Tripod member charPEF is Charlene Lojewski, a union activist who teaches at a New York State correctional facility in the Utica-Rome area.

Tripod member Missey is Kris Aschemeyer, a business owner living in Denton, Maryland.

Tripod member jayen is a single mom living in Massachusetts currently attending school for computer programming.

Tripod member ericmr is Eric Mac Rae.

Tripod member IcecreamC is C. Herndon, a student in Southern California.

Tripod member Veroglass is Linda Varos, Executive Director of Marketing and Creative Services at VEROGLASS in Erie, Pennsylvania.

Tripod member lilypad2 is Margo Shirley Traywick, a retired English teacher living in Ashdown, Arkansas.

Tripod member ScaMingLee is a twenty-year-old female who has had a rather interesting life living near San Francisco, Seattle, and Columbia, Missouri, while perpetually searching for a decent job.

Tripod member Louise_Cis Louise Chamberlin, an herbalist who lives in northeast Nebraska.

Tripod member Roosevelt_s is an educator and consultant living in Boston.

Tripod member Samdo is Linda Snyder, an artist and housewife living in Goliad, Texas.

Tripod member Nick_Condyles is a computer scientist and systems security analyst who resides in Richmond, Virginia.

Tripod member tree_shaman is Mark Smith, a poet and writer living in Orlando, Florida.

Tripod member DearAbbey is Maekie Der Veer, a Norwegian born restaurateur and soon-to-be published author now living in Sydney, Australia.

Tripod member nsrosenthal is Neil Rosenthal, an aspiring poet and computer network operator from Hartsdale, New York.

Tripod member Maria99 is Maria T. Gaetano, a college student, runner, soccer player, and avid writer living on the Eastern Shore of Maryland.

Tripod member LatcoEnt is Laurie Wells, a private investigator/peace officer in Texas.

Tripod member dj is Dick Jacobs, an author and writer living in Dallas.

Tripod member Emma is Emma Jane Taylor, an editor and writer living in Williamstown, Massachusetts.

Tripod member deborahstone (Deborah Stone) is an artist living and working in small town New Hampshire.

Tripod member HopeK is Hope Koseff, a Radio Market Research Specialist in New York City.

Tripod member kzentek is Karenne Zentek of Connecticut. She is a wife, mother of twins, and nurse.

Tripod member toby_not_the_dog is Toby Lees, a creative corporate executive in midlife crisis.
Tripod member Kathy7 is Kathy Strong, a graduate student in literature living in Dallas.
Tripod member Applecheeks is a fifty-year-old computer science student at Southeastern Louisiana University.
Tripod member MonicaD, a.k.a. Monica DelaRosa, is a multimedia producer in Philadelphia.
Tripod member kebara is Anne Gilbert, a writer living in Seattle.
Tripod member Txhern is Richard Craven, a starving artist living with his lover in Dallas.
Tripod member LParsons is a forty-two-year-old librarian in Cleveland.
Tripod member carolannie is a poet and novelist who lives near the Adirondack Mountains and the Canadian border.
Tripod member peacepigeon, a native of the Midwest whose real name is Karole, uses Tripod to publish her own Web page advocating abstinence.
Tripod member JD Conrad is a native of Louisville, Kentucky, a semiprofessional technomancer, and would-be Renaissance man.
Tripod member realife_records is Dan Magnolia, an indie music producer and web developer living in the Washington, D.C, area.
Tripod member Jlewis is Jon Lewis, President of Lewis Enterprises.
Tripod member Sarashay is a writer, performer and artist who lives in the Atlanta area and otherwise prefers to be anonymous.
Tripod member Traegorn is Eric Dorn, a student in Wauwatosa, Wisconsin.
Tripod member InTempo is Maric Anne, a translator and computer salesperson living in the Dominican Republic.
Tripod member Bonquilt is Bonnie Hensley, a registered nurse and avid quilter from western Washington state.
Tripod member paytonc is Payton Chung, an idealistic student from Chicago.
Tripod member sonny321 is a married mother of two (soon to be three) children living in Arlington, Texas.
Tripod member nostrand is Shaun Su, currently an epidemiologist/SAS program analyst in New York City.
Tripod member Andrew_D_G is Andrew Getraer, geothermal power developer, entrepreneur, writer, husband, and father of three boys, living in Wellesley, Massachusetts.
Tripod member jkcummi is Kyle Cummings, a computer systems analyst and father of two living in Baltimore.
Tripod member meian is a college student.
Tripod member MaryBeast is Mary Barnes, a network administrator and lesbian mother of two living in Washington, D.C.
Tripod member Aiyana is Vicki Lessard, a struggling writer and animal lover who lives in Lebanon, Maine.
Tripod member hardpack uses the E-zine *babble* to support his day job.
Tripod member Apel is Warren Apel, a molecular biologist, screenwriter, political activist, and Web designer.
Tripod member jngamble is Jack N. Gamble, a self-employed computer consultant and programmer living in Seattle.
Tripod member Melosh is Michael Melosh, a Web page designer and RASSMer living in Knoxville, Tennessee.
Tripod member GloriaF is a RE home/commercial broker and venture capital funding source for all your lending needs.
Tripod member WashingtonG is trying to retire and has seen it all.
Tripod member Nurse is Ernestine Sykes, a registered nurse certified in critical care with a special interest in nutrition and preventive medicine.

Tripod member PhoenixElaine, a scientist and poet, is a native of North Carolina transplanted to Philadelphia.

Tripod member Nightdriver is Greg Anderson, a customer representative living in Dallas.

Tripod member BernieLucas is a radio DJ/production director and volunteer cable access television producer living and working in the Washington, D.C. area.

Tripod member Elision is Lisa, a designer living in Tidewater, Virgina.

Tripod member bluegrassrainbow is a forty-nine-year-old clinical chemist and collector of fine porcelain china, living in Lexington, Kentucky and working at UK Medical Center, University of Kentucky.

Tripod Member rokey is Rokiatu Rahim, a youth programmer living and working in his hometown of Greensboro, North Carolina.

Tripod member New_Mexican is a fifty-five-year-old political consultant in Albuquerque, New Mexico, with a son in the army and two cats tearing up the house.

Tripod member TheWriter writes and edits.

Tripod member Absynthe is an incurable chocoholic and university student from the bustling metropolis of Toronto, Canada.

Tripod member Lazydaze is Tripod contributor Carol Anderson, from the Redington Beaches, Florida.

Tripod member RrakkaDog is Chaz Stacy, a student in northern Kentucky.

Tripod member nobody19 is Josh Morris, a frequent IRCer, musician, and programmer.

Tripod member OlindaM is Olinda Morar, a homemaker and Internet surfer living in Harare, Zimbabwe.

Tripod member nyeah, a.k.a Joe Willis, is a twenty-one-year-old housekeeper.

Tripod member KatherynJ is Katheryn Jager, a business process manager from Austin.

Tripod member kimmer is Kim Amick, a law student in San Francisco.

Tripod member RbarthJr2 is an artist and carpenter, living and working in eastern North Carolina.

Tripod member emraldangel is Angel, a writer, author, and Web designer living in New York City.

Tripod member LScholes is a freelance writer working and living in Oxford, Mississippi.

Tripod member trascal is a nurse and poet living in Nebraska.

Tripod member CSproat is Cornelia Sproat, an interactive artist living in Philadelphia.

Tripod member LauraEllen727 is Laura Ellen Sweimler, a college student in Mertztown, Pennsylvania.

Tripod member kool is Jacob Wolfsheimer, a teenager living in Potomac, Maryland.

Tripod member Lorissa is Rosita Harper, a university teacher in the Midwest.

Index